WORKING AGAINST THE GRAIN

WORKING AGAINST THE GRAIN

Women Sculptors in Britain c.1885–1950

Pauline Rose

LIVERPOOL UNIVERSITY PRESS

First published 2020 by
Liverpool University Press
4 Cambridge Street
Liverpool
L69 7ZU

British Library Cataloguing-in-Publication data
A British Library CIP record is available

ISBN 978-1-78962-156-3 cased

Typeset by Carnegie Book Production, Lancaster
Printed and bound by TJ International Ltd, Padstow, Cornwall, PL28 8RW

To my husband Dave:
I cannot thank you enough for your
encouragement, understanding and love

Contents

Plates

11. Phoebe Stabler, *Untitled (Mother and Child)*, c.1907, bronze (photo: George P. Landow, The Victorian Web, http://www.victorianweb.org/sculpture/stabler/1.html)
12. Josefina de Vasconcellos, *Dove from the Ark Nesting after the Flood*, undated, Hoptonwood stone. © Josefina de Vasconcellos and Leeds Museums and Galleries. Henry Moore Institute Archive. 2003.44 (photo: the author)
13. Rosamund Praeger, *Harvest*, c.1905, polychromed plaster. National Museums Northern Ireland. By permission of the National Trust for Northern Ireland, the National Society for the Prevention of Cruelty to Children, and the Ulster Society for the Prevention of Cruelty to Animals (photo: Joseph McBrinn)
14. Kathleen Scott, *Neville Chamberlain*, 1936, bronze, 55 × 22 × 26 cm. Courtesy of the Kennet family (photo: the author)
15. Emmeline Halse, *Monument to Henri Van Laun*, c.1897, terracotta and marble. Brookwood Cemetery, Woking (photo: Robert Freidus, The Victorian Web, http://www.victorianweb.org/sculpture/funerary/186.html)
16. Lilian Maud Wade, *Monument to 2nd Lieutenant Rex Moir (1898–1916) and his father Sir Ernest William Moir (1862–1933)*, before 1923, bronze, Brookwood Cemetery, Brookwood, Woking (photo: Robert Freidus, The Victorian Web, http://www.victorianweb.org/sculpture/funerary/128i.jpg)
17. Kathleen Scott, *These Had Most to Give*, 1922–23, bronze. Scott Polar Research Institute, Cambridge. By permission of the Kennet family and the Scott Polar Research Institute (photo: © Bryan Lintott)
18. Anne Strauss, *Family Group*, c.1930, tulip wood, 53 cm. Private collection. By permission of Martin Strauss (photo: Inga Fraser)
19. Frances Burlison, *Beaumont College War Memorial*, 1921, bronze and ashlar stone, Windsor (photo: Peter Bird via the War Memorials Register)
20. Mary Pownall Bromet, *Watford War Memorial*, 1928, bronze figures on Portland stone plinth and pedestals, between 150 and 240 cm. high (photo: © Gordon Haws)
21. Frances Darlington, *Ancilla Domini, the visit of the Magi*, c.1914–18, coloured plaster relief panel. St Wilfrid's Church, Harrogate. By permission of Darlington Estate. Courtesy of Harrogate Borough Council and Simon Miles Photography (photo: © Simon Miles)
22. Ellen Mary Rope, *The Guardian Angel*, 1897, painted plaster. St Margaret's Church, Leiston (photo: © Chris Nottingham)

Illustrations

Acknowledgements

Numerous individuals and organizations have been vital to the realization of this book, especially given the challenge presented in locating works and unearthing commentary on these mostly unknown women sculptors. The Arts University Bournemouth assisted by way of remission from teaching and funding for the illustrations. The Henry Moore Foundation's production grant to Liverpool University Press enabled this book to be well illustrated and competitively priced. Guidance from my editor Alison Welsby has been invaluable, and it has been a pleasure working with Sarah Warren of Carnegie Book Production. I would also like to thank the two anonymous peer reviewers who were so supportive of this book. Finally, Dr Margaret Garlake has been just an email away for many years now, and no doubt will be surprised at how much I have valued that.

Especial thanks are due to a number of individuals who have been helpful and patient in many ways from answering my queries to supplying images: Lord Alexander Antrim; Dr Odile Ayral and Gary Dwyer; Louise Bartlett, Senior Church Buildings Adviser, Diocese of Exeter; Charlotte Beare; Lt. Col. Roger Binks, Scottish National War Memorial, Edinburgh; Hope Brooks, Edna Manley Foundation, Jamaica; Dr Sophie Bowness; Caroline Criedel, Curator of Collections, University of Victoria Legacy Art Galleries; Donald Davies, Durban Art Deco Society; Viscount Randal Dunluce; Neil Faris; Mark Forrest, Dorset History Centre; Ted Few; Inga Fraser, Tate Britain; Gordon Haws; George P. Landow, the Victorian Web; Bryan Lintott, the Scott Polar Research Institute; David Llewellyn; Hector McDonnell; Louise Marchal; Dr Joseph McBrinn, Belfast School of Art, University of Ulster; Simon Miles; Nick Moir; Gary Nisbet; Chris Nottingham; Diana Phillips; Antonia Reeve; Arthur Rope; Phyllida and Tim Shaw; Dr Mark Stocker, Curator, Historical International Art at the Museum of New

Zealand Te Papa Tongarewa, Wellington; Alice Strang, Senior Curator, Scottish National Gallery of Modern Art; Martin Strauss; Ken Swtizer; Ed Trelinski, Housemaster, Cotton House, Rugby School; Richenda Walford, London Remembers; Margaret and James Ward; Dr Helen Wilson; Gwen Yarker; the late Elizabeth Young; Louisa Young.

Many galleries, museums and archives granted me access to images and documents: Aberdeen Art Gallery and Museums; Cambridge University Library; Dorich House Museum; Dorset History Centre; The Fine Art Society; Harrogate Ladies College; Harrogate Museums; The Henry Moore Institute; The Hepworth Wakefield archives; Historic England; Historic Royal Palaces, London; The King's School, Worcester; Leeds Museums and Art Galleries; Leicester Arts and Museum Service; Manchester Art Gallery; Manchester Museum; McLean Museum and Art Gallery; Museums Sheffield; National Museums Northern Ireland; The National Library of Scotland, Edinburgh; The National Portrait Gallery, London; The National Museum of Wales, Cardiff; The New Hall Art Collection, Murray Edwards College, Cambridge University; Ripon Museum Trust; The Robbins Library, Rochester University; The Royal Academy of Arts, London; The Royal Parks, London; St Dunstan's Archive, London; St Paul's Cathedral archive, London; Salisbury Cathedral; The Scott Polar Research Institute, Cambridge; Southwark Local Studies Library, London; University of Victoria Legacy Art Galleries and University of Victoria Libraries Special Collections and University Archives; The Victoria and Albert Museum, London; The War Memorials Register; The Imperial War Museum, London; The Whitworth Art Gallery, Manchester; Winchester College Archive.

1

Introduction: 'A bevy of fair sculptresses'

> One of the phenomena of the present day is the number of female artists now practising sculpture and the allied arts ... with excellent taste and dainty fancy. Colour, as being more sensuous, has proved a more frequent attraction to feminine skill and devotion; but the last twenty years have witnessed the advent of a bevy of fair sculptresses where fifty years ago there was only one. Mrs. Thornycroft lived long enough ... to see a score of candidates for the position she used to fill almost without challenge ... there are not wanting among the rising school a few ladies who seek to carry their practice of sculpture on to the higher plane; but the majority of them appear satisfied with a lighter vein. This remark does not apply to those still included in the ranks of the students, who, filled with enthusiasm, and undisturbed (to all appearance – which is so misleading!) by paralysing thoughts of marriage, are very earnestly following up the traditions of the art with the ardour of a Verrocchio, the passion of a Michael Angelo, the frenzy of a Carpeaux. They are most of them necessarily affected by the prevailing wave of Latinity; but as the best French sculpture comprises nearly all that art can boast of vitality, grace, and elegance, we cannot lament that Englishwomen should steep themselves in it, so long as they do not sacrifice the instinctive promptings of their own nationality.[1]

This equivocal appraisal of aspiring British female sculptors made in 1901 by leading critic Marion Harry Spielmann conveys many of the prejudices that they faced. His comments were based on several assumptions and generalizations, all rooted in the issue of gender. He repeated the widely held belief that women artists were naturally attracted to colour and thus to painting. However, if they did produce sculpture it would likely be unambitious and derivative since they were regarded as suggestible and easily influenced. There was widespread resistance to women following a career, especially if they were married, and apart from this social convention the idea that women's creativity would automatically be fulfilled through marriage and family responsibilities was commonplace. One might suppose this to be a populist view but the same argument was also expressed in art journals: in an 1884 article in the *Magazine of Art* it was claimed that women's true role was to be 'the presiding genius of the home. Here all her artistic proclivities may be brought into full play, as the beautifier and refiner of the household dwelling-place.'[2] Nonetheless Spielmann did acknowledge the significant number of women who were making sculpture, and his views were widely accessible through his editorship at the *Connoisseur* and the *Magazine of Art* during the period 1887–1904, as well as his contributions to several other prominent journals. He was a significant individual whose comments on a number of women sculptors will appear throughout this book.

Ben Read suggested that the art historian has two broad choices: to re-evaluate well-trodden ground with the intention of building on or arguing against the work of other art historians or to test out new theoretical frameworks; or to be an 'archaeologist, who goes back to the past to discover traces of those subsequently ignored and forgotten'.[3] Female sculptors certainly provide much material for the latter approach and it is in this spirit that my project began, specifically inspired by the launch on 25 February 2011 of a groundbreaking online sculpture database. Unveiled at the Victoria and Albert Museum, *Mapping the Practice and Profession of Sculpture in Britain and Ireland 1851–1951* was the first in-depth investigation of sculptors active in Britain and of their related trades. Its ethos has been to synthesize material concerning training, exhibiting, societies, the role of workshops and foundries and so on, as well as to incorporate modellers and makers of jewellery, medals and architectural decoration. At the launch event I was particularly struck by a comment that women practitioners represented about one-third of all sculptors active in this hundred-year period, a figure that both surprised and intrigued me. However, in the nineteenth century there were more female painters than sculptors and so art historical research and writing has understandably concentrated on this larger group, potentially creating the impression that the experience of women painters should be taken as representative of all female artists. Thus the status and specificities of sculpture and sculptors is further devalued through generalizations and omissions. Another obstacle for sculpture studies is that in the period immediately preceding the timeframe of this book, painting tended to receive preferential treatment in exhibitions, and so attracted more reviews and critiques. This in turn would have encouraged collectors to focus on painting as the more favoured discipline. Although towards the end of the nineteenth century sculpture was increasing in popularity, the subsequent preoccupation with early twentieth-century modernism resulted in both Victorian painting and sculpture being overlooked by many art historians.

In trying to uncover the careers of British women sculptors we find that contemporary commentators regularly treated them differently from their male peers, and that this continued right through and beyond the period covered in this book. Appraisals of male sculptors would rarely include any reference to their gender: however, the work of female sculptors has routinely been approached from this perspective. Commentators apparently found it necessary first to question their physical and technical capabilities, and then to look for 'feminine' characteristics in their work. It was normal to express surprise that women had the strength to produce sculpture; therefore it was often assumed that their abilities necessarily lay in modestly scaled decorative work, and where their sculpture was praised this was often hedged about with hints of substantial input from male assistants. **Figure 1** shows the impressive model for Paisley's war memorial (1924) with its sculptor Gertrude Alice Meredith Williams (1877–1934), demonstrating just how wrong such assumptions could be in terms of its ambition, quality and scale. This work will be discussed further in Chapter 6. The way in which female sculptors were written about was often extraordinarily patronizing and trivializing, focusing on incidental domestic and anecdotal issues that would rarely be the case in writings on their male colleagues. Although such attitudes may well reflect wider social and cultural norms, it is likely that the effect has been to 'tarnish' the broad reputation of women sculptors in this period, and this in turn will not have been helpful in encouraging subsequent art historical enquiry.

This unsatisfactory treatment of women sculptors did not go entirely unchallenged. As early as 1862 the Irish writer and social reformer Frances Power Cobbe, in an article published in *Fraser's Magazine*, promoted the possibility of women artists succeeding in their chosen profession and of their work becoming 'remarkable for other things beside softness and weakness'. Cobbe's lifelong companion was sculptress Mary Lloyd, who worked with Rosa Bonheur and in the Rome studio under John Gibson in the 1860s where Harriet Hosmer also sculpted. In such a prestigious

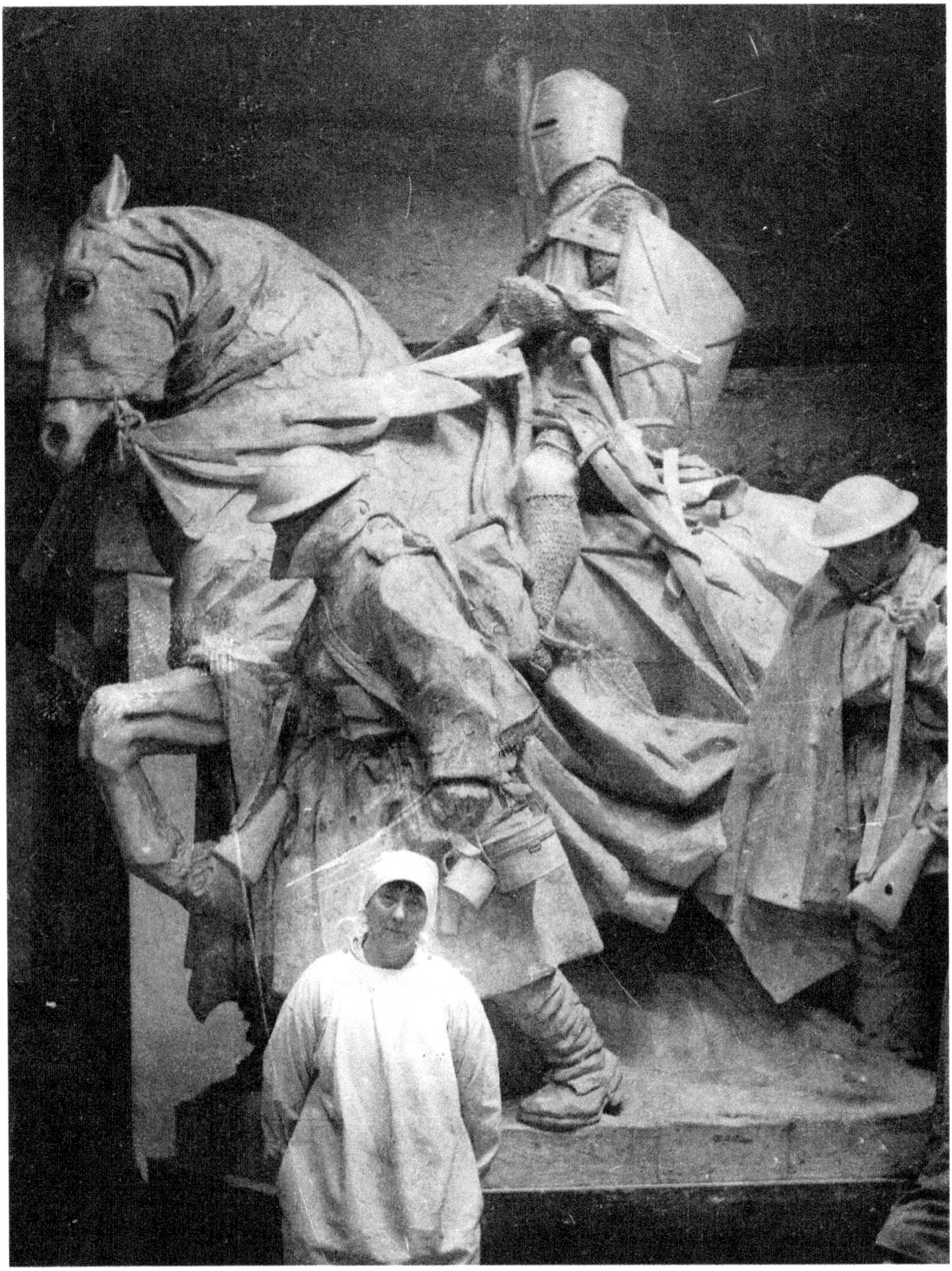

1. *Gertrude Alice Meredith Williams, with the plaster cast of 'The Spirit of the Crusaders', in her studio at 19 Circus Lane, Edinburgh, 1923*

setting female sculpture students could establish invaluable networks among their peers and also with patrons, although of course they were in competition with male students.[4] Despite being published well in advance of this book's timescale, Cobbe's remark underscores the legacy of problematic attitudes with which women sculptors had to contend, since a successful challenge to such entrenched views would take at least another hundred years to materialize. Writing specifically on sculpture, Cobbe remarked:

> Will women's genius ever triumph here? ... Sculpture is in many respects at once the noblest art and the one which tasks highest both creative power and scientific skill. A really good and great statue is an achievement to which there must contribute more elements of power and patience than in almost any other human work, and it is, when perfected one of the most sublime ... If she succeed here, if a school of real sculptresses ever arise, then we think that in effect the problem is solved ... if really good statues come from their studios, statues showing at once a power of conception and science of execution, then we say, women can be artists ... For long centuries women never seem to have attempted sculpture at all ... But in our time things are changed.[5]

In an interesting forerunner of the sentiments held by many second wave feminists, Cobbe argued for the strength of women's artistic work precisely because of the maker's gender. She rebutted criticisms of female artists' work as being too 'feminine', believing such notions to lie in

> the old error that clipping and fettering every faculty of body and mind was the sole method of making a woman – that as the Chinese make a lady's foot, so we should make a lady's mind; and that, in a word, the old alehouse sign was not so far wrong in depicting 'The Good Woman' as a woman without any head whatsoever. Earnestly would we enforce the opposite doctrine, that as God means a woman to *be* a woman and not a man, every faculty he has given her is a woman's faculty, and the more each of them can be drawn out, trained, and perfected, the more *womanly* she will become.[6]

A major obstacle to researching women sculptors is the lack of accessible personal archives. If we took the existence of an archive as a mechanism by which to calculate the proportion of female sculptors to males we would gain a much-distorted view. This lack of papers kept by women artists again stems largely from social norms, since the usual practice would be for such professional documentation to be carried out (if at all) by a male member of the household. So unmarried female sculptors were potentially at an even greater disadvantage here.[7] Where they have left written material it tends to be in the form of letters and diaries which can be arbitrary in scope and over-personalized in content. In the very few instances where materials relating to their professional as well as private lives have been preserved it is possible to see how some of these women's careers and personal lives were not as clearly demarcated as was often the case with their male counterparts. After much time spent at the Henry Moore Foundation archives in Hertfordshire I have subsequently found no such parallel in terms of organization, scope, breadth and detail in accessible resources for women sculptors. Even material on Barbara Hepworth (1903–75) is uneven and divided between various locations, and so does not give us an equivalent sense of a professional life in all its richness and complexity as is the case with the Moore archive.

The issue of economic and social status was relevant for many of the women I discuss, although, unsurprisingly, less so as we move through the first half of the twentieth century. Sculpture is an expensive practice. For work in marble or bronze the artist would need access to workshop facilities where clay models could be cast in plaster to produce a template for a stone or bronze sculpture. Some pieces could be completed within the domestic sphere but eventually a larger and more professionalized space would be required. If women were less able to access or afford such facilities, then we could argue that this might impact on the scale and ambition of their work. However, we must exercise some caution here: although there are many examples in this book of statuettes made by women sculptors, male sculptors also exploited such small works, since they could be editioned, thus generating a reasonably reliable income with which to make more individual pieces. That said, throughout this project I have sensed that many of these women were sensibly pragmatic in the pursuit of their careers. Few of them were in a financial or social position to deliberately make work that might not find a buyer or was not part of a paid commission. In addition to acknowledging the realities of the marketplace, many female sculptors appear to have been quite comfortable in having a flexible attitude towards operating as an 'assistant' or as a 'professional', and moving between the 'fine' and 'decorative' arts as opportunities presented themselves and as financial concerns demanded.[8]

In the early years of the period covered in this book female sculptors needed to negotiate carefully the various parts of their lives, both domestic and professional, and to bear in mind society's expectations of them as respectable women. If they were married they might encounter difficulties in being full-time sculptors, but conversely could benefit from access to potential patrons through their husband's connections. In contrast an unmarried woman sculptor theoretically had a degree of freedom to work when and how she wished, but she would be more socially and financially isolated. In publicizing themselves and their talents all women sculptors needed to tread carefully and maintain a level of decorum. However, as can be seen on the *Mapping the Practice and Profession of Sculpture* database, many women did work as professional sculptors in the late nineteenth and first half of the twentieth centuries. My initial search quickly resulted in a list of over 150 names that fell within my chosen timeframe. However, virtually none of them have received the examination and analysis required for significant exhibition catalogues, monographs and inclusion in surveys of British art. To date only Hepworth, Gertrude Hermes (1901–83) and Dora Gordine (1895–1991) have attracted this sustained attention.[9] Apart from their sculpture not being displayed and written about, this lack of attention in itself has the effect of implying that women sculptors' work is not worth looking at. However, there are also some major practical reasons for this lack of visibility beyond the virtual non-existence of archives from which to construct the rationale and information for an exhibition or a publication. In the first two or three decades of my period exhibition catalogues routinely comprised either a list of works, or pages of photographs, with a very cursory accompanying text. We cannot gain a sense of how these sculptures were regarded and contextualized. These catalogues reveal the existence of a very large number of women sculptors, but pursuing such references any further presents huge challenges: where works survive, they are largely held in regional collections and often not on display, or are dispersed among the artist's family and heirs.

The assumed limitations imposed by gender were frequently voiced in publications: in 1925 an entry in the *Studio* noted of sculptor Violet Brunton that 'her work is an example of the almost super-masculine strength which marks the best of modern feminine art'.[10] Perhaps of more concern should be clear evidence that sexist perceptions of female sculptors have not disappeared. In a 1988 radio broadcast with Mary Spencer Watson (1913–2006), the interviewer stated that he could see in his mind a vision of a 'petite 12-year old girl working away with massive tools on a great block of stone', referring to Spencer Watson's early interest in stone carving in Dorset's Purbeck quarries (see Chapter 5).[11]

Undoubtedly some women might not have the physical strength of men, but to imply that brute force is the sole or most important attribute for a sculptor is flawed. These constant juxtapositions of heavy (manly) labour with the (frail) female form have been unhelpful, but this type of response was widespread, as will be seen in the pages that follow. The measuring of women's abilities against masculine norms is part and parcel of a patriarchal society: as Virginia Woolf commented in 1929 'the history of England is the history of the male line, not of the female. Of our fathers we know always some fact, some distinction ... But of our mothers, our grandmothers, our great-grandmothers, what remains?'[12] In nineteenth-century histories of prominent and successful women it was the norm that their femininity be highlighted, along with other desirable qualities such as moral rectitude and faithfulness. Such generalizations are now obsolete: for example, we know that accounts of Florence Nightingale that presented her as self-sacrificing and caring glossed over her core determination to be a woman who effected change. However, middle-class families during most of the timespan covered by this book encouraged their daughters to show due deference to their male counterparts and not to display unseemly ambition. The majority of the women I discuss who were still working in the 1940s were raised either in the late nineteenth century or at the latest in the 1920s. Hence these attitudes were still widespread, and therefore the legacy of Victorian and Edwardian ideals permeated most of their lives.

The sociological and economic reasons for women's low profile in histories of art, and for the difficulties they encountered in pursuing the career of a professional artist, have been thoroughly addressed in recent decades. Scholarly attention to British sculpture is a relatively recent affair and for the most part has been a history of male sculptors. In contrast, women painters have received long-overdue attention and there are several important writings on the general situation of women artists within a male-dominated profession. However, the bias in much art historical writing towards work that is seen as innovative creates another problem, since the majority of the women included in my book cannot be placed within a twentieth-century modernist framework. To some extent this may reveal a pragmatism on their part, a wish or a necessity to make a living from their work, and thus the need to recognize the preferences of patrons as opposed to those of art critics. Indeed, if we want to understand the tastes of a particular period, then the large body of artistic production which was not avant-garde and which did not attract pages of commentary on the basis of its difference from the norm is a much more accurate reflection of contemporary taste. That said, there has often been a simplistic separation of artists into 'modernist' or 'traditional' categories, reinforced through a lineage of British art critics and historians who prioritized a modernist model of British art history, from Clive Bell with his dislike of late nineteenth-century British artistic traditions through to critics such as Herbert Read who favoured specific avant-garde practices.

For the history of sculpture, its presence in or omission from written art surveys is significant: it is quite common for books with 'fine art' in their titles to omit coverage of sculpture, and thus 'fine art' is assumed to mean painting. Some recent publications on British sculpture have exposed the subject to academic scrutiny, but the general concern is with an analysis of what might be termed 'modern' styles. The sculptors chosen are usually male and the absence of female sculptors, even if not a deliberate choice, effectively maintains the visibility of male practitioners and the invisibility of their female counterparts. If women sculptors are included in histories of twentieth-century British sculpture this has overwhelmingly been on the basis of their adherence to the modernist (masculine) canon. So in this book I examine female sculptors working across a broad spectrum of practice; thus someone as well known as Barbara Hepworth is placed within a wider community of practice than is normally the case. However, even she was consistently defined in relation to, or as following after, a male sculptor – Henry Moore – which contained and constrained her practice within a narrow and reflexive framework. Modernist accounts are inherently selective, and of course many highly successful male sculptors have also been marginalized through this focus on a particular artistic approach. However, women were likely to be doubly excluded through this aesthetic selectivity as well as their gender. One example of the latter is evident right at the start of the twentieth century. Editions of the long-running internationally orientated arts and crafts publication the *Studio* magazine discussed the sculpture of very few women, even those whose work was closely aligned to that of the male sculptors who were reviewed within the journal's pages. In contrast, a much lesser known and short-lived publication from the same period, *Academy Architecture and Architectural Review*, illustrated work by a surprisingly large number of female sculptors and has proved very useful for the discovery of completely unknown individuals, albeit only through illustrations of their work.[13]

By focusing on British women sculptors over a period of around half a century, this book explores how they became professionalized, the type of sculptural practices with which they engaged, and how their work was defined in both visual and written form. Women sculptors working in Victorian Britain are beginning to receive attention; those active during the second half of the twentieth century were operating in more favourable economic and social climates, which led to more secure careers and greater acknowledgement from critics and historians. This leaves the period which my book investigates. The decision to use 1950 as an end date is because the post-war period signalled a moment of fundamental cultural change. Britain was damaged, physically and economically, and the shifts in politics and social structures in the 1950s mark that time as fundamentally different from what had gone before. On a positive note there would emerge better opportunities for women to train and pursue a career in the fine arts, and thus they become less invisible in accounts of art history. My decision to move my original start date of 1900 to an earlier point was driven entirely by what I discovered in the course of my research, which revealed a significant number of sculptors whose careers straddled the turn of the century and who I felt deserved inclusion in this book.

I also wanted to represent a broad range of sculptural practice for two main reasons. First, books on sculpture, other than monographs, often focus on a particular genre – the figure, the memorial, and so on – and I found that several of the women sculptors who I selected worked across these categories. Secondly, and connected to this last point, many of these women produced work which in other contexts might be defined as 'decorative art' and thus would be most unlikely to appear in books on fine art, let alone on sculpture. For example, West Country wood carver Violet Pinwill (1874–1957) ran a large ecclesiastical workshop in Plymouth in the early decades of the twentieth century, the majority of her company's output comprising screens, pulpits and so on for Cornish and Devon churches. **Plate 1** shows her virtuoso Stoke Fleming pulpit in Devon, produced when she was just 17. Decorative ecclesiastical work such as the carved doors of great European cathedrals indisputably form part of the Western canon of art. So Pinwill was working within a recognized genre, but only very recently have one or two historians in her home county of Devon started to catalogue her carvings. The *Mapping the Practice and Profession of Sculpture* project revealed data on early exhibitions at venues such as the Royal Academy. At this august institution we might expect displays to have been exclusively of 'high' art objects. In reality exhibitions included much work that now might be characterized as design or applied art – door furniture, fountains and so on – and these objects were produced by both men and women. The boundaries between fine and applied art appear to have been surprisingly porous in the late nineteenth and early twentieth centuries.

There are no existing survey publications on British female sculptors. The Henry Moore Institute's *Sculpture in 20th Century Britain* (2003) began the process of looking at British sculptors from a similar perspective to my book, but discussion of women practitioners was still slight. It is interesting to examine the 100 thumbnail images used to illustrate each year on the book's timeline. For the 1900–25 period no work by a female sculptor is shown; the 1925–50 period includes just two examples. This absence of women's sculptures in reproduction exacerbates their invisibility. In my own book on Henry Moore (2014) I referred to the commissioning of sculpture for the 1951 Festival of Britain: architects were asked to suggest contemporary sculptors with whom they could work, and the only name that they could offer was that of Moore.[14] Given the history of writings on British sculpture, I would suggest that both in 1951 and now, the only female British sculptor that most people could name would be Barbara Hepworth.

In this book I will discuss and illustrate the work of some of these women who practised as sculptors and the differing ways in which they negotiated the tricky balance between their profession and competing domestic demands. This is not a comprehensive survey: visual and written material is patchy and uneven. Also I wanted to include some sculptors on whom there is seemingly nothing published as well as individuals who remain largely unknown but had successful careers. In this spirit it is an introduction to a field of study.

Notes

1 M. H. Spielmann, *British Sculpture and Sculptors of To-Day* (London: Cassell, 1901), p. 12.

2 L. Scott, 'Women at work: their function in art', *Magazine of Art*, 7 (1884), pp. 98–99.

3 Benedict Read, Preface, in *Ellen Mary Rope: The Poet Sculptor*, exhibition held at the Williamson Art Gallery & Museum, Birkenhead, 22 February–2 March 1997, and H. Blairman & Sons, 11–27 March 1997 (London: Joanna Barnes Fine Arts and H. Blairman & Sons, 1997), p. 1.

4 Shannon Hurtado, *Genteel Mavericks: Professional Women Sculptors in Victorian Britain* (Berlin: Peter Lang, 2012), p. 35.

5 Frances Power Cobbe, 'What shall we do with our Old Maids?', *Fraser's Magazine*, 66, November 1862, pp. 594–610, in Susan Waller, *Women Artists in the Modern Era: A Documentary History* (Metuchen, NJ: The Scarecrow Press, 1991), pp. 142–43.

6 Waller, *Women Artists in the Modern Era*, p. 145.

7 Hurtado, *Genteel Mavericks*, p. 51.

8 Waller, *Women Artists in the Modern Era*, p. x.

9 Jane Hill, *The Sculpture of Gertrude Hermes* (London: Lund Humphries in association with the Henry Moore Foundation, 2011); Jonathan Black and Brenda Martin, *Dora Gordine: Sculptor, Artist, Designer* (London: Dorich House Museum, Kingston University, in association with Philip Wilson Publishers, 2007). There have been numerous publications on Hepworth.

10 *The Studio*, 89 (February 1925), pp. 105–06.

11 Richard Cartridge, Interview with Mary Spencer Watson, Radio Solent, 15 April 1988. Dorset History Centre, Dorchester, D/MSW.9209.

12 Virginia Woolf, 'Women and fiction', in *Virginia Woolf, Collected Essays*, vol. 2 (London: Hogarth Press, 1966), p. 141. Essay originally published in *The Forum*, March 1929. Quoted in June Purvis, *Women's History: Britain, 1850–1945* (London: Routledge, 1995), p. 1.

13 https://archive.org/details/academyarchiteco2unkngoog (accessed 25 November 2019).

14 Pauline Rose, *Henry Moore in America: Art, Business and the Special Relationship* (London: I. B. Tauris, 2014).

2

Context

2.1 Artistic context

Sculpture 'inhabits' our world in a way that a painting does not: its physicality encourages an equally physical response. It is possible that this insistent presence has for some observers made sculpture less appealing than a painting which, although also an object, encourages less attention to its physical characteristics and limits, but instead acts as a vehicle to engage and transport us through illusion, narrative or imagination. I suspect that this might explain a bias among some art historians towards the two-dimensional rather than the three-dimensional artwork. On more than one occasion I have experienced surprised responses from my peers when I reveal my attachment to British sculpture, and once was congratulated with a heartfelt 'Well done!' for what apparently was seen as a brave, although perhaps somewhat esoteric interest. Jacqueline Lichtenstein's 2008 book *The Blind Spot: An Essay on the Relations between Painting and Sculpture in the Modern Age* examines a shift in the hierarchy between the senses of sight and touch during the seventeenth and eighteenth centuries, and the ideas and theorists that she discusses are relevant to the subsequent reception of sculpture and to the period covered by my book. Previously, vision had been regarded as the 'model and the metaphor of knowledge', but this was to be challenged by a new attention to how our senses and ideas might be related. It was believed that sight could be conceived in a similar way to the sense of touch, and hence there developed an approach to the visual via a 'tactile experience'. This alignment between sight and touch produced particular results, chiefly with regard to the hierarchy of the arts, which had been constituted on the basis of a hierarchy of the senses. Sight was privileged in the Renaissance period, not the least to support painting as the superior discipline to sculpture. Whereas the painter could produce an illusion of anything, the sculptor's use of three dimensions, imitating 'the reality of what we touch rather than what we see', pushed such practice into second place. Of course this could produce the reverse argument in sculpture's favour, in that 'its imitation was less deceitful and illusory than that of painting, which represented bodies on a flat surface'.[1] Referring to the second half of the eighteenth century, Lichtenstein notes that if we relied wholly on texts on sculpture we would get a misleading view of the discipline. In part this was because sculptors tended not to write about their work, in contrast to painters, who could build on a lineage of autobiographical texts going back to the Renaissance. This resulted in subsequent research favouring painting due to this body of supporting material.[2] This is a similar point to my own criticism that 'art' has too often stood to mean only painting, and Lichtenstein suggests that this is because, until recently,

> many reasons – historical, artistic, philosophical, and theological – could be invoked to explain the astonishing priority enjoyed by painting in Western thinking. A very ancient tradition lies behind the selection of painting as the model around which the definition of art was constructed, a tradition that goes back to Plato and Aristotle.[3]

One might suggest that this debate to which Lichtenstein refers only began to subside in the 1960s when writing about, and exhibiting of, sculpture came to the fore; however, painting undoubtedly still retains the greater popular appeal.

Lichtenstein also comments on the status of casts or marble copies, which were not treated as in some way counterfeit but instead were accorded the same status as their originals. This could never happen with painting, and thus sculpture was 'not an art of the unique but of the multiple instance: an art of the replica'.[4] The effect that the reproducibility of sculpture might have on its status in some ways mirrored the early debates about photography and the latter's claims that, despite the use of a machine, photography might still constitute 'art'. For some observers sculpture might be too literal and defined, not leaving space for the imagination: again this was one of the issues for early photography, and there have been periods when both practices were regarded as based on and therefore diminished by mechanical processes. Additionally in its display sculpture can be more affected by external conditions than painting, conditions often beyond the control of its maker. A painting hangs against a wall; a free-standing sculpture can be positioned in almost unlimited ways so that its sightlines become multiple and arbitrary. Another issue for the status of sculpture in the period addressed by Lichtenstein was that modernity was identified with colour and thus painting; therefore sculpture was seen as unable to reflect modern life. Further, the linking of the ideal nude with sculpture hastened its critical demise as this Greek standard became outmoded and irrelevant.[5] However, Lichtenstein argues that to equate the 'death' of the nude with the 'death' of sculpture is unsound, as sculpture moved towards a more naturalistic expression, loosening the conventions of the antique ideal, and this approach can certainly be seen in the work of many of the women sculptors discussed in my book.[6]

What we can see happening in the second half of the nineteenth century is an expansion of the role and nature of sculpture. With the many advances made by Britain in the areas of global power, industry, urbanization, wealth creation and the development of a public civic culture came an enhanced role for sculpture. Its tangible form helped make visible the celebration and commemoration of British achievements. Stylistic changes were also on the horizon, and it was in this context that the so-called 'New Sculpture' made its presence felt. The term was coined by critic Edmund Gosse in a series of articles written in 1894, and as an artistic approach it continued into the 1930s.[7] It therefore impacted strongly on the work of many of the women sculptors I will be looking at. It not only had stylistic implications but also displayed an expansion of genres and an interest in blurring the boundaries between so-called high and decorative art, significantly appropriate for my rationale. The New Sculpture practitioners not only looked to architectural collaborations but also connected with the art market through the production of small works and editioning.

The variety of materials that emerged did lay down a challenge to how, or indeed whether, one might separate 'fine' from 'applied' art. It is interesting that many of the individuals associated with the New Sculpture movement were trained craftsmen and so the materials they employed were ones already associated with the decorative arts.[8] This was one aspect that linked the New Sculpture to the Arts and Crafts movement: the desire to move away from reusing forms from earlier styles, as well as to make work that better respected the intrinsic properties of the material being worked. Marble should retain its 'stony' qualities and bronze its fluidity. In broad terms the New Sculpture privileged aesthetic concerns and the Arts and Crafts movement was more concerned with ways of working, with an attention to materials and a collapsing of artistic genres. So it is possible to see how both phenomena might coalesce in the practice of an individual sculptor.

The Arts and Crafts Exhibition Society commenced in 1888 but grew out of slightly earlier precedents such as the Century Guild of Artists and the Art Workers' Guild. Many of their discussions focused on issues of ethics and production in relation to art, on the relationship between artists, architects and craftsmen. Topics debated by the Art Workers' Guild in the 1880s and 1890s included the relationship between art and industry, and specifically for sculpture its relationship with decoration, reproductive processes and the role of colour.[9] These societies reflected the popularity of a taste for the decorative in the art of the day, with the medieval period serving as their model through craft being conceived as representing an artisanal society. They also provided a forum within which individuals could network and argue against the Royal Academy's privileging of painting as the pre-eminent art form. Importantly, the Arts and Crafts Society included women practitioners. In 1904 there was a symposium on Art Nouveau at which delegates included not only decorative artists such as Walter Crane but also sculptors such as Alfred Gilbert and William Hamo Thornycroft, and similar discussions took place at meetings of the National Association for the Advancement of Art.[10] Although Art Nouveau does not appear to have had a direct impact on sculpture, to seek the views of sculptors on the decorative aesthetic of Art Nouveau suggests that some common ground between decorative art and sculpture was possible.[11]

Arising out of the Arts and Crafts movement was a wish to improve the lives of ordinary people, with an emphasis on the domestic sphere which was especially important to some of the women sculptors I will discuss. The movement comprised a substantial breadth of bodies with similar ideas. So it was not about a particular style, but rather an underpinning ethos, and one that presented the craftsman as worthy of the same status as the fine artist. Hitherto utilitarian objects might now also be conceived of as fine art objects. Between the 1880s and the early 1900s, the period of greatest influence of the Arts and Crafts movement, many such objects came to be viewed as 'art', for example the products of art furnishers, artistic garden seats, art carpets, and so on.[12] One of the leading male sculptors of the day, Alfred Stevens, has been characterized as interested in architectural sculpture rather than portraiture, and in decorative household fittings rather than monumental works.[13] This challenges the assumption that (male) sculptors were necessarily focused on what might be assumed to be the most prestigious work. In fact, between 1890 and 1910 there was a strong drive to revive architectural decoration, not the least to secure sculpture's relevance to everyday life. Such ambitions also encouraged the production of bronze statuettes on a commercial scale, which would make sculpture both affordable and physically appropriate for domestic display in homes and gardens.[14] This phenomenon is the subject of Chapter 4.

The Arts and Crafts movement encouraged a functional alliance between sculpture and architecture, in that sculpture would itself move from being adornment to displaying intrinsic architectonic characteristics, combined with forms organically derived from nature.[15] A striking example of this type of sculpture can be seen in a key work by Katharine Maltwood (1878–1961). Her 1911 *Magna Mater* was designed as a triptych (**Plate 2**). The central crouching figure with bound arms conveys a feeling of despair: the man appears physically strong, like a labourer, and on either side of him are groups of people bound together along a rope. This work exists in both Portland stone and bronze versions, and the former was exhibited at the Royal Academy in 1911. Its title translates as the great mother, clearly linked to Maltwood's interest in ancient religion, and the text accompanying the work stated: 'Great travail is created for every man from the day he goes out of his mother's womb till the day he returns to the Mother of all things.' The work has been described as depicting a 'Blake-like figure' representing nature, surrounded by a mass of struggling humanity, the whole enclosed in a frame which some critics saw as referencing Egyptian architecture. Comparisons were made between the sculpture's vigour and the work of Eric Gill and Jacob Epstein.[16] The piece was very well received by the critics, the *Sunday Times* reviewer describing it as impressive and possessing a 'truly monumental quality'.[17] Writing about Maltwood in his 1931 book *The Art of Carved Sculpture*, Kineton Parkes described this work as

> a fine relief with architectural setting ... A central sitting figure, with arms on the drawn-up knees and face resting on the arms in thought, is supported by two side panels of many representations of children, women and men in ascending spirals and representing allegorically the activities of life on earth. It is a fine conception, carried out with great technical skill.[18]

The sculpture was bought by Alice and Elbert Hubbard who were leading figures in the American Arts and Crafts movement. Maltwood had studied under George Frampton at the Slade between 1896 and 1897.

Her training there enabled her to learn a wide range of techniques and to have contact with leaders of the Arts and Crafts movement. In the late 1890s she continued her studies in Italy and Paris where she studied the works of Rodin, and was particularly impressed by the Rodin Pavilion at the 1900 Exposition. In Italy she sketched and made notes on many famous Italian artworks as well making studies from nature. As had been the case with members of the Arts and Crafts movement, she very much admired the Florentine Renaissance artists such as Donatello and Michelangelo.[19]

Another Arts and Crafts concern was with the revival of a native interest in illustration and literary allusions, and an engagement with the applied arts that had its source in the Morris workshops as well as in John Ruskin's theories, later consolidated by the Art Workers' Guild and the Arts and Crafts Exhibition Society. Unlike the emphasis on form which could be seen in contemporary French sculpture, English practitioners frequently turned to more decorative work, often encompassing symbolic or allegorical themes. Sculptors working in this manner, as well as producing portrait busts and idealized groups for display at the Royal Academy, made shallow reliefs and general architectural decorative work. They began to use new materials and many followed the Arts and Crafts ideology of doing all the work themselves without the use of assistants.[20] However, in many accounts of twentieth-century sculpture any hint of 'the decorative' appears to have marginalized sculptures that displayed such characteristics. This is despite the fact that there appear to have been overlaps between the developing early modernist sculptures, the Arts and Crafts movement and the New Sculpture.[21]

This once more suggests that it is problematic to polarize traditional and avant-garde, Victorian and modern, not the least because neither artists nor audiences were likely to conceive of such art in this oppositional manner. Rather than a linear model of progression, we should view the art of any period as perpetually in conversation with and modifying that which preceded it. David Getsy has described the emergence of a heightened sense of naturalism that forced a sophisticated attention to the material qualities of a particular sculpture, and to how the sculptor could exploit these in order to encourage active engagement between the viewer and a work. With regard to women sculptors, his analysis of what a professional sculptor might be at this time inadvertently demonstrates the problems facing women practitioners due to their lack of access to key networks. He describes (male) professional sculptors in the early decades of the twentieth century as usually operating within the existing framework through which sculpture was both made and viewed, that is to say academies, established exhibiting societies and committees that controlled commissions. Sculptors' training was expected to lead to the creation of sculptural projects for 'civic life'.[22] The role of sculpture as an expression of civic values was firmly embedded in Western culture until at least the period of the Cold War, and despite continuing debates about exactly what such public works might mean, sculptors who produced them did at least have a recognizable niche within fine art. Clearly if male sculptors were expected to focus on such work, but often did not, then women sculptors working outside the appropriate institutional and commissioning networks were in an even more difficult situation. Once again the supposed distance between academic sculptors and those characterized as modern was questionable. For example, public commissions were not always awarded to Royal Academicians, but in reality were an important source of income for avant-garde sculptors. What was significant was how a sculptor was perceived, rather than their actual allegiance, either as part of the art establishment or opposed to it.[23] So the privileging of modernist practices as the only or the preferred narrative in the writing of twentieth-century art history ignores artistic interconnections and overlaps, and the attempt to place an artist's work in one of only two possible categories lacks subtlety.

Getsy also notes another aspect which can certainly be recognized in the work of numerous female sculptors of this period by proposing that many professional British sculptors in the early years of the twentieth century did not follow the fashion of the day but instead deliberately worked within a more established stylistic and intellectual framework. This, of course, made them open to attack as being outmoded, and within this 'more restrained and cautious environment' he included Kathleen Scott (1878–1947) as one of the sculptors whose work stood out due to 'its commitment to the definitions of professional sculpture and for its continued efforts to work within these parameters in the face of a vibrant and burgeoning modernism'.[24] Scott will be a key figure in my book. An example from her series of striking life-size bronze male youths is *The Kingdom is Within* (1925–26) which was shown at the Royal Academy in 1927 and at the Paris Salon (**Figure 2**). Bought by Conservative MP Sir Paul Latham in 1933, the sculpture was photographed beside a swimming pool at his home, Herstmonceux Castle in Sussex, in a 1935 feature published in *Country Life*.[25] The sculpture long ago vanished from Herstmonceux, although a statuette version without a blindfold is in the North Down Museum in Bangor Castle, Northern Ireland.[26] In its

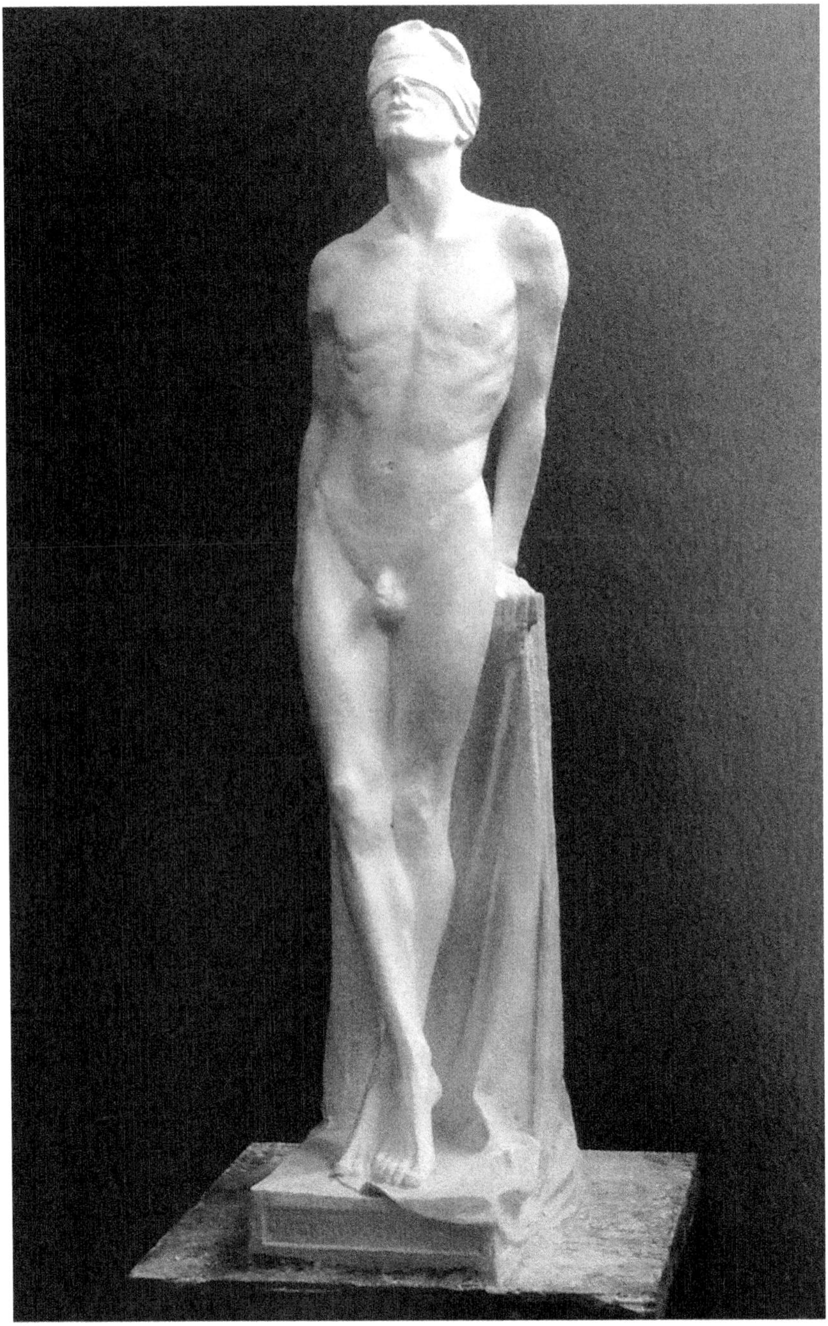

2. Kathleen Scott, *The Kingdom is Within*, 1925–26

beauty and vulnerability this is an impressive work by any standards. It bears comparison with the work of Auguste Rodin, whose sculpture was exhibited in London from the 1880s onwards and whose stylistic influence is present in the work of other female sculptors included in this book. Another popular strand of practice combined an Arts and Crafts aesthetic with a keen interest in early Renaissance forms, as can be seen in the work of Ellen Mary Rope (1855–1934) whose sculptures revealed an allegiance to artists such the Della Robbia family and Donatello. **Figure 3** shows Rope's terracotta *David playing before Saul* (c.1885) which was displayed at the Royal Academy in 1885. The work of many of the women sculptors discussed in this book sits somewhere on a spectrum between early Renaissance sculptural forms which fused classical precedents with increased naturalism, and a Rodinesque fluidity of expression.

There was a great deal of commentary on sculpture in art magazines and periodicals, although the individual art writers and critics who were in a position to construct a critical framework for sculpture comprised quite a small group, who themselves had various interconnections through friendship or locale. It is significant that the majority of writings about sculpture were in the form of articles rather than books, since journalism encouraged more challenging responses, possibly creating a lack of nuance, and too often a dismissal of the past. However, such commentary did help to create significant public interest in sculptural production: so the unveiling of a major sculpture, for example, would be accorded substantial press coverage.[27]

The ways in which sculpture might be expanded as a term is important for my book. Spielmann's 1901 publication *British Sculpture and Sculptors of To-day* included an unlikely figure in Walter Crane, someone normally regarded as a craftsman and a designer, rather than a sculptor. However, Spielmann noted Crane as a 'pioneer' for the 'new breed of sculptor "decorators" who had injected sculpture in Britain with a "fine decorative quality"'. For Spielmann, it was the linear character of Crane's output, rather than its three-dimensional quality, that resulted in his 'brilliant work'.[28] This spirit of cooperation was widespread beyond design, impacting wider critiques of both the makers and objects of art. Such an expansion of the boundaries of sculpture would be ongoing and will be explored in this book. Many of the sculptors I discuss worked across such areas, producing ceremonial objects, door knockers and statuettes, as did their male colleagues.

An example of a work that we might associate with the Arts and Crafts movement is Countess Feodora Gleichen's (1861–1922) unusual bronze

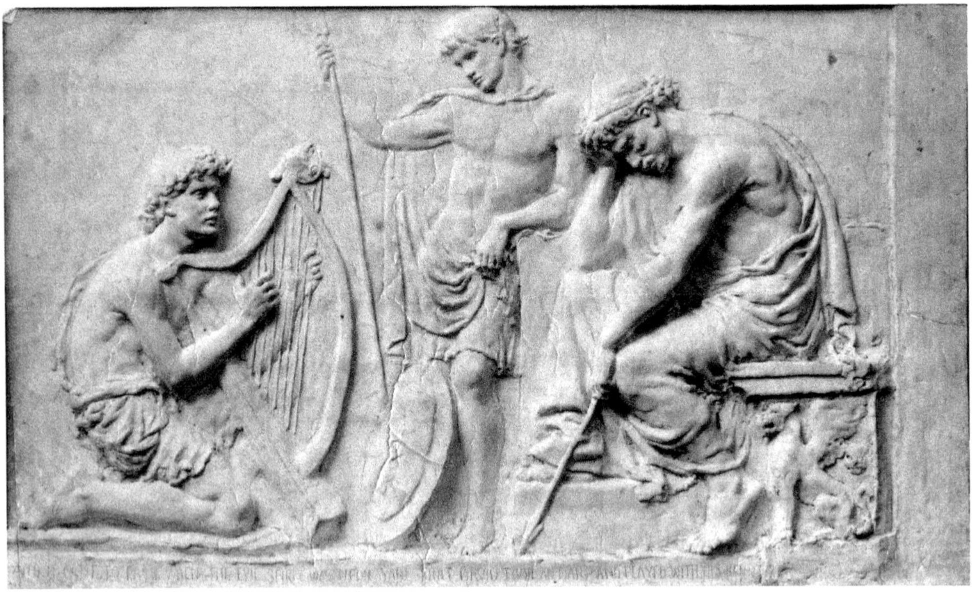

3. Ellen Mary Rope, *David playing before Saul*, c.1885

figure of *Satan* (c.1894) on a marble throne, which was exhibited at the Royal Academy (**Figure 4**). Gleichen, a great-niece of Queen Victoria, completed her studies in Rome in 1891 and at the Slade, where she was a pupil of Alphonse Legros. She produced mainly portraits, allegorical figures and decorative objects, exhibiting at the Royal Academy between 1892 and 1922, the New Gallery in 1894, and the New Dudley Gallery in 1907. The winged and armoured knight attracted critical attention, although Spielmann was not entirely convinced by it, describing it as 'a fanciful and weird design ... the work reveals undoubted skill and invention, although it is somewhat overloaded'.[29] More to his liking was Gleichen's 'beautiful hand-mirror of jade and bronze', first shown at the Royal Academy and then at the 1900 Paris Exhibition, where it won her a bronze medal, and which he felt displayed a greater understanding of design and decoration.[30] Therefore as a writer on British sculpture he was not at all opposed to considering decorative items.

Within the Arts and Crafts movement professional networks and exhibitions demonstrated the overlapping of 'Victorian' and 'modern' sculpture. The Art Workers' Guild, although without a large number of sculpture members, did have clear influence. Sculptors Edward Onslow

Ford and George Frampton served as chairmen, and among its members were William Hamo Thornycroft and Alfred Gilbert. Importantly, discussion topics indicate that the Guild regarded sculpture as an area of fine art practice that was malleable and open to change. Artistic definitions were perhaps surprising: for instance, Frampton was regarded as a 'craftsman', an 'art worker', and apparently was quite happy with such labels, open to new ideas and materials, working across a wide range from wax to metal, as well as plaster and stone.[31] It is striking that the emphasis on Frampton's craftsmanship, and his dexterity with and understanding of his materials, would later be echoed in the 'truth to materials' mantra associated with the twentieth-century avant-garde. This really should alert us to the somewhat imprecise way in which this much-repeated phrase has become attached to both the avant-garde and more particularly to carving.

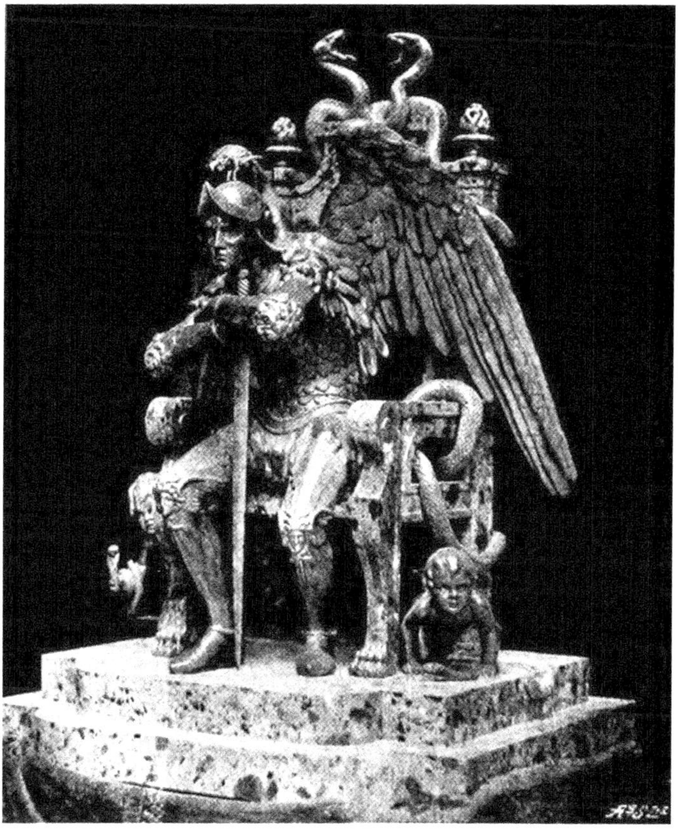

4. Feodora Gleichen, *Satan*, c.1894

The emphasis on the latter has bedevilled accounts of early twentieth-century British sculpture, the phrase having become overloaded with a signification that goes well beyond a description of sculptural method, and has as a result become generalizing and imprecise, losing much of its original meaning. The ways in which a sculptor achieves the final manifestation of their work is to varying degrees driven by, enhanced by and dependent on the materials used. Only a narrow definition has equated carving with modernity, and modernity with (ironically) traditional materials such as stone and marble. However, it was a term that had wide currency among artists and writers following the First World War, in the belief that the sculptor should retain total control over every stage in the production of a work. This was counterpoised against, and presented as superior to, the practice of sculptors who made clay models and then left the making of the sculpture in marble or bronze to specialist carvers or to bronze foundries.[32] The choice of sculptural materials has been used to demarcate the Victorian and the modern period, the former being associated with bronze, and the latter with stone. But in looking at sculptors working around the start of the twentieth century we see many who used a range of media, sometimes even within an individual work, while sculptors such as Epstein and Gill, well known for their stone carving, also used bronze and other materials, and thus the significance of this division between casting and carving is questionable. However, in the second quarter of the twentieth century many critics, in their wish to emphasize a modern practice, focused on the sculptor's decision either to model or to carve. This division was then expanded to present the modeller as trapped in nineteenth-century naturalism, as opposed to the 'high seriousness' of the modern sculptor who engaged with the physical demands of stone carving.

The choice of medium also inflected perceptions of the sculptor's character, and this focus on effort and the projection of an individual personality would not be helpful for female sculptors who were contending with social and cultural expectations of them as women. By engaging with direct carving in the 1920s and 1930s, the sculptor was characterized as a workman, and as unequivocally masculine. The difficulties for women sculptors in this context are clear both in terms of what they might practically achieve and the critical responses to their sculptures. Since the doctrine of carving impacted on male sculptors as well, the depth of this problem becomes even more apparent. That said, carving as a method of working undoubtedly enjoyed a resurgence after the First World War, but Ben Read has described how one might approach this history in a rather more subtle way than has frequently been the case. Concerning the harnessing of carving to early twentieth-century modernist sculpture, Read has alerted us to the fact that part of a Victorian sculptor's training would be to work as an assistant to a practising sculptor, and one of his tasks would be to carve marble for the main artist. In the 1930s Henry Moore produced models for casting in parallel with his small carvings and so this demarcation in sculptors' work between carving and modelling needs to be treated with some caution.[33] As Read has noted, critic Kineton Parkes' 1931 publication *The Art of Carved Sculpture* revealed a more nuanced history and as a contemporary source is of great significance. The predictable figures of Eric Gill, Jacob Epstein, Frank Dobson, John Skeaping and Moore are present. Also included was Barbara Hepworth, who for so long has been treated as the only British woman sculptor of note working in the early twentieth century. However, other names also appeared, such as Edna Manley (1900–87) and Ursula Edgcumbe (1900–85), both of whom are little known today.

Edna Manley was born in Cornwall and relocated to Jamaica in 1921, her father being British Jamaican. She had private art lessons with Maurice Harding, followed by study at Regent Street Polytechnic and St Martin's School of Art (alongside Moore and Hepworth). From around 1925 she was making sculpture mainly from native wood. She exhibited in London with the Society of Women Artists and the London Group, as well as at a number of venues including the Goupil Gallery. She was a significant sculptor in British art, although the cost of shipping her work to Britain for exhibition inhibited this, but she did establish herself as the leading twentieth-century figure in Jamaican art, where her use of black models and her exploration of Jamaican iconography marked out her work as culturally distinct. In 1927 she exhibited at the French Gallery and it was reported in the Jamaican *Gleaner* newspaper that the show had opened to great acclaim. Manley's work was favourably compared to that of Epstein and it was suggested that her use of 'beautiful native woods' almost constituted a new medium in English and European sculpture.[34] Her 1929 statue *Eve-Ceremonial Dance* was described in the Jamaican press as 'deeply penetrating in the perception of character true to the unsophisticated Jamaica [*sic*] type, and powerfully executed'.[35] This sculpture was exhibited at the Goupil Gallery in 1930, attracting notable critical acclaim; however, when it was acquired by the Graves Gallery, Sheffield in 1937 it was dismissed by a local councillor as 'absolute tripe' (**Plate 3**).[36] Kineton Parkes described this impressive life-size figure as

> a very fine piece with a most attractive original lyricism, untainted by any art movement, carved out in the wilds. An Englishwoman ... with a noted faculty for sculpture ... Untrammelled as she is by the currency of modernistic ideas and having an original and productive mind, as well as enthusiasm and industry ... she is sensitive enough to feel not only what separates modelling from carving, but what separates carving in stone from carving in wood.[37]

The gift to the Graves Gallery may have resulted from the friendship between Manley and John Rothenstein, the gallery's first director. It was the first notable sculptural acquisition by the city and many were critical of its unconventional treatment of the nude. The Graves Gallery possesses a letter to the sculptor dated 7 June 1937 (unsigned, but probably from Rothenstein):

> It was charming of you to apologise for any trouble your 'Eve' has caused, but quite needless. In view of the prejudice against any but a stereotyped representation of the nude in the North of England, the work like 'Eve' is always a tempting target. In this case, however, the attack which was thoroughly irresponsible has failed to score, and while a certain number of people view it with reserve rather than displeasure, the consensus of opinion is that the City is very fortunate to have it. It is actually the first piece of serious sculpture to be acquired by the City and it is natural that the size combined with the ... [text missing] of approach which it reveals, should produce a rather staggering effect. Personally I am delighted with it, but what is more important I am convinced that when this bit of nonsense has abated, 'Eve' will become a valued landmark in the City.[38]

Sculptors connected to the Arts and Crafts movement used the sculpted relief as a vehicle for experimentation, as well as a financially expedient practice. This trend continued well into the twentieth century, as can be seen in a sculpture by Ursula Edgcumbe who worked in the studio of James Havard Thomas from the age of 15, prior to studying under him at the Slade where she won the Scholarship for Sculpture in 1918. In 1921 she moved from modelling in clay to carving, and worked as an architectural carver, especially for George L. Kennedy. Her 1921 Hoptonwood stone relief *The Finding of Moses* is reminiscent of early Renaissance sculptural reliefs in its slightly awkward perspectival rendering of the crib (**Figure 5**). Edgcumbe was among the first artists to join the National Society of

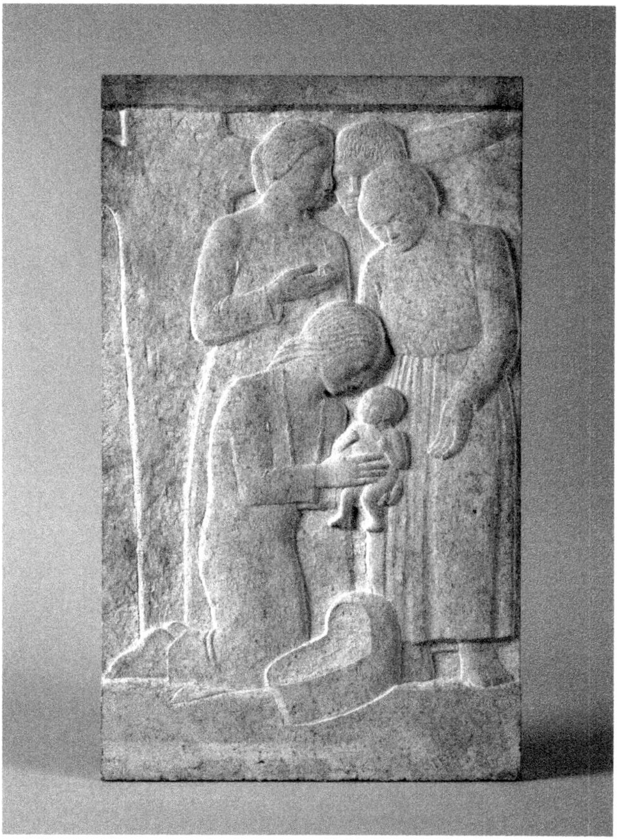

5. Ursula Edgcumbe, *The Finding of Moses*, 1921

Painters, Sculptors, Engravers and Potters when it was established in 1929, and regularly exhibited with them. She held a one-woman show at Leger and Son in 1936 and the catalogue reveals the range of her carving, as she worked with most of the English freestones but had a strong preference for dark Italian marbles when making small work.[39] The problems raised by dividing artists into 'traditional' and 'modern' are exemplified by a sculptor such as Edgcumbe, since other examples of her work seem to better align with the ways in which the latter category has been defined. Her 1931 *Seated Female Figure* (sometimes referred to as *Seated Woman*) is essentially in the early manner of sculptors such as Gill, but rarely appears in such histories, whose construction has of course depended largely on the preferences of influential male critics and writers (**Plate 4**). It was revealing to see this sculpture displayed in the first room of Tate Britain's 2015 exhibition *Barbara Hepworth:*

Sculpture for a Modern World as an example of the popularity of carving in the 1920s and 1930s. Since Hepworth is routinely presented within a modernist, innovative framework, this would encourage viewers at that exhibition to understand the Edgcumbe piece on the same terms. It was striking to see that her sculpture held its own in terms of quality and presence, making a stark point about the wildly differing fortunes of female sculptors' reputations.

Publications such as Herbert Read's *A Concise History of Modern Painting* (1959) and *A Concise History of Modern Sculpture* (1964) would consistently support a narrow range of sculptors, in particular Moore and Hepworth, presenting them as having overcome the supposedly parochial nature of British art which Read believed had existed in the nineteenth century. But it was never that simple: an emphasis on stylistic distinctions has placed a false divide between works deemed traditional (old-fashioned) or modern (experimental). The turn of the century and the death of Queen Victoria has for too long stood as a barrier between what went before and what came after. Clearly this is unrealistic, caused by arbitrary dates. While influences from earlier generations on subsequent ones, such as that of Reynolds and Turner on painters active in the mid to late nineteenth century, have rightly been acknowledged, for too long the same connections were rarely made between Victorian painters, let alone sculptors, and those active in the early twentieth century. However, scholars are beginning to examine this issue, challenging the supposed boundaries that have demarcated modernism from its immediate past and presented it as a 'rigid and over-determined narrative'.[40]

2.2 Training

In his *British Sculpture and Sculptors of To-Day* Spielmann stated that a resurgence in British sculpture could largely be ascribed to the influence of Jules Dalou and Edouard Lantéri, as well as to the impact of Alfred Gilbert.[41] The names of these sculptors in their role as teacher recur in the biographies of many of the women sculptors discussed in my book. French sculptor Dalou was in London between 1871 and 1879, holding the position of Professor of Sculpture at the South Kensington School of Art during this period. He was friends with Lantéri who taught at the National Art Training School between 1880 and 1917, a long period of influence. Lantéri used his teaching notes to publish a three-volume book *Modelling: A Guide for Teachers and Students* (1902–11), which became a standard work of reference. Dalou had been a student alongside Rodin in Paris and the fluidity of Rodin's style certainly infiltrated English sculpture at the turn of the century. Women had already experienced some success within the Arts and Crafts movement in designing textiles, metal and leather work, and ceramics, which in part gave them a way into the sculptural and allied professions. The introduction of clay modelling techniques from France by Dalou was one feature in the creation of the New Sculpture movement, and modelling was a technique suited to the production of small bronze figures, portrait busts and groups appropriate for display in the home. Edwardian women sculptors undoubtedly benefited from these developments. Alfred Gilbert worked with Lantéri, and from 1882 he was exhibiting to great acclaim in London, after 1901 teaching in London, both as Professor of Sculpture at the Royal Academy of Arts and regularly lecturing elsewhere.

For the majority of the nineteenth century women sculptors faced great difficulty in gaining an artistic education equal to that of their male peers. However, art school training was gradually opened up to women in the final quarter of the century. The Royal Academy Schools were one of the first to reluctantly admit women from 1860, although they were not allowed access to the life room until the 1890s. The move to admit female students came about when the institution relocated to Burlington House. In its former premises, space was at a premium and this was one reason why male students received preferential treatment. In Edinburgh the Royal Scottish Academy accepted women from 1854 but also barred them from life classes. The Government School of Design, founded in 1837 and known as the Central School of Design from c.1852, accepted women students, but as their curriculum was devised in order to produce industrial designers and art teachers, drawing from the nude was not a normal part of their studies. Some women sculptors, for example Princess Louise (1848–1939), did follow the design instruction at the National Art Training School, but it was not until the opening of the Slade School of Art in 1871 that women finally could undertake a high level of fine art training.[42] The Slade opened through a bequest from businessman and art collector Sir Felix Slade, devised to establish a fine art college as part of University College, London, which had itself been founded in 1826 'upon the principle of accepting students from any race, class or religion and was a driving force of progression in accepting female students on the same terms as men'.[43] By the 1890s women were able to engage with the academic art school system and were also increasingly able to travel to study in private studios or academies. Women sculptors who were exhibiting in the period covered by this book had mostly benefited from formal art training.

Few women were trained in the Royal Academy's Sculpture School. However, it seems that a proportionately greater number of them as compared with female painting students at the Academy pursued their practice after training. It is possible that awards from the Lady Feodora Gleichen Fund (1922–51) may have helped, although they were small sums. Administered by the Academy from 1926, this fund had been established to provide grants for female sculptors when they had concluded their education, as well as to buy works from them. Gleichen had been the first woman to be elected to the Royal Society of British Sculptors (RBS). Although the intention had been to use the money to provide a studio and grants to enable women sculptors to focus on their work for a few years, the fund was not sufficiently large and so instead its income was used each year to buy sculptures from women artists at a value of £150. The awards seem to have generally been given to younger and less well-known women sculptors at the Royal Academy exhibitions.[44]

The first woman to become an associate member of the Royal Academy was Annie Swynnerton in 1922, and the first woman full Royal Academician was Laura Knight in 1936. Since the buying public looked for the letters RA or ARA after an artist's name as a guarantee of quality, artists without this distinction would be less likely to make a sale. This discriminated against women artists and thus perpetuated the notion that their work was not of a 'good' quality. Admitting female students to the Royal Academy Schools was also quite probably prompted by self-interest, since by the end of the nineteenth century the Academy was faced with significant competition for students from the Slade.[45] The Royal College of Art (RCA) was established in 1896 with a view to producing good designers who would be of benefit to the country either through working within industry or by educating the taste of potential consumers. This contrasted with the other schools, since the Royal Academy used privately sourced funds to train students in the fine arts, and the Central School of Art and Design was funded by a local authority and trained mostly part-time students 'in skills that had a direct relationship to their careers as artisans in the crafts and design'.[46] At the RCA the ideals of the Arts and Crafts Exhibition Society and of the Art Workers' Guild fed into the School of Sculpture. Generally contemporary art was not discussed, as was also the case at the Royal Academy, although there were a few occasions when the RCA responded to contemporary events such as contributing work for the 1924 British Empire Exhibition at Wembley, which focused on demonstrating the trading benefits of the Empire.[47] For clarification, the Royal College of Art went under various titles during the period covered by this book: the relevant ones that crop up in biographies and reviews are the National Art Training School from 1853, the South Kensington School of Art, which was an informal title, and finally the Royal College of Art from 1896. In my text I will use whichever title is referred to in my sources.

Other developments facilitated artists moving across into the arena of the decorative or applied arts. The British Institute of Industrial Art (BIIA) was formed in 1920 and Gertrude Hermes showed a panel of her door furniture at the Institute's first exhibition.[48] By 1924 works had been selected to form a permanent collection of modern industrial art to be housed in the Victoria and Albert Museum, and between 1922 and 1929 displays of contemporary industrial art were staged in the museum's North Court. The BIIA was wound down and by 1933 was absorbed into the new Council for Art and Industry. It is during this period that we can see some of our female sculptors crossing into the arena of the decorative or applied arts. In 1920 the Federation of British Industries established an Industrial Art Committee, and the work of these bodies seems to have supported an area of mutual ground for the fine and decorative arts. In 1929 Herbert Read noted the experiments taking place at the RCA, referring to the possibility of 'canvas free artists'.[49] One of his favoured sculptors, Barbara Hepworth, a graduate of the sculpture school, designed constructivist textiles for the Edinburgh company Mortons and also decorated contemporary ceramics for Foley's.[50] Therefore there was some blurring of the boundaries between different forms of visual practice, and within the practices of individual modernist artists. These shifts will be evident in the work of some of the women sculptors covered in the following chapters. However, it is fair to say that these aspects of many artists' work have in the past been downplayed. Twentieth-century art history has tended not to look favourably on diversity within an artist's output: indeed variety has frequently attracted the negative accusation of inconsistency.

The School of Architecture at the RCA provided all college entrants with training to appreciate the connections between different visual art forms, of which architecture was considered to be the key. Many art schools during the period 1900–40 offered architectural training for both painting and sculpting students, and within the RCA School of Architecture there was a strong interest in the Arts and Crafts movement and links with the Art Workers' Guild, reinforcing a belief in the unity of architecture and art, both applied and fine. This belief is evidenced in the work of several of the women sculptors I will be discussing. The drawing together of these creative disciplines was promoted by many individuals. Walter Crane, one of the founder members of the Art Workers' Guild and an influential member of the artistic craft circle, published *Ideals in Art* in 1905, in which he argued his belief that the handicrafts could allow for greater artistic creativity, that 'we must turn our artists into craftsmen and our craftsmen into artists'.[51] In a similar vein, William Lethaby, who was Professor of Design at the RCA between 1900 and 1918, was very influential within the sphere of art education and the Arts and Crafts movement, arguing that it was vital that designers be capable makers, that artists and designers have a good knowledge of the traditions of their genre and that all work should be produced by reference to nature.[52]

Work produced in the School of Sculpture at the RCA remained largely figurative, in the tradition of Lantéri, and as continued by Francis Derwent Wood, Ernest Cole and Gilbert Ledward. The focus was on figure and architectural composition; studies in the round and in relief of the head and body from life; drawing from life; and stone carving, wood carving and pointing. Carving was seen as an integral part of the course, and modelling for pottery and metalwork was linked to the School of Design. Collaboration with the School of Architecture was also encouraged. In 1930 sculptor Richard Garbe was appointed to the School and its work became more contemporary in character, with the stone carving tutor Barry Hart and the assistant ex-student Henry Moore encouraging modern work. Fine art was considered to be more 'intellectual' than design and therefore the Design School was considered by many to be second class, with staff sending weaker students there. Such a view probably accounts for the high number of female students in the Design School, as well as the fact that women were expected to find forms of employment other than as artists.[53] There were large numbers of female students at the RCA generally; however, their employment was restricted. Until 1944 only unmarried women could hold a teaching post and the number in industry managerial posts were few. Some women who entered the crafts did gain recognition, but the majority did not.

By the 1920s carving was widely taught in art schools and was especially taken up by women students. It certainly was not the case that Henry Moore and Barbara Hepworth were exceptional in using this method, yet this is a narrative that has persisted.[54] Classes in stone and wood carving at art schools commenced around 1900 and often the tenets of the Arts and Crafts movement permeated the nature of such teaching. However, the choice of material could be critical. A sculptor working in wood risked comparison with the large number of amateurs who favoured that material, since it needed skill but no great physical strength. In this way wood carving became 'domesticated' through association with amateurism. In contrast, enormous numbers of men were employed in the trades associated with stone carving – quarrymen, stonemasons and sculptors – and thus it was perceived as inherently a masculine practice. After 1900, however, there were some changes in attitude towards the use of wood in sculpture, ironically in part due to its mass appeal. So in the 1920s, for example, apart from Hepworth, male sculptors such as Eric Gill, Richard Garbe, Henry Poole, Henry Moore, Leon Underwood and Alan Durst all worked with wood, and in 1924 a substantial number of wood sculptures were shown at the Royal Academy. Therefore the picture was complex – wood carving was still associated with amateurism, but it was also being used by fine artists.[55]

In some instances women outnumbered men among groups of art students, but the curriculum that they experienced could be markedly different since their male tutors did not view them in the same light. It was vital for both sexes that a student made contact with established figures within their profession. However, this was not facilitated for female students because of the masculine values inherent in art school training. Women seeking a creative career were often guided towards the applied arts; however, large numbers of men also worked in this area, and so such activities, which included woodwork, were perceived by many to be inherently masculine. Moreover these occupations were not attractive to middle-class female students, being commercial, workshop-based enterprises. If women wished to work in these areas, the only realistic route for them was to operate independently and show their work in specialist exhibitions or those staged by women artists' groups.[56]

One way in which aspiring female sculptors could attempt to break out of the restrictions of the British art school system was by spending a period studying in Paris. The city presented hitherto unexperienced freedoms to both sexes, although arguably more so in the case of young men. Nonetheless, studying at one of the private academies such as Académie Julian or Académie Colarossi presented real spaces for women to study: the former school ran special life classes for women, but at Colarossi there were mixed classes. We have a description from Kathleen Scott (then Kathleen Bruce) of her first day at Colarossi in 1901:

> New figure models were chosen every Monday morning ... At the end of the studio passed one by one a string of nude male models. Each jumped for a moment on to the model throne, took a pose and jumped down. The model for the day was being chosen. Before reason could control instinct, I turned and fled, shut myself in the lavatory and was sick.[57]

One clear disadvantage for these women sculpture students becomes evident when we look at Paris and its master sculptors. This was the length of training that the latter had undergone. Rodin, for example, had worked for many years as an artisan sculptor: this very long technical apprenticeship was difficult for women to access for social and financial reasons. Most female students necessarily came from middle- or upper-class families, having continued their education beyond the age at which those from less fortunate backgrounds would leave school. With this came certain expectations as to how they should conduct themselves, that they should not push themselves forward. If female sculptors followed the expected route of marriage, the undoubted responsibilities of running a home, caring for a family and providing emotional support to a wage-earning husband were, perhaps with some justification, seen as inevitably impeding their career. Nonetheless, in the first quarter of the twentieth century women sculptors represented nearly 40 per cent of new entrants to the profession, reflecting the marked increase in female students studying at art school in the 1880s and 1890s.

2.3 Societies and exhibiting

At the end of the nineteenth century and into the early years of the twentieth, sculptors wishing to exhibit had to do so at large exhibitions in London and at regional art venues where their work was scrutinized for selection by juries. Female sculptors whose careers commenced in the 1920s were the first of their sex to display their work at smaller events such as exhibitions staged by the Seven and Five Society and the London Group, and to gain one-person shows at art dealers' galleries. For example the sculptures of Elizabeth (Betty) Muntz (1894–1979) were shown at the Warren Gallery in 1928 (just before Henry Moore's

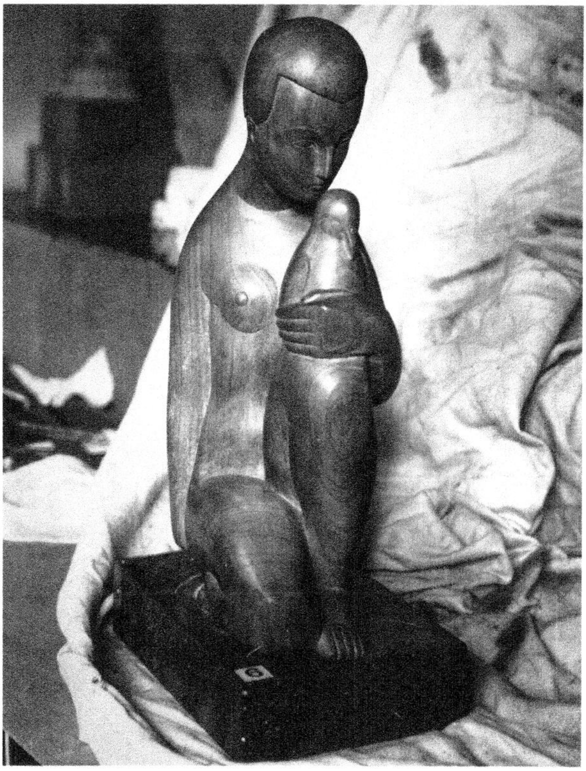

6. Elizabeth Muntz, *Valentine with Bird (Seagull)*, c.1927

one-man show there). **Figure 6** shows her *Valentine with Bird (Seagull)*, dating from around 1927. Born in Toronto, Muntz moved to Europe and studied in the studios of Antoine Bourdelle, subsequently arriving in England in the mid-1920s. She was privately taught by Frank Dobson and joined the Seven and Five Society, exhibiting with them between 1926 and 1929. In 1932 she moved permanently from London to Chaldon Herring in Dorset. Muntz's Warren Gallery show attracted favourable attention, with a review in *The Times* noting that her strength was her sensitivity to materials, avoiding 'the cheaply "glyptic" effect of pronounced tool marks' and working with 'the decorative quality of the grain'.[58] Barbara Hepworth showed at the Beaux Arts Gallery in 1928 and at Arthur Tooth and Sons in 1930: however, it was noticeable that she and John Skeaping were presented as a sculptural (as well as marital) partnership. Hepworth differed from many other female sculptors who either delayed marriage and children, or remained single, being only 22 when she married Skeaping. Other women sculptors also managed to combine a professional and family life, for example Edna Manley, Dora Gordine and Anne Strauss (1902–88). A notable benefit of these partnerships, which were usually with fellow artists, was access to valuable networks and patrons. Hepworth in particular capitalized on this, marrying first a sculptor, then painter Ben Nicholson. Hepworth's and Skeaping's 1927 joint studio show drew the attention of curator Richard Bedford and collector George Eumorfopoulos, and such patrons helped secure exhibitions in dealers' galleries.[59]

Within the main institutions such as the RBS, the Chelsea Arts Club, the Royal Academy Schools and the RCA a relatively small number of sculptors held positions of influence. Most were academicians, thus confirming the power of the Royal Academy, which derived from its wealth, the high profile of the Summer Exhibition, its control of trusts and the Chantrey and Leighton funds for purchasing artworks, as well as from royal patronage. At the Royal Academy sculptors' interests faced competition from those of the painters and architects, and as a result the formation of the RBS in 1904 was intended to promote and support British sculptors and the profession in general.

It commenced with 51 members, who represented the most prominent sculptors of the time, and royal patronage was bestowed in 1911. The establishment of this body not only marked a concerted effort to raise the status of professional sculpture, but also showed that by the start of the twentieth century sculpture was prominent in British artistic life. From the outset the RBS prioritized the issue of professional identity, realized through the regulation of competitions, the devising of a form of ideal contract to protect sculptors when working to commission, and lobbying the government for changes in copyright law. It also campaigned for improvements in the display of sculpture in provincial museums, and Manchester City Art Gallery was one that responded positively by including a gallery dedicated to the display of sculpture in plans for the rebuilding of the museum in 1910. Within the RBS members were both allies and competitors, but information disseminated by the Society gave all its members access to sculpture competitions and war memorial commissions in the early 1920s.

The prime context in which sculptors met prospective patrons was through exhibiting, but it was difficult for most sculptors to obtain a solo show: they needed the right connections. Since most of them had to rely on inclusion in the Royal Academy Summer Exhibition they were dependent on the tastes of a small number of senior academicians. The proportion of sculptures to paintings exhibited was low, but sculptors were tied by the fact that no other venue came anywhere near to the Royal Academy's average of showing 214 sculptures every year.[60] To exhibit outside the Academy meant that a sculptor had to belong to a society, most of which were for painters. The International Society of Sculptors, Painters and Gravers was unusual in representing all major art forms and operating on an international basis, and with the election of Rodin as president in 1905 the profile of the sculptor members was enhanced. The RBS was the only society that tried to put on solely sculptural shows, but it met with some difficulty in finding suitable premises. So it took a more collaborative approach and directed its efforts towards promoting the presence of sculpture at international exhibitions, the chief ones being the 1911 International Exhibition in Rome and the 1924 British Empire Exhibition. The formation of the Chelsea Arts Club had involved some sculptors, with 65 joining the Club between 1900 and 1925. One bonus for sculptors here was the possibility of joining forces with architects, who were present in the Club in about the same numbers as the sculptors. In addition, the British School at Rome's council and executive committees contained prominent collectors such as Viscount Esher, Alfred Mond and Stephen Courtauld, who were in an ideal position to purchase or commission sculptures. Even though by the early decades of the twentieth century women artists had gained access to the same art training as men, and continued to exhibit in the same venues and under the auspices of the same societies, it is the case that their gender remained an issue. Sex discrimination operated in both overt and covert forms, and it was undoubtedly advantageous for a woman sculptor to have the backing of a male patron or family member. Women also supported each other, but given the general lack of records for women artists this is yet another area that is hard to explore.

Women had to be persistent in waiting for exhibiting opportunities, regardless of praise for their abilities. For example, the sculptor Dame Ethel Walker (1861–1951) had exhibited at the Royal Academy from 1898 onwards, but it was only in the early 1940s that she was described as 'our greatest woman artist'.[61] Today she is little known. She was eventually elected to the Royal Academy, but this came 40 years after she had joined the New English Art Club. The London Group held its first exhibition in March 1914 at the Goupil Gallery, moving to the Mansard Gallery in Heal's department store from 1917 to 1924, then to the Royal Watercolour Society Galleries between 1925 and 1927, and thereafter exhibiting at the New Burlington Galleries. The Mansard Gallery was important because of Heal's position as a leader in modern design. The gallery was positioned on the top floor of the store, with an adjacent garden and a courtyard with a fountain, and its first highly successful exhibition was curated by Roger Fry. In the context of the Mansard Gallery, the London Group had the opportunity to present their work as a suitable component of modern design in contemporary home interiors. Among later members of the group were Gertrude Hermes and Barbara Hepworth. The majority of London Group artists had been educated at the Slade, an exception being Elizabeth Muntz. Writing in 1931 Kineton Parkes noted that

> while the London galleries have done much during the last twenty years to encourage the British sculptors to exhibit their carved work, the exhibiting societies have not been so enterprising. A notable exception is the London Group, which, since its inception in 1914, has given to the quite young men and women the opportunity of demonstrating their ideals.[62]

One way for women to increase the exposure of their work was through the formation of all-female exhibiting societies. After the First World War the largest of these groups was the Society of Women Artists, which had been established in 1857 and received royal patronage from 1865. It was run essentially as an academy and thus was similar in ethos to the Royal Academy; formed initially as the Society of Female Artists, between 1869 and 1899 it was known as the Society of Lady Artists. Membership peaked in 1930 at 134 members. Like the Royal Academy it offered full and associate membership, and divided members into the categories of fine artists or craft workers. The Society was clearly well regarded, since the post-1920 records indicate its competitiveness, with about half of the works submitted each year being rejected. However, it appears that in some ways the Society maintained the status quo, since women artists working in a modernist idiom were either not invited or did not submit work to open exhibitions. The effect of exhibiting through invitation also meant that artists who had not yet gained a reputation were disadvantaged, since they were unlikely to be approached. Additionally, the majority of the Society of Women Artists' members were painters: sculpture was included in their exhibitions but only at the level of about 20 or 30 items out of a total exhibit of 500 or more.[63]

The Women's International Art Club (WIAC), established in 1900, differed in that its members did not wish to receive royal patronage and saw themselves as essentially a cooperative of female artists. In Scotland the Glasgow Society of Lady Artists had been formed in 1882 and in

1924 a further group was formed in Edinburgh, the Scottish Society of Women Artists. The aim of the women who formed these associations was to give female artists greater opportunities to show their work rather than to challenge the contemporary (masculine) norms of the art world. These societies enabled their members to form professional networks, and naturally they were concerned to address the economic position of women artists and to do whatever was possible to enable their careers. This meant that they placed an emphasis on the professional conduct of the societies and on setting high standards for artwork. The WIAC focused its efforts on its annual exhibitions which were open to members and invited guest artists. In 1932 it elected Ethel Walker, a long-standing member, as its honorary president. She was clearly seen as an artist of stature, since the Club's minutes record that it was hoped that her election would bring the Club to the attention of the public and attract greater press coverage. The WIAC's membership was at its highest in 1937 when it reached 186, and by 1950 it formalized the membership at 150.[64] In 1932 the Club organized a special section for Decorative and Architectural Arts.

The activities of the Glasgow Society of Lady Artists were well regarded as contributing to Glasgow's cultural life. Unusually the Society was founded by a man, the headmaster of Glasgow School of Art, Robert Greenlees, with the aim of enabling female students to continue in their profession after art school. The early days were exceptional, with the members having their own premises from which they were able to exhibit. However, in order to absorb running costs they had to co-opt lay members, who eventually outnumbered the artist members.

The Scottish Society of Women Artists (SSWA) was also founded by a man, William McDougall, who in this instance had in mind the promotion of the work of his daughter Lily and her female colleagues. He remained its president until 1930, although the Society was run and managed by a female committee. In his inaugural address McDougall suggested that the idea for the Society had arisen from 'a general new-found confidence from men in what women could achieve after their contribution to the war effort'. He argued that the work that women had taken on during the war had proved their ability to 'contribute to the life of the world', not the least since they had performed many roles which hitherto were inaccessible 'on the plea of sex discrimination'. He believed that it was now fair that women should be given equal opportunities in peacetime. The tone of his address was somewhat qualified, perhaps indicating that his words were aimed at a male rather than female audience, and with an emphasis on encouraging women to develop as citizens. When widely reported in the Scottish press, his argument was understood as being largely economically driven, and this interpretation is understandable when we read McDougall quoted as advocating 'a good show window' for female artists which would

> add materially to the economic response. It was no good hiding the fact that many of them had to live by their profession, and therefore must sell, having not yet discovered a method of living on air. Others had no need to do so, though all classes of course, liked to dispose of their work, knowing in this practical way it was admired and coveted.

It does seem as if he was trying to persuade those (men) who had a low opinion of women's intellectual capacity when he continued:

> In art they could create the vogue and the more of it they disseminated in educating the people the happier and more refined they would be even though its source emanated from the brain of a woman the more of beauty brought into the home and appreciated the better. For that reason alone was room for a Society which could provide what was required even from a woman's standpoint.

Thus this perception of the beneficial effects of art is placed in the context of a domestic and decorative sphere, naturally understood to be feminine. Therefore 'women's role is here seen primarily as beautification of the environment and the Society's role to make room for that expression'.[65]

The SSWA displayed a concern with the status of craft in the interwar years: in its annual exhibitions such work now comprised about half the total number of works on display.[66] From 1925 it held one exhibition for craft and one for fine art; however, from 1941 applied art was subsumed into the Society's single annual exhibition. It has been difficult to judge whether the craft exhibition arose through demand or from a wish to follow the tenets of the Arts and Crafts movement, and the possibility remains that supporting craft could simply have been a mechanism by which to confirm women's function to beautify the home.[67]

These societies were clearly important fora for women, but the opportunities for women sculptors to exhibit their work were mixed: in a market where painting was generally preferred to sculpture difficulties arising from their gender were exacerbated. A nineteenth-century legacy was a perception that women's creativity might be more suitably realized through craft rather than art objects, or through design rather than painting or sculpture.[68] Therefore their choice of medium and genre would affect how they were regarded by critics. Society was comfortable with the idea of the female amateur artist, but it is clear that as early as the mid-nineteenth century many such women had great ambitions, and this elicited responses from critics that veered 'between criticism and gallantry, between scholarship and small talk, in their treatment of women's work. Often the women ... too showed a like confusion at the contradictions of their own position.'[69] The following chapters will show examples of this, particularly striking in the case of Kathleen Scott. Despite her great success as a professional sculptor, this type of critical response, which mixed flattery and descriptions of domestic trivia with rather weak attempts to critique her work, was not counteracted by Scott's repeated personal self-deprecation.

Notes

1 Jacqueline Lichtenstein, *The Blind Spot: An Essay on the Relations between Painting and Sculpture in the Modern Age* (Los Angeles: Getty Research Institute, 2008), pp. 3–4.
2 Lichtenstein, *The Blind Spot*, pp. 9–10.
3 Lichtenstein, *The Blind Spot*, p. 10.
4 Lichtenstein, *The Blind Spot*, p. 25.
5 Lichtenstein, *The Blind Spot*, pp. 149–52.
6 Lichtenstein, *The Blind Spot*, pp. 153–54.
7 Edmund Gosse, 'The New Sculpture 1879–1884', *Art Journal*, 1894, pp. 138–42, 199–203, 277–82, 306–11.
8 S. K. Tillyard, *The Impact of Modernism 1900–1920: Early Modernism and the Arts and Crafts Movement in Edwardian England* (London: Routledge, 1988), p. 151.
9 Martina Droth, Jason Edwards and Michael Hatt, *Sculpture Victorious: Art in the Age of Invention, 1837–1901* (New Haven, CT: Yale University Press, 2014), p. 370.
10 Location unknown. There was coverage in the *Magazine of Art*, 1904, in three parts: Francis S. Blizard, 'L'Art Nouveau: What it is and what is thought of it: a symposium', Part I, pp. 209–13; Part II, pp. 259–64; Part III, pp. 324–27.
11 Martina Droth, 'The Statuette and the Role of the Ornamental in late Nineteenth Century Sculpture', PhD dissertation, University of Reading, 2000, p. 121.
12 Tillyard, *The Impact of Modernism*, p. 12.
13 Susan Beattie, *The New Sculpture* (New Haven, CT: Yale University Press, 1983), pp. 2–3.
14 Beattie, *The New Sculpture*, p. 8.
15 Rosemary Alicia Brown, *Katharine Emma Maltwood, Artist, 1878–1961*, monograph for exhibition at the Maltwood Art Museum and Gallery, University of Victoria, June–July 1981 (Saanich, BC: Maltwood Art Museum and Gallery, 1981), p. 16.
16 Brown, *Katharine Emma Maltwood*, p. 21.
17 *Sunday Times*, 30 April 1911, n.p., quoted in Brown, *Katharine Emma Maltwood*, p. 21.
18 Kineton Parkes, *The Art of Carved Sculpture, Vol. 1, Western Europe, America and Japan* (London: Chapman and Hall, 1931), p. 122.
19 Brown, *Katharine Emma Maltwood*, p. 20.
20 Brown, *Katharine Emma Maltwood*, p. 16.
21 Tillyard, *The Impact of Modernism*, p. 158. Quoted in Sarah Victoria Turner, '"Reuniting what should never have been separated": The Arts and Crafts movement, modernism, and sculpture in Britain 1890–1914', *Nineteenth-Century Art Worldwide: A Journal of Nineteenth-Century Visual Culture*, 14.2 (2015), http://www.19th-artworldwide.org/summer15/ turner-on-the-arts-and-crafts-movement-modernism-and-sculpture-in-britain (accessed 25 November 2019).
22 David Getsy, 'The identity of the sculptor 1900–25', in Henry Moore Institute, *Sculpture in 20th Century Britain: Identity, Infrastructures, Aesthetics, Display, Reception* (Leeds: Henry Moore Institute, 2003), vol. 1, p. 12.

23 Ann Compton, 'Affirmative action: *British Sculptors and Sculpture* and the monographic form in twentieth-century sculpture studies', *Sculpture Journal*, 22.2 (2013), p. 82.
24 Getsy, 'The identity of the sculptor', p. 13.
25 C. Hussey, 'The restoration of Herstmonceux Castle', *Country Life*, 77 (7 December 1935), p. 606, quoted in Mark Stocker, '"My masculine models": the sculpture of Kathleen Scott', *Apollo*, 150:451 (1999), p. 125. Latham died at the age of 50, having had a tragic life, being charged for indecent behaviour while a Royal Artillery officer and attempting suicide before his trial and imprisonment.
26 Stocker, '"My masculine models"', p. 125.
27 Turner, '"Reuniting what should never have been separated"'.
28 Spielmann, *British Sculpture and Sculptors of To-Day*, p. 157, quoted in Turner, '"Reuniting what should never have been separated"'.
29 Spielmann, *British Sculpture and Sculptors of To-Day*, p. 18. For many years the sculpture was referred to in Birmingham as *Mercury*, the Greek messenger of the gods. The association with Mercury may have been due to a similarity between the two characters' attributes. Another reason for the mistaken identity was probably connected with the sculpture's location on the Gazette building which, between 1904 and 1929, served as the publishing offices of the *Birmingham Gazette* and associated newspapers, including the *Sunday Mercury*. In February 1981 it was stolen from above the main entrance: soon recovered, it was stored at Elliot, Son & Boyton, agents of Wingates Investments Ltd, the owners of the building at that time. Its current whereabouts is unknown. The sculpture was badly weathered and had sustained some damage. George T. Noszlopy, in Jeremy Beach (ed.), *Public Sculpture of Birmingham, including Sutton Coldfield* (Liverpool: Liverpool University Press and Public Monuments and Sculpture Association, 1998), pp. 173–74.
30 Spielmann, *British Sculpture and Sculptors of To-Day*, p. 161.
31 Fred Miller, 'George Frampton, A.R.A, art worker', *Art Journal*, November 1897, p. 321, quoted in Turner, '"Reuniting what should never have been separated"'.
32 Ann Compton, 'Crafting modernism: Hepworth's practice in the 1920s', in Penelope Curtis and Chris Stephens (eds), *Barbara Hepworth: Sculpture for a Modern World* (London: Tate Publishing, 2015), p. 14.
33 Benedict Read, 'Introduction', in The Fine Art Society, *Carving in Britain from 1910 to Now* (London: The Fine Art Society, 2012), pp. 7–8.
34 'Edna Manley's Exhibition Big Success in London', *The Daily Gleaner*, 5 March 1937, p. 25.
35 'English Reception of Edna Manley's Sculpture Show', *The Daily Gleaner*, 20 March 1937, p. 53.
36 Graves Gallery, Sheffield, biographical details on the artist contained in their descriptor for Manley's *Dance of Life*, 1932.
37 Parkes, *The Art of Carved Sculpture*, pp. 104–06.
38 Unsigned letter to Mrs E. Manley, 7 June 1937. Graves Gallery, Sheffield.
39 *Sculpture by Ursula Edgcumbe*, J. Leger and Son, London, 16 April–2 May 1936.

40 Martina Droth and Peter Trippi, 'Change/continuity: writing about art in Britain before and after 1900', *Nineteenth-Century Art Worldwide: A Journal of Nineteenth-Century Visual Culture*, 14.2 (2015), http://www.19thc-artworldwide.org/summer15/droth-trippi-introduction-writing-about-art-in-britain-before-and-after-1900 (accessed 25 November 2019).
41 Theophilus Paul Cowdell, 'The Role of the Royal Academy in English Art 1918–1930', PhD dissertation, University of London, 1980, pp. 131–32.
42 Hurtado, *Genteel Mavericks*, p. 29.
43 Louise Marchal, *Finding Frances: The Biography of Frances Darlington (Sculptor)* (Thirsk: The Marble Press, 2013), p. 85.
44 Katy Deepwell, 'Women Artists in Britain between the Two World Wars', PhD dissertation, Birkbeck College, University of London, 1991, p. 149.
45 Elizabeth Farningham, *Emmeline Halse, Sculptor, 1853–1930* (Doncaster: L. E. Farningham, 2002), pp. 7–8.
46 Hilary Cunliffe-Charlesworth, 'The Royal College of Art: Its Influence on Education, Art and Design, 1900–1950', PhD dissertation, Sheffield City Polytechnic, 1991, p. 2.
47 Cunliffe-Charlesworth, 'The Royal College of Art', pp. 89–91.
48 Hill, *The Sculpture of Gertrude Hermes*, pp. 40–41.
49 Cunliffe-Charlesworth, 'The Royal College of Art', p. 96.
50 Cunliffe-Charlesworth, 'The Royal College of Art', p. 101.
51 Walter Crane, *Ideals in Art* (London: George Bell, 1905), p. 9.
52 Lethaby, entry on design, *Encyclopaedia Britannica* (London, 1911), p. 95, quoted in Cunliffe-Charlesworth, 'The Royal College of Art', p. 308.
53 Cunliffe-Charlesworth, 'The Royal College of Art', pp. 319–20.
54 Penelope Curtis and Chris Stephens, 'Introduction', in Penelope Curtis and Chris Stephens (eds), *Barbara Hepworth: Sculpture for a Modern World* (London: Tate Publishing, 2015), p. 9.
55 Compton, 'Crafting modernism', pp. 16–18.
56 Deepwell, 'Women Artists in Britain between the Two World Wars', pp. 115–16.
57 Kathleen Kennet, *Self-Portrait of an Artist* (London: John Murray, 1949), p. 26.
58 'Art exhibitions', *The Times*, 31 October 1928, p. 12.
59 Compton, 'Crafting modernism', pp. 13–14.
60 Ann Compton, 'Infrastructures: formation and networks 1900–25', in Henry Moore Institute, *Sculpture in 20th Century Britain: Identity, Infrastructures, Aesthetics, Display, Reception* (Leeds: Henry Moore Institute, 2003), vol. 1, pp. 24–26.
61 *The Daily Telegraph*, 27 October 1942, quoted in Deepwell, 'Women Artists in Britain between the Two World Wars', p. 131.
62 Parkes, *The Art of Carved Sculpture*, p. 85.
63 Deepwell, 'Women Artists in Britain between the Two World Wars', p. 274.
64 Deepwell, 'Women Artists in Britain between the Two World Wars', pp. 235–36.
65 Deepwell, 'Women Artists in Britain between the Two World Wars', p. 252.
66 Deepwell, 'Women Artists in Britain between the Two World Wars', p. 233.
67 Deepwell, 'Women Artists in Britain between the Two World Wars', p. 256.
68 Pamela Geraldine Nunn, 'The Mid-Victorian Woman Artist: 1850–1879', PhD dissertation, University College London, 1982, p. 15.
69 Nunn, 'The Mid-Victorian Woman Artist', pp. 34–35.

3

Presentation and Reception

3.1 Photography and film

Many of the sculptures illustrated in this book are either lost or in private collections. Having to rely on photographic reproductions of sculpture raises several problems that are less acute in the case of painting. For the latter, the decisions to be made by the photographer are few: the aim is for the painting to fill the photographic frame and present a centred viewpoint, replicating the ideal position of a viewer standing in front of the original. Reproductions of paintings allow us to view their content, albeit on a different scale, and the most severe problems are variations in colour, tone and resolution. A fundamental problem inherent in photographs of sculpture is that the singular view of the camera, and thus of the photographer, is partial and selective, based on many decisions concerning angle, distance and lighting, and this can have a dramatic effect on how we understand and imagine the actual sculpture to be. Critically, we are trying to do this via a two-dimensional representation of a three-dimensional artwork. However, the reality is that the art historian often has only the photograph for reference: as Donald Preziosi has argued, 'art history as we know it today is the child of photography'.[1] It is interesting that we re-examine artists continually, but the same photographs of their work are recycled, as if they have somehow escaped their cultural context and have remained neutral.[2] Because core images have been reproduced many times they effectively become autonomous substitutes for the artworks they supposedly record. I am acutely aware of this issue in writing this book: my images vary greatly in terms of when they were taken, whether colour or black and white film was used, whether they have sustained water damage through less than ideal storage conditions, where they were initially intended to be seen and whether it has been possible to access original prints or electronic images.

Geraldine Johnson has commented on Heinrich Wolfflin's opinions on the use of photography for the study of art and specifically on his three groundbreaking articles published in 1896–97 and 1915 in which he argued that in researching sculpture we should pay close attention to the specifics of photographic representations. Although art historical books were being widely published at the time, he believed that it was still hard to locate good photographs of sculpture, and was apparently still complaining about this in the 1930s and early 1940s. He was critical of those who when photographing sculptures tried to produce a creative effect, in particular portraying sculptures from the side, which in his opinion failed to show the 'correct', that is to say frontal, view.[3] Although this suggests that he preferred as 'neutral' a photographic representation as possible, he contradicted this assertion in the ways in which he used photographs of sculpture as the basis for formal analysis, as if they were indeed the works of art being examined. The photographs of which he approved reflected his own approach to Italian Renaissance art: a head-on photograph of a sculpture became the model for the later recording of most artworks.

Johnson points to the growth of connoisseurship in the late nineteenth and early twentieth centuries as being reliant on increasing access to photographic images, in particular ones that showed details of individual artworks, and of course connoisseurship in turn could influence the form of a photographic image.[4] Pre-dating the routine use of the close-up view in the photographing of modernist sculpture, by the end of the nineteenth century photographers were drawing attention to sculptural details that they believed were important, and thus were significantly affecting the viewer's understanding of such works. The creation of sculptural close-ups has since the inception of photography been based on the idea that in the detail is to be found both the artwork and the artist's unique qualities. Mary Bergstein's writings on the photographing of sculpture draw attention to the irony that photography and sculpture have had a long relationship, one that is 'complicit', yet 'determined by an inherent asymmetry; whereas photography does not especially lend itself to being sculptured, sculpture ... is a highly photogenic art form ... What the photograph ... and the art book do to sculpture is to transform it ... into pictorial art.'[5] In such photographs other viewers are absent: this encourages a more immediate connection on our part when looking at such images – the viewpoint becomes our viewpoint, the experience is offered as if unmediated. However, in the early years of photography the use of sculpture as subject allowed the photographer to experiment, to both record and create 'time and space as an artist might shape marble or plaster'. Because of this, the two media have been described as having much in common.[6] Nonetheless, the subjectivity of the photographer undercuts the supposed neutrality of such images. In considering the photographing of the sculptural object, Bergstein has pinpointed the complex issues of authorship at play. Photographers cannot create an entirely neutral image: in reality they probably select the view or detail that most interests them. So perhaps it is more honest to say that photography interprets sculpture rather than reproduces it.

Production processes and economic contexts are vital components in the history of illustrated books. Photographs of sculpture and other artworks remained a relative rarity in art historical publications before the mid- to late 1880s for technical and financial reasons. The inclusion of illustrations in books in the 1920s increased sales, as did colour reproduction after the Second World War. People began to have greater access to books through libraries and the output of publishers who were prepared to bear the burden of small profit margins. In the printed book our experience of the photographs is both pictorial and serial: photographers wishing to tell a specific story will adopt the approach of the film-maker and suggest a linear reading through the layout of their images.[7] In his first book on sculpture published in 1928 Stanley Casson made use of borrowed photographs and sourced many images through the Italian firm of Alinari, which had been founded in the mid-nineteenth century, and which virtually monopolized the supply of photographs of sculpture and architecture until the 1930s. In these photographs sculpture was treated in a very specific manner – usually 'from a frontal viewpoint, always strongly lit and frequently set against a dark background with no hint of real context, so that the striking tonal contrast made for a dramatic – even theatrical – effect'.[8] For his second book published in 1930, Casson borrowed most of the images directly from the sculptors, many of whom were now photographing their own work. This meant that they could control how they wished to present both themselves and their sculptures. In such photographs they often included some reference to the place where their work had been made, in order to position it in a particular context, and would also pay close attention to the use of lighting to emphasize surface texture and volume.

Films about sculpture are particularly interesting and complex since the three-dimensional medium lends itself to the moving image in a way that painting does not, allowing for dramatic treatment, distortions of scale and multiple viewpoints as the camera pans around it. Indeed, it is possible that one of the perceived weaknesses of sculpture for some viewers (and thus maybe for some critics and art historians) is an uncertainty as to the correct position from which to view it. In contrast, a still photograph of a sculpture appears to solve this issue by imposing a viewpoint on the observer. By the end of the period covered in this book the growing interest in sculpture was exploited by the media, both through still and moving images, and the artist and the artwork as 'celebrity' are a product of this time. In turn, still photography and film could also affect a sculptor's practice: if they were a high-profile figure then the ways in which these media could present both them and their work would have been almost impossible to ignore or avoid. With the development of television, huge numbers of viewers were able to see artworks they would probably never actually encounter. Television also had the ability to reach out to them, to transport them to the heart of an artist's practice, their studio: such documentaries were and remain highly compelling.

The impact of photography and film was addressed in Tate Britain's *Barbara Hepworth: Sculpture for a Modern World.* The broad aim of this show was to reconnect Hepworth with international concerns and contexts, and to balance out the prior emphasis on St Ives as both the source of her ideas and the key to understanding her sculpture. In doing so, the exhibition paid particular attention to sculptures that she made in the 1920s, before moving to Cornwall; the artistic ramifications of her relationship with and marriage to Ben Nicholson; and also how she controlled the presentation of her work to the public. The exhibition clearly demonstrated Hepworth's understanding of the various ways in which photography could not only be used to record sculpture but also to 'imagine' it in different settings. She was attuned to how both film and the organization of the printed page could affect viewers' understanding of her sculptures. **Figure 7** shows Hepworth at work in January 1930: it comprises the right-hand side of an original photograph that included her husband John Skeaping to the left. He appeared as the more dominant presence, working on a full-length figure that occupied the centre of the photographic composition. We can only speculate as to why he was edited out of this image. It is tempting to imagine that this might have been done by Hepworth herself as an assertion of her artistic and personal autonomy.

The constraints posed by the practicalities of photographic representations of her work were addressed in a 1946 interview published in *Studio* magazine. Hepworth was asked about her thoughts on the effect of lighting when she was conceiving a sculpture, and also her feelings concerning suitable settings and backgrounds. She replied that the photographs included in the published interview were taken in her studio or her garden, and that she regarded the photographs just as records and not functioning so as to show her sculptures in an ideal setting, although this argument is somewhat contradicted by her use of collaged photographs, which I will discuss shortly. She described different scales of sculpture as being appropriate for domestic, landscape or architectural settings:

> I have never felt that sculpture was too formidable to live with. The chief error in the past has been the pretentious way of showing it and the conventional habit of associating sculpture with symbolic or commemorative monuments, and very rarely for the purpose of enjoying its inherent qualities. Quite large sculptures can be placed in small rooms where their presence gives a new sense of enjoyment – a new aesthetic experience which cannot be got through any other art.[9]

These aspects of sculpture's domestic possibilities will be explored in Chapter 4.

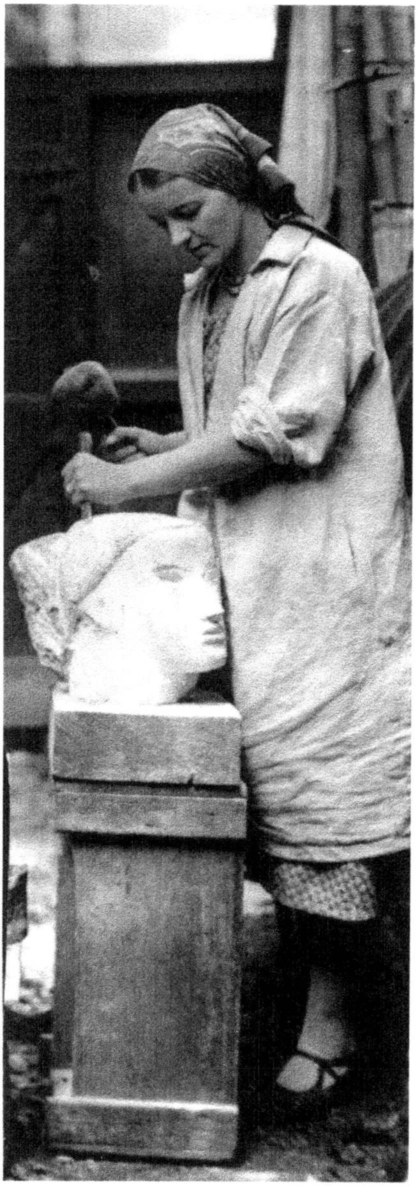

7. Barbara Hepworth carving *Head*, 1930–31

The first film about Hepworth's sculpture was made in 1953, and although slightly out of my timeframe it is a useful indicator of the ways in which artists were presented on film.

It was shown at the *Barbara Hepworth: Sculpture for a Modern World* exhibition as an important example of how Hepworth and her work were conceived. Entitled *Figures in a Landscape*, it is clear from the outset that this film followed established approaches of locating both Hepworth and her practice within the specifics of the Cornish landscape. This colour film shows Hepworth's sculptures against the landscape and architecture of the St Ives area: in her studio garden, on a beach and in the countryside. Some of the analogies are rather forced: for example, the emphasis on the crashing sea and the rocks, and how the sea shapes the rocks, proposing a parallel with the sculptor 'shaping' her work. Words such as 'ordering', 'smoothing' and 'hammering' are used in the commentary – all interchangeable between the actions of the sea on the land and the actions of the sculptor on her materials. Visual analogies are drawn between Hepworth's upright figures and Cornwall's standing stones, giving the former a primeval heritage. When we are shown Hepworth's sculpture situated within the landscape the analogy becomes complete, as is the case when similar sculptures are aligned with shots of Cornish mine shafts. However, Hepworth was not completely happy with the film's distortions of sculptural scale, most particularly produced through the camera zooming in and back from individual works. She also seems to have felt that the narration and music were rather intrusive, and this may well have made her feel uncomfortable, given her desire to control the representation of her work as much as possible.[10] **Plate 5** shows a still from the film, being both pictorial and biographical in its placement of Hepworth and her work against the backdrop of St Ives.

Nonetheless, despite any reservations she may have had, Hepworth continued to document her work through photography and film, paying close attention to the boundaries between her art and these media.[11] Prior to the making of this film, Hepworth and Ben Nicholson had been assembling album images of themselves and of their work, and this use of photography to establish artistic identity was taken forward into various publications. In the 1930s the reproduction in books of Hepworth's sculpture became the main forum for her public display and reception in Britain as well as overseas, and she was careful to ensure that she obtained high-quality images of her work as it was produced. Hepworth was attuned to the importance of being in control of how her work was presented to the public, through both visual and written means. She did not conceive of the camera as a passive instrument: she carefully oversaw the professional recording of her work and in her own photography was acutely aware of the need to explore and represent the three-dimensionality of her medium. From the late 1930s she also used photography to envisage her sculptures in different settings, pasting photographs of existing works on to images of gardens, modernist houses and sometimes just against the sky.[12] She often worked in collaboration with landscape architect Christopher Tunnard, and some of the resultant images were published in an article entitled 'Art Out-of-Doors' in *Architectural Review* in April 1939. Here it was argued that

> sculpture is not always designed for a particular setting, but an ideal arrangement for it usually exists in the artist's mind ... The debased tradition of garden and civic decoration is no doubt partly the cause of the general lack of interest in out-of-door aspects of the art. The composite illustrations on this and the facing page are an attempt to relate some specimens of sculpture to a background which in scale and atmosphere might produce mutually helpful associations.[13]

Hepworth had a sophisticated understanding of the impact of context in relation to sculpture, and **Figure 8** shows a photo-collage from 1939 with her *Helicoids in Sphere* (1938). The sculpture appears to be imagined as 'punctuating' the end of the path that winds its way towards us from the wooded background. Hepworth believed that sculpture could be revelatory through its placement and that the power of site could be aligned to a 'sense of the hidden and the discovered which landscape can provide'. She imagined 'putting her own sculpture in out of the way places ... coming across other sculptures as if they might have been lost for centuries, and of being the explorer who is the first to bring the light of discovery, the light of seeing, to this unseen installation'.[14] After moving to St Ives, from 1944 Hepworth chose the backgrounds for photographs of her sculptures, such as overlooking St Ives Bay. After she acquired Trewyn Studio in 1949 the garden and the view of the church tower beyond became a recurrent context and frame for her work. Earlier photographs had presented a neutral context for the sculptures, but when Hepworth started photographing them herself in 1934 she became more sensitive to the role played by a background.[15] On the reverse of the early prints are notes that show her understanding of the effects of cropping and the importance of the backdrop, as much as the usual attention to lighting. Hepworth clearly understood the problems arising from photographing sculpture, but at the same time this led her to use the medium in creative ways. For example, in her private albums she would

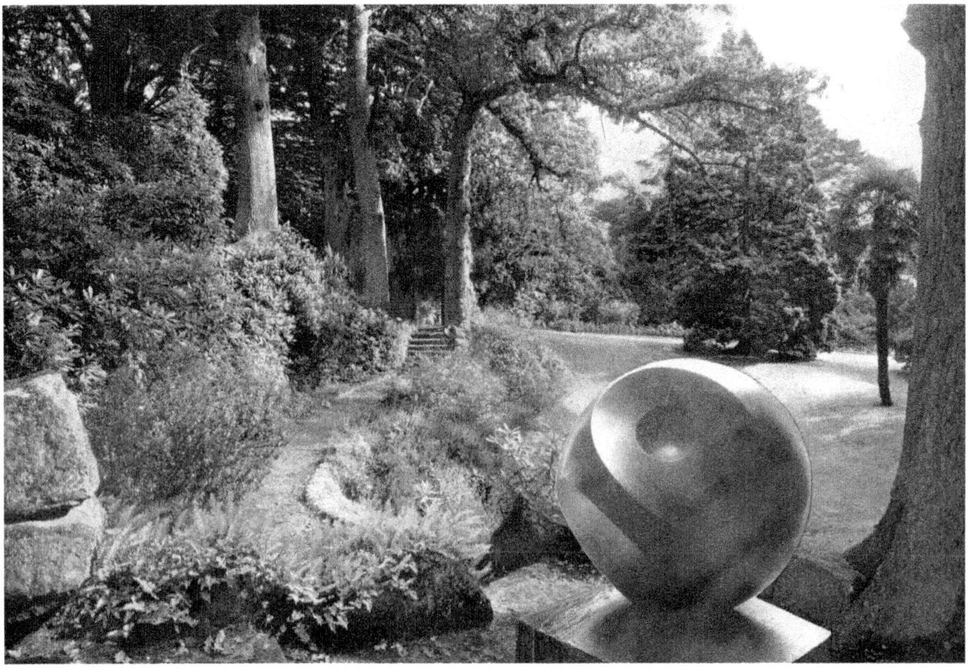

8. Barbara Hepworth, photo-collage with *Helicoids in Sphere*, 1938, in the garden of Redleaf, Penshurst, 1939

often show the same sculpture sequentially, from differing viewpoints, thus attempting to suggest a more comprehensive understanding of the work. In Herbert Read's 1952 monograph on Hepworth there are several instances of different views of the same sculpture presented on one page, seemingly intended to evoke being able to see a work from several viewpoints.[16]

With the development of the internet, the issue of reproductions and their veracity has become even more acute, magnified beyond anything that could have been foreseen, resulting in wild variations in terms of detail, colour, scale, cropping and resolution. The multiple versions of any given artwork that exist electronically can result in a lack of sensitivity to quality: each reproduction becomes a signifier and each additional version essentially takes us further away from the original. When this is added to the difficulties inherent in the photographic representation of a sculpture, as well as in its frequent inaccessibility, the problems are significant.

3.2 Narrating the artist and her studio

Interviews with artists often take place in the context of their studios, accompanied by photographs of their working and/or domestic environment. Female artists have not been the subject of biographies to the extent of their male colleagues, but the illustrated interview has been a way in which all artists' lives can be laid bare to an avid public and represents 'a sensational, duplicitous simulation of the artist's privacy'.[17] In this way the artist becomes an object to be 'consumed' by readers. Studio homes have been particularly potent sources for journalism, presenting readers with the illusion of 'getting to know' the sculptor, and where ordinary objects and situations can become imbued with significance. There is also a very particular resonance for the viewer looking at photographs of sculptures in their studio context rather than displayed in galleries. Even though the photograph distances the viewer, this is compensated for by setting up a narrative, presenting us with a context through which to interpret the work. Although the studio is a special place in which to 'stage' art, and despite the sense that these photographs may give us greater access to the sculptor's thoughts and processes, of course they are carefully constructed presentations. This is unsurprising since all photography 'frames' its subjects, but the issue here is when such images are presented as a neutral record of the sculptor's activities. The persistent use of still photography and of film as a means to 'know' an artist is now treated with some caution. However in the early twentieth century it is likely that such images would have been taken more at face value, and the visual and linguistic presentation of those female sculptors whom journalists and critics presented to the public are highly revealing in the ways in which they characterize the sculptors and their environments. In comparison to painted portraits of artists, where the various components can be orchestrated on the canvas, photographs suggest a greater sense of intimacy and reality, a privileged insight into a creative practice. Photographs published in the mass media are capable of simultaneously romanticizing the artist as well as suggesting to the reader that what they are seeing is reality. Images of the sculptor's studio encourage us to seek relationships between the objects on display: if the sculptor is also present, then an additional set of relationships is established. If we regard a portrait as essentially a collaborative effort between creator and subject, then in working with a photographer a sculptor could enable seemingly incidental views of herself within her home and studio to establish a very particular sort of portrait of both her and her work.

Sculptors have shown a keen interest in the photographic construction of their image, thoroughly exploiting the indexical nature of the photograph, and most sculptors since the invention of photography have posed for the camera alongside one or more of their works. However, from looking at photographs of some female sculptors, they seem not to be entirely at ease when posing for (usually) male photographers. Many such images appear awkward in contrast to photographs of male sculptors, which convey greater confidence, reading 'as a statement of accomplishment'.[18] **Figure 9** showing sculptor Anne Acheson (1882–1962) in 1929 is striking in its modesty, in terms of her relaxed pose, her distance from her sculptures and the setting apparently being a very ordinary corner of a living room. The artist and her works do not merge in the way that they do in images of male sculptors such as Henry Moore (**Figure 10**). In part this may have something to do with the gender of

9. Anne Acheson, 7 March 1929

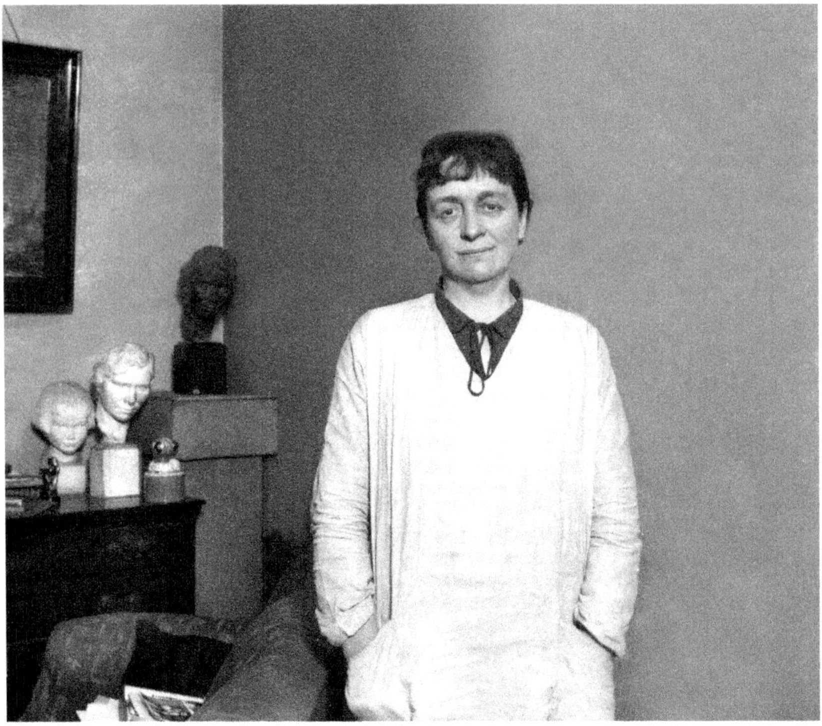

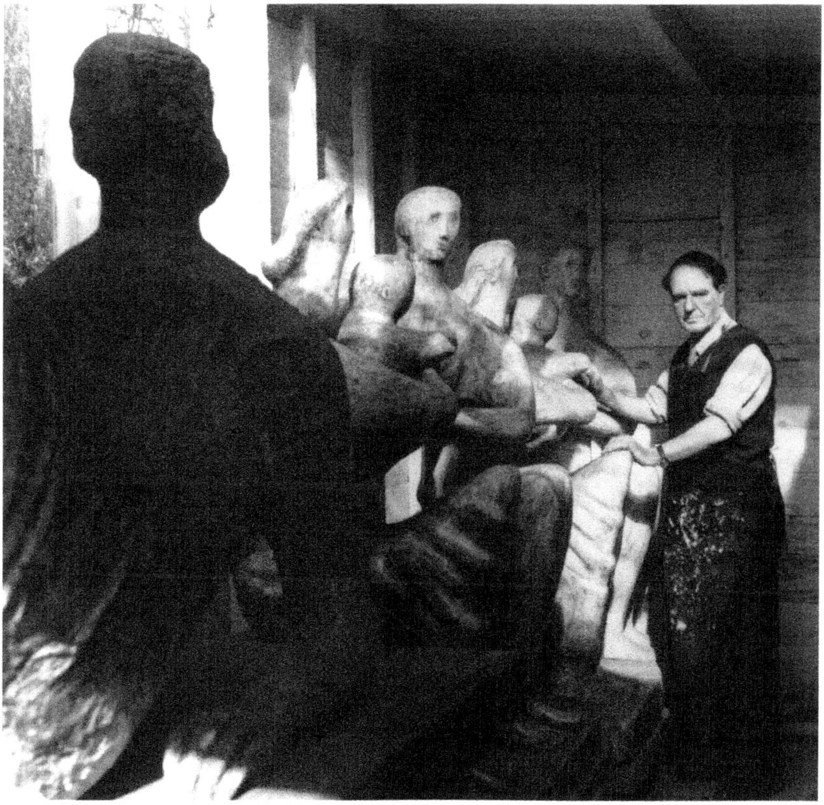

10. Ida Kar, *Henry Moore with two casts of 'Family Group' 1948–49*, 1954

Acheson and the small scale of her work. In the photograph of Moore the sculptor's head is relatable to those of his arranged sculpted figures, and the composition and lighting are singularly more dynamic than in the Acheson portrait. But perhaps the strongest impression in the image of Moore is that of ownership – we are left in absolutely no doubt that he is the maker and master of these sculptures. The photograph 'speaks' to us in a very different way to the one of Acheson.

The women discussed in this book made works depicting both sexes, but the lack of visual dominance in images of them with their sculptures appears to go further than a gendered relationship between the sculptor and their work. The ways in which these women stand (or frequently sit) renders them more passive and less commanding over their creations than their male colleagues. In many instances the female

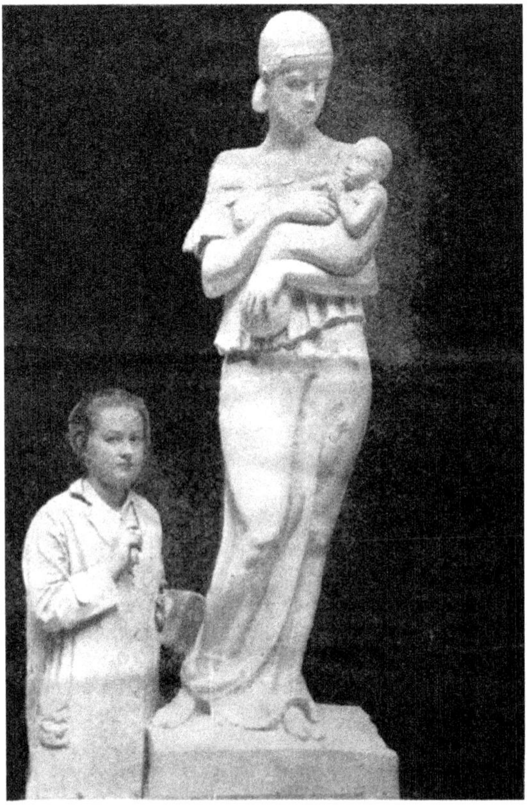

11. Angela Sykes (later Lady Antrim), RA, 1929 show, *Mother and Child*, in *Good Housekeeping* (US), February 1931, p. 37

sculptors look slightly uncomfortable at being asked to pose with their works. In a photograph of Angela Sykes (1911–84) with her sculpture *Mother and Child*, published in *Good Housekeeping* in 1931, the sculptor is truly dwarfed by her production. It is interesting to compare this image to that of Gertrude Williams (**Figure 1**) where the latter, even if her work towers over her, still presents a confident individual, whereas Sykes looks nervous and rather uncomfortable (**Figure 11**). However, Sykes, later to become Countess of Antrim in 1934, would become very successful, often working in stone and on a very large scale. She studied in Brussels under sculptor Marnix D'Haveloose and then at the British School at Rome, and the influence of Rodin is evident in her work. She exhibited widely, but her son Hector described her as a pragmatic businesswoman who 'had to pay the electricity bill'.[19] One source dates the sculpture shown in **Figure 11** to when Antrim was only 16 years old which would make its date 1927.[20] So the image reproduced in *Good*

Housekeeping is either an older photograph from 1927 or a retrospectively posed composition. The accompanying review recorded that the sculptor had been successful in exhibiting her stone *Mother and Child* at the Royal Academy:

> This piece was notable for the expression of solicitude on the countenance of the youthful mother, and the attitude of the sleeping infant in her arms, truly indicated repose. Texture was cleverly suggested in the folds of the simple garments worn by mother and child ... Miss Sykes has ideas and is already mistress of her technique ... the coming years should give us a sculptress of steady and enduring fame.[21]

Figure 12 shows the first full-page photograph in the 2007 publication *Dora Gordine: Sculptor, Artist, Designer*.[22] Here the sculptor is in her Paris studio in 1933 with her sculpture *Dyak/Headhunter* (1931–32) (**Figure 71**). The effect of this image is to diminish the sculptor both through her position and the overall composition. It would be surprising to see a

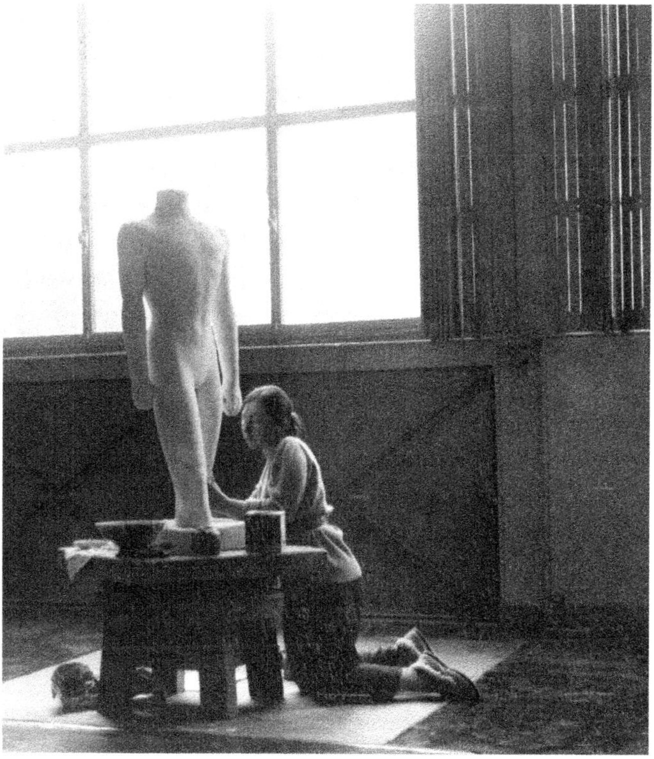

12. Dora Gordine in studio, 1933

photograph of a male sculptor on his knees, and in this instance the highlighting of the sculpted figure against the window makes it/him the animated subject here rather than Gordine. Her studio home, Dorich House, on the southern side of Richmond Park, was designed when she was at the peak of her career and the space clearly embodied her social and professional concerns. A 1930s modernist structure which made the most of light and space, Dorich House was the subject of an article in *Country Life* in 1938 where it was described as 'idiosyncratic and unique ... As a sculptor [Dora Gordine] thinks naturally in terms of space and volume ... she knew what she wanted in [her] house and studio, and ... why she wanted it.'[23] The gallery and modelling studio were situated on the first floor, created to demarcate an area where Gordine could meet patrons and potential buyers. Thus through the layout of the house she displayed an understanding of the need to separate the domestic from the professional sphere, although having a gallery within a house apparently worked in oppositional yet successful ways. The gallery functioned as a frame for her sculpture, both distancing it and thus legitimizing her representations of the nude, but at the same time bringing the work closer to the viewer so that the boundary between art and life was blurred. Photographs of Gordine's studio-house also provide useful evidence of the contemporary expanding market for small domestic sculptures.[24] In a 1950 radio broadcast entitled 'Sculpture and Everyday Life' Gordine said:

> I am a full-time professional artist. Many people think that professional life is grand and important and despise the essential occupation of a housewife. This is a grave mistake; it is just as important to be a good housewife as it is to be a professional artist ... and many people have to be both ... Beautiful homes in which hospitality can be given to friends have always been among the most important foundations of civilised life.[25]

This statement is interesting since it is entirely gender-specific, and acknowledges the range of demands placed on the married female professional artist.

Like many other women sculptors Barbara Hepworth also had to endure constant references to her gender, even if these were at times somewhat oblique. In 1933 Adrian Stokes reviewed her work at the Lefevre Galleries, remarking that

> these stones are inhabited with feeling, even if, in common with the majority of 'advanced' carvers, Miss Hepworth has felt not only the

> block, but also its potential fruit, to be always feminine. These sculptors approach the block with such gravity that more ebullient, more masculine, forms evade them ... Her carving is astonishingly mature: whereas the appreciation and critique of sculpture remain fatuous.[26]

In 1947 William Gibson wrote about Moore and Hepworth for *Britain Today*, describing how early in her career Hepworth moved away from distortions of the human figure to a form of geometric abstraction which she then maintained. He contrasted this with Moore, whom he described as having experimented with such geometric abstractions but who then returned to the human figure. He attributed their approach to sculpting to their gender:

> Even in her earliest carvings Miss Hepworth displayed a *delicate* adjustment of carved surface and edge which has since become one of her principal means of expression. In contrast, Mr. Moore showed in his latest exhibition a wooden figure with the surface so *roughly* finished as to have been impossible in the work of his fellow artist without considerable loss of meaning ... the formal interest predominates in the one (BH), the dramatic interest in the other (HM).[27]

I have emphasized the gendered terminology implied in this appraisal, and it is just one example among many in which Hepworth was assessed in relation to Moore. Herbert Read wrote frequently on Hepworth, including the Foreword to the 1932 catalogue *Carvings by Barbara Hepworth and Paintings by Ben Nicholson*, published on the occasion of their November/December exhibition at Arthur Tooth and Sons. Read's written support would be of great importance in establishing Hepworth's position, although he routinely compared her with Moore. He described the two sculptors as essentially moving in a similar direction until about 1935, when they diverged. However, from the beginning there existed a fundamental difference in their temperaments:

> Barbara Hepworth evokes a landscape ... It is a '*sense of mystery*' that gives her the power to project 'some universal or abstract vision of beauty' onto her plastic medium ... Moore ... goes to nature for a vocabulary of form ... and gives as the aim of his art, *vitality* ... The two ideals, distinct in their essence and expression, are denoted by the words '*beauty*' and '*power*', and these two words express the divergence that was to take place in the development of the two sculptors.[28]

Again, I have highlighted the ways in which Read differentiated Hepworth's and Moore's work in an essentially gendered manner – in both pieces it is implied that Hepworth's practice is more ethereal than that of Moore.

We might expect a focus on gender when encountering a female sculptor to be the province of male commentators, but this was not always the case. Art patron Margaret Gardiner met Hepworth in 1930 and recalled that

> the unexpected strength of her grip when we shook hands startled me. It seemed at variance with the general impression of delicacy that she gave; in fact, though slim, she was sturdily built. She was beautiful – brown haired with a high, sloping forehead, finely drawn eyebrows, dark-lashed brown eyes, a straight, determined nose and a firm mouth. Her skin was pale and very clear and everything about her seemed outlined, defined. She was neatly dressed and she carried a neat umbrella – she was altogether different from the picture of artists that I had gained from meetings in Vienna and Paris. There seemed to be nothing of their free and easy ways about Barbara as she sat there, upright, smiling and silent, looking about her ... and we drank the first of many hundreds of cups of tea.[29]

Unsurprisingly, Hepworth was aware of the endemic marginalization of female artists. Fighting to gain a similar level of exposure as Ben Nicholson and Henry Moore, she believed that she had been overlooked by the British Council, which was of great importance in promoting British artists' work overseas. She told Herbert Read in 1943 'I have never been included in one of their exhibitions but up till now I have thought of various reasons for this omission – such as: 1. being a woman; 2. being abstract; 3. young; 4. a wife & mother etc. etc.'[30] This was a fairly accurate assessment of the context in which she was working; it would only be with her wartime retrospective exhibitions, and particularly in the 1950s, that greater exposure would come her way. In 1950 her work was shown by the British Council at the Venice Biennale, but yet again it was compared with that of Moore, who had won the Biennale sculpture prize in 1948.

Where the female sculptor's gender is not used to 'explain' her work, another approach is to present the work as in some sense 'reliant' on external factors, beyond her own talent. Hepworth again was subject to this treatment. Early in the 2011 publication *Barbara Hepworth: The Plasters. The Gift to Wakefield* there is a list of artists, critics and architects (all male) and it is proposed that Hepworth drew on all of 'these influences and foils' in the creation of her own work.[31] Even today it is noticeable that writings on women artists sometimes betray an uncertainty about how to position their work other than in relation to, or even filtered through, the ideas and practice of masculine precedents. In characterizing Hepworth in this manner she is, no doubt unintentionally, presented as some kind of conduit, a passive vessel. In her 1975 obituary in the *Guardian* she was described as possibly 'the most significant woman artist in the history of art to this day', and that this was all the more remarkable since she worked in the field of sculpture. Again, the implication is that her work is important because she was female and because her medium was sculpture. This is a reductive approach. More positive was this author's attribution of Hepworth's success to her 'driving energy and the right kind of ambition, as well as a rare and particular talent', but then the obituary returned to the question of Hepworth's gender. Smaller sculptures were described as conveying a 'pervading, unselfconscious femininity. However stringent the forms she used, her work is always marked by an ultimate kindness and gentleness, and often by a particular gesture of sheltering embracing. When she uses two or more elements grouped together there is an unmistakable sense of human intercourse.'[32]

In some ways Hepworth colluded in a gendered interpretation of her sculpture. Although she complained about the 'little woman' label, she also quite reasonably argued for femininity as a positive force in sculpture, proposing that a woman's approach was different from, rather than inferior to, that of a male sculptor. Nevertheless, critical evaluations of her work invariably compared her with Moore and Nicholson: she was presented as literally following the two men since she was younger, but also because of her gender. Rarely was her work assessed on the basis of its own quality. Despite arguing for the experience of a woman as distinct, a positive trait, Hepworth acknowledged that her gender and motherhood had been a brake on her reputation. Although she encouraged, even protected, a formalist account of her work, a reassessment of her work from the 1970s onwards within a wider feminist discourse has enabled a more nuanced approach to her practice.[33]

Like Hepworth, Gertrude Hermes was most often photographed at work. As with Hepworth, commentary on Hermes could be superficial in its focus on the sculptor's persona, with one visitor describing her as leading 'a slightly disorganised life in a Chelsea terrace house, admitting she had clean forgotten I was coming to see her'. As was often the case, the reviewer tried to draw comparisons between Hermes and her sculpture, suggesting that there was 'no trace of sentimentality in … her work, which is clean and clear-cut – a little like the artist, who is tall, slim and attractive, with cropped hair. Before I arrived, she had been working on a bust ... and was clad in a sweater, cardigan, trousers and men's bedroom slippers.'[34]

A sculptor whose rural location appears to have protected her from the attention of what we might term 'lifestyle' journalism was Mary Spencer Watson, who lived and worked in the Purbecks in Dorset. My cover photograph from the mid-1930s shows her determined focus on the act of carving and vividly captures the commitment of this young sculptor. In a later photograph from 1950 we see her standing surrounded by her works (**Figure 13**). Her hand is on *The Muse* (1950). Many of the sculptures shown appear to be in progress. The photographs of her studio present the artist and her work as contained within the physical boundaries of both this working space and the photographic frame. There are many similar photographs of Spencer Watson with her work, and in all instances she is presented as a serious, professional sculptor.

London-based Kathleen Scott was photographed many times. Images of her supposedly at work are rather unconvincing due to her clothing, and underscore the performative nature of such photographs (**Figure 14**). However, her fixed gaze on her work is striking, producing

13. *Mary Spencer Watson in her studio*, 1950

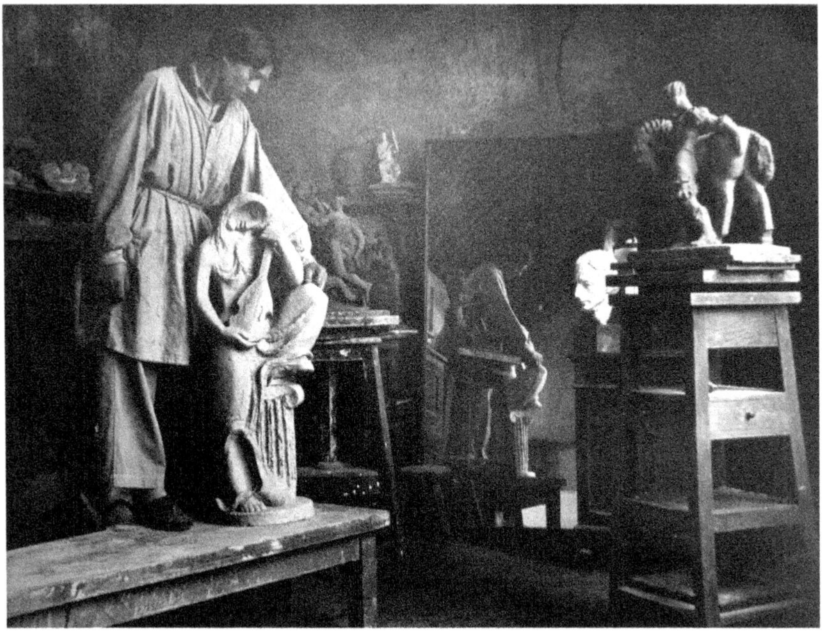

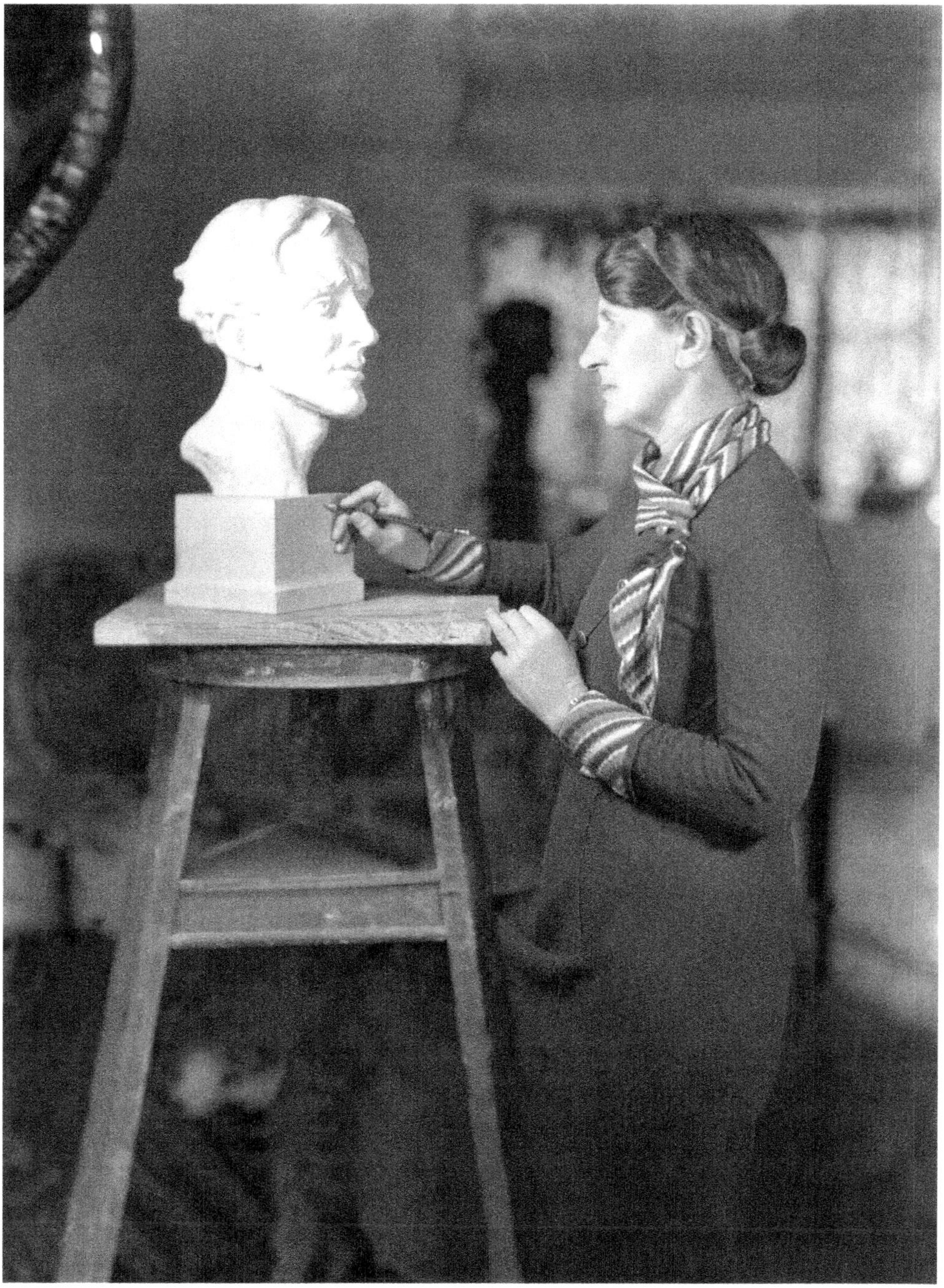

14. Kathleen Scott by Bassano Ltd, 18 April 1934

the effect of an exchange between sculptor and sculpture: the latter is animated through such deep concentration and we as observers are drawn into this close relationship. Portraits of a sculptor at work in the studio have tended not to reveal the mechanics of producing a work, but instead construct an image of how the sculptor wished to be regarded by potential patrons. In this photograph we gain a sense of Scott's privileged social status, which she shared with most of her sitters.

As part of a series entitled 'Other People's Homes', in 1932 Derek Patmore wrote in *Queen* about Scott, the article including a range of evocative photographs. He began by stating that it was obvious that sculpture was the most demanding of the arts, and thus it was especially remarkable that a woman practitioner should achieve worldwide fame. Once he had made this predictable comment, Patmore proceeded to write in great detail about the sculptor's home and her large outdoor studio 'which stands invitingly amongst trees beyond a lily pool'. He described her as hard-working and with a rare gift for portraiture, characterizing her sculptures as exhibiting qualities of nobility and strength. 'No wonder Rodin greatly admired her work, and even deigned to call her "colleague!" However, Lady Hilton Young is very reticent about herself and her work.' In 1922 Scott had married Edward Hilton Young, MP, 1st Baron Kennet, following the death of her first husband, Robert Falcon Scott in 1912. In 1927 the family moved to Leinster Corner, on the Bayswater Road, overlooking Kensington Gardens, where she converted the coach house into a two-storey studio. The *Queen* article occupied a double-page spread in the magazine and had a sub-heading 'Lady Hilton Young has Successfully Captured the Atmosphere of a Country House in Her London Home'. Patmore referred to the long list of Scott's achievements, positioning her 'in the front rank of English sculptors'. When he remarked to her how few sculptors there were in Britain, Scott is quoted as replying: '"Yes; there are only three. Jagger, Reid Dick and myself."' Patmore proceeded to describe the lyricism of Scott's work and how several examples of her sculptures could be seen in her home: an image of the dining room was captioned 'Corner of the dining room, showing how the groups of sculpture harmonise with the old oak furniture of the room'. To the right of this image we can see a cast of *The Kingdom is Within* (**Figure 2**, **Figure 15**).

Patmore's description of the house and its rooms explicitly defines them as an appropriate context for the sculptures, referring to 'simple cream walls and comfortable armchairs and settee covered in gay blue, pink, yellow, and cream floral cretonne form an effective background

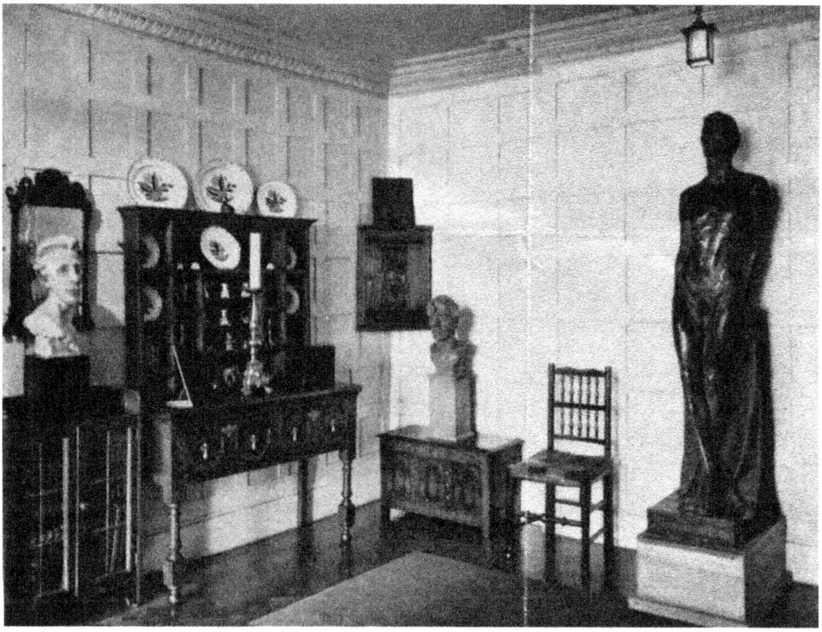

15. Derek Patmore, 'Inside the dining room', in 'Other People's Homes – No. 10: The Studio of a Famous Woman Sculptor', *Queen*, 3 February 1932

for the pieces of sculpture'. His emphasis is overwhelmingly on the context in which Scott lived and worked rather than on her sculptures as individual artworks. Patmore referred his readers to the illustration of the dining room in which could be seen one of her most important works, a bronze statue of a blindfolded young man, originally intended to function as a war memorial. He described in great detail the location of the house and its style as 'deliciously early Victorian, with its delicately wrought iron balconies and shelter over the front door' and that her studio in the garden was

> one of the most beautiful and workmanlike I have ever seen ... It is so planned that on the darkest of London days the studio inside is filled with light ... it is a veritable little gallery of celebrities. For she has done most of the famous people of the day either in bronze or stone.[35]

There were other photographs in this extensive review, and together with the text they provided readers with a vivid sense of Scott's combined living and working situation, with no distinction being drawn between the two. Her sculptures were firmly subsumed into the sculptor's context and as individual works of art they were hardly addressed at all.

As with Hepworth, Scott's gender would be a frequent issue for commentators. For example: 'Sculptors are almost invariably big, powerfully-built men, but Lady Hilton Young is rather petite. She is exceptionally strong, however, for one of her sex, and keeps fit with outdoor exercise.'[36] Writing in 1926, a reviewer described Scott's time in Paris when reportedly she lived on £75 a year, was completely independent and thus demonstrated early in her career 'qualities ... akin to a man's'.[37] It was noted how,

> smashing away at marble with chisel and mallet, Mrs. Hilton Young ... is winning for her sex a triumph over the most arduous branch of the most arduous art. No form of artistic expression needs more muscle or calls for greater demands upon the strength than this. Yet the widow of the dauntless Antarctic hero faces the rough block received from the mason with a courage, and chisels it with a strength and facility that some of the strongest of the best sculptors must envy.[38]

In 1923 Scott showed at the Grosvenor Gallery. A review entitled 'A Woman Sculptor' stated that this exhibition was a surprise on two counts. First, three years previously, when Scott had been interviewed as to whether women were sufficiently qualified to be elected ARAs she had said that 'women had never excelled in art; and when asked why she thought so, laughingly rejoined "We are an inferior race I suppose"'. When she remarried many had assumed that this 'woman who had achieved a certain amount of fame in the difficult art of sculpture, and seemingly in spite of her own intention, would thenceforth give up all exercise of her talents'.[39] The 1923 show was expected to be very successful, and another reviewer believed that the main characteristic of Scott's work was 'its intense virility. It might well be the work of a male sculptor, and one could imagine that a spectator, ignorant of the artist's sex, might take "K. Hilton Young" to be a man.'[40]

In the *Observer* in 1923 it was recounted how Scott worked her own marble, which would inevitably leave a trace of the artist's hand, and her bronzes were described as delicate, explained perhaps by being worked on with files after the casting process. This particular reviewer described how he had sat for Scott some years previously, and he observed in this extraordinarily whimsical account that

> there was a sudden transformation when the sculptor's blouse went on, and a creature entirely new to me fell to work with extraordinary

> intensity slapping clay on to the armature or central support. It had the adroitness of a bird nest-building; the quick, freezing eyes that scrutinised me were as little human as a squirrel's, and all the movements were as rapid and instinctive as a squirrel's. The busy creature hopped as it worked; it kicked its feet forward and backwards; it whistled, it sang. Then suddenly it stopped, after about an hour, and said 'I'm tired'. The same thing went on next day for another hour, and the work was finished.[41]

Very few critics had much to say about Scott's sculptures; instead the continuing popular novelty of the female sculptor fuelled numerous articles in newspapers and women's magazines. An example from February 1922 in the *Sketch* announced that Scott was to remarry. The accompanying illustration shows a photograph of Scott in the style of Pre-Raphaelite portrayals of women. Along two edges of the page we see images of four famous works, and in the middle of these a head-and-shoulders photograph of her fiancé (**Figure 16**).[42] A similarly constructed page in the *Tatler* 12 years later showed Scott with her family, and in this instance her position was subordinated to that of her second husband. On both occasions she was depicted alongside either men or sculptures of masculine subjects. From her autobiography and various statements she appears to have much preferred men to women, and was clearly able to form close friendships with leading men from the areas of politics, exploration and the arts. She adored her two sons and one wonders whether a daughter would have been so welcome. She was a powerful, attractive and yet non-threatening woman who clearly charmed the men who became her subjects.

In sharp contrast, a 1949 illustrated article about Dorset artist Elizabeth Muntz described her in terms appropriate for 'Hardy country' and presented a quite different version of a female sculptor: 'Along the lonely cliff road overlooking the sea that in the distance pounds the bleak headland of Portland Bill, comes a shaggy brown pony. Astride it, in a duffle coat and gum boots, with scarf flapping in the chilly north-west wind, is Elizabeth Muntz' (**Figure 17**). Muntz was on her way to carve in situ a memorial to novelist Llewelyn Powys, made from a single one-ton block of Portland limestone and located on the cliff-top near White Nothe in Purbeck. The photograph is captioned as follows:

> Every day a sculptor makes her pilgrimage to a desolate Dorset cliff-top where she carves a memorial in fulfilment of an author's dying wish. To get to work, Miss Muntz rides Merrylegs two miles from the village. In saddlebags is food and the sculptress spends four hours on cliff-top in weather both fair and foul.

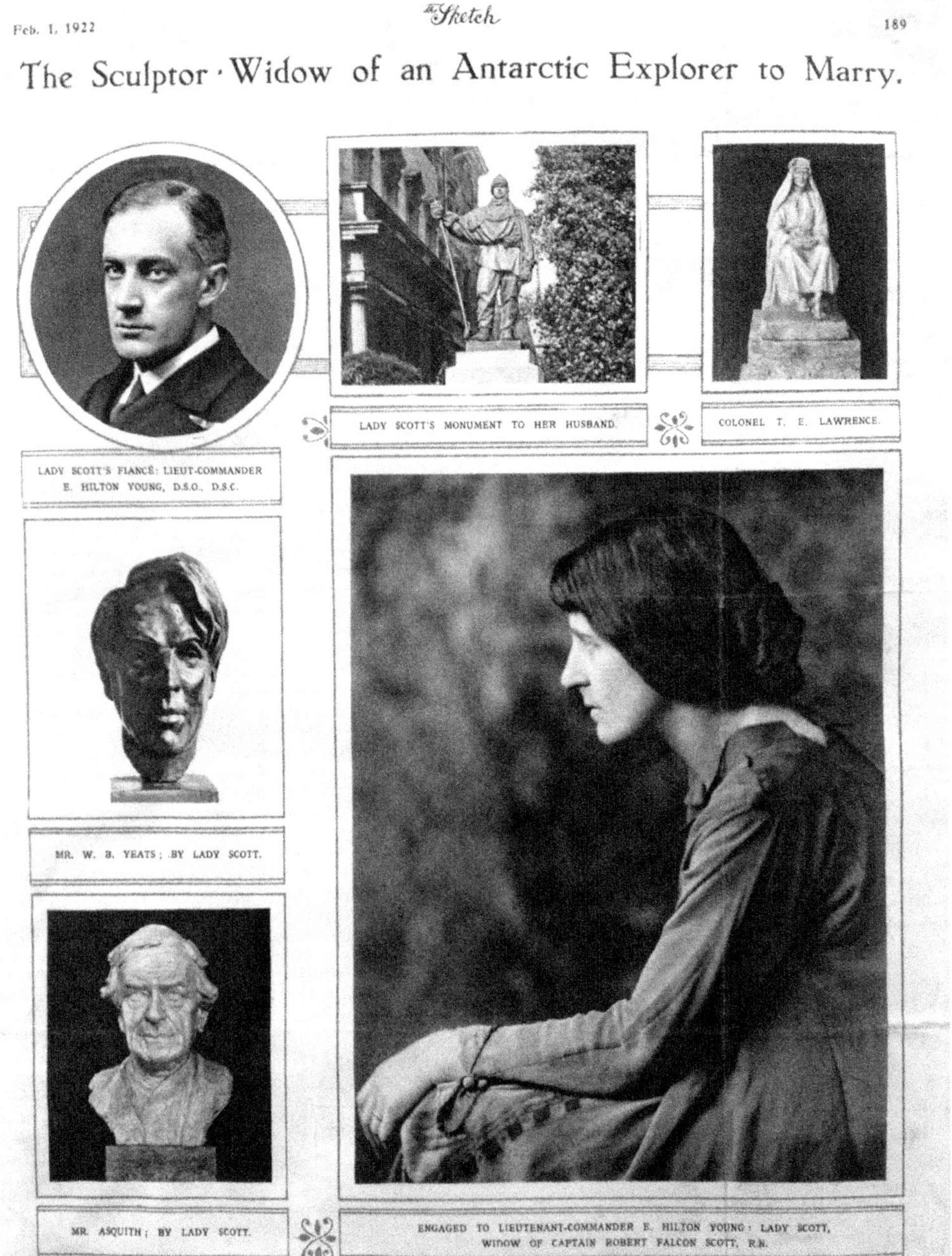
Feb. 1, 1922 The Sketch 189

The Sculptor-Widow of an Antarctic Explorer to Marry.

LADY SCOTT'S FIANCÉ: LIEUT.-COMMANDER E. HILTON YOUNG, D.S.O., D.S.C.

LADY SCOTT'S MONUMENT TO HER HUSBAND.

COLONEL T. E. LAWRENCE.

MR. W. B. YEATS; BY LADY SCOTT.

MR. ASQUITH; BY LADY SCOTT.

ENGAGED TO LIEUTENANT-COMMANDER E. HILTON YOUNG: LADY SCOTT, WIDOW OF CAPTAIN ROBERT FALCON SCOTT, R.N.

16. 'The Sculptor Widow of an Antarctic Explorer to Marry', *The Sketch*, 1 February 1922, p. 29

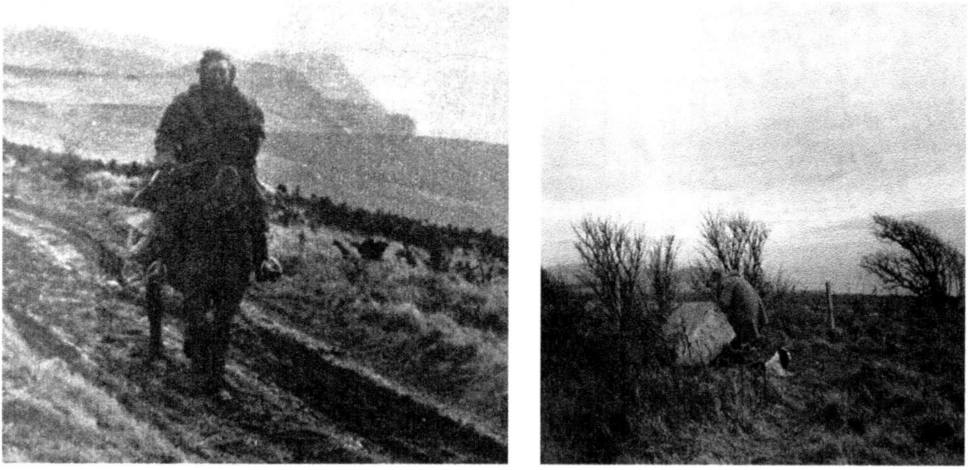

17. *Illustrated London News*, 5 February 1949

The pattern of the day is the focus of the article:

> Elizabeth Muntz ... works steadily, apart from a break for food, for about four hours a day. Six hours is the longest spell so far. Sculpturing with mallet and cold chisel needs undivided concentration and a hand as steady as the rock above which it is clenched. After several hours of standing buffeted by the stiff wind which sweeps across this part of the downs, and none too warm despite heavy clothing, she is more than ready for the comfort of her cottage.[43]

The tone of this review clearly placed Muntz in a different social and geographical context than that enjoyed by Scott, and also depicted her as a sculptor who actively engaged with nature and the elements. In another source, Muntz's studio-home was described as being the oldest 'tucked-away cottage' in her village, where some of her carved figures were 'placed quite naturally in the grass and among the flowers'.[44] An image of her at work in her garden in what appears to be the summer of 1949 conveys what was, and remains, an idyllic location (**Figure 18**). Thus texts and photographs conflate Muntz with the Dorset landscape, in sharp contrast to those of Scott which locate her within a privileged metropolitan elite.

Women artists have tended not to write about their work and so this means of accessing their thoughts poses another obstacle to our understanding of them. Various types of personal writing give us

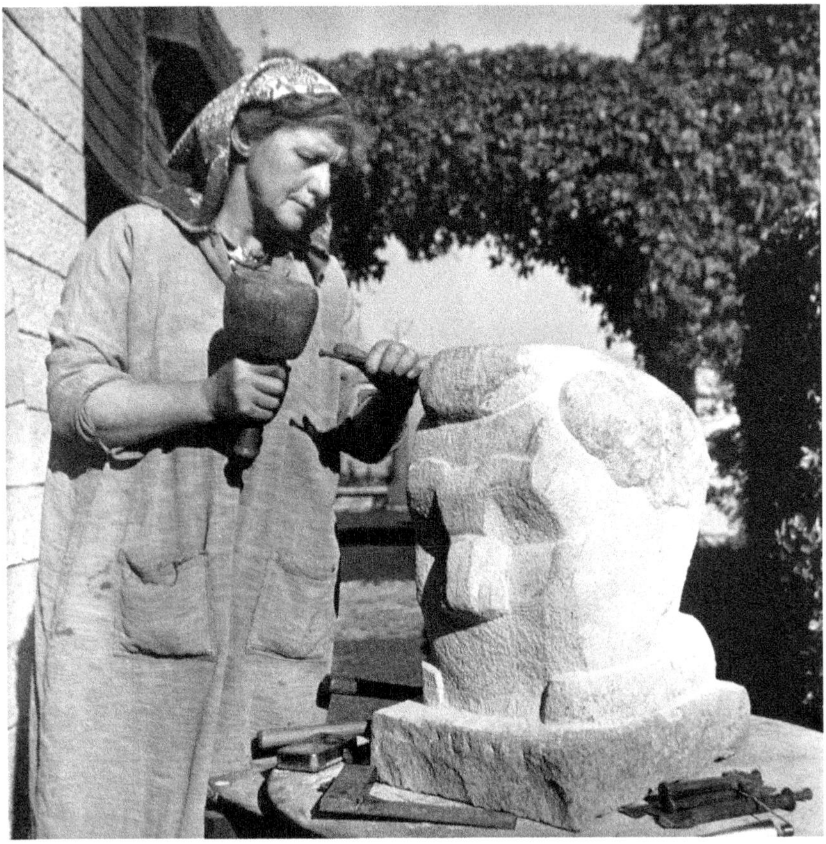

18. *Miss Muntz roughing out portrait of T. F Powys, 1949*

different versions of events; autobiographies are written with a future readership in mind and their authors are likely to be highly aware of how they wish to construct their legacy. Letters, in contrast, are less self-conscious. Only a few of the women discussed in this book made public their aims, although some did speak on television or radio. For example, Dora Gordine had a clear understanding of the importance of publicity and promotion and in November 1938 was one of the earliest artists to be seen on the then two-year-old BBC television. She hoped that this new medium would raise people's awareness of the arts. In her second appearance she proposed that sculpture had 'a vital, exciting message, if only people could be brought more closely in touch with what is being done. In that way, television ... is going to help tremendously.'[45]

Her hopes would not be realized for about 20 years and she herself never owned a television. Between 1945 and 1950 she gave three well-received radio talks which included one on 'Sculpture and Everyday Life'.[46]

Kathleen Scott's autobiography is deeply frustrating, as she hardly mentions her sculpture at all. Published two years after her death in 1947, having been written during an illness in 1932, it was selective in terms of what could be put into the public realm. The book's Introduction is signed 'K' and was probably written by her second husband, Lord Kennet. Here it was made clear that some material could not yet be published, since Scott was candid in writing down her thoughts about the people she met. It was emphasized that Scott had to negotiate the calls on her time made by her family, social life and her art, but that her energy enabled her to work in her studio, if not regularly, then with 'concentration and speed'.[47] Elsewhere Scott did have something to say about her choice of subjects but it remained somewhat superficial and repetitive:

> Most artists like best to produce what they know best. What they know best is commonly what they love best; and what they love best is what is to them the most beautiful. So they have in their minds a sequence which may be taken in any order – knowledge, love, beauty; beauty, knowledge, love. I expect that it is for that reason that the models who suggest themselves to me, for instance, and that I like best to work from, are the figures of little round children and eager striplings, and the heads of men whose features suggest high power or intellect. All that means is that those are the models which I think are the most beautiful.[48]

The sculptor's biography, *A Great Task of Happiness: The Life of Kathleen Scott* (1995), was written by her grand-daughter Louisa Young, based on Scott's diaries, which encompassed the period 1910–46. The book is generally short on detail and analysis of Scott's sculptural career, instead largely covering social engagements and personal relationships. This mirrors the content of the diaries themselves, which are disappointing due to the little Scott has to say about her work.

Barbara Hepworth's writings are slightly different, revealing her professionalism and commitment to working hard. In the 1970 publication *Barbara Hepworth: A Pictorial Autobiography* she described her preference for 'working holidays', a pattern established by her father on family trips to Robin's Hood Bay, Yorkshire, and that she did not regard it as problematic to run her domestic life in tandem with her professional: 'a woman artist is not deprived by cooking and having children, nor by nursing children with measles (even in triplicate) – one is in fact nourished by this rich life, provided one always does some work each day'.[49] In the 1930s Hepworth's work developed substantially alongside increased output. However, this was a difficult time for the art market following the 1929 stock market crash. Despite this, art publishing was growing, and titles that dealt with modern sculpture began to exceed those on classical Greece. Hepworth's publications, such as her *Pictorial Autobiography*, contained photographs of Howarth and the hills near Keighley, rooting the sculptor in her native Yorkshire, a localizing geographical treatment that was also applied to Henry Moore, in particular by John Hedgecoe.[50] Importantly, Hepworth drew attention to the support of Herbert Read in this book through the inclusion of facsimiles of most of the texts that the critic had written about her work. This could be seen as a strategy to make it public that Read supported her as well as Henry Moore. Ironically of course, this had the effect of locking Hepworth into a 'Read/Moore paradigm' which for many years after her death closed down investigation into her practice, rather than encouraging the opposite. Read's promotion of Moore as the exemplar in British modern sculpture had established the norm that Hepworth could only then be measured against.[51]

In the same way that interviewers appear to have focused on women sculptors' domestic contexts and responsibilities, and how they managed to be professionals with such 'distractions', many of the artists themselves reinforced this by doing just the same. Hepworth wrote of how she worked in a studio that was 'a jumble of children, rocks, sculptures, trees, importunate flowers and washing'.[52] Of course, if we focus too much on such descriptions then what is achieved is a reinforcement of the notion of an interior, basically private and domestic practice. We would be unlikely to find a male sculptor writing in the same manner. Henry Moore might well refer to collected stones and pieces of wood, but these would not be made ordinary, as the detritus of everyday life, but rather elevated to the status of sources for creative inspiration.

The practicalities of life during wartime were revealed in Hepworth's correspondence, such as in an undated letter to Sadie Martin written from Little Park Owles, Carbis Bay, in Cornwall. Hepworth and Nicholson had evacuated there, staying with Margaret Mellis and Adrian Stokes. She wrote that they were settling down and she hoped soon to be able to get time to make some sculpture: 'I have made myself a corner in which to work. If we can garden ½ time and work the other ½ I guess both ends will meet.'[53] However, underpinning Hepworth's *Autobiography* was her desire to settle certain key dates: 'My dates have been much altered by writers on Henry Moore. And of course, apart from being a woman, it has not been easy always having great bears breathing down one's neck.'[54] Clearly Hepworth understood the effect that Moore's reputation was having on her own, in part eliminating or at best marginalizing her in accounts of 1930s British modernism. She also felt that, unlike Moore, her work had attracted insufficient critical attention.[55]

Maybe unwittingly, many female artists have shored up the binary opposite of male/female; how female sculptors were able to present themselves, both in written and visual form, has been significant in shaping perceptions of them. The persistence of gendered norms has in the past affected the interpretation of sculptures made by women, and the combined impact of image and text, or film and narration, has been powerful.

3.3 Theorists and contexts of display

The ability of sculpture to be replicated was a recurring theme in nineteenth-century commentary, one that would be echoed in early twentieth-century debates about the supposed superiority of (direct) carving over (indirect) casting. In 1864 sculptor Harriet Hosmer wrote about the collaborative nature of sculptural production, which encompassed studio assistants and foundry workers.[56] Women sculptors such as Hosmer exposed this practice, in part to prove that they could indeed produce sculpture despite their supposed physical inferiority, though of course this could reinforce a perception of sculpture's inauthenticity as a result of the number of individuals who might have worked on a single piece. This is despite the fact that we know that it had been the norm for prominent male painters and sculptors to employ workshop assistants. Although press coverage of sculpture increased markedly towards the end of the nineteenth century, the tone was often hostile. The belief in the superiority of painting over sculpture still lingered, and can be traced back to Sir Joshua Reynolds's Discourses at the Royal Academy (1769–90). Contemporary critical and theoretical writings reinforced this attitude; for example, in Ruskin's *The Seven Lamps of Architecture* (1849) the author more or less ignored sculpture, apart from a positive commentary on how it might be used in a decorative capacity in conjunction with architecture.[57] There was a widely held view among sculptors that the Royal Academy had failed to educate people on how to understand sculpture and not to perceive its absence of colour as a fundamental problem.

Martina Droth has suggested that the late nineteenth-century's preference and nostalgia for older periods of art seems to have been linked to uncertainty as to how sculpture should be used and regarded in the modern world. It appeared increasingly isolated, in part due to a decline in decoration required by contemporary architectural designs; if it could not be aligned with the values understood as implicit in architecture, such as permanence, stability and dignity, then sculpture ran the risk of appearing 'weak and vulnerable'. A building did more than provide a physical and aesthetic framework through which sculpture was mediated – it provided the viewer with a context through which to understand the work:

> Sculpture was so intrinsically and ideologically identified with architecture that its existence outside of this context necessarily altered the ways it was looked at and interpreted and ... redefined notions of what sculpture was and what it was for. As soon as it became free-standing, physically detached and isolated, its point of reference shifted inward, to its own intrinsic aesthetics; it acquired an autonomy and specificity that called for a new contextual evaluation.

Thus the interpretation of sculpture was increasingly seen to be dependent on its context. At the turn of the century the sense that sculpture had lost context encouraged a reconsideration of how it was experienced, and the argument that sculpture was necessarily defined by architecture was challenged. Instead, sculpture might now be regarded as 'an idea that extended, breathed and resonated in space' and this impacted on how it was viewed, commented on and displayed.[58]

With a crisis in the supply of public commissions, sculptors were obliged to show their work within an artistic rather than public context in order to gain recognition. Several women sculptors regularly exhibited at the Royal Academy Summer Exhibitions, including Anne Acheson, Kathleen Scott, Phoebe Stabler (1879–1955) and Gertrude Williams, all of whom are discussed in this book. These particular women produced major commissions in the form of portrait busts of famous individuals and memorials. Another exhibiting venue was provided by the establishment of the Grosvenor Gallery in May 1877. Its policy was to invite a range of artists whose styles differed but whose work was interesting. Founded by Sir Coutts Lindsay and his wife Lady Blanche, the gallery's design imitated the fashionable domestic interior, and to support this effect visitors were provided with access to a library, billiard and dining rooms, all of which underscored the desired ambience. The gallery became famous as one of the few exhibition spaces in London where both male and female artists could present their work. Queen Victoria's daughter Princess Louise, Duchess of Argyll, exhibited there regularly, showing both sculptures and paintings between 1878 and 1889.[59] In venues such as the Grosvenor Gallery a broad mix of individuals would be on the guest list for receptions and private view events, ranging from bankers, aristocrats and entrepreneurs to painters and actors. The gallery only showed work by invitation and aimed to differ from what was seen as the unsatisfactory display methodologies of the Royal Academy.[60] However, it closed in 1890 when the marriage of its owners failed.

Despite such innovations the Royal Academy remained the supreme showcase and as such provided a standard against which artists were measured, although crowded displays and the concept of the 'sculpture hall' persisted. This physical isolation of sculpture was criticized by Edmund Gosse, who believed that, unlike a painting which was self-contained, a sculpture was dependent on (and indeed affected by) its surroundings. For Gosse, this placement could be better realized in the home. As late as April 1927 a reviewer in the *Spectator*, commenting on the policies and display strategies of the Royal Academy, noted that the institution largely remained unchanged in the work it favoured, and that the layout of the central room devoted to sculpture was incoherent: 'life size studies set beside others on a larger scale cause a confusion to the eye which could be avoided if the studies above life size were juxtaposed with those definitely below them'. However, he particularly selected for praise Kathleen Scott's *The Kingdom is Within* (**Figure 2**) writing: 'here all is wrought in detail; the tip-toe poise gives tension to the muscles in the slender limbs, down which the eye goes sliding. This is the only large piece of statuary which develops the sensuous charm of bronze as a material.'[61]

Writing in 1904, Clara Erskine Clement, an American writer and traveller, argued that sculpture had become more 'democratic'. While continuing its traditional role of commemorating great men and deeds, it also reflected 'common, every-day life', and drew on poetic sources such as myths and legends. She noted the existence of a large number of female sculptors who were receiving important commissions related to the great expositions, and producing memorial statues, monuments and fountains which demonstrated the quality of their work.[62] A few years later, Margaret Thomas, a travel writer, poet and artist, published a book entitled *How to Understand Sculpture* (1911). Here she attempted to rebalance the general appreciation of painting, describing sculpture as requiring of its viewer a study of the medium's 'more sober fascinations ... a special education and knowledge of form [in order] to understand her cold and classic charms, her pure impassive dignity'.[63] She recalled a recent visit to the Tate Gallery where there was 'a small but interesting collection of British sculpture', but, as ever, the rooms containing paintings were crowded and the sculpture gallery was silent and only used as a route to get from one display of paintings to another.[64]

In this final section I want to look at some of the key writers on sculpture within the period covered by this book. Edmund Gosse was an early critic who reacted positively to trends in late nineteenth-century British sculpture, facilitated by his friendship with the sculptor William Hamo Thornycroft. Gosse's writings enabled him to draw his readers' attention in particular to the movement he named 'The New Sculpture', a term repeated in his key essay of the same name.[65] In his 1890s piece 'The Place of Sculpture in Daily Life' Gosse urged the public to decorate their homes with statuettes, and he also promoted the touching of sculpture, something that had become forbidden in the Victorian museum space in the latter half of the nineteenth century. When Gosse first wrote about the New Sculpture in the *Art Journal* in 1894 he characterized its main features as a naturalism in the display of figures, an attention to the surface of the sculpture, the choice of literary subject matter, picturesque qualities and intimacy of scale.[66] Between 1919 and his death in 1928 he regularly wrote in the literary pages of the *Sunday Times*, which he called his 'pulpit'. Writing in the *Saturday Review* Gosse commented on all matters to do with contemporary sculpture, although Academy criticism was his strength, but in these articles he was covering a large number of sculptures and so detailed analysis was not feasible. Gosse tried to engage the public to take an interest in, and collect, sculpture. So apart from academic criticism he wrote articles on 'Living English Sculptors', examined public monuments and suggested means of improving their quality.[67] In 'Equestrian Sculpture for London' (1884) Gosse argued that English sculptors did not have the imagination of their French counterparts, among whom sculpture was flourishing under state patronage. He implied that in Britain such patronage was resisted, being still linked to an absolutist monarchy which dictated taste and realized schemes at public expense.

Gosse was also critical of the habit in England of putting out sculpture commissions to competition, believing this to be a parochial attitude and a wasteful process: money so used could be more usefully spent on the final memorial. Instead it was diluted by being spent on the models submitted by the competing sculptors. 'Philistinism often prevailed when decisions were made; ignorant memorial committees were seduced by the smooth and conventional models of mediocre artists rather than rougher sketches of great men.'[68] He pointed to the fallacy that sculpture could not withstand the British climate, and that it was necessarily unaffordable. His words fell on deaf ears as he repeatedly made the same points, and by the end of the 1890s he withdrew from commentating on sculpture. However, he had repeatedly advocated the publication of cheap bronze statuettes so as to bring sculpture into the ordinary home, and believed that the statuette 'liberated' sculpture from neoclassical norms and provided an affordable form. I will return to Gosse and the statuette in Chapter 4.

Marion Spielmann edited the *Magazine of Art* between 1886 and 1904, wrote on art for the daily paper *The Graphic*, supported the Royal Academy, and through his writings sought to establish a national school of British art in response to developing trends in France, especially the impact of Impressionism. Although conservative in taste, he wielded great influence on people's thinking about art since he wished to present artists as having shared values with their public, namely 'respectability, a work ethic, and success'. Spielmann believed that painting dealt with realist and genre subjects, whereas sculpture was the perfect medium through which to express allegorical, classical and ideal subjects. He tried to describe a British school of sculpture and is known to have taken Rodin to visit various English sculptors' studios, thus revealing his sculptural preferences. However, he was also a champion of artistic freedom since he joined those who defended Epstein's nude sculptures on the façade of the British Medical Association building, even though he personally found them 'too grim and sculpturesquely brutal for my taste'.[69]

In his 1901 publication *British Sculpture and Sculptors of To-Day* Spielmann opened by drawing his readers' attention to the lack of a book on recent or contemporary British sculpture, the topic only being covered by the occasional magazine article. This had prompted him to write a book that promoted what he saw as the important developments in British sculpture during the last quarter of the nineteenth century, which had resulted in 'works of extraordinary merit and beauty … excellent alike in design and execution'. He supported the work of Alfred Gilbert, in particular the sculptor's use of metal, and although Spielmann suggested that it was 'more or less as "bibelot" on a large scale, it belongs at least to the domain of fine art'.[70] This hints at the cross-fertilization between fine and applied art forms that would become a feature of many sculptors' practice in the early twentieth century. Spielmann constructed a lineage for the New Sculpture movement. Since it sought to avoid the classical notion of the 'ideal', instead aiming for realism and picturesque qualities, he brought the new and old together by arguing that an important aspect of the New Sculpture was 'the effort towards such realism and picturesqueness of treatment as do not detract from the dignity of the conception'.[71] In *British Sculpture and Sculptors of To-Day* he focused on living artists, which was a break with that book's most significant antecedent, William Bell Scott's 1872 *The British School of Sculpture*, which covered only dead sculptors, represented by engravings of their works. Spielmann's aim in writing about living sculptors was not just to insert them into the sculptural canon but also to market their work to the public.

In 1902 he helped organize the exhibition *Sculpture for the Home* at the Fine Art Society to encourage the purchase of small New Sculpture bronzes, and New Sculpture artists received long entries and photographic reproductions in his 1901 book.[72] Although the New Sculpture was rooted in ideas brought to England by Jules Dalou and Edward Lantéri, Spielmann was insistent that such work was thoroughly 'British'.[73] He did not like what could be seen as the extremes of classical art or of realism, regarding the first as lifeless and the latter as vulgar. In an effort to encourage interest from the public he, like Gosse, suggested to readers that they should buy statuettes to decorate their homes, and he also advocated the establishment of a national sculpture gallery and a fine arts department for artists and connoisseurs in order that London's sculpture might rival that of Paris.[74] He believed that British sculpture demonstrated the medium's best qualities, 'nobility, style, ideal poetry, and dignified treatment', and that with these characteristics it avoided what he termed, but did not explain, 'the pitfalls' of French sculpture.[75]

It appears that Spielmann wished to extend the definition of what sculpture might be, although within the conventions of the day he was necessarily constrained. He showed awareness of why some observers might find viewing sculpture unsatisfactory, arguing that vision favoured colour over form and thus painting over sculpture. 'To produce bad sculpture is … easier than to execute bad painting; and the power to discriminate between the bad and the good in sculpture appears to be a rare gift.' He also wrote about the problems faced in the creation and reception of sculpture, describing painting as 'frankly illusive' whereas to the untrained eye a sculpture might seem to be merely 'imitative'.

He argued that this was not the case, since a sculpture had to meet 'the highest requirements, with the poorest means'. He characterized the physical process as relatively easy but the idea as demanding. 'Whilst almost anyone can mould pliant clay into a copy of a man, few can conceive and embody an elevated idea, not by imitation of a model, but by the fine treatment of form and the noble character of expression and design.' Sculpture did not have painting's advantages of colour, tone and atmosphere; the latter could encompass any subject matter, whereas the subjects for sculpture were restricted.[76]

Spielmann structured his book in chronological order, apart from coverage of female sculptors, who had their own section. It is interesting that he foresaw how this might be interpreted when he stated that this should not be read as implying inferiority, but he did not explain his decision. Some of his chapters were based on types of sculptural practice, one such interesting classification being 'The Sculptor-Decorators'. Here he wrote that many of the famous sculptors whom he had already discussed in his book had often put to one side their idealized or realistic work and instead indulged in decorative practice, which was highly fashionable in Britain and Europe. This is important since it reflects the reality that most sculptors diversified more than is generally recorded in art histories.[77] When he turned to the female sculptors, Spielmann noted that now that they were gaining access to proper training, and particularly to study from the nude, they were 'making their mark in England' and were avoiding the stifling 'cold heaviness' of classicism.[78]

Spielmann was critical of a lack of national attention to the display of sculpture: it was not present in the Victoria and Albert Museum, and although at the Tate Gallery there was a good room that could display figures and groups, it was quite small. The country had no venue where it would be possible to mount a permanent, representative display of British sculpture. However, he tempered this criticism by adding 'but ... the art of the sculptor ... looks better in decorative surroundings – in the open, or appropriately placed in fine houses – so that, for the present at least, the snub to sculpture is more sentimental than real'.[79] Spielmann was aware that sculpture was often used to embody certain sweeping values; in many public and private art collections, which had often commenced with the acquisition of sculpture, the latter now seemed to be required to play 'a leading role as a means of articulating the museum's grandest vision of itself as the eternal custodian of the highest expressions of culture and even of civilization itself'. However, despite sculpture's usefulness as emblematic of high culture, in practical terms it was difficult to display due to its size and so its exhibition outside of the sculptor's studio was problematic and expensive.[80]

In 1922 Kineton Parkes published his important two-volume *Sculpture of To-Day*. Here he argued that contemporary sculpture was

> dealing with truth more than with the embroideries of truth; it is studying nature more than it is studying artifice ... it is on the right lines now, and has been struggling to get on the right lines for more than half a century. Its eventual success admits of little doubt. It is true that in England sculptors were slothful in taking up the lead given them by Alfred Stevens ... but those days of sloth have passed.[81]

Like Margaret Thomas, he also commented on the fact that the public focused on paintings rather than sculptures when they visited exhibitions, and in part he blamed the galleries for relegating sculpture to 'odd corners' and for generally displaying insufficient amounts. He also noted the cost of sculpture in that it was a good deal cheaper to have your portrait painted rather than sculpted, and that the materials used by a painter were far cheaper than those a sculptor required. He argued that sculpture as an art form was very direct but that many viewers did not know how to approach it. The main problem seemed to be that, unlike painting, sculpture did not present a narrative, and the latter gave painting popular appeal. However, he believed that many modern sculptors' work did 'tell stories'. 'Monumental sculpture is often pictorial ... as the vast majority of people are not very cultivated, sculpture should at least bear some of the burden of general enlightenment, and at the same time achieve a greater measure of appreciation for itself in its higher forms.' Apart from this rather lofty attack on the 'uncultivated', Parkes blamed many groups of people for what he saw as the misunderstanding of sculpture, from sculptors themselves to architects, from public offices of works to fine art organizations, from memorial committees to patrons.[82]

Parkes slated the Victorian period for its sculpture and was also critical of the ways in which all sculpture was currently cared for. He characterized Alfred Gilbert's *Eros* in Piccadilly Circus as being ruined by its state of neglect, describing it thus:

> sodden masses of newspaper and pieces of broken wooden flower boxes are strewn in and around the fountain, and blowsy flower-women degrade their wares and throw them when decayed into the basin, into which dingy men, smoking short pipes and horrible tobacco, also spit at intervals. Gilbert gave England a new vision of beauty in the memory of

> one of that great country's most beautiful characters, Lord Shaftesbury, and it has degraded it into a cesspool, and is like to destroy it utterly.[83]

Parkes then turned his attention to the library at South Kensington, stating that books by living authors were readily purchased, but where contemporary English sculpture was concerned it appeared that it was subject to widespread dislike and lack of recognition. He deplored this state of affairs, believing that contemporary English sculpture stood comparison with that of other countries. He too was critical of the display of sculpture, noting that at the Royal Academy in 1920 there were about 160 sculptures and medals exhibited, of mixed quality, as was to be expected of any such large-scale display. However, he still believed that even at the Academy English contemporary sculpture was treated with 'contempt' and that this was not only 'feeble' but 'foolish and dangerous', and he was disappointed that Burlington House was the only place in which to view a large amount of sculpture.[84]

In 1931 Parkes would return to the subject of sculpture and the Royal Academy, arguing that an 'academy does not postulate progress; at its best it registers contemporary modes. When there is an advance, it is due to its rebellious members, who frequently succumb at last to academic pressure and cease to function as pioneers.'[85] He also felt that sculpture did not receive sufficient attention in art journals, many of which he described as having ceased publication through 'indifference' to their contents, such as *The Art Journal, The Magazine of Art* and *The Artist,* although still in publication were *The Burlington Magazine, The Connoisseur, The Studio, Colour* and *Drawing and Design.* He argued that there was better exposure in the United States and Europe, and that consequently in these countries there were more sculptures to be found in the home, and more shops selling sculpture; much more sculpture was shown at the Salons than at the Royal Academy.[86]

In 1930 Stanley Casson published a book on twentieth-century sculptors, giving as his rationale a growing interest in sculpture on the part of the ordinary person. This had resulted in more sculptors being trained and therefore increased sculptural production. Out of this would result critiques of the practice and discussion of its guiding principles. The somewhat didactic approach in this book was not unusual, as the early 1930s saw several publications in which particular approaches to sculptural practice were emphasized. The most obvious 'fault-line' remained the supposed neat division between the (traditional) method of modelling in clay for subsequent casting in bronze and the (modern) method of direct carving. Where the latter was emphasized, the aim was to shape public perception of the artist as physically powerful. Casson referred to the frequent distinction made in the 1920s between carving and modelling, the supposed direct engagement of the carver with their material as opposed to the more removed position of the sculptor who sent a clay model to the bronze foundry.[87] He was critical of this view and saw such oppositions of tradition and innovation, and of modelling and carving, as being essentially rhetorical.

Also in 1930 G. A. Jellicoe wrote about 'Modern British Sculpture' for the *Studio*. He deplored a tendency to literalism on the part of the public, arguing that aiming for exact visual likeness alone did not produce art, but rather a commercial product. He believed that sculptors understood that obtaining a superficial visual likeness was insufficient: to be a work of art, a sculpture needed more. As well as being expressive through its form, it needed to be sympathetic both to its materials and to its eventual surroundings. He praised Elizabeth Muntz's sculpture as demonstrating formal qualities that showed

> mastery over the truth that it is that which lies within that gives sculpture its energy and force ... Barbara Hepworth show[s] the same feeling for form, though less pronounced ... Gertrude Hermes is less playful but more profound in grasping the movements of animals and expressing them in planes.[88]

Figure 19 shows Muntz experimenting with semi-abstracted forms, and is probably the sort of work that Jellicoe had in mind. Muntz's *Dancing Children* (1925–27) was reproduced in the same article and was shown at the 1928 Seven and Five show. She had a solo exhibition at the Storran Gallery in 1938, showing sculptures in bronze, stone and terracotta, and in February 1951 her work was displayed at the Burlington Galleries as part of the London Group exhibition. She was friends with Eric Kennington, and like her friend and near neighbour in Dorset, Mary Spencer Watson, she also taught at Bryanston School. Despite now being hardly known, her work was widely reviewed. An undated account in *Apollo* described her as 'one of the few sculptors in this country whose work shows real merit and genuine feeling for its material whether it be wood, stone, bronze, or lead'.[89] Not all reviews of Muntz's work were favourable: a 1926 article in *Apollo* linked her work to that of her mentor Dobson, but in dismissing her *Torso* it is unclear whether the reviewer also disliked Dobson's work when he described Muntz's sculpture as 'Dobsonesque' and as having its 'good points destroyed by ridiculous

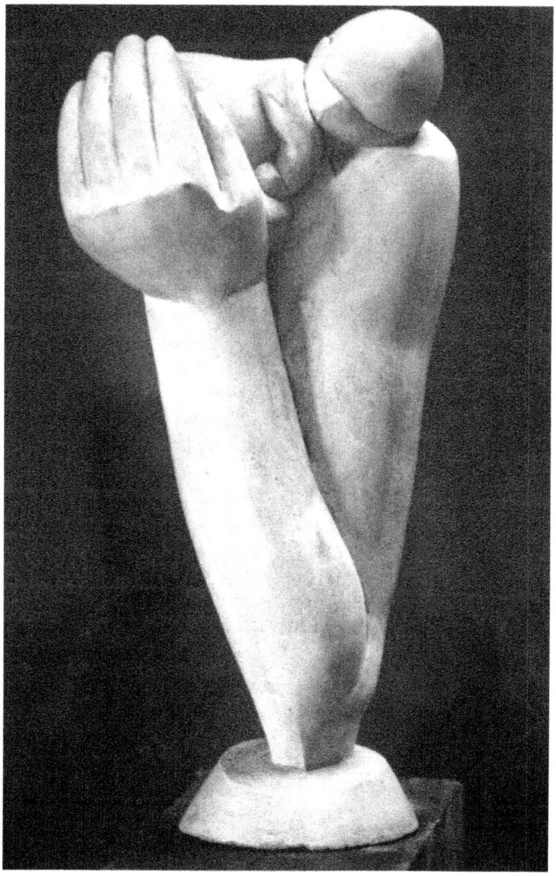

19. Elizabeth Muntz, *Arm and Baby*, c.1924

truncations'.[90] However, in 1931 Kineton Parkes argued that this piece, alongside *Child with a Fawn* (**Figure 20**), showed a plastic sensitivity: even when Muntz carved she displayed the attributes of the proficient modeller.[91] The work that was a matter for disagreement is likely to have been *Reclining Torso* from 1921 (**Figure 21**).

In his 1931 book *The Art of Carved Sculpture* Kineton Parkes made a clear distinction between carving and modelling, preferring the former, and argued that the materials of clay and stone were so different that they should remain separate. He asserted that all sculpture should draw closely from nature, including decorative sculpture, although he acknowledged that it was more difficult to obtain naturalism through carving. Instead simplification of forms might be more effective, and thus by contrast modelling allowed for greater realism.[92] However, he

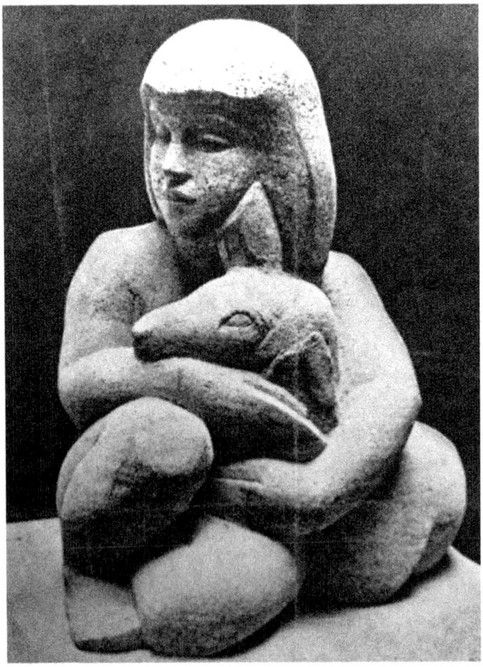

20. Elizabeth Muntz, *Child with a Fawn*, 1925–27

21. Elizabeth Muntz, *Reclining Torso*, 1921

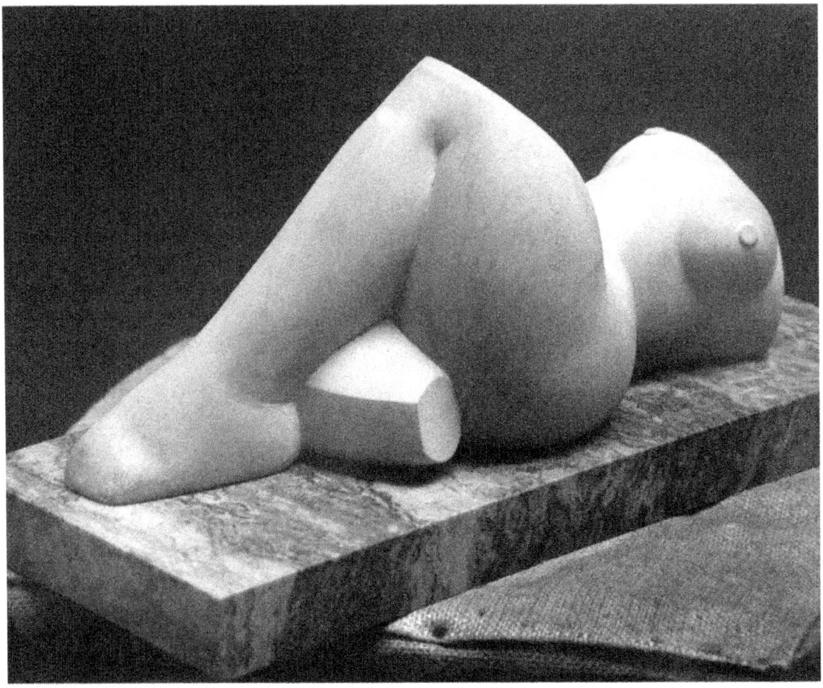

believed that the sculptor as direct carver comprised the Pygmalion figure of the popular imagination: 'A picture of a sculptor armed with a lump of clay and a modelling tool is seldom seen, and yet Pygmalions – the artists with mallet and chisel – are rare. The great majority of sculptors are modellers and modified carvers only.'[93] To support his preference for carving he described how, during the previous decade, the carved work that had been exhibited at the Royal Academy had reinvigorated the practice of sculpture. According to Parkes, many sculptors were realizing that clay was not 'not the be-all and end-all of sculpture', and that whereas modelling (from his perspective) only required the sculptor to put something into the 'shapeless clay', direct carving required more craftsmanship. He asserted that the Royal Academy needed to receive and display fewer modelled sculptures and more carved works, but interestingly also 'less ideal work and more applied, either in metals or in pottery'.[94] So once again there was a sense that the definition of what a sculptor might produce was being expanded, even if modelling attracted criticism from some quarters.

22. Elsie Henderson, *Recumbent Fawn*, 1925

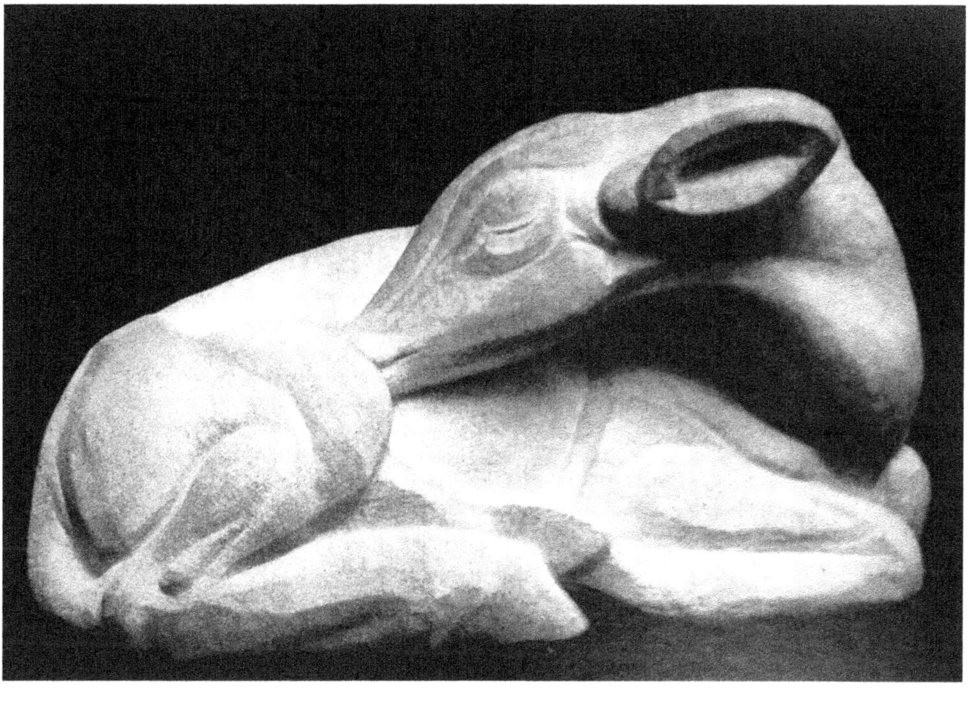

Despite this emphasis on carving, Parkes's book does have the great advantage of including a number of women artists – Phyllis Clay (1880–1947), Ursula Edgcumbe, Elsie Henderson (1880–1967), Barbara Hepworth, Arnrid Johnston (1895–1972), Katharine Maltwood, Elizabeth Muntz and Edna Manley – thus underscoring female sculptors' engagement with this supposedly masculine and avant-garde practice. Elsie Henderson studied at the Slade between 1903 and 1905, and from 1908 at the Académie Colarossi in Paris. During the First World War she studied lithography at the Chelsea Polytechnic. She set up her own press, focused on animal imagery, and exhibited at the Leicester Galleries and the Royal Academy in 1924. There followed solo shows at the Redfern Gallery in 1929 and the Storran Gallery in 1935.[95] Referring to Henderson's early directly carved animal studies of lions and deer made from artificial stone, Kineton Parkes believed her work to be compact and essentially linear, and specifically referred to works made for the garden. He discussed and illustrated a sculpture of a sitting deer, *Recumbent Fawn*, made in 1925 from Portland stone

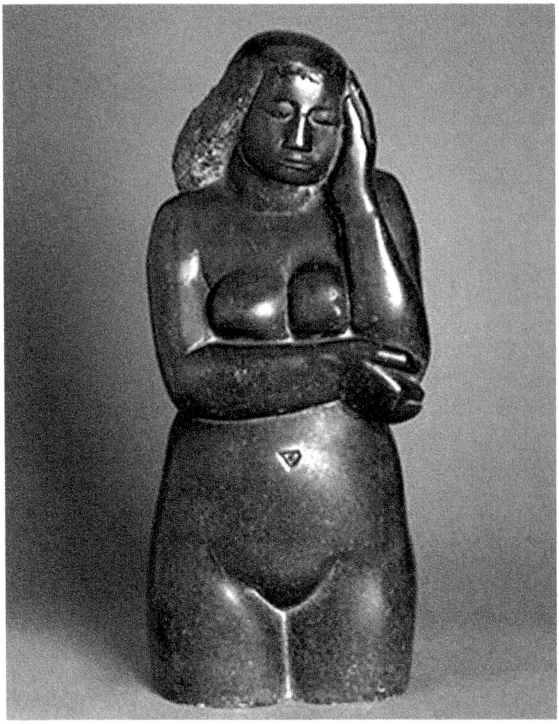

23. Barbara Hepworth, *Contemplative Figure*, 1928

(**Figure 22**).[96] A recent Hepworth sculpture also included in Parkes's book was *Contemplative Figure* (1928) (**Figure 23**). In the 1920s and 1930s Hepworth sculpted birds and maternal themes, as did many other female artists, but only using stone or marble (apart from the 1929 Burmese wood *Infant*). This had the effect of harnessing her domestic themes to the masculine act of stone carving. When she commenced carving in wood in 1929, the female figure was her subject, thus aligning her use of this particular material with a well-regarded sculptural subject.[97] This early figurative sculpture shows how much her pre-war work had in common with that of other women sculptors in my book.

Born in Sweden, Arnrid Johnston was friends with Ursula Edgcumbe when they both studied at the Slade School of Art. Her work was included in the 1927 *Living British Artists* exhibition at Leeds City Art Gallery; she also showed at the London Group's 1930 *Open-Air Sculpture* exhibition at Selfridges and the 1931 Whitechapel Art Gallery show. Johnston's *Triangular Obelisk* of c.1930, constructed for Walden House in Pimlico in Portland stone, is a much-weathered but still impressive work (**Figure 24**). Parkes described Johnston as producing a considerable amount of carving in various materials, and he believed this sculpture to be her most important. It comprises a three-sided group depicting children playing and a base containing groups of deeply carved animals. Parkes noted that a green serpentine sculpture *In Pasture* and *A Bird Bath* by Johnston were on display at the London Group's Selfridge Roof Garden Exhibition.[98]

In 1916 Katharine Maltwood's memorial tablet *A Vision* (1916) was exhibited at the Arts and Crafts Society, Burlington House. She carved two versions: a plaster went to a private purchaser in London and an alabaster work was made for the sculptor's mother, and is now in the Maltwood Collection in Canada (**Figure 25**). In his book Parkes reproduced the alabaster version, and this is probably the work referred to by Sir Claude Philips, who wrote in the *Daily Telegraph* that Maltwood was

> equally at home in the difficult arts of high and low relief; the aspiring rhythm of her composition, starting from a basis of static, and changing as it moves upwards into one of dynamic intensity, is novel and expressive. Even the Italian Gothic framework ... studiously simple as it is, proves close and sympathetic study of style and accuracy in detail.[99]

This was a productive period for Maltwood, her work showing both the influence of the Italian Renaissance in terms of her religious pieces, and

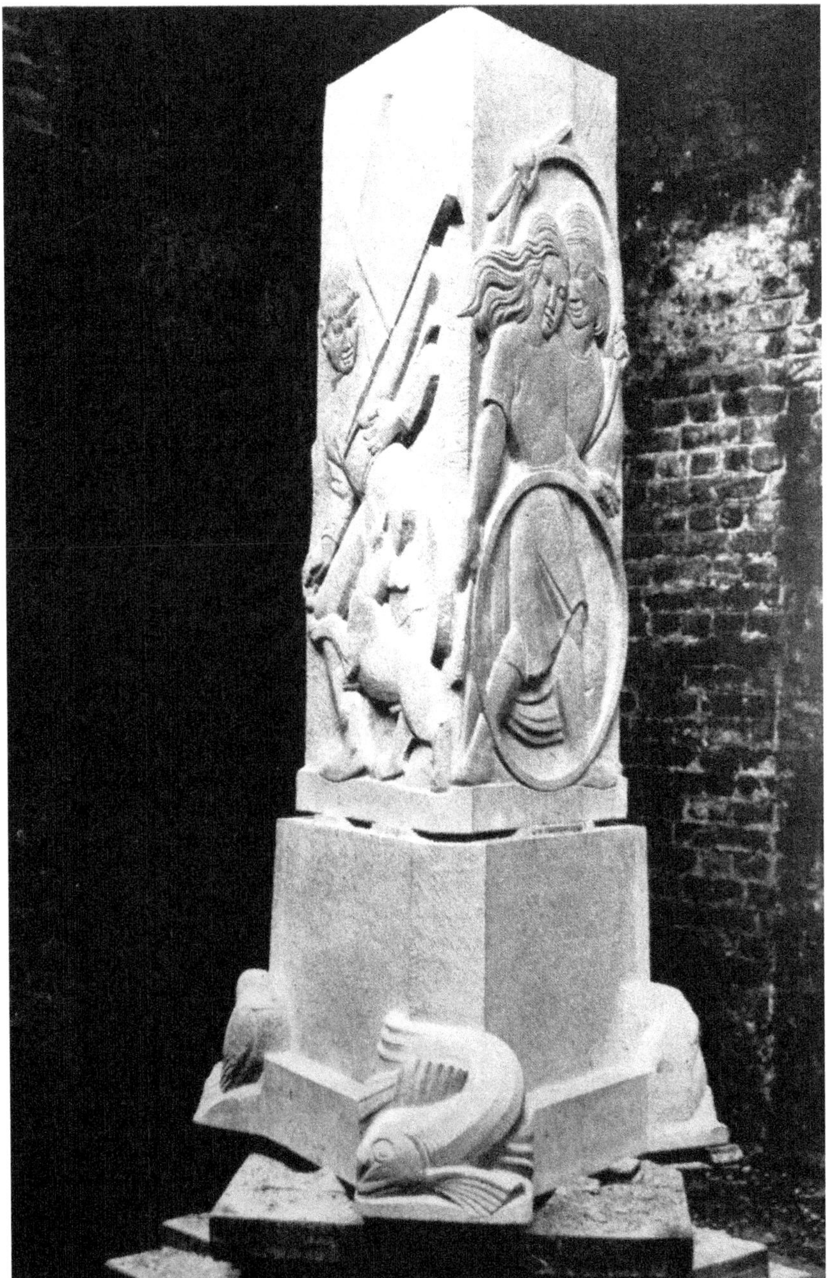

24. Arnrid Johnston, *Triangular Obelisk*, c.1930

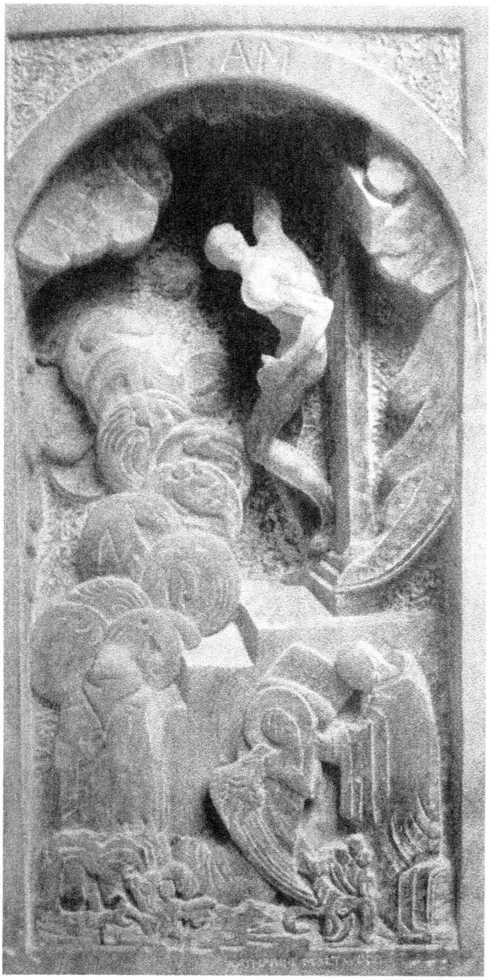

25. Katharine Maltwood, *A Vision*, 1916

her linking of sculpture to architectural frameworks, yet at the same time her figures are reminiscent of Rodin's sculpture in their fluidity and expressiveness.

In 1933 Eric Underwood's *A Short History of English Sculpture* was published, and like Parkes he too separated carving from modelling. He wished to demonstrate a continuous lineage for English sculpture, stretching back to Romanesque and Gothic carvers, and the designers of early Celtic crosses, in the belief that contemporary sculptors owed a debt to these antecedents.[100] He emphatically asserted that the meaning of the word 'sculpture' was 'carving' and thus not modelling for a bronze work. He also believed that sculpture could be separated into two categories by purpose, architectural sculpture and isolated pieces that fulfilled the equivalent function of the 'easel picture'.[101] Ten years later Arthur J. Broadbent's *Sculpture Today in Great Britain, 1940–1943* focused on a very narrow timeframe. He asserted that sculpture both in Britain and abroad had become increasingly popular during the last decade. A greater range of people were now beginning to understand it. As a result, the commissioning of a portrait bust was no longer the privilege of the wealthy. Sculpture as a domestic decoration was increasing and people were learning how to distinguish between the cheap reproduction and the exclusive work of the artist. Sculpture had become something to have in the home to enjoy, to pass on as an heirloom.[102] Included in this publication were illustrations of sculptures by eight women sculptors, including Joyce Bidder (1906–99) and Gwynneth Holt (1905–95).

Overall, between the 1890s and 1930s we can see in this selection of key publications evidence of a growing preference for sculpture that is carved rather than modelled. Women sculptors often received negative commentary in art journals, ranging from arguments that owing to their gender they were incapable of reaching the highest standards to claims that their work itself was gendered 'feminine' and should thus be interpreted in terms of its sensitivity, delicacy and restraint. Reviews of work exhibited by women's art societies frequently focused on the artists' gender, as well as overlaying commentary on the works on display with events taking place in wider society in terms of women's push for equality with men. This had the effect of further marginalizing women sculptors' practice.[103] Moreover, when reviews were published on group exhibitions mounted by women artists, critics routinely rounded up diverse work into a single category of 'women's work'. None of these exhibitions were regularly reviewed in prominent art journals. *Apollo* was the exception in covering exhibitions by the Society of Women Artists and the Women's International Art Club from its inception in 1925 until 1928, when it ceased regular review of such exhibitions.[104] Since women's practice was largely omitted from the art journals in which the contemporary fine art debates were conducted, they were also omitted from an important source of art historical research. Instead the exhibitions by women's art societies were reviewed in the national press, and thus their critical reception was constructed in different ways from that of the specialist art press. The main fora for the review of the London societies' shows was *The Times* and the *Daily Telegraph,* and it is typical of such publications that the opening of the show by a dignitary received as much attention as the work of the artists on display. In 1920 a reviewer in the *Athenaeum* demonstrated the criticism that existed of women exhibiting separately from men after they had gained the vote, and how it was expected that their work would communicate something that was gender specific:

> In the present exhibition we have the right to expect something more definite, something which would justify sex segregation; in a word, something characteristically feminine. We could pardon mediocrity, badness even, if it were specifically feminine mediocrity or specifically feminine badness. We go to the Society of Women Artists to see women's art but we do not find it.[105]

In an interesting use of terminology to be employed many years later by Griselda Pollock and Roszika Parker, a writer for *Apollo* in 1926 made a play on the labels 'master' and 'mistress'. The reviewer argued that women had faced fewer impediments in pursuing an artistic career compared with other professions; indeed that there now existed many more female than male artists and 'the "Old Masters" should have been superseded by a galaxy of "Old Mistresses"'. However, the reality was 'unfortunately, entirely on the side of Nature's ungallant, but inexorable, law. In other words, the woman artist is, like a crowing hen, an exception that proves the rule. If therefore there are few modern "masters", the proportion of modern "mistresses" is commensurately infinitesimal.'[106] In contrast to this somewhat sour commentary, in 1928 the *Manchester Guardian* carried an article entitled 'Women Sculptors to the Fore' in which it was recorded that over 600 sculptures had been submitted to the Royal Academy for exhibition, and that of these a large proportion were by women.[107]

This chapter has considered the critical and display contexts within which the women sculptors I discuss were operating. These were complex and fraught with prejudices and omissions. The generalizations proposed concerning the gender of a sculptor, and thus the innate qualities of their work, persisted throughout the period covered. Some women sculptors were included in key texts, but they were very much in the minority. They and their work were just as likely to be encountered in mass circulation periodicals, which might bring a certain degree of popular fame, but might just as easily enable them to be dismissed as ultimately not worthy of serious critical attention.

Notes

1 Donald Preziosi, *Rethinking Art History: Meditations on a Coy Science* (New Haven, CT: Yale University Press, 1989), p. 72.
2 Ralph Lieberman, 'Thoughts of an art historian/photographer on the relationship of his two disciplines', in Helene E. Roberts (ed.), *Art History: Through the Camera Lens* (London: Gordon and Breach, 1995), p. 219.
3 Geraldine A. Johnson, 'Renaissance sculpture and the visual historiography of art history', *Art History*, 36.1 (2013), p. 27.
4 Johnson, 'Renaissance sculpture', pp. 31–32.
5 Mary Bergstein, 'Lonely Aphrodites: on the documentary photography of sculpture', *The Art Bulletin*, 74.3 (1992), p. 475.
6 Roxanna Marcoci, *The Original Copy: Photography of Sculpture, 1839 to Today* (New York: Museum of Modern Art, 2010), p. 25.
7 Marcoci, *The Original Copy*, p. 128.
8 Valerie Holman, 'A fruitful symbiosis: sculptors and publishers in Britain between the wars', *The Space Between: Literature and Culture, 1914–1945*, 7.1 (2011), p. 117; Stanley Casson, *Some Modern Sculptors* (Oxford: Oxford University Press, 1928).
9 Barbara Hepworth, 'Approach to sculpture', *Studio*, 132.643 (October 1946), n.p., in Sophie Bowness (ed.), *Barbara Hepworth: Writings and Conversations* (London: Tate Publishing, 2016), pp. 34–36.
10 Inga Fraser, 'Media and movement: Barbara Hepworth beyond the lens', in Penelope Curtis and Chris Stephens (eds), *Barbara Hepworth: Sculpture for a Modern World* (London: Tate Publishing, 2015), p. 78.
11 *Figures in a Landscape* (1953), directed by Dudley Shaw Ashton, British Film Institute.
12 Curtis and Stephens, 'Introduction', p. 10.
13 'Art out-of-doors', *Architectural Review*, 85.509 (1939), pp. 200–01.
14 Penelope Curtis, 'The landscape of Barbara Hepworth', *Sculpture Journal*, 2 (1998), pp. 106–12.
15 Curtis and Stephens, 'Introduction', p. 11.
16 Fraser, 'Media and movement', pp. 73–75.
17 Julie F. Codell, 'The art press and the art market: the artist as "economic man"', in Pamela Fletcher and Anne Helmreich (eds), *The Rise of the Modern Art Market in London, 1850–1939* (Manchester: Manchester University Press, 2011), p. 139.
18 Jon Wood, *Close Encounters: The Sculptor's Studio in the Age of the Camera* (Leeds: Henry Moore Institute, 2001), p. 11.
19 Telephone conversation between author and Countess of Antrim's son Hector McDonnell, 7 August 2012.
20 http://www.glenarmcastle.com/top-garden-attractions (accessed 25 November 2019).
21 Anon. review, *Good Housekeeping*, February 1931, n.p.
22 Black and Martin, *Dora Gordine: Sculptor, Artist, Designer.*

23 M. Barron, 'Dorich House Kingston Vale', *Country Life*, 5 November 1938, pp. 456–57. The house also featured in *Ideal Home*, October 1946, pp. 36–40. Brenda Martin, 'A house of her own: Dora Gordine and Dorich House (1936)', in Brenda Martin and Penny Sparke (eds), *Women's Places: Architecture and Design 1860–1960* (London: Routledge, 2003), p. 127.
24 Fran Lloyd in Black and Martin, *Dora Gordine: Sculptor, Artist, Designer*, p. 90.
25 'Sculpture and everyday life', *Mainly for Women*, BBC Home Service, 10 January 1950, BBC Written Archive, Reading. Quoted in Black and Martin, *Dora Gordine: Sculptor, Artist, Designer*, p. 163.
26 Adrian Stokes, 'Art. Miss Hepworth's carving', *The Spectator*, 3 November 1933, n.p.
27 William Gibson, 'Art – two English sculptors', *Britain Today*, 129 (January 1947), pp. 30–31.
28 Herbert Read, *Barbara Hepworth: Carvings and Drawings* (London: Lund Humphries, 1952), p. ix.
29 Margaret Gardiner, *Barbara Hepworth: A Memoir* (London: Lund Humphries, 1994 [1982]), p. 9.
30 Barbara Hepworth, letter to Herbert Read, 12 January 1943. Herbert Read fonds (SC100), Special Collections, University of Victoria Libraries. By permission of Hepworth Estate.
31 Simon Wallis, in Sophie Bowness (ed.), *Barbara Hepworth: The Plasters. The Gift to Wakefield* (London: Lund Humphries and The Hepworth Wakefield, 2011), p. 7.
32 'Great abstract art', Barbara Hepworth obituary, *The Guardian*, 21 May 1975, quoted in Barbara Hepworth, *A Pictorial Autobiography* (London: Tate Gallery, 1998 [1970]), p. 29.
33 Matthew Gale and Chris Stephens, *Barbara Hepworth: Works in the Tate Collection and the Barbara Hepworth Museum St. Ives* (London: Tate Publishing, 2001), p. 21.
34 William Foster, 'A clear look at the Royal Academy after 200 years', *Homes and Gardens*, 49.11 (May 1968), pp. 58–59.
35 Derek Patmore, 'Other People's Homes – No. 10: the studio of a famous woman sculptor: Lady Hilton Young's house in Bayswater', *Queen*, 3 February 1932, pp. 11–13.
36 'Lady Hilton Young', *Newcastle Daily Journal and North Star*, 21 December 1928. University of Cambridge Manuscripts Library, GB/NNAF/P 162494, NCUACS 87.8.99.167/1, Press Cuttings.
37 Viola Tree, 'Continuing the special series of Women of the Day. No. 5 – Mrs. Hilton Young, formerly Lady Scott', *Eve*, 16 June 1926, n.p. University of Cambridge Manuscripts Library, GB/NNAF/P 162494, NCUACS 87.8.99.167/1, Press Cuttings.
38 'When woman wields the chisel', *The Daily Mail*, 8 April 1927. University of Cambridge Manuscripts Library, GB/NNAF/P 162494, NCUACS 87.8.99.167/1, Press Cuttings.
39 'A woman sculptor', *The Westminster Gazette*, 3 October 1923. University of Cambridge Manuscripts Library, GB/NNAF/P 162494, NCUACS 87.8.99.167/1, Press Cuttings.

40 'Mrs. Hilton Young's sculptures', *Eastern Daily Press*, 19 October 1923. University of Cambridge Manuscripts Library, GB/NNAF/P 162494, NCUACS 87.8.99.167/1, Press Cuttings.
41 'Lady Scott as sculptor', *The Observer*, 21 October 1923. University of Cambridge Manuscripts Library, GB/NNAF/P 162494, NCUACS 87.8.99.167/1, Press Cuttings.
42 'The sculptor widow of an Antarctic explorer to marry', *The Sketch*, 1 February 1922, p. 189. University of Cambridge Manuscripts Library, GB/NNAF/P 162494, NCUACS 87.8.99.167/1, Press Cuttings.
43 George Graves, 'By pony to her studio', *Illustrated London News*, 5 February 1949, n.p. Elizabeth Muntz Archive, Dorset History Centre.
44 Roger Peers, *Exhibition: The Sculpture of Elizabeth Muntz at the Dorset County Museum* (Dorchester, 1971). Elizabeth Muntz Archive, Dorset History Centre.
45 Dora Gordine, *Picture Page*, 24 November 1938. BBC Written Archives, Reading. Quoted in Black and Martin, *Dora Gordine: Sculptor, Artist, Designer*, p. 13.
46 Dora Gordine, 'A sense of time', *The World Goes By*, BBC Home Service Radio, 10 January 1950. BBC Written Archives, Reading.
47 'K', 'Introduction', in Kennet, *Self-Portrait of an Artist*.
48 '"My masculine models" by Mrs. Hilton Young', *Weekly Dispatch*, 3 April 1927. University of Cambridge Manuscripts Library, GB/NNAF/P 162494, NCUACS 87.8.99.167/1, Press Cuttings.
49 Hepworth, *A Pictorial Autobiography*, p. 20.
50 John Hedgecoe, *Henry Spencer Moore* (London/New York: Nelson/Simon and Schuster, 1968); John Hedgecoe, *A Monumental Vision: The Sculpture of Henry Moore* (London: Collins and Brown, 1998). See also Rose, *Henry Moore in America*.
51 Katy Deepwell, 'Hepworth and her critics', in Katy Deepwell (ed.), *Women Artists and Modernism* (Manchester: Manchester University Press, 1998), p. 101.
52 Maria R. Witzling (ed.), *Voicing our Visions: Writings by Women Artists* (London: The Women's Press, 1992), p. 273.
53 Letter from Barbara Hepworth to Sadie Martin, undated. Archives, National Gallery of Modern Art Two, Edinburgh, GMA A70/2/15, Leslie Martin Personal Papers, Correspondence with Barbara Hepworth.
54 Letter from Barbara Hepworth to Ben Nicholson, 31 May 1970. Quoted by Penelope Curtis in Penelope Curtis and Alan G. Wilkinson, *Barbara Hepworth: A Retrospective* (Liverpool: Tate Gallery, 1994), p. 147.
55 Deepwell, 'Hepworth and her critics', pp. 76–78.
56 Harriet Hosmer, 'The Process of Sculpture', *Atlantic Monthly*, December 1864, pp. 734–38.
57 Angela Dunstan, 'Nineteenth-century sculpture and the imprint of authenticity', *Interdisciplinary Studies in the Long Nineteenth Century*, 19 (2014), https://www.19.bbk.ac.uk/articles/10.16995/ntn.704/ (accessed 25 November 2019); John Ruskin, *The Seven Lamps of Architecture* (Orpington: Allen, 1880), p. 124.
58 Martina Droth, 'Conditions of display 1900–25', in Henry Moore Institute, *Sculpture in 20th Century Britain: Identity, Infrastructures, Aesthetics, Display, Reception* (Leeds: Henry Moore Institute, 2003), vol. 1, pp. 43–44.

59 Lucinda Hawksley, *The Mystery of Princess Louise: Queen Victoria's Rebellious Daughter* (London: Chatto and Windus, 2013), pp. 160–61.
60 Louise Campbell, 'Women, architecture and the Aesthetic Movement', in Brenda Martin and Penny Sparke (eds), *Women's Places: Architecture and Design 1860–1960* (London: Routledge, 2003), p. 4.
61 'Art: The Royal Academy', *The Spectator*, 30 April 1927. University of Cambridge Manuscripts Library, GB/NNAF/P 162494, NCUACS 87.8.99.167/1, Press Cuttings.
62 Clara Erskine Clement, *Women in the Fine Arts from the Seventh Century B.C. to the Twentieth Century A.D.* (Boston: Houghton, Mifflin, 1904), https://archive.org/details/womeninfineartsooclemgoog (accessed 25 November 2019).
63 Margaret Thomas, *How to Understand Sculpture* (London: G. Bell and Sons, 1911), p. 1.
64 Thomas, *How to Understand Sculpture*, pp. 99–100.
65 Mark Stocker, 'Edmund Gosse on sculpture', *University of Leeds Review*, 28 (1985–86), p. 283.
66 Gosse, 'The New Sculpture', p. 138.
67 Stocker, 'Edmund Gosse on sculpture', pp. 295–99.
68 Stocker, 'Edmund Gosse on sculpture', pp. 305–06.
69 Julie Codell, 'From English School to British School: modernism, revisionism, and national culture in the writings of M. H. Spielmann', *Nineteenth-Century Art Worldwide: a Journal of Nineteenth-Century Visual Culture*, 14.2 (2015), pp. 5–7, http://www.19thc-artworldwide.org/summer15/codell-on-modernism-revisionism-and-national-culture-in-the-writings-of-spielmann (accessed 25 November 2019).
70 Spielmann, *British Sculpture and Sculptors of To-Day*, pp. 1–2.
71 Spielmann, *British Sculpture and Sculptors of To-Day*, p. 2, quoted in Tillyard, *The Impact of Modernism*, p. 145.
72 Codell, 'From English School to British School', pp. 7–8.
73 Spielmann, *British Sculpture and Sculptors of To-Day*, p. 2.
74 Spielmann, *British Sculpture and Sculptors of To-Day*, pp. 8–9.
75 M. H. Spielmann, 'The fine art section', in *Souvenir of the Fine Art Section, Franco-British Exhibition, 1908*, under the auspices of the British Art Committee (London: Bemrose and Sons, 1908), p. 93.
76 Spielmann, *British Sculpture and Sculptors of To-Day*, pp. 3–4.
77 Spielmann, *British Sculpture and Sculptors of To-Day*, p. 157.
78 Spielmann, *British Sculpture and Sculptors of To-Day*, pp. 159–60.
79 Spielmann, *British Sculpture and Sculptors of To-Day*, pp. 8–9.
80 Christopher R. Marshall (ed.), *Sculpture and the Museum* (Farnham: Ashgate, 2011), pp. 1–4.
81 Parkes, *Sculpture of To-Day*, p. 7.
82 Parkes, *Sculpture of To-Day*, pp. 11–15.
83 Parkes, *Sculpture of To-Day*, pp. 16–17.
84 Parkes, *Sculpture of To-Day*, pp. 18–20.
85 Parkes, *The Art of Carved Sculpture*, p. 90.
86 Parkes, *Sculpture of To-Day*, pp. 225–26.
87 Casson, *Twentieth Century Sculptors*, preface.

88 G. A. Jellicoe, 'Modern British sculpture', *The Studio* (January 1930), pp. 26–31.
89 Review in *Apollo*, n.d. Elizabeth Muntz Archive, Dorset History Centre.
90 *Apollo*, 4 (July 1926), p. 44, quoted in Deepwell, 'Women Artists in Britain between the Two World Wars', p. 211.
91 Parkes, *The Art of Carved Sculpture*, p. 103.
92 Parkes, *The Art of Carved Sculpture*, pp. 5–6.
93 Parkes, *The Art of Carved Sculpture*, pp. 12–13.
94 Parkes, *The Art of Carved Sculpture*, p. 93.
95 'Elsie Marian Henderson', *Mapping the Practice and Profession of Sculpture in Britain and Ireland 1851–1951*, University of Glasgow History of Art and HATII, online database 2011, http://sculpture.gla.ac.uk/view/person.php?id=msib2_1207701112 (accessed 25 November 2019).
96 Parkes, *The Art of Carved Sculpture*, pp. 124–25.
97 Compton, 'Crafting modernism', p. 18.
98 Parkes, *The Art of Carved Sculpture*, p. 125.
99 Brown, *Katharine Emma Maltwood*, p. 24.
100 Eric G. Underwood, *A Short History of English Sculpture* (London: Faber and Faber, 1933), p. vii.
101 Underwood, *A Short History of English Sculpture*, p. 8.
102 Arthur J. Broadbent, *Sculpture Today in Great Britain, 1940–1943* (London: John Tiranti, 1944).
103 Deepwell, 'Women Artists in Britain between the Two World Wars', p. 222.
104 Deepwell, 'Women Artists in Britain between the Two World Wars', p. 287.
105 'The Society of Women Artists', *The Athenaeum*, 5 March 1920, p. 312.
106 *Apollo*, 3 (April 1926), p. 245.
107 *The Manchester Guardian*, 4 April 1928, quoted in Deepwell, 'Women Artists in Britain between the Two World Wars', p. 152.

4

On a Domestic Scale

4.1 The popularity of the statuette

> When we think of modern art ... we do not generally think of domestic imagery or objects for the home ... While ... most makers of buildings, furniture, sculpture and paintings supplied the rapidly expanding market for domestic structures and decoration, these workers and their products did not meet avant-garde definitions of 'architecture' and 'art' ... the home has been positioned as the antipode to high art ... in the eyes of the avant-garde, being undomestic came to serve as a guarantee of being art.[1]

This analysis reveals the likely tensions created by the placement of sculpture in the domestic realm. Despite this assumed conflict, a concern with interior decor in nineteenth-century Britain did see artists and traders attempting to shape the public's preferences. Around the turn of the century, particularly for the middle classes, money spent on furnishing their home represented a solid material and symbolic investment. From the late nineteenth century onwards the statuette was consistently promoted as a domestic ornament, and it was quite normal for journals such as the *Magazine of Art* to contain illustrations of how such sculptures might appear when placed in the fashionable home interior. Essentially 'lifestyle' magazines, these journals promoted the idea of collecting art as a way for a new buying public to exhibit their good taste.[2] A wealth of publications and advertisements encouraged this trend, with contemporary representations of domestic interiors and of the modern home filtered through references to historical designs. It appears that the impetus was to realize ideas and forms in a manner that acknowledged people's sense of a society in a state of flux.

In the nineteenth century writers and manufacturers saw how art could benefit the development of good design. Alongside a wish that art and artists should be autonomous ran a parallel desire that industry adopt the principles of artistry and the handmade. Between 1850 and 1945 there was a significant growth in popular publications aimed at a broad cross-section of women, which would form a considerable gender-specific part of the publishing industry.[3] Such journals often carried articles on women artists, and so readers might encounter women sculptors and their work alongside articles on home decoration, helping to draw together these two areas. Since the emphasis in many articles on female artists focused on the specifics of their gender and domestic context, this would further encourage a merging of biography with interior design in the mind of the reader. Therefore there was clearly a broadening and deepening of people's understanding of the ways in which a relationship between art and the home might be conceived and achieved, even if some art critics remained ambivalent as to whether such art was being correctly valued and understood, or used as mere adornment. An interesting letter written by William Hamo Thornycroft to his fiancée in 1883 argued that a statuette furnished a room in a way that a painting did not. He wrote:

> It is the frames of pictures that furnish a room, so are part of the room like a piece of sculpture ... but the picture itself be it good or bad does not furnish. If it is a good picture it takes the eye out of the room ... But a nice piece of statuary of the proper colour for the room ... does furnish, for the *room* is *its* atmosphere.[4]

This is a very perceptive understanding of the difference between the two-dimensional and three-dimensional art forms.

The distinction between a sculpture or statue, and a statuette, was understood in the nineteenth century, although the development of the New Sculpture towards the end of the century effectively blurred such boundaries, the statuette providing an object that could theoretically be mass-produced yet still bear the imprint of the sculptor's hand. For women sculptors this new interest in small-scale works offered a great opportunity. It is possible to attribute the marked rise in women sculptors practising in the 1890s not only to the popularity of the statuette but to modelling as the most direct means of expression, concurrent with a revolution in the bronze-founding industry. These developments negated the claim that women could not make sculpture due to the latter's scale and thus the physical effort supposedly required. The possible challenge that this increase in women sculptors might present to their male peers was effectively rebuffed in an 1896 interview with George Frampton, who was confident in his prejudice that

> no matter how poetic the idea, how ethereal the finished bas-relief or statue ... the art of the sculptor in its noblest form demands strenuous labour so that you may regard it as being tolerably secure from invasion by the new woman, or the mere dilettante; for it is a most perfect instance of fine art inextricably allied with fine craft.[5]

However, when we look at the statuettes made by women they do have particularly favourable characteristics that can in part be linked to the sculptors' gender. Many male sculptors who produced statuettes did so on the basis of reducing the scale of a monumental figure. By contrast, the statuettes made by women sculptors mostly appear to have been originally conceived as such, not as scaled-down versions of larger works, since women were less likely to be awarded monumental commissions. Another advantage of the statuette for all sculptors was that its small scale allowed for a degree of freedom from what might be expected of life-sized works: they could afford to experiment. Additionally, the expansion of the bronze foundry industry was significant in supporting the development of these small sculptures, which in formal and thematic terms were often more coherent than large-scale works.

Royal Academy exhibition catalogues from the mid-1890s show that there was a significant increase in the number of women exhibiting. Virtually no women showed sculpture in the late 1880s, but in the 1896 catalogue 24 out of approximately 80 exhibitors were women. Although the fashion for modelling may have encouraged more women to make sculpture, once they began to exhibit, many of them, including Margaret Giles (1868–1949), also took up carving. They also worked with supposedly masculine subjects: for example, Ruby Levick (c.1872–1940) exhibited a statuette group of boys wrestling (1897) (**Figure 26**). This sculpture has been likened to Frederic Leighton's influential *Athlete Wrestling with a Python* (1877), also reproduced as a statuette, not just through its title but also in the expression of physicality. There are few photographs of the Levick work in existence, very little research material can be found, and its present location is unknown, if indeed the work has survived. Levick's plaster model is inevitably not as finished as the Leighton sculpture but perhaps has more energy, and it too was cast in bronze. The two nude male figures are engaged in a powerful struggle, and this intertwining of limbs encourages the possibility of looking at the sculpture from a variety of viewpoints: through the concealment of

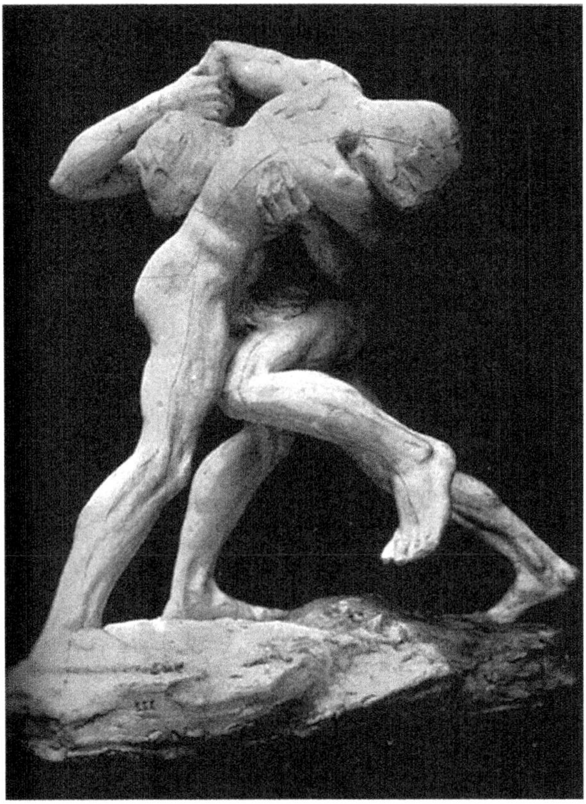

26. Ruby Levick, *Wrestling Boys*, 1897

parts of the bodies the focus is on the overall sense of struggle. Whereas in the Leighton sculpture the contest is implied through the presence of the snake and the taut muscles, Levick's representation is earthier and less 'classical'.[6] In its 1897 review of the National Competition for British students of art and design, the *Studio* began its discussion of sculpture with this on Levick: 'The sculpture is up to its high level again. Ruby Levick ... has a really fine group of two wrestlers, not merely vigorous in conception but handled with something like mastery.'[7]

Clearly the home has always 'displayed' objects of a personal nature, but the presentation of sculpture in the home became more specific in the early twentieth century, and we saw in Chapter 3.3 how many writers on sculpture addressed this issue. Journals such as the *Studio* informed viewers about how they should show sculptures, and books on interior design started to explicitly discuss how such works might be displayed. The move towards a more intimate sculpture appeared alongside a stress on modelling and detail, largely through the medium of bronze, and such smaller works were in opposition to the grandeur of preceding statues. The viewer was required to move closer. This development in the British statuette was very different from other such forms, particularly those current in France, where the statuette was largely conceived as a multiply reproduced small version of larger and already popular works. Prior to the growth in production of statuettes at the end of the nineteenth century, such small sculptures had not been taken seriously by British critics because of their scale and reproducibility. However, the New Sculpture statuette was better received when positive links could be made between its scale, decorative qualities and the domestic sphere. This relationship could be conveyed in art exhibitions, blurring the boundaries between these differing display contexts. Following the Grosvenor Gallery's co-option of a domestic context for its displays, this fashionable trend was subsequently adopted by the Fine Art Society.

Sculpture and domesticity also converged at international exhibitions, such as the 1908 Franco-British Exhibition of Science, Art and Industries, as well as in museums and galleries. In 1900 architect Harry Bulkeley Creswell, who regularly wrote for the *Architectural Review*, published an article which called for a new way of displaying sculpture in Britain's museums and galleries, drawing specifically on the domestic interior as a template for conceiving of exhibition spaces in which to display sculpture.[8] Creswell's ideas on display could be seen at the 1902 Fine Art Society's *First Exhibition of Statuettes by the Sculptors of Today, British and French*, which showed a significant number of works by well-known sculptors in a setting that had a domestic flavour. The catalogue incorporated Marion Spielmann's essay 'Sculpture for the Home', which proved just how much statuettes had become associated with a domestic context, since he characterized them as 'intimate, private possessions that made possible a closer connection with the viewer'.[9] This new relationship suggested that sculpture was to be evaluated in a fresh way, and Spielmann wrote that 'sculpture has hitherto had little attraction for us as a nation. We have usually regarded it with awe, sometimes with admiration, but rarely indeed has it inspired "the man in the street" with a desire for possession.' It was significant that such small sculptures, when displayed in venues such as the Fine Art Society galleries, occupied the same spaces as carpets, furniture and mantelpieces, and so the distance created by the conventional display of sculpture was overturned. Such intimacy encouraged a new relationship, a new way of looking and understanding.

Observers who disliked this relocation into the decorative and domestic sphere tended to regard such sculpture as traditional and outmoded in approach. A concern with a detailed, finished surface was characterized as superficial, and unfavourable comparisons were made with contemporary fashions on the Continent, especially in Paris. But the reverse could be argued: this transformation of how sculpture was to be encountered and located could be regarded as a modernizing trend. Through its small scale and decorative quality it challenged and also proposed just what a sculpture might be.[10] As Spielmann proclaimed in his *British Sculpture and Sculptors of To-Day*, 'without doubt, he who makes statuettes has little ground for complaint, for he has properly met the objection that in our modern houses we have no room for sculpture; every drawing-room and dining-room in the land is now a fit gallery for his graceful and inspiring work'.[11]

As part of the late nineteenth-century British sculptural revival, art magazines were dominated by the writings of Edmund Gosse, Alfred Lys Baldry, Cosmo Monkhouse, Claude Phillips and Marion Spielmann. They wrote about painting as well as sculpture but in a different way, since they could assume the former's popular appeal. In their desire to educate people about sculpture and try to make it as accessible as painting, Gosse and Spielmann in particular began to target the ordinary citizen, hoping that a popularization of sculpture would result in a new buying public. The statuette would be vital for this mission and if it became both accessible and affordable this would naturally benefit both sculptor and buyer. For Gosse, the statuette 'symbolized the liberation of sculpture from the marble Neo-classical pomposities of John Gibson', and in his last major article, 'The Place of Sculpture in Daily Life', Gosse argued that if the buying public could overcome the perception that sculpture was not appropriate for the ordinary home then they would see just how much refinement could be achieved by the placement of a statuette in a room.[12]

However, the promotion of the statuette raised a paradox: it was both fine art and decoration when unremittingly promoted as an object for the domestic interior. Art journals of the day reveal the contradictions inherent in the objects that they were dealing with. For example, the *Studio* defined itself as 'The Illustrated Magazine of Fine and Applied Art'. However, in its content the emphasis was on applied art, doing little to bring together fine and decorative art. Often it focused on the craftsman rather than the specialist practitioner, and in many instances sculpture was only discussed in relation to applied art. A search through its pages reveals that many very important sculptors, whether male or female, are rarely mentioned. Thus the journal was essentially supporting the use of sculptural elements as part of the applied and decorative arts, but not the converse, which might be problematic for a fine art practice.[13] At a time of debate about the necessity of raising the standard of architectural decoration, and about the relationship between art and industry, the Art Union of London, founded to promote the highest aesthetic standards in the decorative arts, seems to have aligned itself with the New Sculpture movement, working to establish high technical standards for the production of statuettes.

As it emerged in the 1880s the New Sculpture moved away from the severity of neoclassical forms in order to encompass colour and decoration, and its relationship to the Arts and Crafts movement produced some difficulties in defining such work. New Sculpture statuettes had commercial appeal, not least since they could be marketed as superior to mass-produced decorative items. It became possible for the middle class to be able to afford to buy into this market, not least since statuettes were often on sale in commercial outlets such as department stores. However, this raised serious issues concerning value. The statuette's popularity could be a result of its ability to simultaneously embody the gravitas of sculpture with the intimacy of ornament, but its display within a domestic setting as essentially decoration upset deep-rooted divisions between sculpture/art and decoration/ornament. Reductions from existing works were still desirable as they came with a sense of 'authentication', as deriving from a work made by a recognized sculptor. This was an attractive proposition for a buyer who might effectively aspire to a 'representation' of a well-known full-size sculpture, with an artistic pedigree, but costing less than would be the case with a unique statuette. However, a popular market in reductions never really materialized and so it was sculpture designed from the outset to be made to a small scale that was successful at the end of the nineteenth century.

Exhibitions were vital in establishing the statuette as a new and aesthetically particular art form. Here the Arts and Crafts Society was important in offering a context in which the distinctions between fine and applied art might be tested. Alongside such objects as door knockers and light brackets it was possible to see fine art sculpture, and so the latter essentially moved into the category of accessories. The following examples show the range of work undertaken by women sculptors who engaged with the statuette, and the subsequent part of this chapter will deal with the decorative items referred to above. I have grouped the statuettes into four broadly related themes: the body and the nude; allegory; mother and child and religious subjects; and portraits and animal studies.

The body and the nude

In the 1890s Margaret Giles was awarded many prizes in the National Art Competitions, including during her student years, and among other venues she exhibited at the Royal Academy between 1895 and 1900, with a final work appearing after a 33-year absence in 1945. In total she exhibited 26 works at the Academy. The *Studio* reported that she won a gold medal for an unnamed relief at the 1893 exhibition of students' work at South Kensington. The same periodical's review of the 1893 Arts and Crafts Exhibition pointed out as 'especially worthy of notice ... a combined lamp and finger-post, by Margaret Giles, which would be a welcome relief from such objects as the groups opposite the Criterion, or defacing the centres of most of our cross-roads'.[14] Giles's statuette *Hero* (1901) has been described as a departure from conventional representations of the female nude in art, demonstrating innovative aesthetic standards and conceptions of the female figure (**Plate 7**). Here the body is active and powerful, in marked contrast to the conventional norms of the female as victim or at least as passive. Giles's nude bears some resemblance to a Michelangelo figure in its heavy musculature and strength, but rejects the usual classical features of dignity, stillness and balance, opting instead for an energetic rendering of the female form. Through this approach she was reinterpreting conventional treatments of the female nude as formulated by male sculptors.[15] *Hero* established Giles's reputation and its sketch model was entered for the Art Union's 1894 competition, where sculptors were invited to submit designs for a statuette. The winning model would be cast in bronze and added to the lottery prizes. Leighton agreed to act as an advisor and had the final power of selection, choosing Giles's work from 36 sketch models, and she was awarded £150 in 1896. That year the work was displayed at the Royal Academy and in 1897 the first two bronzes cast by Singer and Sons were on the prize lists. The purchase of *Hero* by the Art Union has been described as perhaps its

> most significant single act in its self-appointed role as sponsor of modern sculpture. Many vital strands of the new movement are gathered together within the yearning, solitary figure: the development of symbolist expression and the concept of popular art, educational reform, the influence of Dalou, through Lantéri, on modelling technique, and the renaissance of commercial bronze founding.[16]

A major part of *Hero*'s importance to the history of British sculpture derives from its relation of scale to basic conception. The form of Giles's statuette would encourage an owner to view it from many positions, to be able to fully understand it as an artwork in the round. The way in which the sculpture is animated is carried out in a manner entirely appropriate for, and dependent on, its scale.

Ruby Levick worked in several media, particularly gaining attention for her statuettes and garden sculptures, architectural reliefs and stained-glass windows. Prior to 1905 she executed decorative panels at the Roman Catholic Chapel of St Edmund in Hunstanton, Norfolk, a reredos and relief panels for St Brelades, Jersey, and decoration for a shop front in Sloane Street, Chelsea.[17] She also worked as an assistant to Gilbert W. Bayes and was associated with the New Sculpture and the parallel rising popularity of the statuette. Spielmann noted her regular displays at the Royal Academy from 1893 and he particularly drew attention to her studies of male athletes. He wrote that the bronze statuette groups *Boys Fishing/Fishermen Hauling in a Net* (c.1900) (**Figure 27**), *Wrestling Boys* (**Figure 26**) and another work entitled *Football* 'are all clever and well modelled; the last-named composition is full of life and vigour'.[18] At the South Kensington School Levick was awarded the prize for figure design, the medal for a study of a head from life, as well as medals and other awards in the National Competition.

In 1905 T. Martin Wood wrote an article on Levick for the *Studio*. It reflected the usual prejudice against women sculptors: although he acknowledged that they were receptive students, he believed that this caused them to make work that was unambitious and that they were easily sidetracked into imitation. He argued that in order to produce original art, women needed to make work that expressed their femininity, reflecting on

> the subtleties of sentiment that belong to women ... The artistic material that they choose receives from their hands an exquisiteness in exchange for strength ... Where so much charm is contained as there is in femininity in art, it is more than a thousand pities that so many women artists should forsake the qualities which they could easily give to their work in struggling ambitiously after achievements in which, by the nature of things, men easily dominate.

Wood believed that once Levick left art school, and thus implicitly the competition with male students, her work revealed 'the intimate qualities that we so much prize'.[19]

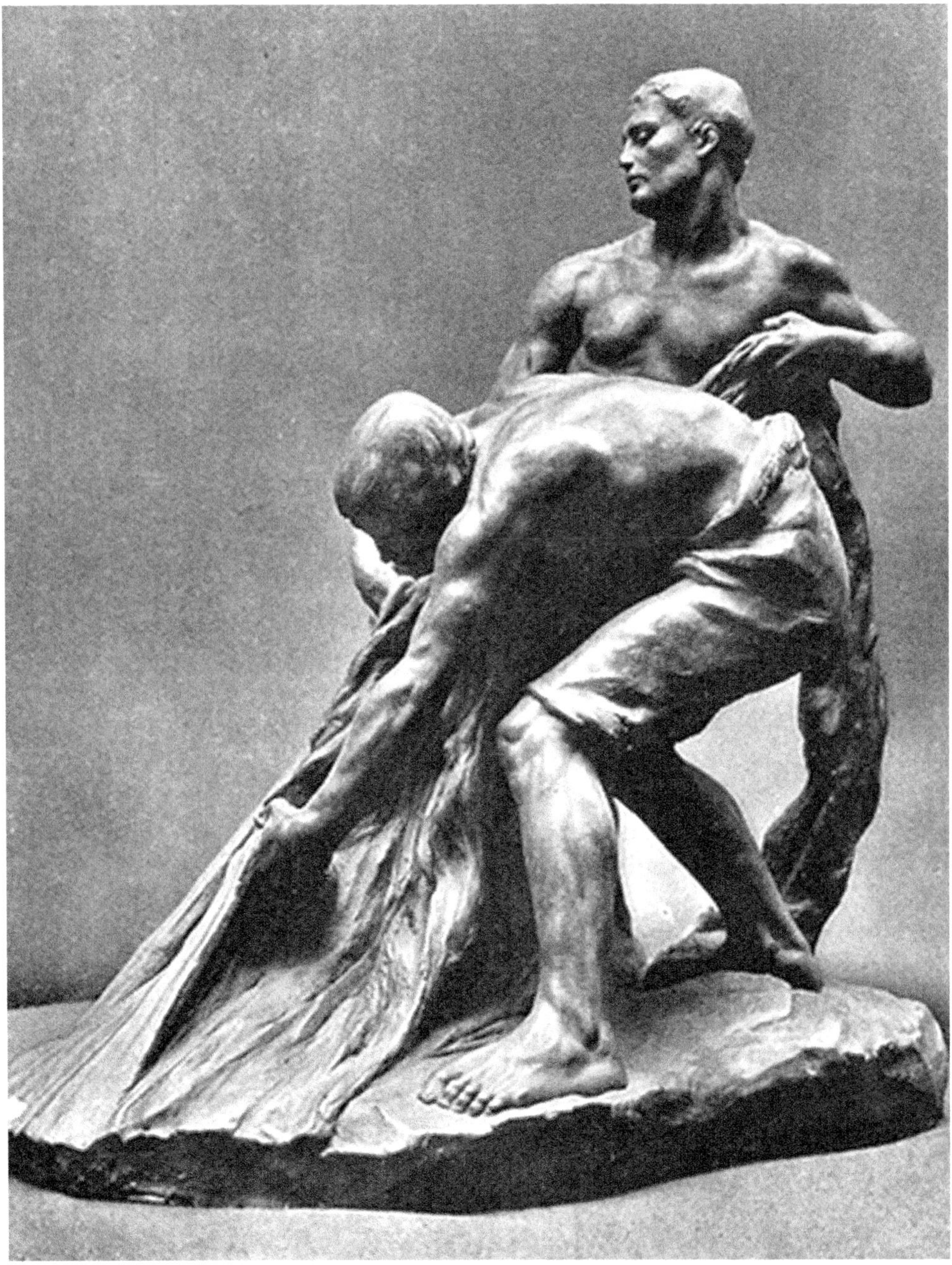

27. Ruby Levick, *Boys Fishing/Fishermen hauling in a net*, 1900

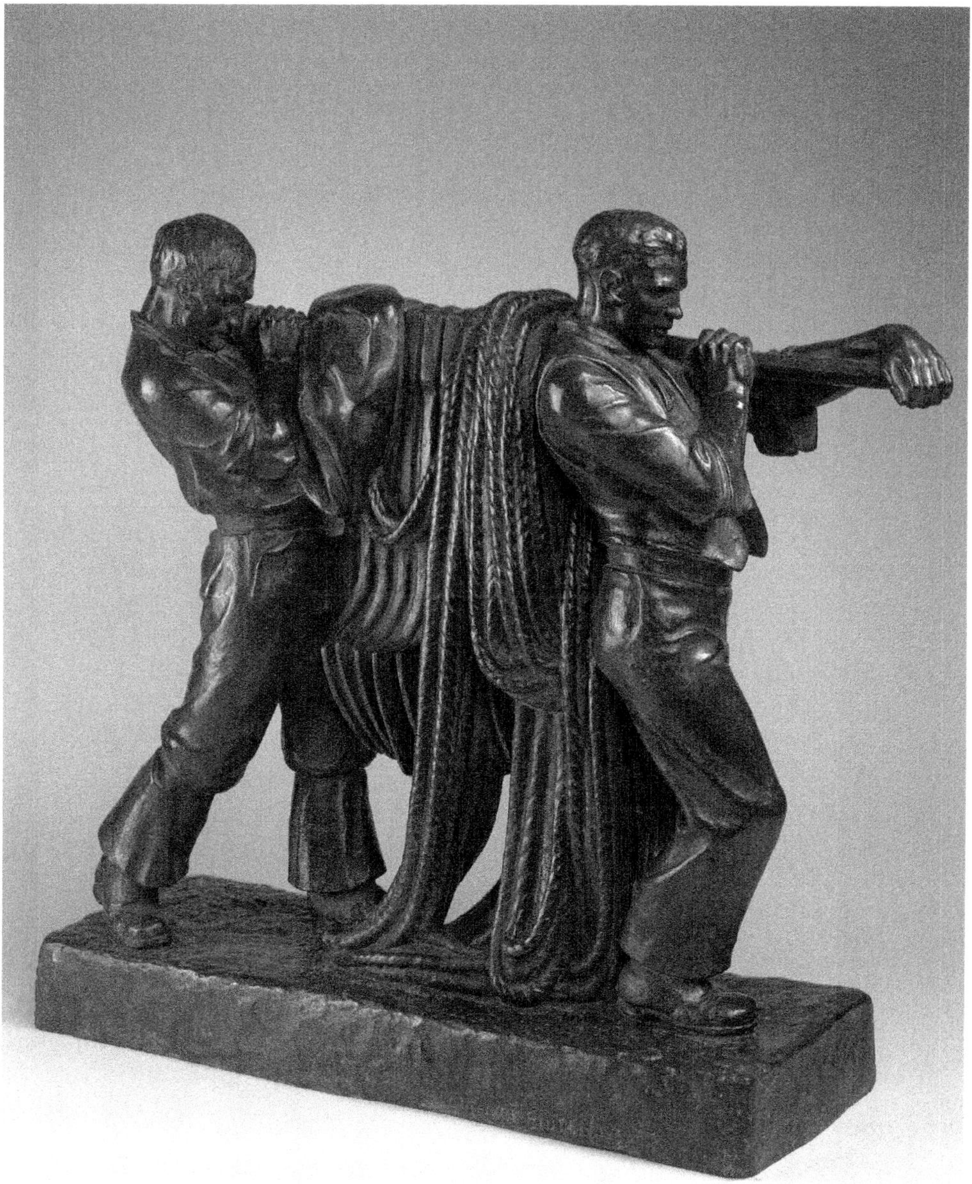

28. Joyce Bidder, *Labour,* 1932

Joyce Bidder studied at Wimbledon School of Art with Stanley Nicholson Babb, becoming one of his most talented students. In 1943 he nominated her for membership of the RBS, where she eventually became a Fellow. Bidder worked in various materials – marble, bronze, terracotta, ceramic, wood and ivory – and she first exhibited at the Royal Academy in 1932 with *Tackled*, followed in 1933 with an even more ambitious group, *Labour*, a work that vividly renders the effort exerted by the two men (**Figure 28**). Her sculptural groups express a sense of empathy with the working man and are also aligned to a clear understanding of the international language of conservative modernism.

Allegory

Josefina de Vasconcellos (1904–2005) and Phoebe Stabler produced two unusual heads: the former's *Prayer* is a stylish and striking undated work (**Figure 29**) as is Stabler's sculpture *Memory* (c.1917), which seems particularly out of kilter with most of her practice, being engagingly enigmatic and experimental (**Figure 30**). Vasconcellos lived in Cumbria for much of her working life. She was a student at the Royal Academy and in Paris studied under Antoine Bourdelle, at that time one of Rodin's assistants, and subsequently under the brilliant stone carver Libero Andreotti in Florence. Her father worked for the Genoa Consulate and used his influence to help her to gain access to an all-male team, where she worked on large-scale projects that included stone carvings for public buildings.[20] She exhibited regularly at the Royal Academy, the Paris Salon and the RBS, and was a founder member of the Society of Portrait Sculptors. In 1930 she was runner-up for the Prix de Rome and appeared to be on the brink of a successful career, being in 1946 the first woman to be elected a Fellow of the RBS. In the winter of 1946–47 she showed 46 sculptures at a joint exhibition with her husband, painter Delmar Banner, at the Royal Watercolour Society Galleries. Her materials were wide ranging, comprising works in wood, stone, bronze, slate, marble and lead, and sculptures that ranged from abstract pieces to portrait heads. Apparently her large works were too big to be displayed in the gallery and so she gained permission for them to be positioned out of doors on a bombsite at 35 Piccadilly:

> A photograph in *The Times* newspaper shows how crowds gathered round the sculptures. Thousands of people saw them and found the presence of art among the rubble strangely encouraging at a time when Britain was weary and worn after the effect of six years' privation and

> hardship ... Lady Scott ... purchased one of Josefina's sculptures and wrote to her full of praise: 'Sorry I couldn't get to your private view – I was in the throes of casting, which I do very badly and couldn't leave a hash I was making. However I went today and would like to send showers of congratulations. Prodigious workers you both seem to be! I liked so very much of the work ... there were a lot of people there.'[21]

Vasconcellos generally received positive press reports.

Twenty years previously in his *Sculpture of To-Day* Kineton Parkes noted that Phoebe Stabler carved direct and worked in a variety of materials, referring specifically to a large stone *Head of a Woman*, exhibited at the Royal Academy in 1916, and a sculpture titled *The Dreamer* shown at the Academy in the following year. This appears to be the work now referred to as *Memory* (**Figure 30**), and Parkes noted its alignment to contemporary sculptural modernism.[22] Stabler studied at the School of Architecture and Applied Art, University College,

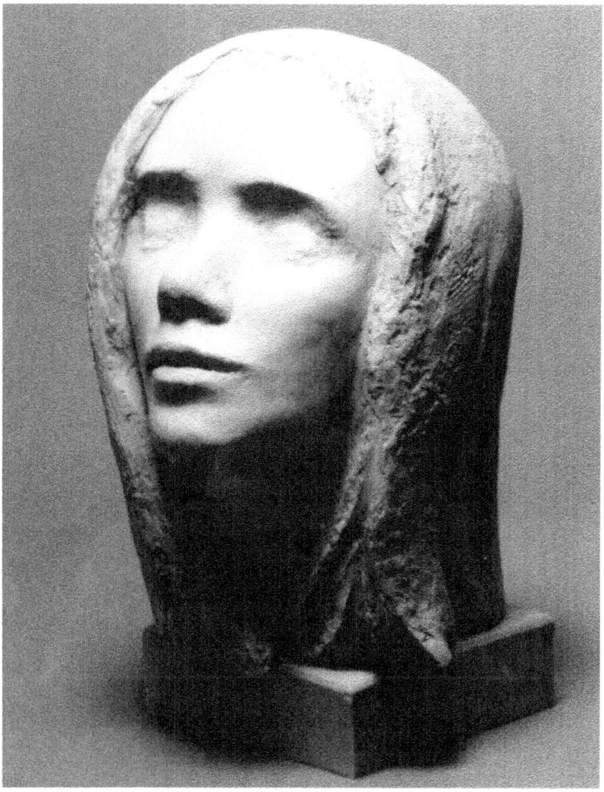

29. Josefina de Vasconcellos, *Prayer*, undated

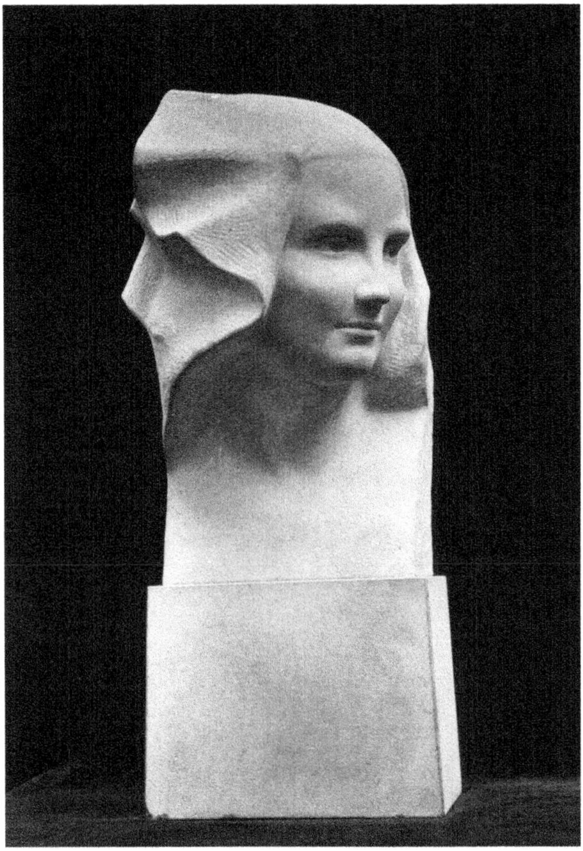

30. Phoebe Stabler, *Memory*, c.1917

Liverpool, from 1901 to 1904 and then at the Royal College of Art. In 1906 she married silversmith Harold Stabler.

Joyce Bidder also produced allegorical work such as *The Croziers of Spring* (1934), a strikingly beautiful piece later exhibited at the Royal Academy in 1948 (**Plate 8**). At first glance it might appear fairly traditional, but the stylization, especially evident in the head and the repeated decoration of the curled tops of young ferns (croziers) which forms both foreground and backdrop when the sculpture is viewed from this angle, make it far from an academic piece.

Edith Elizabeth Downing (1857–1951) studied at the South Kensington Schools under Lantéri and then at the Slade School of Art between 1892 and 1893. Born in Cardiff, for most of her career she was based in Chelsea, and unusually for a woman in the early 1900s she earned a living from her sculpture. She normally worked on solid marble without pointing, as well as in bronze, producing portrait busts, figures and decorative pieces. She exhibited regularly at the Royal Academy between 1891 and 1910, at the Royal Glasgow Institute, the Society of Women Artists and the Paris Salon, and some of her works were shown at the Arts and Crafts exhibitions in London. Downing produced many statuettes, one of which was *Boy with Cherry* (1907) (**Plate 9**).

Sir William Goscombe John's name appears in correspondence associated with some Welsh female sculptors, including Downing. He was a strong supporter of the establishment and growth of the National Museum of Wales in Cardiff, to which he donated many pieces of his own work. He also appears to have communicated with women sculptors whose work would enter the collection: for example, in a letter to the National Museum of Wales Downing stated that John had advised her to contact the museum since she wanted to bequeath some of her sculptures to Cardiff as well as to the Tate Gallery. However, she understood that 'there are obstacles in the way, that "sponsors" are necessary and wealthy and influential friends also'.[23] Just what she meant by this enigmatic comment is unclear – perhaps she felt her gender might be an issue, or maybe she was simply describing the reality of the art collecting world. However, she clearly had John's support, since he recommended to the museum that Downing use his bronze foundry, A. B. Burton of Thames Ditton.[24]

Lilian Maud Wade (c.1870–1923) worked as a studio assistant to Edouard Lantéri around 1911 and exhibited at the Royal Academy eight times between 1900 and 1916: on each occasion she showed one work, drawn from a mixture of statuettes, reliefs, medallions and portrait busts. Her statuette *Victory* (**Figure 31**), shown at the Academy in 1907, was possibly a maquette for a significant memorial (**Plate 16**). She is yet another female sculptor about whom there is very little information but who clearly produced a wide range of work, all to a high standard.

Elsie March (1884–1974) was one of nine children, six of whom were artists. It is probable that she learned sculpting through assisting her brothers with large memorial works on which they all worked as a team, as borne out by photographs of them together (**Figure 91**). She and her brothers Vernon and Sydney were certainly the main sculptors in the family. The large sculptural commissions awarded to Sydney were probably worked on with his family, as each had their own area of expertise. From 1901 the siblings had a studio at Goddendene, near Farnborough in Kent, which was expanded over subsequent years to include furnaces, casting facilities, a small railway, a hoist to move heavy

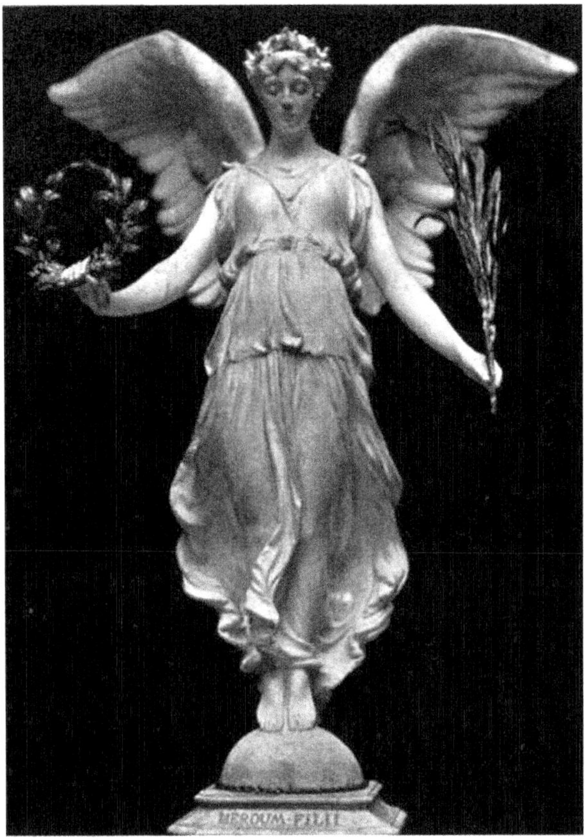

31. Lillian Maud Wade, *Victory*, c.1907

materials and a studio which had moveable walls.[25] In 1919 Elsie March exhibited two works at the Royal Glasgow Institute of the Fine Arts annual exhibition; she showed nine works in all at the Royal Academy and in 1942 won the Feodora Gleichen Award for a terracotta *Mother and Child*. An earlier and unusual work is her 1903 *Mother and Child* in which a stylized tree sweeps up behind the two figures. Sadly the image of this work is an example of the difficulty of sourcing good photographs: when acquiring images for my book this sculpture was on loan and museum staff were not able to access it to record it from a more sympathetic angle (**Figure 32**).

Frances Darlington (1880–1940) enrolled at the Slade School of Art in September 1897 and was taught by George Frampton. She progressed to the South Kensington Schools, studying under Lantéri, who in 1900 had been made Professor of Modelling, an aspect of Darlington's

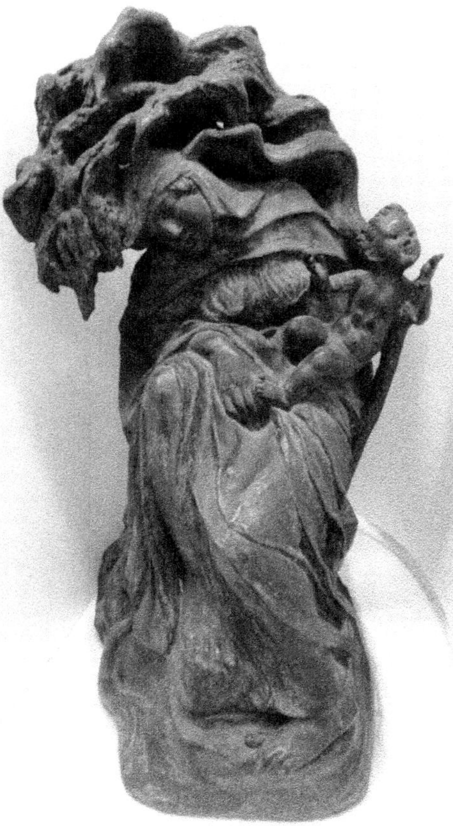

32. Elsie March, *Mother and Child*, 1903

work which would attract the greatest public praise.[26] She may also have studied under Gerald Moira who was mainly a mural painter; however, he had collaborated with sculptor Frank Lynn Jenkins to realize a type of coloured low-relief plaster decoration. This technique was used by Darlington for two of her most important commissions in Harrogate (**Plate 21** and **Figure 84**).[27] As with many women artists of her generation, it appears that Darlington was reticent when it came to self-promotion. She also seems to have been wary of marriage, having seen how it closed down the artistic activities of friends such as Edna Waugh, who has been described as a 'child protégé ... at the Slade (beginning) at the age of 14, she had been the formidable Tonks' star pupil'.[28] In 1904 Darlington's statuette *The Unforeseen* (c.1904) appeared on the front cover of the July issue of the journal *Womanhood* and was shown at the Royal Academy in the same year (**Figure 33**). The subject

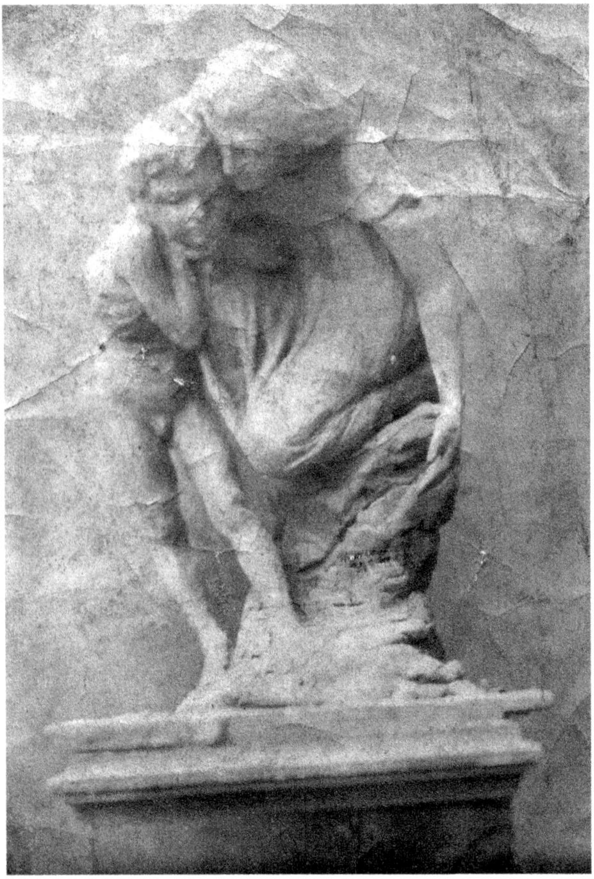

33. Frances Darlington, *The Unforeseen*, c.1904

comprises two children discovering a crab and appears to be drawn from Darlington's childhood. *Womanhood* had been founded in 1898 and was published for nine years, edited by Ada S. Ballin, a campaigner for women and a scholar who had attended University College London. For Frances to have her sculpture presented so prominently on the cover of this magazine established her professional status and associated her with other women of similar academic and intellectual standing.[29] She was gradually establishing a reputation and more work appeared in various catalogues and reviews in 1904.

Mother and child and religious subjects

Like most Victorian sculptors, Margaret Giles seems to have devoted a large part of her attention to portrait and memorial work. Her sculpture was undoubtedly varied: she worked in different styles over a relatively short period, and where we have photographs of her works there are hints that she changed her style to suit the material and the sculpture's intended use or site. Spielmann described Giles as one of the strongest female sculptors. 'Her memorial sculpture ... is graceful and sympathetic, and her exhibit in the Academy of 1901, "After Nineteen Hundred Years, and Still They Crucify" is an important and original group of very considerable power, admirable in feeling, and careful and gracious in modelling' (**Figure 34**).[30] Gertrude Williams's *Sleeping Mother and Child* (c.1903) is a compelling work, the fluidity of the two suggested figures being particularly effective (**Figure 35**). In 1906 Lucy Gwendolen Williams (1870–1955) exhibited *Queen of Dreams* (1905–06), a 10¾ inch bronze statuette, at the Walker Art Gallery (**Plate 10**). This is a particularly successful work on a small scale, appearing right for its size, and embodying an expressive rendering of the relationship between the two figures. Lucy Williams trained at Wimbledon Art College with Alfred Drury in the early 1890s and then attended the Royal College of Art from about 1895, where she studied under Lantéri. Drury had advised her to take up sculpture and remained an important influence throughout

34. Margaret Giles, *After Nineteen Hundred Years and Still They Crucify*, 1901

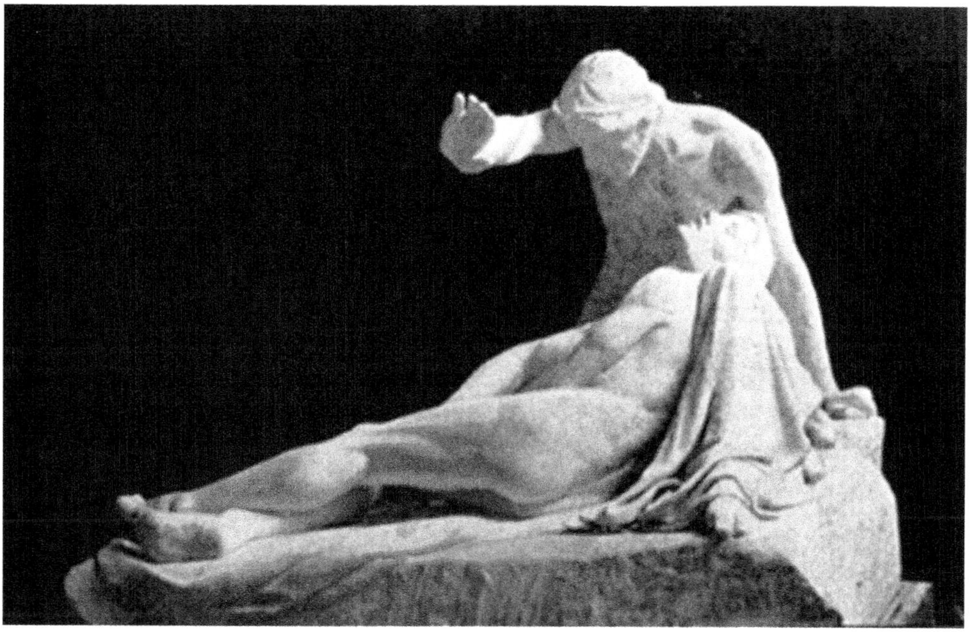

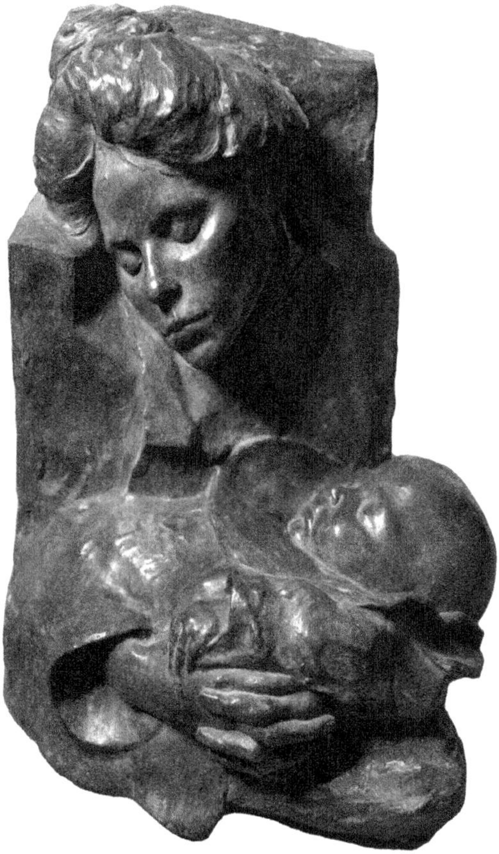

35. Gertrude Alice Meredith Williams, *Sleeping Mother and Child*, c.1903

her career, the naturalistic idealism of her sculptures recalling his work. She was awarded the silver medal for sculpture in the 1894 National Art Competition. Very little information is available on her; however, her sculptures were extensively reproduced in *Academy Architecture and Architectural Review*. She exhibited at the Royal Academy from 1893 while she was still a student, and later showed at the Paris Salon and at a number of international exhibitions, including in Rome where her patrons included Queen Alexandra and Queen Margherita of Italy.[31] *Queen of Dreams* shows a half-length young woman wearing a winged headband, with drapery surrounding her waist, and overall is a typical New Sculpture work. The material used is fairly unusual, being spelter, a zinc alloy that is cheaper and easier to work than bronze, although here it is finished so that it looks like bronze.[32] Phoebe Stabler does not appear to have made as many statuettes as some of the other sculptors discussed here, but one skilful example, her *Untitled (Mother and Child)* from c.1907 shows her also dealing with this theme (**Plate 11**).

Rosamund Praeger (1867–1954) attended Belfast's Government School of Art, and in 1888 enrolled at the Slade School of Art to study fine art and fine art anatomy, where she was taught by Legros, whose impact on the resurgence of bronze casting, especially in the making of bas-reliefs, was to have a strong influence on both Praeger's style and medium. Her work falls into four categories: architectural work for churches, schools, hospitals, banks, libraries and domestic dwellings, obtained mainly through her network of patrons from within the Presbyterian community; memorials to individuals and five First World War memorials; portraiture; and many small-scale domestic sculptures in either statuette or bas-relief form, sometimes brightly coloured, and including medals, toys, fountains and garden sculpture. Praeger knew Ellen Mary Rope and under her guidance became increasingly interested in modelling and sculpture. She won prizes for painting and drawing from the antique, composition and sculpture, and in her final year of study was awarded a silver medal for life drawing. Legros and Rope encouraged Praeger to study in France, and she went to Paris in the autumn of 1892 rather than returning to the Slade. Here she saw the work of Rodin as well as of female sculptors such as Camille Claudel. London and Paris provided Praeger with important professional contacts.[33]

In 1891 she had her first sculpture accepted by the Royal Academy and in 1893 settled permanently in the north of Ireland. A pottery version of Praeger's *St. Brigid of Kildare* was exhibited at the Irish Decorative Art Association in 1904. She had links to the Della Robbia Pottery in Birkenhead, which worked with many leading figures from the Arts and Crafts movement. Praeger was fascinated with the Irish-born St Fiachra, known as the 'Garden Saint of France' (**Figure 36**). The small, domestic style of her statue of the saint (c.1910) resembles figures by Rope of the Madonna, some of which were designed for Christmas cribs in the early 1900s. In 1912 Praeger had her first major solo show in Pollack's Gallery, Belfast, and in the same year produced *The Philosopher*, a seated toddler deep in thought which brought international acclaim. Shown in its plaster version at the Liverpool Autumn Exhibition in 1912 and in marble at the Royal Academy in 1913, it subsequently sold about 20,000 casts. The financial rewards from this work enabled her to establish two working studios in Holywood in December 1913, giving her the facilities to make a range of objects which included full-size figures, archways

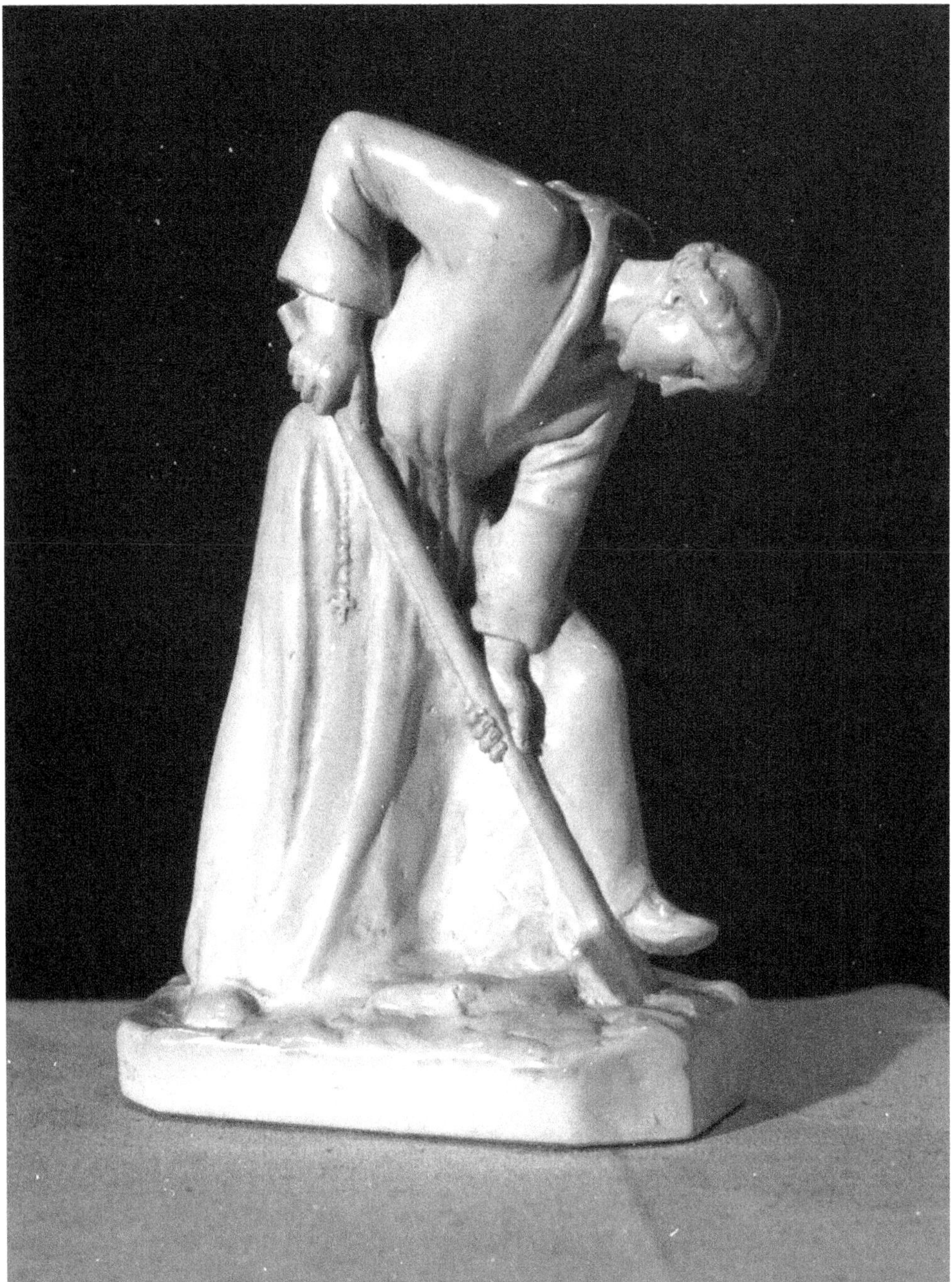

36. Rosamund Praeger, *St Fiachra*, c.1910

for public buildings, plaster casts of fountains, and many individual objects made in plaster or stone on request. Praeger appears to have had a keen business sense, attuned to the potential market for her small genre works. She referred frequently in her correspondence to the 'doll factory' where she reproduced multiple copies of *The Philosopher* and other images of children in different sizes and materials.[34] Despite all this activity, her work is little known. She was a significant professional presence in the art world of Northern Ireland, constantly advocating the role of women in the arts.

René Hetherington (d. 1979) studied at Leeds College of Art and the Royal College of Art. She was elected to the RBS in 1949 and later won the Feodora Gleichen Award. Hetherington's unusually stylized *Angel of the Annunciation* (c.1930) (**Figure 37**) is in the New Hall Art Collection, whereas most of her sculptures are in private collections.

A review of Gwynneth Holt's work particularly drew readers' attention to her ivory sculpture *Annunciation* (1946) (**Figure 38**), describing it as a lovely statuette which showed 'an inquiring mind, ever ready to experiment in new mediums and with new technique, coupled to a technical skill that is excellent ... "Annunciation" ... has all that one asks from such a figure – warmth, line, beauty and a fine, free-flowing conception.'[35] Holt trained at Wolverhampton School of Art and with Richard Garbe at the Royal College of Art. He is reputed to have given her his ivory working tools at the end of his career. Holt used a range of materials, but her work in ivory was the most prominent. *Annunciation* demonstrates her strong skills in carving: the sculpture shows the Virgin Mary with both of her hands raised to God, accepting the message from Gabriel who is depicted underneath her toes. Holt exhibited at the London, Scottish and West of England Academies, the Society of Portrait Sculptors and the Paris Salon. She was also a winner of the Feodora Gleichen Award for her *Mother and Child* exhibited at the Royal Academy, and several churches in the Essex area contain religious works by her. In 1943 Charles Wheeler proposed her for membership of the RBS and in 1952 she was elected a Fellow.[36] Like many of her female peers, Holt recognized the domination of men within the sculpture profession, believing that 'women are just as intelligent as men, and their contribution to art is just as valuable. They are not given a chance to take art up seriously. What with looking after the house, there is not much time left for concentrating on art.'[37]

A 1972 book on *Modern Ivory Carving* featured Holt's work. The author referred to the timeless nature of this particular medium and the way in which it was worked. Significantly, Holt was the only sculptor included in the book, the other entries concerning the making of chessmen, vases and so on. Holt was described as 'Britain's foremost ivory sculptor' and the author recalled at some length his visit to her cottage in the small village of Broomfield in Essex, recounting how,

> when Miss Holt finally appeared in the 16th-century doorway ... I was too impressed by the interior to say very much for a moment or two. Here was the sort of ambience that would suit even the most fastidious of artists. The plain whitewash and black oak beams of the interior were set off by the sculptor's own creamy colored ivory carvings, displayed on natural wood brackets.[38]

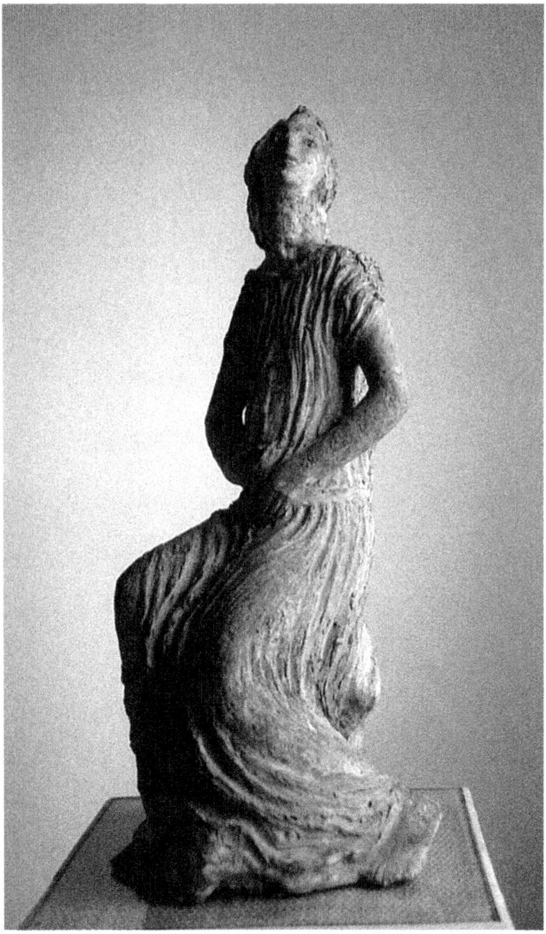

37. René Hetherington, *Angel of the Annunciation*, c.1930

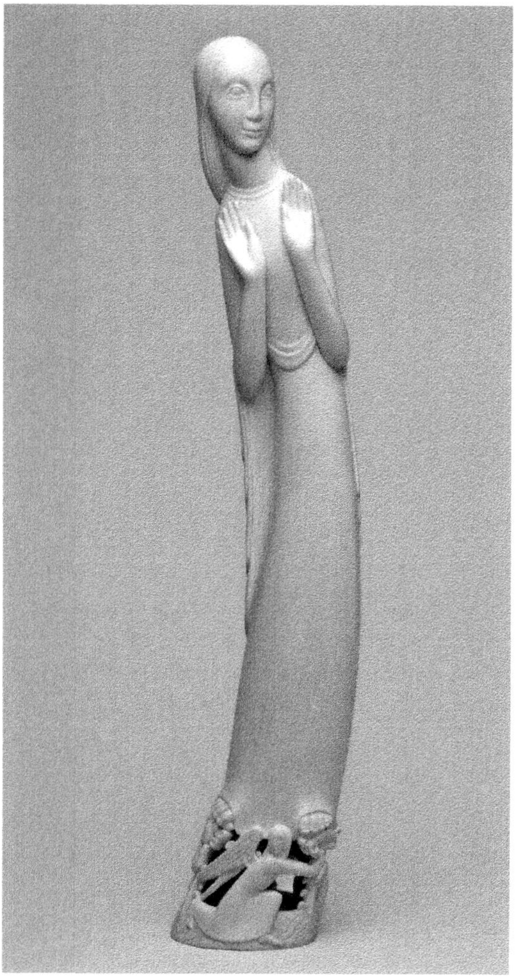

38. Gwynneth Holt, *Annunciation*, 1946

Jocelyn Horner (1902–73) studied at Leeds College of Art and was a contemporary of Hepworth and Moore, who became lifelong friends. In the 1920s she made a series of children's portraits and animal studies. Perhaps surprisingly, she had no intention of making sculpture her career, and in 1937 turned to the welfare of blind people and animals. However, after a 15-year break from sculpting she took up her interest in art again, studied modelling at Leeds College of Art and became a part-time member of staff at Halifax School of Art. Her *Annunciation* (1949) (**Plate 6**) is very much in the spirit of the New Sculpture statuette despite its late date. It was conceived as eliciting a tactile as well as visual response, a point that had been made in an article published in the *Studio* in September 1947, where it was argued that by producing small pieces, contemporary sculptors were 'reviving both the concrete ability to read form by touch, and the demand for the reinvestment of beauty, or at least comeliness, in material things of daily life'. The author stressed that many contemporary sculptors saw slight financial return for their work but were happy to accept this if their sculptures became affordable to people who otherwise would 'be deprived of the joys inherent in the personal ownership of a piece of good carving or modelling'. Moreover he argued that makers of small sculpture were particularly interested in the choice of precisely the most appropriate and often rare materials, and paid close attention to detail and quality, which linked them to English traditions of craftsmanship. He also singled out for praise Gwynneth Holt's 'exquisite *Annunciation*' (**Figure 38**).[39]

Portraits and animal studies

The earliest surviving sculpture made by Frances Darlington is a statuette of her sister Dorothy in her riding habit, dating from 1896 when Frances was only 16 years old (**Figure 39**). Her biographer made a key point when commenting on why the sculptor's work (and, for that matter, that of similar female sculptors) might appear conservative. Darlington grew up among a group of professional and well-educated men. Like them, she had a college education: she had qualified in sculpture just as they had done in law and medicine. Thus her attitude towards her work was likely to follow the training she had received; in the way that lawyers and doctors would adhere to and perfect their training, so there was no reason why Darlington should try to move away from what she had been taught. She was unmarried and therefore had to earn her own living, and so needed to be pragmatic when seeking commissioned work in her home county of Yorkshire.[40] This is an important point: the actual nature of art as a profession has in the twentieth century become overlain with Romantic notions about creative dissidence. Both male and female artists without wealthy relatives or independent incomes needed to be attuned to the marketplace. Many successful sculptors, not just women, did not regard their training as something against which to resist; such an assumption has resulted in many highly professional sculptors, both men and women, disappearing from art history, which broadly since the late nineteenth century has favoured the rebel. Like Gwen John, also from the Slade, Darlington was a successful unmarried female artist who created a career for herself. Unlike John, who had a patron and sold her work through

39. Frances Darlington, *Dorothy in Riding Habit*, 1896

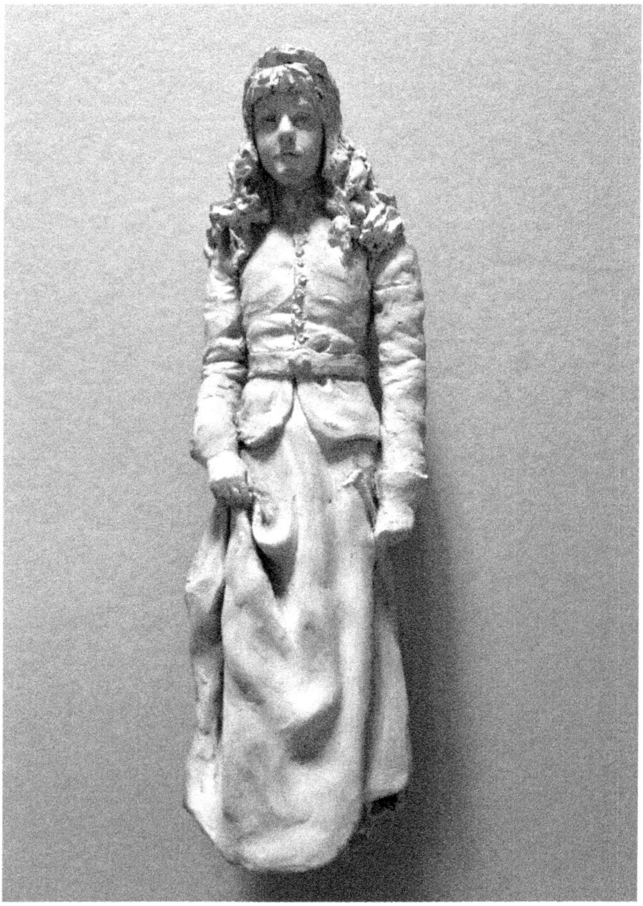

exhibiting, Darlington worked to commission. For a woman to achieve a career in this way, and at this time, is remarkable.

Apart from male sculptors such as Gill and Epstein, Kathleen Scott was one of the most reviewed sculptors during the interwar years, as evidenced by the numerous reports on her life and work in newspapers and magazines. Because she was not a modernist and also frequently made what would subsequently be taken as anti-feminist statements, Scott has been virtually erased from art history. She believed that women should not get the vote, and this position seems to have resulted from a lingering Victorian conservatism as well as a wish not to make a special case for herself. But it is puzzling given her strength of character and clear ambition. Scott also belonged to the generation of artists between the New Sculpture practitioners and modernists such as Moore and Hepworth, an accident of dates that also impeded male sculptors' careers. When Scott's work has been mentioned it is generally summarized as demonstrating a 'rather academic style' and as being 'competent, not innovative, perfectly of her time'.[41] She studied at the Slade between 1898 and 1902 under Henry Tonks, and at this stage showed an aptitude in modelling in clay from life. She was impressed by Rodin's *Burghers of Calais* (1889) which she saw at the 1901 Glasgow Exhibition, and in Paris she enrolled at the Académie Colarossi where she discovered the sculpture class and believed she had found her niche: within three months a statue of a woman and child had been accepted for the Salon.[42] Rodin had a considerable influence on the development of Scott's style, particularly noticeable in her use of naturalistic poses and confident modelling, and although he was not taking official pupils he displayed great interest in her work:

> Every Saturday she visited him at his studio, for help and advice, and often he would return the visits, and take with him his *déjeuner,* which she had to cook for him herself. She tells of the inspiration of his methods, of seeing the innumerable little models of such details as hands and feet that he would prepare and keep in his drawers for reference, and of his patience in regarding his own work, and passing upon it illuminating judgments.[43]

Between 1905 and 1909 Scott exhibited nine sculptures at the Salon de la Societé des Artistes Français, which would have been seen alongside works by Rodin, Bourdelle and Brâncuşi, but she had no time for modernism, saying 'My allegiance is given in sculpture to those exquisite elongated ladies of Chartres, and to their lovely archaic ancestors, the maidens of the Acropolis; and in life ... to the springing grace of the stripling, and the majesty of thought-worn faces.'[44] She particularly disliked the work of Epstein, which she thought ugly. An interesting explanation of Scott's dislike of modernist trends was given in a 1927 article where it was suggested that 'modern styles tend to make a set type, she maintains, and that makes their likenesses uninteresting to record'.[45] She was torn between family and work, saying 'how I love my family and how I love being left alone. It is hard to be a sculptor when there are cooks and nurses and political parties in the world. One imagines one might have been a really fine artist if one had been just selfish and slovenly.' Male sculptors, she accurately observed, often had wives, and thus were able to be single-minded in pursuit of their careers.

After the First World War Scott was in demand for war memorials, regimental plaques and models, and portraits of war heroes, and these works established her prominence in British sculpture. Her career peaked during the interwar years, with six major exhibitions (three of them solo shows), and regular exhibits at the Royal Academy and the Paris Salon where she received the Diploma several times. She gained associate membership of the Societé Nationale des Beaux-Arts, and was elected to the RBS in 1928, regarding which she typically stated indifference. Nonetheless she was elected to the Society's council in 1936. By 1928 her turnover 'was £2,800, and in 1933 she calculated she could earn £9000 by sculpting full-time'.[46] In 1935 she questioned her work rate:

> Why does it matter what one has in the foolish RA? Of course it doesn't and yet ... one goes on until one's limbs ache and one's eyes are dim. I am not ambitious – I want nothing – certainly not money, nor honours – I suppose I must want admiration – yes I expect that must be it, for it can't be just the urge to produce for if merely that I wouldn't care about RAs and such. The *Illustrated London News* had a whole page of my bust of the King – and I am pleased. How silly to be pleased, it does not make me a good sculptor because the ILN reproduces my work.[47]

In 1921 Scott made a porcelain seated figure statuette of Colonel T. E. Lawrence (**Figure 40**). Lawrence was a notoriously shy sitter, but Scott had the ability to entertain her subjects in order to put them at ease.[48] In 1921 he wrote to Scott concerning the forthcoming sculpture:

> Dear Lady Scott. This is very sudden! Once I was 'portrayed in bronze' by Derwent Wood. I met it suddenly in the Academy and felt like the man in Rossetti who met himself in a wood! But then perhaps he isn't very deep. Dobson seems to me better ... if you want an object, I'll agree with pleasure: only it won't be a good speculation: it won't sell afterwards: and my face isn't so-to-speak virgin. John did it, as you say ... also D.-Wood: and Orpen: and now Rothenstein: really the features are quite worn away with so much study of them. If you do it, please hold me as a model, and not as 'the most romantic figure of the war' (American film-artist). I'm tired of the limelight, and am really not stagy at all, and not ever going to be a public figure again. It was a war effort, imposed, involuntary. Don't do me as Colonel Lawrence (he died Nov. 11 1918) but because my shaped head suits your whim. All this sounds very vain and silly ... Apologies for this long stupid screed. Yours sincerely. T. E. Lawrence.[49]

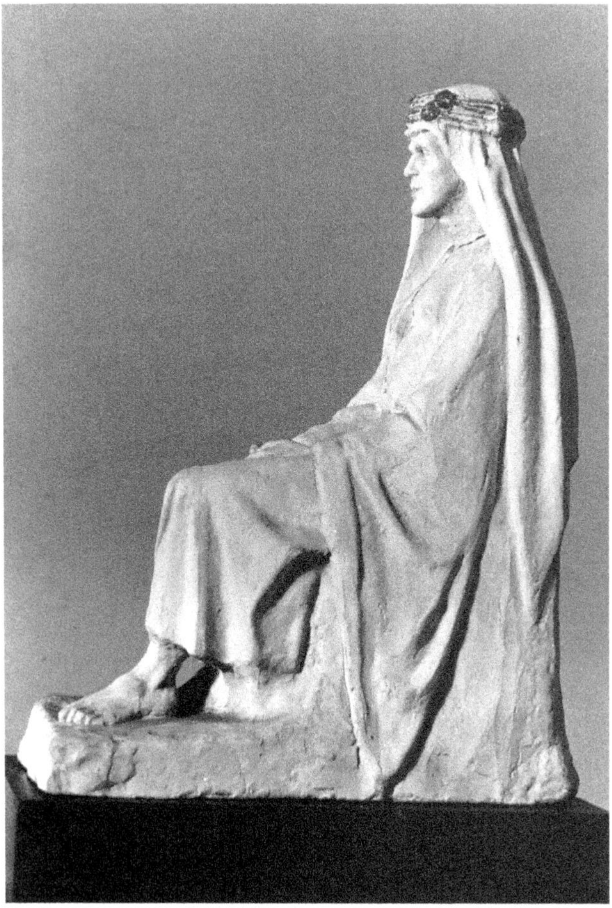

40. Kathleen Scott, *Colonel T. E. Lawrence*, 1921

Scott also sold statuette versions of her full-scale figure sculptures (see Chapters 5 and 6), and several exhibition catalogues reveal the large number of these. For example, in October 1934 she exhibited at the Fine Art Society, showing 33 sculptures, including statuettes of George Bernard Shaw, Lord Knutsford, Reginald Smith, Sir Cecil Smith, Compton Mackenzie, Max Beerbohm, Barbara Harrison, Admiral Arbuthnot, Charles Shannon and Charles Ricketts. In 1936 she showed at Ackermann's Gallery, Bond Street, and the name of Colonel T. E. Lawrence was added to the above list.[50]

Josefina de Vasconcellos worked with animal imagery, as in a particularly beautiful piece entitled *Dove from the Ark Nesting after the Flood* (date unknown) made from Hoptonwood stone (**Plate 12**). Barbara

Hepworth produced similar works among her earlier sculptures, such as *Doves (Group)* from 1927 (**Figure 41**), and it is likely that the Vasconcellos sculpture was also made at around this time. Another similar work from this period is Ivy Gardner Proudfoot's (1894–1975) *Loving Birds (Doves)* (1932) (**Figure 42**). She studied at the Glasgow School of Art, and her reputation was made in the areas of child portraiture and animal sculptures, including garden statuary. She showed regularly at the Royal Glasgow Institute and at the Royal Scottish Academy. *Loving Birds* is carved from a single block of marble with an appealing contrast between the simplified and smooth birds, and the textured surface on which they perch, thus combining aspects of naturalism with abstraction. Seen together, these three works at the least demonstrate an equivalence of sensibility and technical virtuosity.

Gardner Proudfoot also had to endure the usual condescension meted out to women sculptors. In a publication entitled *Round the Studios 1939*, Nan Muirhead Moffat wrote about a visitor to the sculptor's art school

41. Barbara Hepworth, *Doves (Group)*, 1927

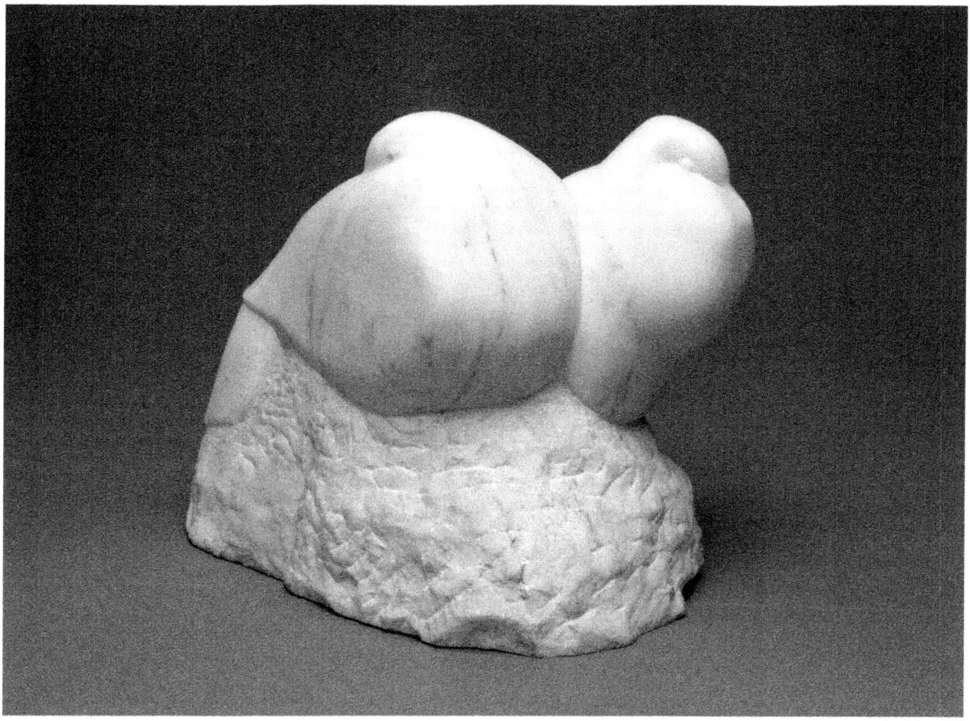

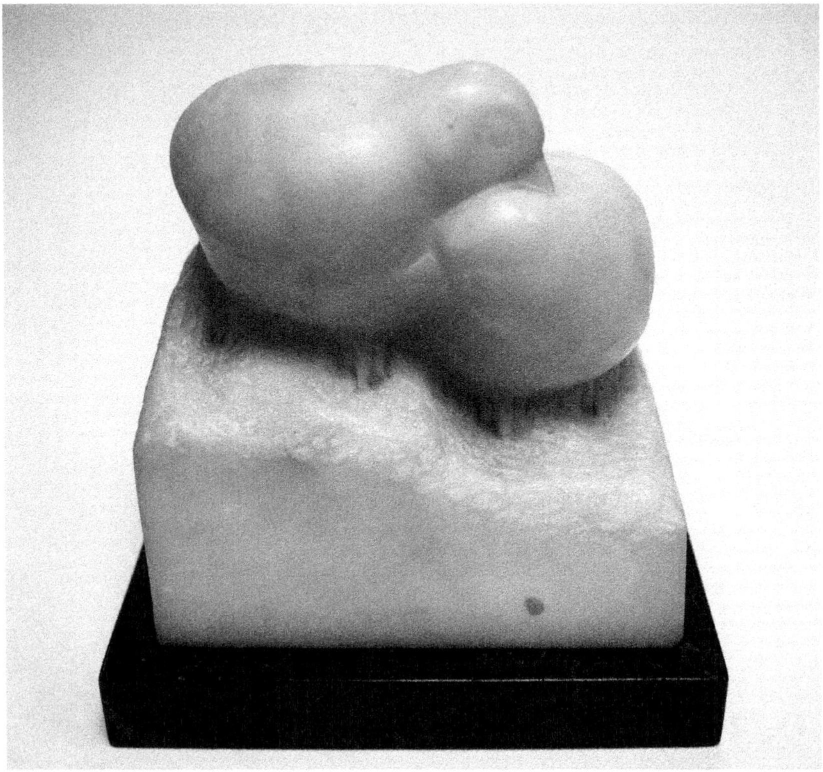

42. Ivy Gardner Proudfoot, *Loving Birds (Doves)*, 1932

studio exclaiming 'And she's such a wee thing!', and Moffat contrasted 'the petite sculptress' with her diploma work, 'two colossal figures for a doorway'. She continued:

> this feminine Follower of Phidias is very fond of blue, and when I sketched her, she was wearing a gentian blue overall. During a break for tea I discovered that she can also make delicious scones and cakes. They are not, I would hasten to add, at all sculptural either in consistency or weight![51]

This continually coy tone must have been difficult for these women sculptors to endure.

From the examples illustrated here, it can be seen that although the statuette probably had its greatest prominence at the turn of the twentieth century and into its early decades, the form did continue for some years. Selling prices, however, remained problematic, since small bronze figures could be priced at over one-twentieth of the annual income of a professional middle-class individual. Therefore their hoped-for role in embellishing the homes of many households was not fully realized. As with the productions of William Morris, the reality was that these works involved skilled craftsmanship, which was not amenable to the creation of a wide consumer base. However, David Getsy has proposed that the statuette form remained important in maintaining artistic experimentation in the early twentieth century:

> British modernist sculpture, though rooted in antagonistic beliefs about style and representation, continued to stress the crucial concerns for the producers and consumers of New Sculpture statuettes: the dynamic relationship between matter and form and the importance of physical contact with the sculptural object. Statuettes were denigrated as the epitome of Victorian bourgeois respectability and kitsch, but these little, precious objects helped to redefine the place of sculpture in everyday life and raised questions which informed modern art in Britain.[52]

In addition to exploiting the formal and physical aspects of small sculptures in this way, practitioners did have the possibility of diversifying even further, into the area of sculptural decoration, the subject of the next section.

4.2 Applied art as sculpture

In 1893 the Arts and Crafts Exhibition Society published a book of essays. In the preface William Morris referred to a resurgence in the decorative arts with which the Society was closely associated, adding that the fact of a 'revival' proved that previously such arts had been 'sick unto death'. He described a lack of beauty in modern life, equating the former with decoration, and urging that this should be remedied.[53] The first of the female sculptors from South Kensington to exhibit with the Arts and Crafts Society were Esther Mary Moore (1857–c.1934) and Margaret Giles in 1893. Moore showed an electric light bracket, and Giles a wax design for a salt-cellar and a model for a street lamp. Florence Steele (1857–1948) exhibited a silvered bronze piano front and a steel and wood casket in 1896, and in 1899 Ruby Levick showed a door knocker design. Florence Steele was commissioned to make tile designs by William Burton of Pilkington's Tile and Pottery Company, several examples of which were shown at the 1900 Paris International Exhibition, and she also produced civic regalia, as can be seen in her *Trophy for Buffs, in Memory of South African War* (1912), essentially a war memorial in miniature (**Figure 43**). Taught by Lantéri at the National Art Training School, her contemporaries included Margaret Giles, Ruby Levick and Esther Mary Moore. She exhibited with the Arts and Crafts Exhibition Society from 1896 and was one of a significant number of women supported by the Art Union of London.

A wide interest in garden design also provided an outlet for sculptural work. An article in the *Gardener's Chronicle* in 1890 recorded that Ruskin was 'more proud of his toil in his garden ... than of his making of great books and renown'.[54] This interest in gardens and their design in part arose from the decline of the landed estates, which led to the development of a newly rich class, as well as the trend for wealthy families to move away from the cities into the country. Architect John Dando Sedding was characterized as a 'plant lover and founder member of the Art Workers' Guild [who] described garden design as a truce struck between man and nature, both sharing the creation of "a picture conceived by man, painted on Nature's canvas with the aid of her materials"'.[55] Articles on gardening even appeared in the *Studio*: for example, in 1901 architect Edward S. Prior wrote a series on garden making for the journal.[56] 1906 saw the publication of *The Studio Yearbook of Decorative Art: A Guide to the Artistic Decoration and Furnishing of the House* in which the topic of garden statues was enthusiastically addressed:

> If it is often overdone in private gardens, the latter certainly have the advantage over public and official sites ... being the property of the individual, they are not burdened by the claims of the nation's life, and are not called upon ... to admit monstrous images of statesmen, ineffectually striving to cloak the hideous banality of frock coat and trousers under the portentous folds of official robes. On the contrary, private gardens are, of all others, places where the sculptor's art is most free to express itself in what Canova declared to be its only language, viz., the nude![57]

All of this critical attention suggested that the outdoor domestic sphere presented a potentially lucrative market that paralleled the vogue for interior sculptural embellishments, and was also attracting serious commentary. However, sculptors working for private clients wishing to adorn their home and garden increasingly faced competition from the growth of firms that could supply a wide range of domestic decorative and sculptural objects.

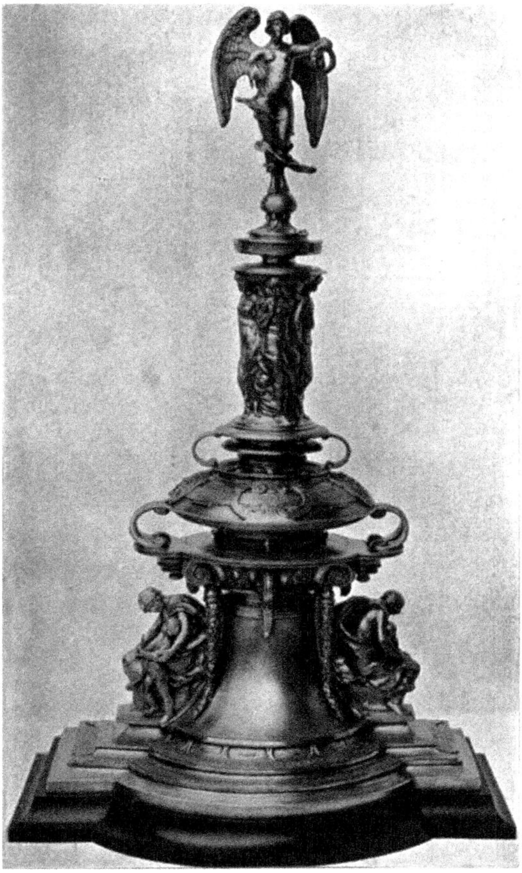

43. Florence Steele, *Trophy for Buffs, in Memory of South African War*, 1912, 'metalwork'

After the First World War initiatives to encourage the acquisition of sculpture designed for the domestic environment were supported by efforts to create a wider interest in the art form, and more specifically to encourage the public to realize the affordability of works made from relatively cheap materials, such as plaster and terracotta. Thus it was hoped that the emphasis could be shifted away from painting, which people already knew how to use decoratively, to sculpture, in order to show how the latter could enter the domestic sphere as a powerful decorative addition and a part of everyday life. In section 4.3 we will see how a display at Heal's department store suggested such possible scenarios by placing small sculptures alongside furniture, wallpaper panels and lengths of fabric, in order that the public might be able to visualize their own use of sculpture at home. In many ways this move perpetuated the values of the Arts and Crafts movement and the ethos of the New Sculpture statuette. There was an emphasis on the role of women, and many of the sculptures shown referred to the female body or the family group. We can now look at a number of areas in which women sculptors might focus their output, or in some cases diversify from their main areas of production such as figures or monumental works.

Home decor

Several women sculptors made decorative panels for domestic interiors. Ella (1858–1946) and Nelia Casella (1859–1950) were sisters who studied under Legros at the Slade in the early 1880s. Over the following decades they made many pieces collaboratively as well as separately. At the Slade they learned the art of modelling in wax, adopting this technique in the creation of medals, miniatures and wax reliefs. They were highly skilled at colouring wax and creating innovative textures which soon attracted critical acclaim. Ella's coloured wax bas-relief *St. George & the Dragon* (c.1897) was exhibited in the Woman's Work Section of the Victorian Era Exhibition in 1897 (**Figure 44**). The sisters showed at both the Royal Academy and the Arts and Crafts Exhibition Society in the 1890s. Their work drew on the Renaissance tradition, in particular the work of Pisanello, and they also gained inspiration from theatrical costumes of the period. Many of their wax relief portraits represented friends from their circle, including celebrities such as Ellen Terry, Henry Irving, Franz Liszt and Bram Stoker.

Ruby Levick made decorative panels in addition to her statuettes. Her *Girl with Flowers* (c.1905) was admired by T. Martin Wood in the 1905 *Studio* article mentioned earlier in this chapter (**Figure 45**). He particularly focused on the panel's refined colour, the treatment of the flowers and child's hair, and the sensitive face; unfortunately no colour reproduction of this work could be located. He characterized Levick's work as bypassing the supposed conflict for a sculptor in choosing between the classical and the realistic, the scholarly and the romantic. In proposing her work as 'sheltered almost in a domestic circle' he acknowledged that this might deflect serious attention, but he urged the viewer to persist, to find within its quietness a sensitivity to its context. He described Levick's work as unaffected, as

> concerned with an outlook which is the outlook from the ordinary home, comes to be so by a modification of the laws that give us the tremendous sculpture of a Rodin, representing the larger forces of the

> modern world ... The range of Miss Levick's sculpture is within the small circumstances of life ... It is curious that, although in painting England admits of and even welcomes art which in its intention is narrow and in its expression limited ... this does not seem to be the case with sculpture. In this art the minds of artists seem hemmed about with traditions – whether of Hellenic beauty, or of Florentine expressiveness, or of the rebellion that in Rodin's art gives form to imprisoned spirituality ... The word big has entered the studios, to complete the ruin of more than one *petit-maitre*.[58]

Given their delicacy, a surprising number of Rosamund Praeger's plaster sculptures have survived. They are generally finished in white, but some have been coloured with a wash or glaze, and several have a bronze paint finish such as her polychromed plaster panel *Harvest*

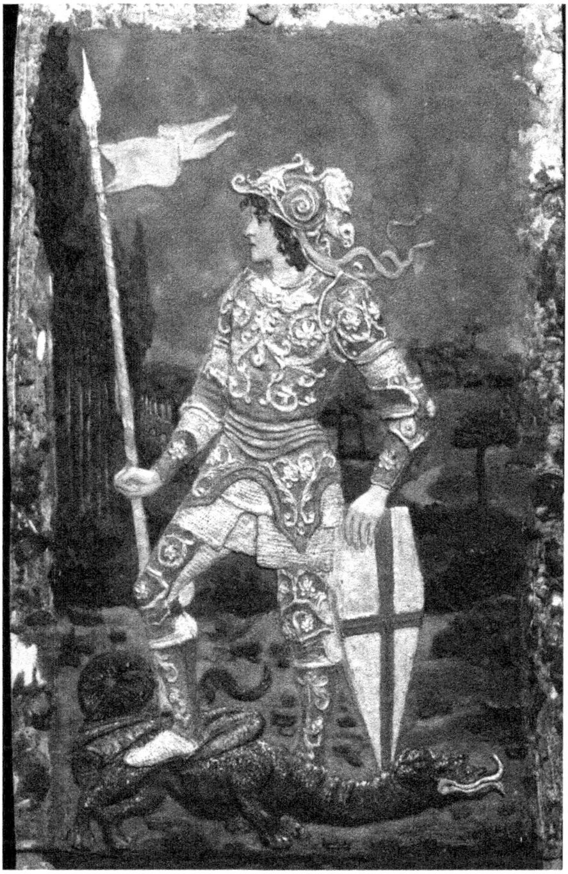

44. Ella Casella, *St George & the Dragon*, c.1897

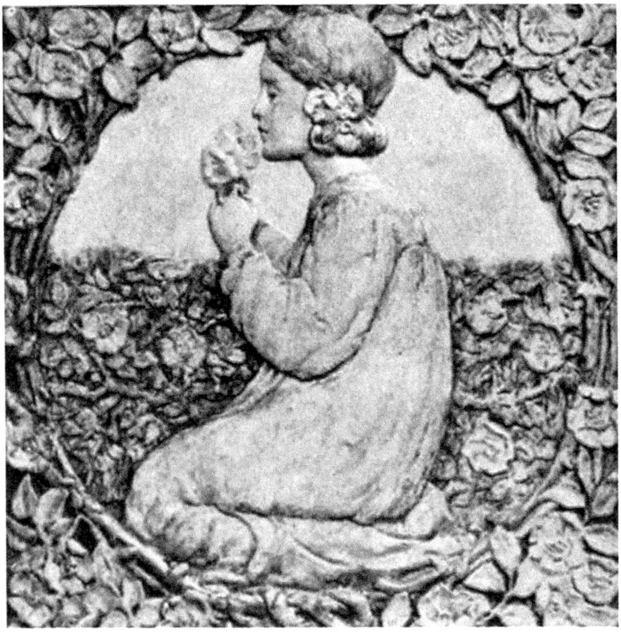

45. Ruby Levick, *Girl with Flowers*, c.1905

(date unknown) (**Plate 13**), which is coloured in ochre and brown. This particular design would be repeated on her *Inglis Memorial* (c.1905) (**Figure 62**).

Another utilitarian area where we see a significant number of works by some of the women discussed is that of door furniture, where they were able to transform such humble objects into beautifully crafted forms. Adèle Hay (active 1897–1904) produced an exquisite bronze door knocker that was shown at the 1899 Arts and Crafts Exhibition (**Figure 46**). A review in the *Studio* described this piece as

> not only a vigorous piece of modelling ... but also a very clever design ... the artist has treated it with no little ingenuity, constituting her ornament solely out of the necessary elements of the subject without recourse to extraneous features ... The general impression conveyed is that of boldness and strength, at the same time that careful attention has been bestowed upon the minutiæ of the saint's armour and of the caparisoning of his horse.[59]

Many sculptors produced pieces that combined the statuette with a functional object such as an electric lamp. A particularly graceful bronze statuette electric lamp was made by Esther Mary Moore in 1900

(**Figure 47**) and in *Hutchinson's Arts & Crafts Magazine* of 1904 reference was made to a 'beautifully modelled figure by Miss Frances Darlington, designed to hold an electric light'.[60] This publication included a black-and-white illustration of the work entitled *The Magic Crystal* (undated), which is an impressive piece of polychrome sculpture, the latter dominating rather than being a decoration for the light (**Figure 48**). It was extremely innovative to incorporate electricity in sculpture, here combining the traditional use of polychromy with the latest technology.[61]

When Phoebe Stabler married she was already well known as a ceramic figure modeller, having begun around 1910–12 to design and model pottery figures. After the First World War she worked for the Ashtead Pottery and then for the firm Carter, Stabler and Adams (later to become Poole Pottery), in which her husband Harold was a partner. Husband and wife collaborated on a number of projects in ceramics, a war memorial in Durban being the most prominent and unusual example, where Phoebe modelled the figures for which she was best known (see Chapter 6.2),

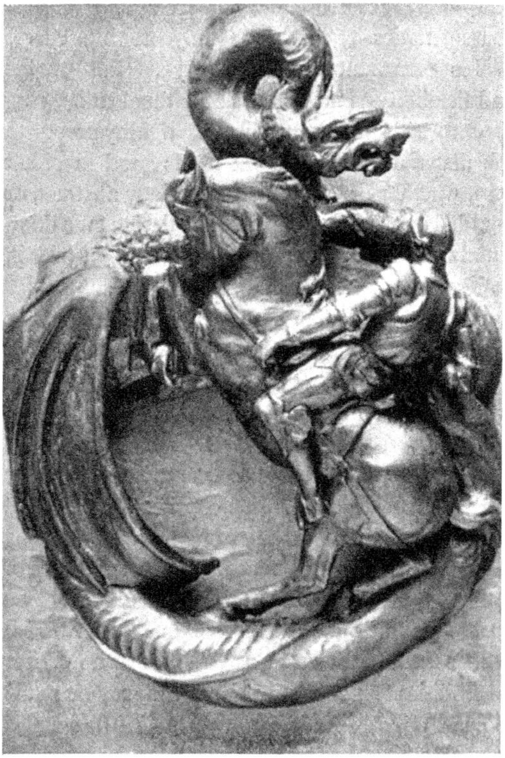

46. Adèle Hay, *Door Knocker in the form of St George and the Dragon*, c.1899

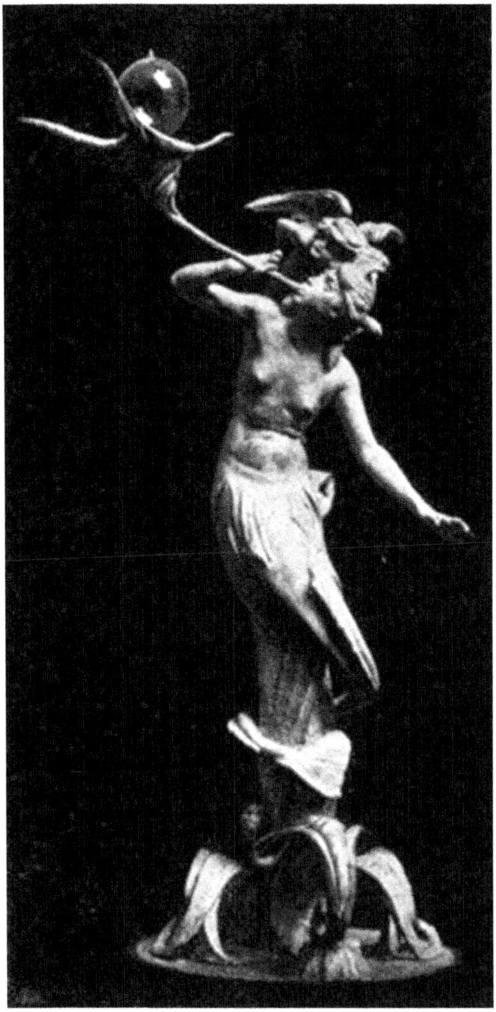

47. Esther Mary Moore, *Electric Lamp*, 1900

and the Della Robbia style has become synonymous with their work. During the 1920s and 1930s she was also established in making stone carvings, and was an important contributor to the 1924 British Empire Exhibition at Wembley, where the Concrete Utilities Bureau of London engaged her to make work demonstrating the sculptural properties of that material. Stabler was described by Kineton Parkes as displaying a 'nice decorative sense' in her work, a characteristic of her 'general garden work in plastic media'. He noted that several pieces of her modelled works were in public galleries and that she had also produced a number

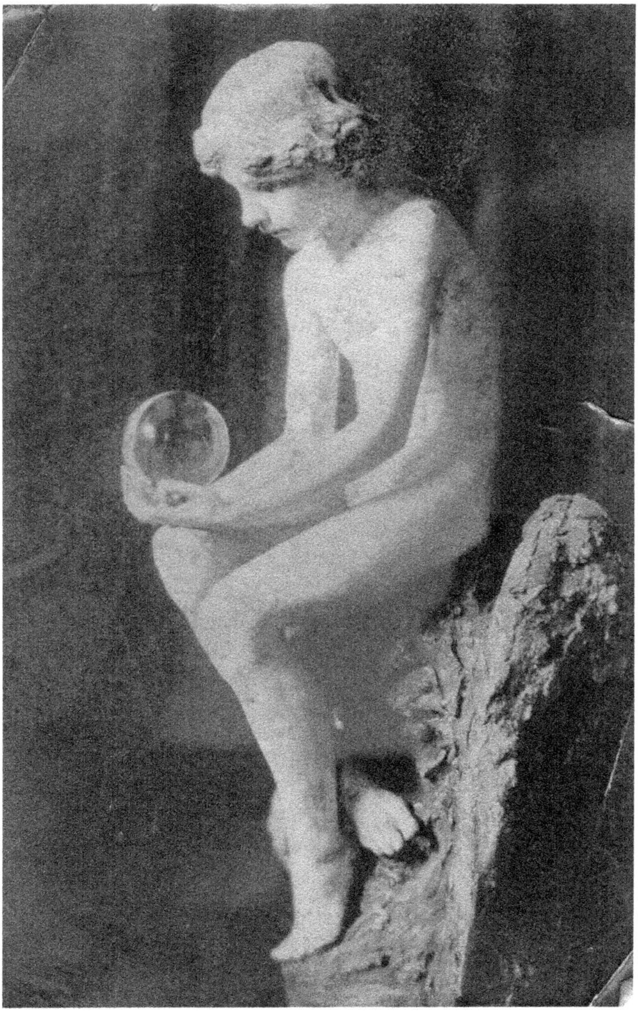

48. Frances Darlington, *The Magic Crystal*, date unknown

of small war memorials.[62] Working together, the Stablers became one of the most prominent and important design partnerships of the early and mid-twentieth century, but they also maintained their individual artistic practices. From 1906 they showed regularly at the Royal Academy, the Arts and Crafts Exhibition Society, the British Industries Fair and similar exhibitions. As members of the Arts Workers' Guild they attended the exhibition of British Arts and Crafts at the Louvre in 1914, and their work was widely reviewed in the *Studio*. One of their first projects was a memorial fireplace commissioned for Rugby School in 1922 which is still

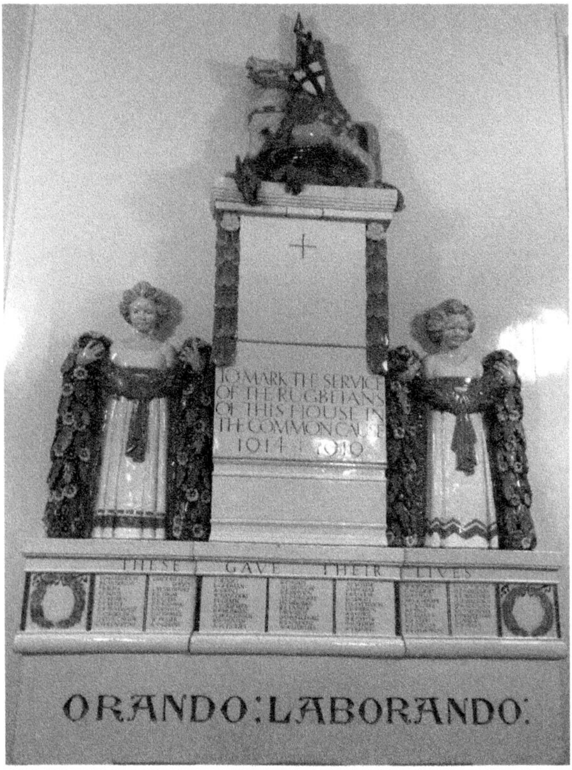

49. Harold and Phoebe Stabler, *Memorial Fireplace, Rugby School*, 1922

in place (**Figure 49**). The figure of St George was modelled by Harold and those on either side of the fireplace by Phoebe.[63] At least one other cast was made and exhibited at the 1924 British Empire Exhibition.

Decorative garden items

Exhibition societies recognized that displaying sculpture in commercial premises would both encourage new audiences and patrons for sculpture as a domestic exterior as well as interior form, and continue an alliance of such sculpture with architecture and design. For its 1930 annual exhibition, the London Group used Selfridges to display its members' work, receiving plaudits from the press for this enterprising move. The work of Barbara Hepworth was among the sculptures displayed on the store's landscaped West End roof garden above Oxford Street. These sculptures were presented as 'contemporary fittings for the modern home and as pleasing garden and grotto ornaments'.[64] Kineton Parkes commented extensively on this exhibition, noting that there were 60 works on display, mostly comprising 'direct work, either carving, burnt modelling or ceramic, a good deal of it by women artists'.[65] However, his appraisal is rather equivocal: he believed that the exhibition displayed no shortage of talent, but clearly did not care for the 'distortion' that he found in some of the exhibits. Rather acerbically, he observed that the

> younger sculptors proved their valour to the younger shop assistants of that part of London, and the lessons they imparted are being disseminated even to the uttermost parts of the outer suburbs, which is all to the good, seeing that the beauty of the outer suburbs is for the most part decimated by the work of the maker of memorials.

Parkes noted works by Arnrid Johnson, Elizabeth Muntz and Edna Manley which he believed ought to attract the attention of architects. He referred to the exhibition as a logical development of a garden sculpture display that had been held earlier at the Horticultural Hall.[66] The latter opened on 17 October 1928 as part of the International Exhibition which was devoted entirely to gardens. In an article published on the eve of the opening the exhibition was described as comprising:

> garden planning, garden statuary, ancient gardens, modern gardens, famous gardens, foreign gardens [which] can be studied at the Exhibition, and there will be conferences on various subjects connected with gardens on each of the four days. Lady Hylton [*sic*] Young is one of a number of women interested in the event, the first of its kind, and has sent some of her beautiful garden statuary work.[67]

The exhibition included a sculpture section which was presented in a layout that mimicked an enclosed garden, designed by William E. Reynolds-Stephens, with William Reid Dick and Gilbert Bayes assisting with the display. Eighty works of sculpture were shown at the exhibition, which was open for eight days.

The early 1900s saw Katharine Maltwood's work maturing and in her practice we can see the influence of several artistic trends from the late nineteenth century; in particular, French ideas fed into her modelling and the anatomical correctness of her sculpture. In 1901 she married John Maltwood, an advertising manager with a considerable fortune, which allowed her to travel widely and amass an art collection while continuing with her own sculpture and writing. Between 1911 and 1930 Maltwood regularly showed her sculptures at the London Salon, the Royal Academy and other London galleries. In 1939 the couple moved to rural Saanich in Victoria, British Columbia.[68] A lead fountain *Boy Tickling Trout* from around 1900 dates from Maltwood's very productive pre-war period (**Figure 50**). It was exhibited in 1922 at the *Daily Express Women's Academy* in Olympia and was later used as a pond ornament at the Maltwoods' various homes.

Although usually known for her memorial and architectural work (see Chapter 6), Gertrude Alice Meredith Williams also made garden figures. No details about possible sales are available, but these pieces show how she too diversified her practice. There were two figure sculptures that appear to have been made during the later part of her career, in each case being listed as situated at North Wyke, Tawton, Devon, where she and her husband retired. One was a bronze design for a garden figure and the second a bronze statue of *Pan*. Neither are dated, although *Pan* was exhibited at the Royal Scottish Academy in 1913 and at the Royal Academy in 1925. There also exists a design for a lead or bronze water spout, which was carried out in the latter material. Again no information is available as to possible sales, but the work was on display at the Royal Scottish Academy in 1929.

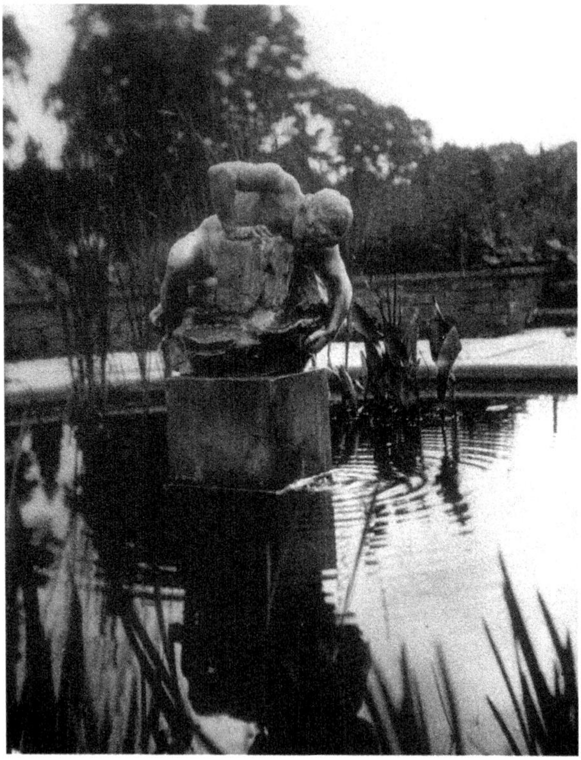

50. Photograph of Katharine Maltwood's *Boy Tickling Trout*, c.1900

In 1939 an article on 'The Lead Tradition in Gardens' was published in the journal *Landscape and Garden*.[69] The historical lineage of the material was referred to and a resurgence in the use of lead as a decorative material described. It was felt that the present-day garden was particularly suitable to being decorated with small, intimate lead sculptures, since such works could provide a focal point in the domestic landscape. Anne Acheson was particularly known for her lead garden figures and is yet another sculptor whose reputation waned. However, she has received recent attention via a television programme and solo exhibition.[70] She was very successful in the 1920s and 1930s, becoming the first female Fellow of the RBS in 1938, having been one of the earliest women to be admitted as an associate member in 1923, as was Phoebe Stabler. The works that she showed at the Royal Academy and also regularly at the Paris Salon included lead garden statues as well as a lead fountain figure, *Boy with Hose-pipe*. Acheson generally made editions of between six and ten sculptures, and although many of her garden pieces are rather sentimental to twenty-first-century eyes, they were immensely popular in their time. Her 1923 garden sculpture *Sally*, which was shown at the 1924 British Empire Exhibition, was particularly admired (**Figure 51**).

An article devoted to 'Lead Garden Figures' was published in *Queen* magazine in August 1923; it was written by Marion Cran, who was a prominent commentator on gardens, an influential member of society and one of Acheson's greatest supporters. She opened by bemoaning the current state of decorative garden sculpture:

> 'And now I must get a figure of some sort to finish it off.' I seem to have heard that sentiment expressed in slightly varying forms a thousand times in my life among the garden-lovers – and it never fails to give me a cold feeling of fear; for though taste in planting is not universal, it is absolutely *prevalent* compared to taste in the choice of garden ornaments. And among the merchants who purvey these luxuries taste would appear to be considered a disgrace. Year after year at the Chelsea Show the same poor range of bad copies of hackneyed models appears to tempt the unwary to buy unwisely. The eye is confounded by everlasting lead boys with dolphins, Mercurys, girls with baskets of flowers, storks and what-nots, cast from moulds so worn or poor that the modelling is almost entirely lost and the image perilously near an amorphous lump. One wearies of the sundials cast in imitation stone to three or four designs which are never of good proportion and seldom free from pretentiousness, and of the small and uninspired bird-bowls carried out so close to the ground that they become in practice a cats' larder.[71]

Cran had recently encountered Acheson's *Sally* at the Royal Academy and bought one of the edition of six. Elsewhere she described for her readers Acheson's approach when sculpting in clay, working quickly yet patiently and often using the children of friends as models. It appears that Acheson was quite reticent in promoting her work, and so Cran's support would have been most useful in gaining sales for her garden figures. In the *Women's Magazine* Cran further described Acheson's famous lead garden babies as shown at many special exhibitions of decorative art, as well as at established fine art venues, believing that they provided their purchasers with something that was not only beautiful but that would increase in value over time.[72]

By the mid-1920s Acheson was sufficiently well known to warrant another full-page feature, this time in the *Lady*. Here she was praised for

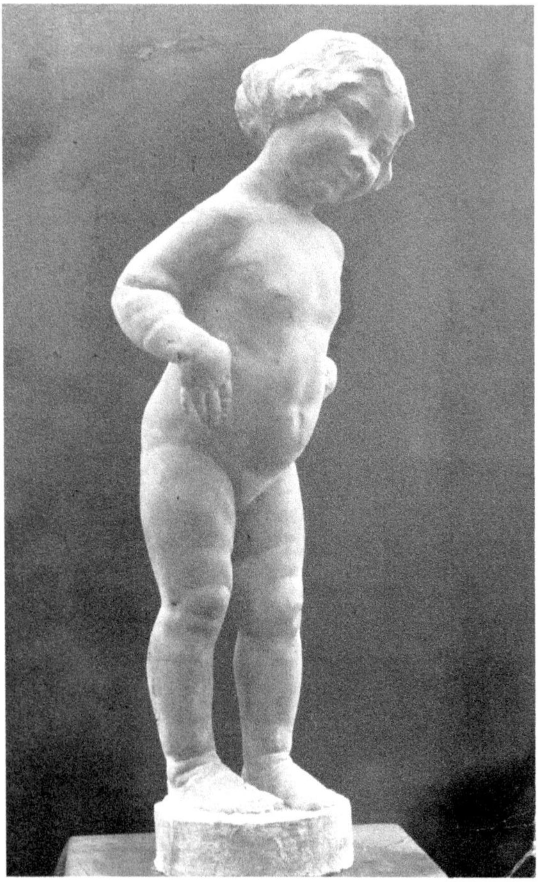

51. Anne Acheson, *Sally*, 1923

having established a fashion with her lead statues of a patron's child or children at the toddler stage, the novelty of capturing the fleeting nature of childhood being particularly emphasized. It was also noted that lead was an ideal medium for garden sculpture since 'its soft, neutral tone merges simply and naturally into the background created by homely English flowers'.[73] In an article published in the *Daily Telegraph* in the late 1920s the popularity of garden statues of children was described as being at its peak. But the author deplored the trend for lesser artists 'hopping on to the Anne Acheson bandwagon'.[74] However, by the late 1920s Acheson was having financial difficulties and her biographer referred to a welcome cheque for £225 for four figures going to America. She also received a commission from the King's School, Worcester, whose headmaster wanted to create a garden in memory of his wife who had died in 1923. Architectural theorist Hope Bagenal designed the garden and Acheson was asked for a suitable figure to sit above a fountain. The school is on the banks of the River Severn and in 1930 Acheson created a figure titled *Sabrina,* the Latin name for the Severn, to represent the mythological goddess or spirit of the river (**Figure 52**).[75] She was still showing lead garden statues at the Royal Academy as well as the Society of Women Artists, but people were generally short of money and Acheson turned again to teaching. In 1938 she won the Feodora Gleichen Award for her lead garden figure *The Thief,* judged to be the best work by a female artist at the Royal Academy that year. She exhibited other fountain figures at the Academy in 1939 and at the Royal Scottish Academy after the interruption of the war. She then left London to return to live in Antrim, Northern Ireland.

It seems that Acheson established a very particular and pragmatic system for obtaining commissions. 'Photographs of different figures would be sent to the potential client, who, if interested, would then be asked for their preferred medium, lead or bronze in the case of the garden figures – after the war Anne added Portland Stone to her portfolio.'[76] Obituaries were full of praise, with *The Times* describing her as accomplished and as producing decorative lead garden figures which were far superior to the prevalence of 'so many monstrosities in terra cotta' that adorned suburban gardens.[77]

Elizabeth Muntz showed with the London Group, including at their Open-Air Sculpture exhibition on Selfridge's roof garden in 1930, where her *Child with a Fawn* (1925–27) was selected for praise (**Figure 20**).[78] This piece had been shown at the Warren Gallery in 1928, attracting praise from Kineton Parkes.[79] Muntz's work varied across the different genres in which she worked, and a much later reviewer wondered whether it was necessary for artists to have a recognizable 'handwriting':

> As with all such questions, one can only attempt an answer in relation to some aim, in some context. Here the most meaningful context would appear to be that of worldly success. One has only to think for a moment of the work of Barbara Hepworth or Henry Moore to see immediately how much a clearly recognisable 'handwriting' has contributed towards recognition and worldwide fame. But what happens if they are asked for architectural work? It has to be, in the one case, a standing form usually pierced, in the other, a seated or reclining form sometimes dismembered. Miss Muntz obviously would never have allowed herself to be subject to such limitations. So she has always had to find what she felt to be just the right approach to each job, to each subject, to each material. This may well be a reason for her work not being as widely known as one would expect.

This perceptive analysis might well be applied to many of the sculptors in this book. The reviewer first quoted Muntz: '"I don't like sculpture which teases the imagination. I can't say I was fond of Epstein"', and then continued:

> The first remark is quite in character, and there must surely be many who will go along with it. But as for Epstein – well, at least one visitor to the exhibition felt the influence of Epstein there, though not as a dominant note. Could Miss Muntz have picked up something unconsciously? Their careers did overlap for a considerable number of years.[80]

An obituary in *The Times* recalled Muntz's first 1928 exhibition at the Warren Gallery, where she exhibited 21 pieces, and particularly focused on her *Reclining Torso* in yellow Mansfield stone (**Figure 21**). Here the influence of Frank Dobson was described in a positive vein, in contrast to the earlier 1926 *Apollo* review. Although it was a carving, the reviewer suggested that Muntz was more naturally a modeller for casting in bronze, and that after the 1920s she went on to produce many interesting things in this and other metals. The *Times* obituary described her work as based on architectural principles, showing a strong sense of construction, and so it was unsurprising that she was popular with architects.[81]

In 1928 Kathleen Scott took part in an exhibition held in the Storey Institute which had been assembled by the Museums Association for circulation to art galleries across the country, and which showed the work of about 70 sculptors. Scott spoke at the opening in Lancaster

52. Anne Acheson, *Sabrina*, 1930

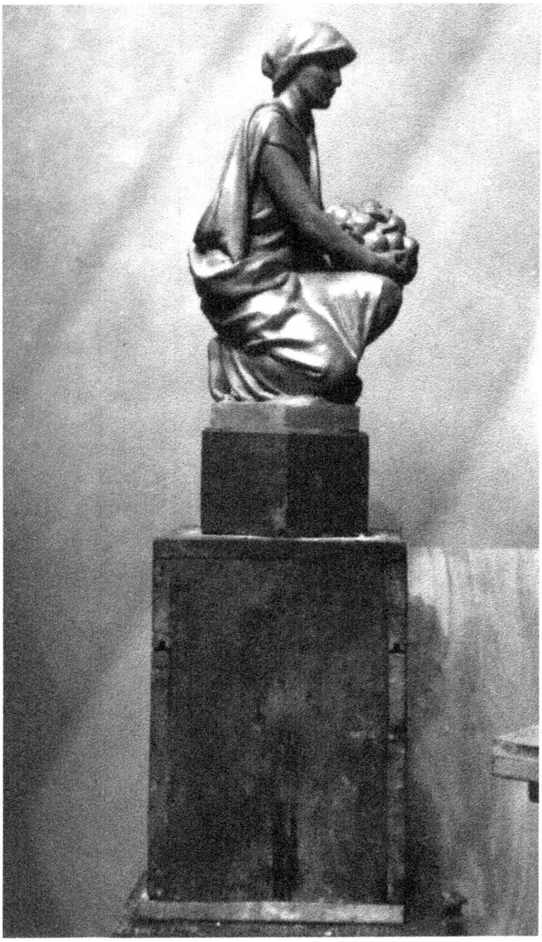

on 20 June 1928. Noting people's preference for a painted rather than sculpted portrait of their husband, wife or children, she suggested that such people believed that a bust was only appropriate if the subject were dead. She deplored the fact that people did not pay attention to sculpture, and that on crowded days at the Royal Academy they 'only seemed to go into the sculpture rooms to sit down, because there was no room anywhere else'. She argued for the 'civilising effect of sculpture in the smallest house or in the garden', saying that 'it was astonishing how it would transform even a cat-run to have a really good bit of sculpture in it'. In her own London garden she displayed sculptures made from bronze, marble and stone, which particularly animated the space in winter. She

advocated that people choose sculpture according to their own taste; they should contact a sculptor directly if they saw their work and wanted something similar – 'they ... should tell him what they wanted, just as they would tell a dressmaker what they wanted'.[82] In November 1934 *Country Life* contained a lengthy article on Scott's decorative sculpture, stating that the best setting for sculpture was generally in the open air. Whether free-standing or as part of architectural decoration, outdoor lighting gave it 'nobility' and emphasized 'its monumental character'. The writer noted the popularity among sculptors of direct carving, preferably carried out in the sculpture's intended location. Stone was acknowledged as the most appropriate material for architectural decoration; however, the writer pointed out that metal also worked well for decorative outdoor work. Shown in the photographs accompanying the article was Scott's *The Kingdom is Within* (1925–26) (**Figure 2**), here recommended as a figure to be set out of doors and whose 'solemn impressiveness would be increased if seen against a wall at the end of an alley'.[83]

As has been seen, the involvement of female sculptors in work that merged sculpture with what might be regarded as design artefacts was quite considerable. Diversifying into decorative objects for gardens also widened the appeal of these works with the buying public, and it is significant that this was achieved while retaining critical approval in the art and design press. For example, in a 1924 *Studio* article the writer was optimistic that the public were warming to sculpture as a decorative art.[84] The final section of this chapter will return full circle to the legacy of the statuette, in the form of a series of exhibitions towards the end of the period covered by this book which were instigated at the highest level as part of an official drive to encourage the production and consumption of sculpture for the domestic environment.

4.3 *Sculpture in the Home*: modernizing the domestic environment

Clearly the statuette and sculptural utilitarian objects for the home and garden remained popular well into the twentieth century. After the Second World War the *Sculpture in the Home* exhibitions made this trend official, for example through the involvement of the Arts Council of Great Britain, while at the same time marking the end of this overt focus on the placement of fine art and decorative sculpture within the domestic environment. Despite the fact that the home as a site for sculptural display was no longer an unusual idea, tensions remained, particularly reprising the debates raised in the late nineteenth century about the relationship between the statuette and mass production. The issue of 'quality control' seemed particularly acute when conceiving of sculpture for domestic display, and it was in the context of these concerns that the series of *Sculpture in the Home* exhibitions developed. Their intended outcome was to introduce high-quality sculpture into such settings and thus mount a challenge to the modernist argument that the two were incompatible. Producing small-scale work was also a practical solution for sculptors suffering from a lack of studio space and materials during and after the Second World War. As was the case with earlier statuettes, making work for the *Sculpture in the Home* exhibitions also gave them an opportunity to produce small pieces that could essentially be maquettes for imagined larger works, would be relatively cheap to make, and if popular could be reproduced in bronze in a range of sizes. The aims of the *Sculpture in the Home* exhibitions can also be seen as continuing the broad democratizing aspirations of the Arts and Crafts movement.

In October 1945 the first *Sculpture in the Home* exhibition was opened in the Mansard Gallery at Heal's department store by Sir Eric Maclagan, former director of the Victoria and Albert Museum. On display were over one hundred works. The Arts Council contributed to the cost and this first exhibition was organized by the Artists' International Association (AIA). Sculptors were invited to engage with an exhibition that would display work accompanied by photographs demonstrating how it could be employed in everyday life in an architectural setting. The initial plan, to utilize photographs rather than furniture as a means of envisioning how sculptures might be placed in the home, was modified when the venue changed from the John Lewis department store on Oxford Street to the Mansard Gallery. The idea of an actual reconstructed interior was quickly adopted; since the gallery was owned by a department store specializing in furniture, this was a logical adjustment. Moreover, displaying sculpture in the context of furniture and textiles had a precedent. In the 1930s the department store Whiteley's of Bayswater and the interior-design studio Duncan Miller had promoted the sale of abstract sculpture by artists such as Hepworth, and this probably confirmed for the AIA that Heal's would be a suitable venue.[85] A department store was seen as a less intimidating venue for an exhibition than a private gallery, although Heal's staff were given a briefing on sculpture before the exhibition opened. Because of the war, exhibiting spaces were makeshift, and as Heal's customers were the middle classes the exhibition organizers had a ready-established audience.

Works for the *Sculpture in the Home* exhibitions had to be affordable (although they cost at least the equivalent of a week's wage), but not so cheap as to undermine the attraction of acquiring a unique piece. The use of materials such as wood, terracotta, stone, plaster and cement kept prices down, and the display of unconvential materials such as cement alongside bronze and stone was also intended to educate viewers on contemporary artistic developments. Support from the newly formed Arts Council of Great Britain demonstrated a degree of backing from the government for the artists and the work of the AIA. It also related to the national post-war agenda: the plan had been for the Arts Council to oversee the exhibition after the display at Heal's and be responsible for touring it around the country. However, this did not happen until the following year, when the exhibition was under the curatorial control of Frank Dobson. Whereas during wartime the focus of the state had been on the arts as a form of entertainment, after the war the emphasis shifted on to the individual artist and the support of new art. In this way the Arts Council's involvement with *Sculpture in the Home* was in line with national policy.[86]

In the catalogue for the first exhibition in 1945, Trevor Tennant wrote that the aim of the AIA in arranging the exhibition had been to lay before the public a high standard of contemporary sculpture in the intimacy of a domestic context rather than in the conventional setting of a gallery. A footnote expanded on this point, revisiting a familiar argument:

> During the last few years there has been a great advance in the understanding and the appreciation of all kinds of painting, but sculpture still lags behind. Many people who are interested in painting fail to appreciate the qualities of three-dimensional form and design obtained in sculpture, which has the advantage that it may be looked at from many points of view.

The fact that visitors moved among furniture rather than plinths would have created a homely setting, producing a different physical and visual relationship with the sculptures than would pertain in a gallery context.[87] It was hoped that the exhibition would help to draw the attention of 'the man in the street' to the aesthetic and decorative value of sculpture in the home. Among the works on display were bronze pieces by Dora Gordine, including her portrait of an anonymous child made in Paris, *Head of a Girl with Pigtails/Girlhood* (c.1926–28) (**Figure 53**). Several other women discussed in this book such as Barbara Hepworth and Mary Spencer Watson also had work

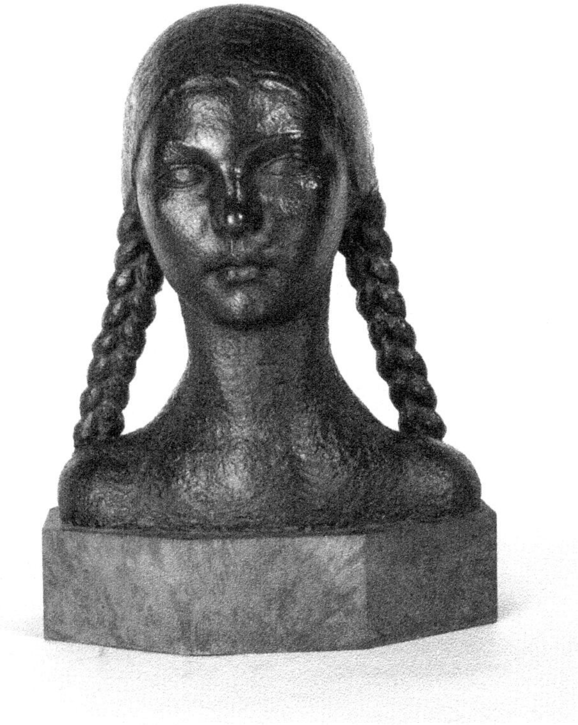

53. Dora Gordine, *Head of a Girl with Pigtails/Girlhood*, c.1926–28

on display, and sculptors Daphne Hardy and Elizabeth Spurr were members of the sculpture committee.

Attendance at the 1945 exhibition was far more than expected, with as many as 4,000–5,000 visitors; however, this did not translate into the hoped-for level of sales, apparently reflecting the current weak retail sector for modern domestic furnishings. It is a confusing picture of public interest, since attendance at the Council of Industrial Design's *Britain Can Make It* exhibition of 1946 at the Victoria and Albert Museum totalled one and a half million. Instigated by Sir Stafford Cripps at the Board of Trade after the new Labour government came into power, the displays of furnished rooms were particularly popular. The 1951 Festival of Britain was also highly successful, attracting eight and a half million visitors. However, rather than widening the buying public, many purchasers of sculpture at the Festival were local authorities and established collectors. Interestingly about a third of the private buyers were women, both single and married, although this may have merely been a reflection of their accepted role as the principal consumers of domestic items. The sculptures that sold were generally smaller and less expensive, costing roughly £20–£50.

The 1946 *Sculpture in the Home* exhibition repeated the display of sculptures in relation to modern furniture, with works being selected by Frank Dobson, who also wrote the catalogue introduction. Unfortunately he quoted the thoughts of Roger Fry on sculpture, that 'it would seem that all good sculpture would at first have to appear a little dull'. Dobson however, hoped that viewers of the *Sculpture in the Home* exhibition, if they exercised 'a little patience', would discover through the sculpture on display 'a world of calm delight'.[88] It was felt that having a sculptor curate the show would help make the displays more accessible to both the public and the collector, and additionally give the sculptures a stamp of approval. This was essentially the first step towards bringing the sculptor 'out into the open' that would culminate in the series of open-air exhibitions of sculpture in Battersea Park, which commenced in 1948 and where sculptors sat on the organizing committees. Both series of exhibitions showed that sculpture did not necessarily have to be commemorative or architectural.

The majority of the works displayed at the *Sculpture in the Home* exhibitions were by contemporary artists, but a few earlier works were also shown so as to establish a sculptural lineage. About a third of the works on display in 1946 had been shown in the 1945 exhibition, and again Dora Gordine was included, as well as Hepworth and Spurr. The 1950 exhibition also continued the theme of displaying sculpture in relation to furnishings, with Gordine, Hetherington, Karin Jonzen, Spurr and Hepworth all showing work. It is possible to interpret this promotion of a viable domestic form of sculpture as a continuation by the English interwar avant-garde of the reformist drive of the Arts and Crafts movement. The type of modernism espoused by critics such as Herbert Read supported a bringing together of the supposedly 'fine' and 'industrial' arts in order to attempt a recreation of the imagined harmonious community of the Middle Ages.[89]

Although the 1958 *Sculpture in the Home* exhibition falls well outside the timeframe for this book it is worth a brief mention, since the catalogue text referred back to the position of sculpture in Britain throughout the period of this series of exhibitions. It was noted that when the 1946 show reached the provincial galleries, collectors were far less likely to buy sculpture for their homes than paintings or drawings. However, it was claimed that the intervening sculpture exhibitions had definitely had an impact and accustomed people to the idea of sculpture for the home.[90] This was important, since one of the founding principles of the Arts Council had been to facilitate an expansion of the buying public,[91] inadvertently echoing the idealism of the Arts and Crafts movement. Many female sculptors were included in these exhibitions: in 1945 they amounted to nearly half of the exhibitors and in subsequent exhibitions they comprised between a third and a fifth of the total numbers. Overall the sculptures were broadly figurative and modernist characteristics were low key, Hepworth being a notable exception. Subjects tended to be religious, allegorical or mythological, or were generally commemorative in nature. Domesticity was a strong theme, with several studies of women, children, family groups, pets and indigenous animals and birds.[92] The sculptures were mostly between 12 and 15 inches high, and in size and subject matter, therefore, were not dissimilar to the turn-of-the-century statuette.

However, as with earlier attempts to promote the statuette as 'sculpture for the home', these post-war efforts did not popularize sculpture for the simple reason that the work was too expensive for most people. Critics were generally positive, but the exhibitions did not ignite the passions that would be evident on the subject of public sculpture. On the other hand, they did give a large number of sculptors good opportunities to exhibit at a time when this was not easy, especially for women.[93]

Notes

1 Christopher Reed (ed.), (introduction), *Not at Home. The Suppression of Domesticity in Modern Art and Architecture* (London: Thames and Hudson, 1996), p. 7.
2 Droth, *The Statuette and the Role of the Ornamental*, pp. 24–26.
3 Penny Tinkler, 'Women and popular literature', in June Purvis (ed.), *Women's History: Britain, 1850–1945* (London: Routledge, 1995), p. 131.
4 Letter from W. Hamo Thornycroft to Agatha Cox, 13 November 1993. Thornycroft Papers, Henry Moore Institute Archives, Leeds, Tii-C-T(H)91), quoted in David J. Getsy, 'Sculpture in the home: the cult of the statuette in late Victorian Britain', in Martina Droth, Jason Edwards, David J. Getsy and Matthew Withey, *The Cult of the Statuette in Late Victorian Britain* (Leeds: Henry Moore Institute, 2000), p. 3.
5 *The Studio*, 6 (January 1896), p. 205, quoted in Beattie, *The New Sculpture*, pp. 195–96.
6 Meredith Moore, 'The struggles of New Sculpture', 08 EL 156/HA 152, *Romans in Togas: Classicism and Empire in Victorian Literature and Art*, Brown University, http://www.victorianweb.org/sculpture/levick/moore.html (accessed 25 November 2019).
7 'The National Competition', *The Studio*, 11 (1897), p. 248.
8 H. B. Creswell, 'A new scheme of arrangement for sculpture galleries', *Architectural Review*, 8 (1900), p. 206, quoted in Droth, 'Conditions of display 1900–25', pp. 50–51.
9 *First Exhibition of Statuettes by the Sculptors of Today – British and French* (London: Fine Art Society, 1902), quoted in Droth, 'Conditions of display 1900–25', pp. 51–52.
10 Droth, 'Conditions of display 1900–25', p. 52.
11 Spielmann, *British Sculpture and Sculptors of To-Day*, p. 9.
12 Edmund Gosse, 'The place of sculpture in daily life', *Magazine of Art*, 1895, p. 329, quoted in Stocker, 'Edmund Gosse on sculpture', p. 307.
13 Droth, *The Statuette and the Role of the Ornamental*, pp. 30–33.
14 'The Arts and Crafts Exhibition, 1893', *The Studio*, I (1893); George P. Landow, *Margaret M. Giles's Hero and the Sublime Female Nude: Introduction*, http://www.victorianweb.org/sculpture/giles/hero.html (accessed 25 November 2019).
15 George P. Landow, *Giles's Hero in the Context of Contemporary Women Sculptors*, www.victorianweb.org/sculpture/giles/hero3.html (accessed 25 November 2019).
16 Beattie, *The New Sculpture*, p. 198.
17 Beattie, *The New Sculpture*, biographical notes, p. 246.
18 Spielmann, *British Sculpture and Sculptors of To-Day*, p. 162.
19 T. Martin Wood, 'A decorative sculptor: Miss Ruby Levick: (Mrs. Gervaise Bailey)', *The Studio*, 34 (1905), pp. 100–07.
20 Linda Clifford, *Sculptor: Josefina de Vasconcellos* (Linda Clifford, 2000), p. 15.
21 Margaret Lewis, *Josefina de Vasconcellos: Her Life and Art* (Hexham: Flambard Press, 2004), pp. 92–93.
22 Parkes, *Sculpture of To-Day*, p. 129.

23 Letter from Edith Downing to National Museum of Wales, 16 December 1928(?). Edith Downing file, Archives, National Museum of Wales, Cardiff.
24 Letter from the Keeper, National Museum of Wales to Edith Downing, 18 January 1929. Edith Downing file, Archives, National Museum of Wales, Cardiff.
25 Terry Cavanagh, *Public Sculpture of South London* (Liverpool: Liverpool University Press and Public Monuments and Sculpture Association, 2007), p. 447.
26 Marchal, *Finding Frances*, p. 92.
27 Ann Compton, *Facing the Future: Sculpture from the Harrogate Collection* (Harrogate: The Mercer Art Gallery, 2014), p. 83.
28 Marchal, *Finding Frances*, p. 116.
29 Marchal, *Finding Frances*, p. 118.
30 Spielmann, *British Sculpture and Sculptors of To-Day*, pp. 162–63.
31 1926 file note, Lucy Gwendolen Williams file, Archives, National Museum of Art, Cardiff.
32 http://collections vam.ac.uk, Museum no. A.5-2009.
33 Joseph McBrinn, *Sophia Rosamond Praeger, 1867–1954, Art, Literature, Science*, The Naughton Gallery, Queen's University, Belfast, 29 June–18 August 2007 (Belfast: The Naughton Gallery, 2007), p. 16.
34 Catherine Gaynor, 'An Ulster sculptor: Sophia Rosamond Praeger (1867–1954), *Irish Arts Review* (2000), p. 36.
35 'Here is Eve in Plaster', publication unknown, 30 December 1946. Wolverhampton City Art Gallery.
36 Joan Weedon, 'Gwynneth Holt R.B.S. An Appreciation', *Eynsham Record*, 14 (1997), pp. 33–37, issuu.com > eynshamrecord > docs > eynsham_record_1997 (accessed 12 February 2020).
37 Holt quoted in *The Aberdeen Bonn Accord*. Essex Record Office, Chelmsford, papers relating to Thomas Huxley-Jones and Gwynneth Holt, n.d.
38 Carson I. A. Ritchie, *Modern Ivory Carving* (New York/London: A. S. Barnes and Company/Thomas Yoseloff, 1972), pp. 13–14.
39 Kenneth Romney Towndrow, 'Small sculpture in the home', *The Studio*, 134.654 (September 1947), p. 58.
40 Marchal, *Finding Frances*, p. 169.
41 Mark Stocker, '"Young male objects": the ideal sculpture of Kathleen Scott', *Sculpture Journal*, 22.2 (2013), pp. 119–27. S. Reynolds, *Paris–Edinburgh: Cultural Connections in the Belle Époque* (Farnham: Ashgate, 2007), p. 70; A. Garrihy, 'Scott, Kathleen', in D. Gaze (ed.), *Dictionary of Women Artists*, vol. II (Chicago: Fitzroy Dearborn, 1997), p. 1253.
42 Louisa Young, *A Great Task of Happiness: The Life of Kathleen Scott* (London: Macmillan, 1995), p. 28.
43 'Sculptor and Traveller', *Review of Reviews*, November 1922.
44 Young, *A Great Task of Happiness*, p. 218.
45 'From a woman's notebook: Lady Scott', *Manchester Evening News*, 22 April 1927. University of Cambridge Manuscripts Library, GB/NNAF/P 162494, NCUACS 87.8.99.167/1, Press Cuttings. Scott valued the admiration of artists whom she respected. These included Charles Sergeant Jagger, William Reid Dick, Sir Charles Wheeler, Glyn Philpot, Wallace Wood and Eric Gill.

46 Stocker, '"My masculine models"', p. 49.
47 Young, *A Great Task of Happiness*, p. 236.
48 'A new bust of the king?', *Evening* Star (n.d., probably early 1935). University of Cambridge Manuscripts Library, GB/NNAF/P 162494, NCUACS 87.8.99.167/1, Press Cuttings.
49 Letter from T. E. Lawrence to Kathleen Scott, 2 February 1921. University of Cambridge Manuscripts Library, GB/NNAF/P 162494, NCUACS 87.8.99, Kennet Manuscripts, E-H, K. Letters. Kennet 131/1–12. T. E. Lawrence. 131/1. Reproduced by kind permission of the Syndics of Cambridge University Library and the Kennet family.
50 *Register of Sculpture by Kathleen Lady Kennet (Lady Scott) 1878–1947*, compiled by Lord Kennet, 1948, by permission of the Kennet family.
51 Nan Muirhead Moffat, *Round the Studios 1939: Portraits of Twelve Lady Artists at Work* (1939). Archives of National Gallery of Modern Art Two, Edinburgh.
52 Getsy, 'Sculpture in the home', p. 4.
53 William Morris, preface, in Arts and Crafts Exhibition Society, *Arts and Crafts Essays by Members of the Arts and Crafts Exhibition Society* (Rivington: Percival and Co., 1893), p. vi.
54 John Ruskin, article in *The Gardener's Chronicle*, 29 November 1890.
55 John Dando Sedding, *Garden Craft Old and New* (London: Kegan Paul, 1895).
56 E. S. Prior, 'Garden Making', *The Studio*, 21 (1901), p. 88.
57 *The Studio Yearbook of Decorative Art: A Guide to the Artistic Decoration and Furnishing of the House* (1906), pp. 266–70.
58 Wood, 'A decorative sculptor: Miss Ruby Levick', pp. 100–07.
59 'Arts and Crafts', *The Studio*, 18 (1899), p. 260.
60 *Hutchinson's Arts & Crafts Magazine, A Practical Magazine for the Studio, The Workshop and the Home*, 102 (1904), n.p.
61 Marchal, *Finding Frances*, p. 120.
62 Parkes, *The Art of Carved Sculpture*, pp. 123–24.
63 Padaruth Raksha, *The use of ceramics as an aesthetic element in Durban architecture (1914–2012)*, 2013. http://hdl.handle.net/10321/945, p. 55 (accessed 12 February 2020).
64 Andrew Stephenson, 'Conditions of display 1925–50', in Henry Moore Institute, *Sculpture in 20th Century Britain: Identity, Infrastructures, Aesthetics, Display, Reception* (Leeds: Henry Moore Institute, 2003), vol. 1, p. 115.
65 Parkes, *The Art of Carved Sculpture*, p. 104.
66 Parkes, *The Art of Carved Sculpture*, pp. 87–88.
67 'Gardens', *Leeds Mercury*, 16 October 1928, n.p. University of Cambridge Manuscripts Library, GB/NNAF/P 162494, NCUACS 87.8.99.167/1, Press Cuttings.
68 In 1940 she was made a Fellow of the Royal Society of Arts. In 1944 the Maltwoods purchased The Royal Oak Inn and renamed it The Thatch, turning it into a spacious country home, well suited to displaying their art treasures and with a studio for Katharine on an upper floor. She was a patron for local artists, especially Emily Carr. The Maltwood's collection, including Katharine's sculptures, was bequeathed to the University of Victoria in 1977.
69 C. B. Gray, 'The lead tradition in gardens', *Landscape and Garden*, January 1939, p. 171.

70 *Groundbreakers – Anne Acheson: The Art of Medicine*, Morrow Communications and Clean Slate Television production for BBC Northern Ireland, broadcast 4 November 2018; *Anne Acheson: A Sculptor in War and Peace*, Craigavon Museum Services, Millennium Court Arts Centre, Portadown, 5 April–8 May 2019, including Pauline Rose, 'How to be a Woman Sculptor'.
71 Marian Cran, 'Lead garden figures', *The Queen*, 9 August 1923, p. 65.
72 David Llewellyn, *The First Lady of Mulberry Walk: The Life and Times of Irish Sculptress Anne Acheson* (Leicester: Matador, 2010), p. 83.
73 Margot Hirons, 'The art of Anne Acheson – adorning the family garden with lead and bronze statuary', *The Lady*, 11 August 1927, p. 165.
74 Llewellyn, *The First Lady of Mulberry Walk*, p. 85.
75 Llewellyn, *The First Lady of Mulberry Walk*, p. 99.
76 Llewellyn, *The First Lady of Mulberry Walk*, pp. 183–86.
77 Llewellyn, *The First Lady of Mulberry Walk*, p. 212.
78 'Art exhibition. Open-air sculpture', *The Times*, July 1930: exact date and page unknown. Elizabeth Muntz Archive, Dorset History Centre.
79 Parkes, *The Art of Carved Sculpture*, pp. 103–04.
80 L.M., 'The work of Elizabeth Muntz: Dorset County Library', *Stone Industries Magazine*, January/February 1972. Elizabeth Muntz Archive, Dorset History Centre.
81 'Miss Elizabeth Muntz', *The Times*, 2 April 1977, page unknown. Elizabeth Muntz Archive, Dorset History Centre.
82 'Sculpture in the home: Lady Hilton Young's plea. Decoration for house and garden', *Manchester Guardian*, 20 June 1928. University of Cambridge Manuscripts Library, GB/NNAF/P 162494, NCUACS 87.8.99.167/1, Press Cuttings.
83 'Sculpture for garden ornaments', *Country Life*, 8 November 1934. University of Cambridge Manuscripts Library, GB/NNAF/P 162494, NCUACS 87.8.99.167/1, Press Cuttings.
84 'S.B.W', 'Handicrafts at the Women Artists' Exhibition', *The Studio*, 15 April 1924, pp. 200–02.
85 Robert Burstow, *The Sculpture in the Home Exhibitions: Reconstructing the Home and Family in Post-War Britain* (Leeds: Henry Moore Institute, 2008), p. 5.
86 Clare Milligan, 'Sculpture in the Home: A Case Study for Post-war British Life, Culture and Aesthetics', MA dissertation, University of Leeds, 2003, pp. 15–17. The Henry Moore Institute Archives.
87 Milligan, 'Sculpture in the Home', pp. 15–17.
88 Frank Dobson, Introduction, *Sculpture in the Home – 1st Arts Council Exhibition, 1946*. The Henry Moore Institute Archives.
89 Robert Burstow, '"Sculpture in the Home": selling modernism to post-war British homemakers', *Sculpture Journal*, 17.2 (2008), p. 48.
90 Foreword, *Sculpture in the Home, 4th exhibition* (London: Arts Council of Great Britain, 1958). The Henry Moore Institute Archives.
91 Penny Sparke, 'Domesticity in post 1945 England and the role of Sculpture in the Home', paper given at the *Sculpture in the Home* study day, Henry Moore Institute, Leeds, 5 December 2008, HMI archives.
92 Burstow, *The Sculpture in the Home Exhibitions*, pp. 3–4.
93 Burstow, *The Sculpture in the Home Exhibitions*, pp. 12–13.

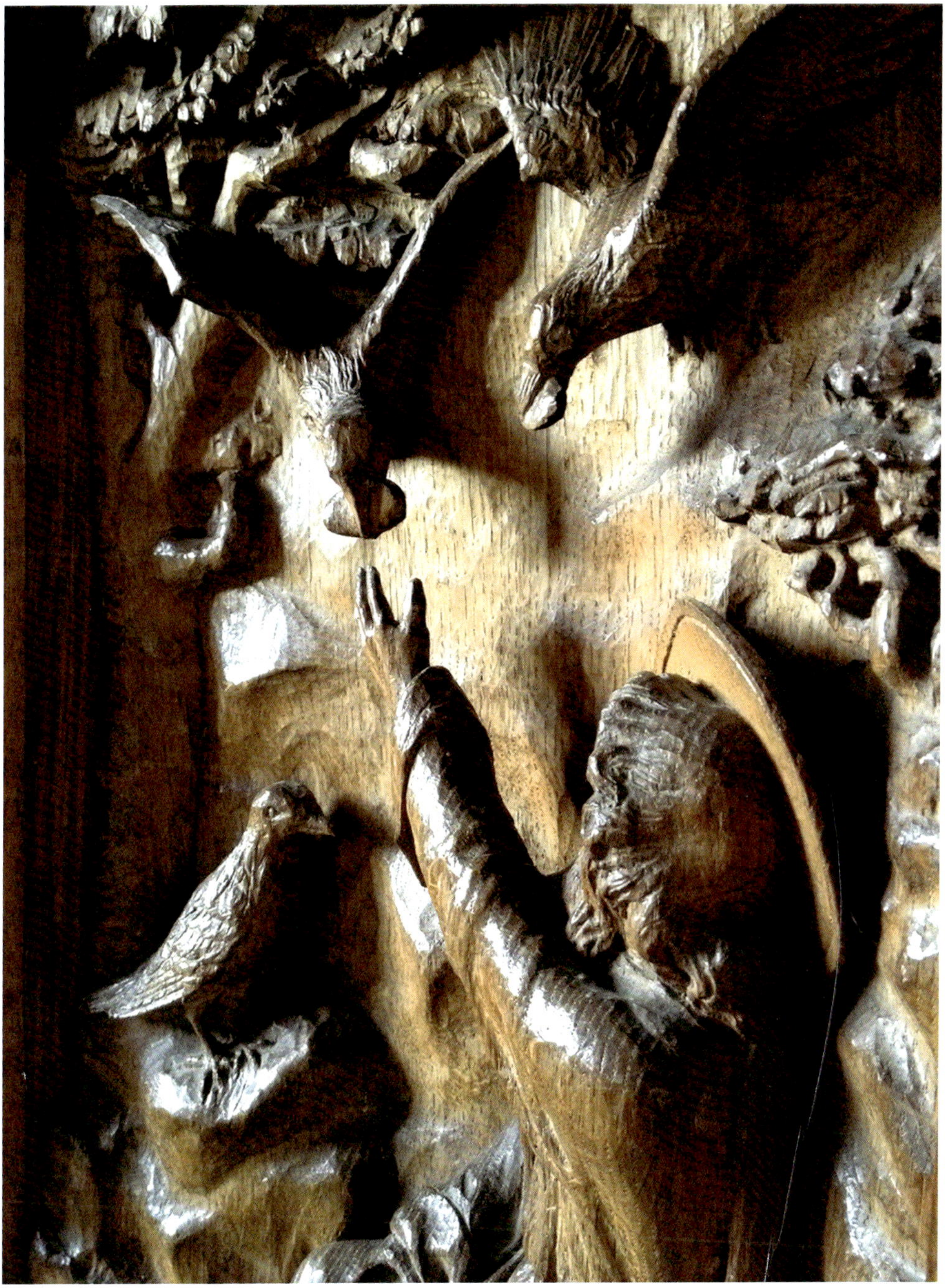

1. Violet Pinwill, pulpit, St Peter's Church, Stoke Fleming, detail, 1891

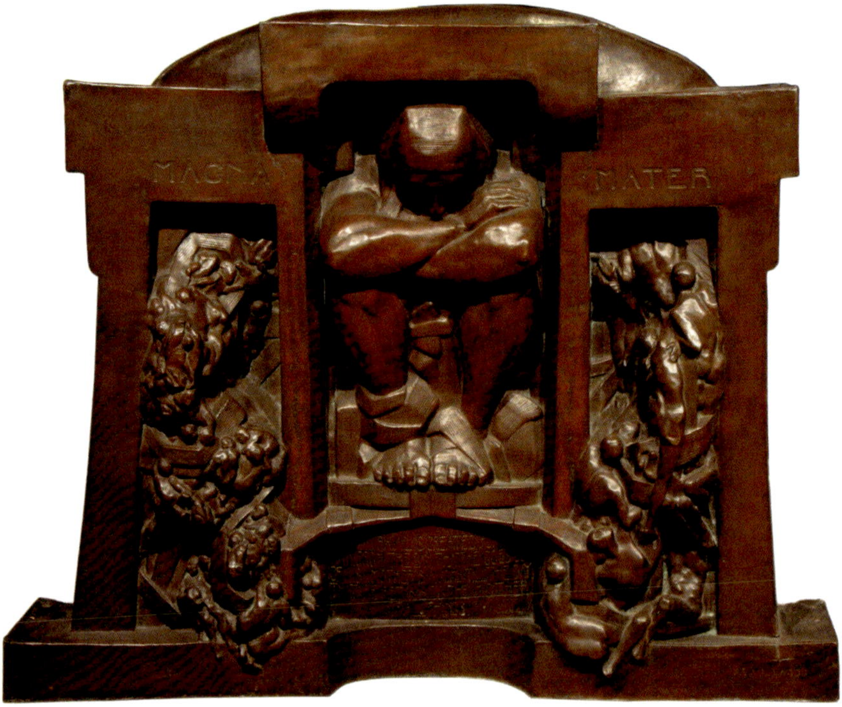

2. Katharine Maltwood,
Magna Mater, c.1910–11

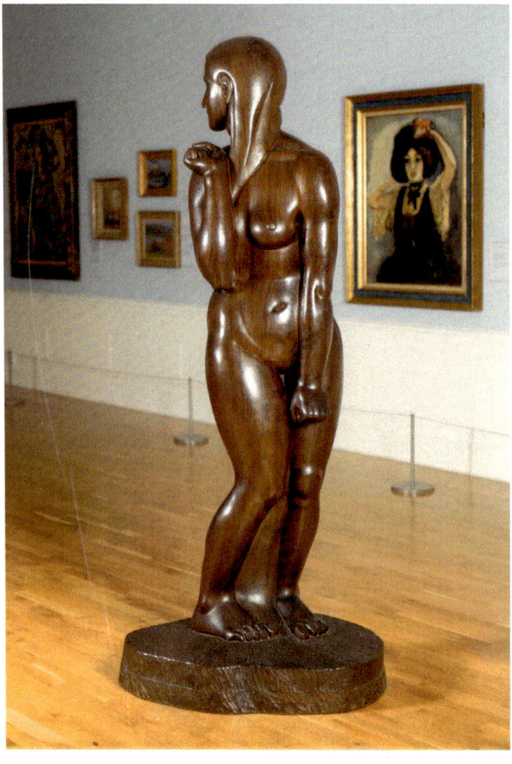

3. Edna Manley,
Eve-Ceremonial Dance, 1929

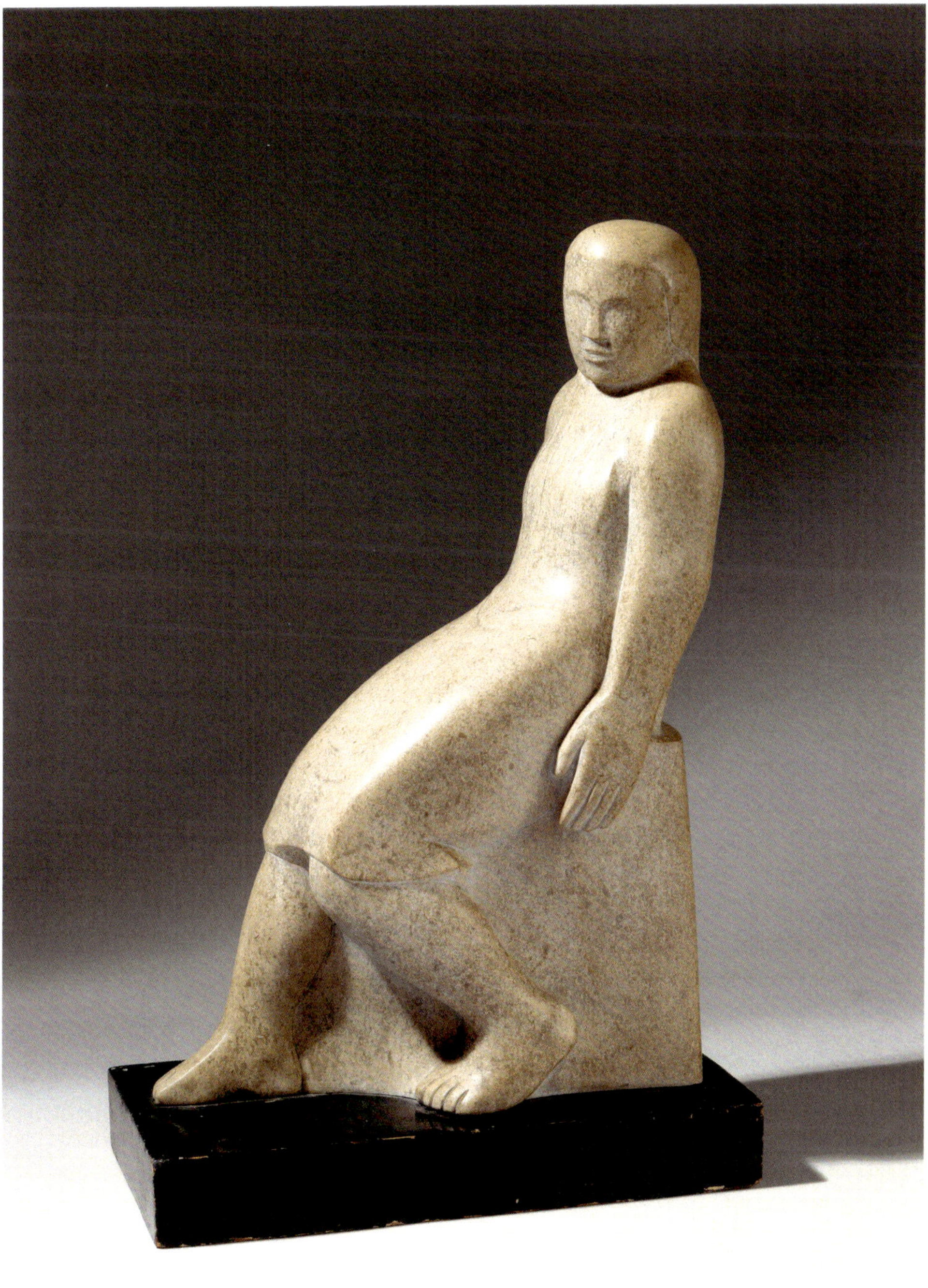

4. Ursula Edgcumbe, *Seated Female Figure*, 1931

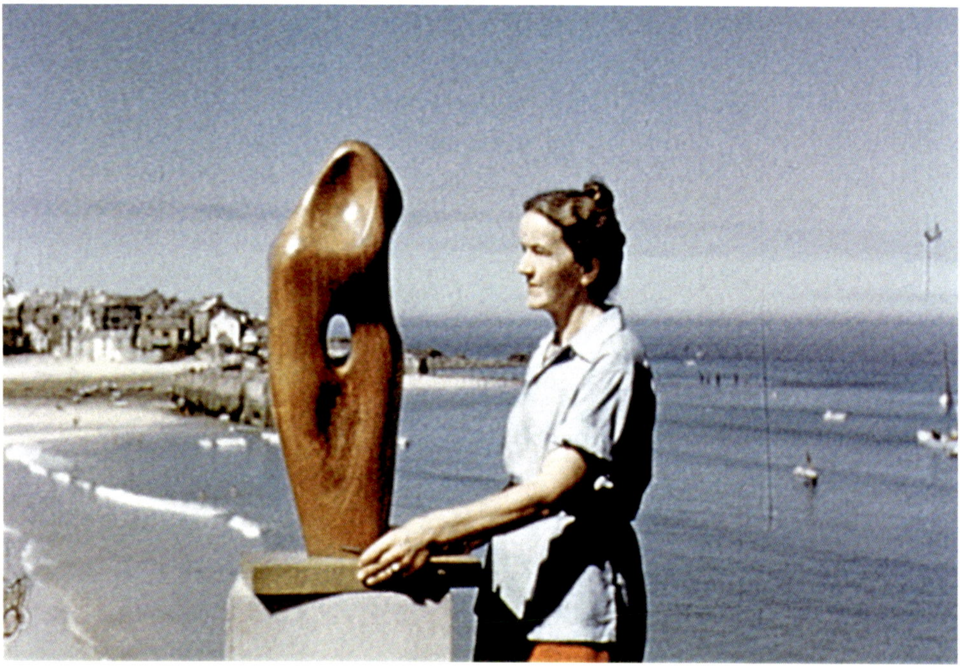

5. Still from *Figures in a Landscape*, 1953

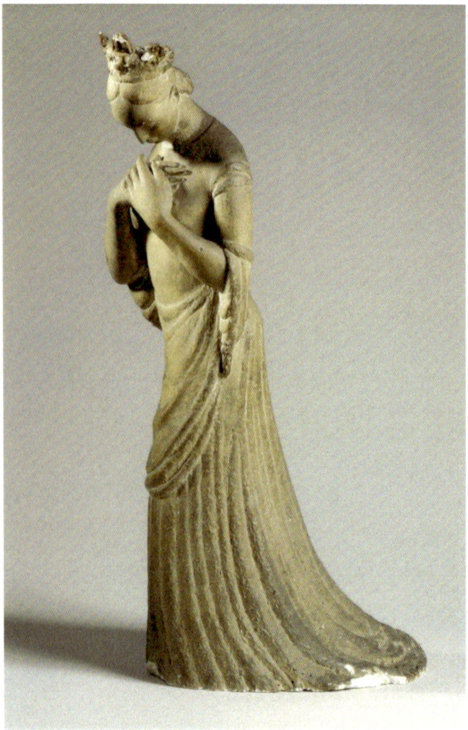

6. Jocelyn Horner, *Annunciation*, 1949

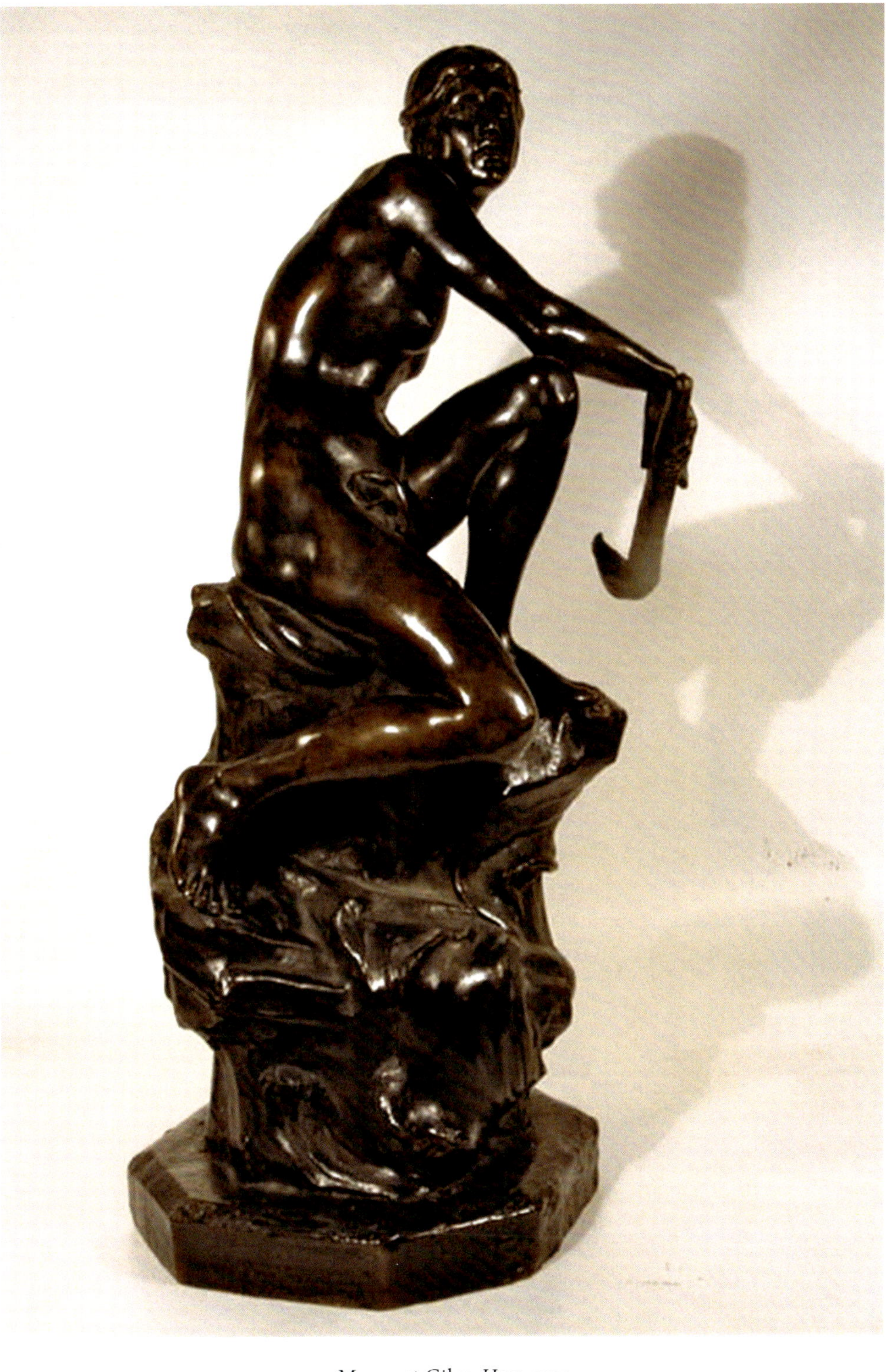

7. Margaret Giles, *Hero*, 1901

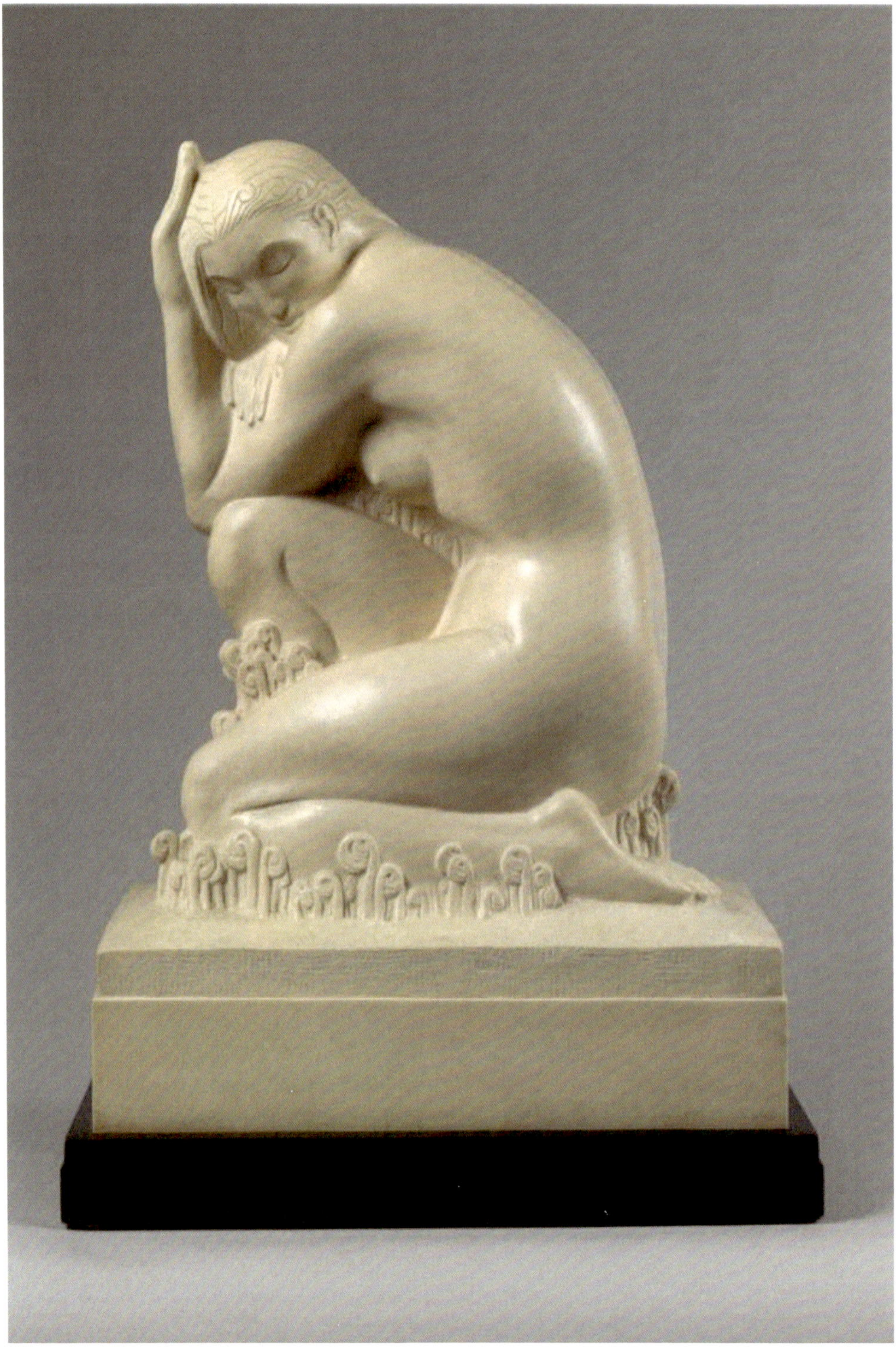

8. Joyce Bidder, *The Croziers of Spring*, 1934

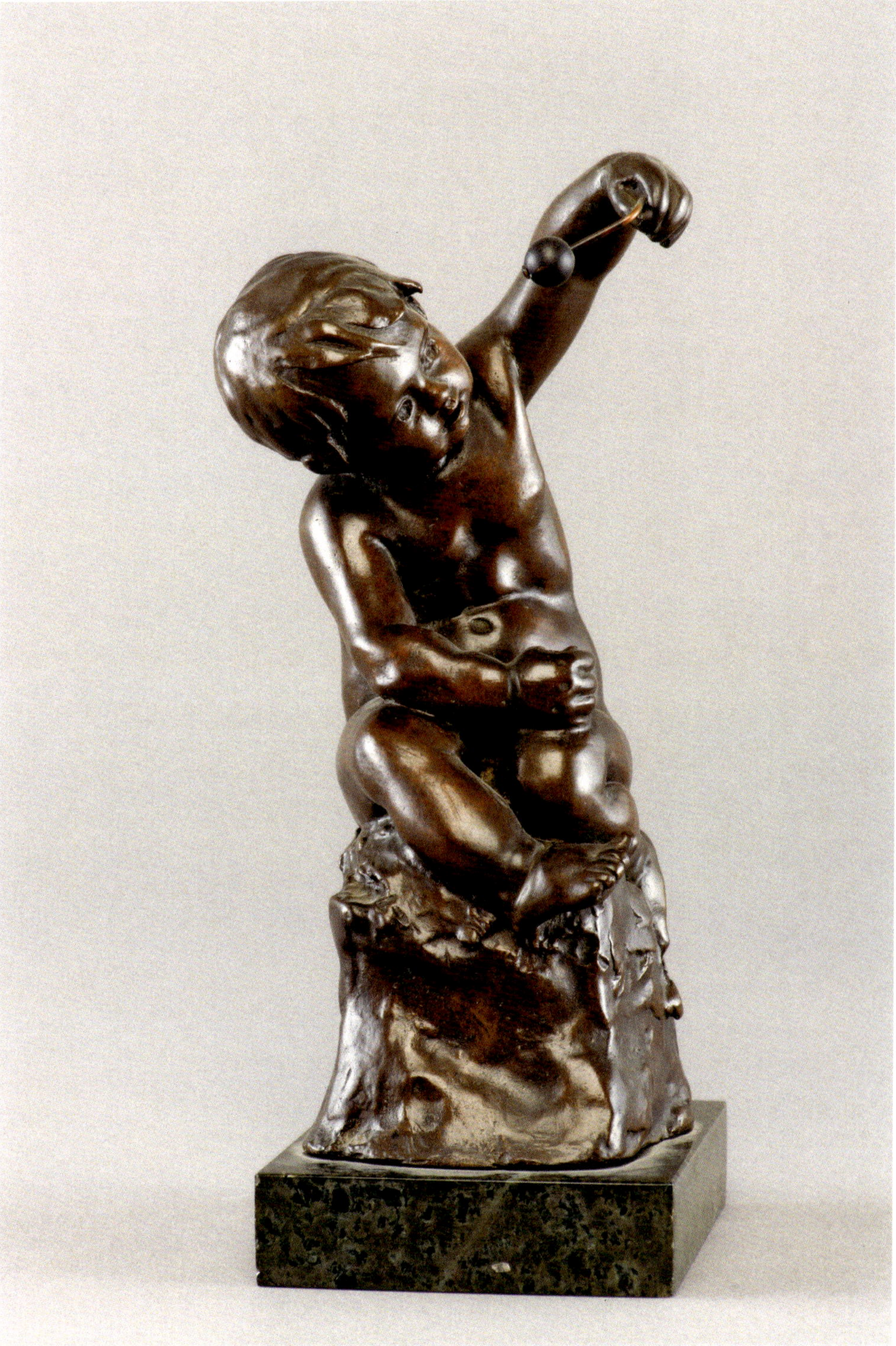

9. Edith Downing, *Boy with Cherry*, 1907

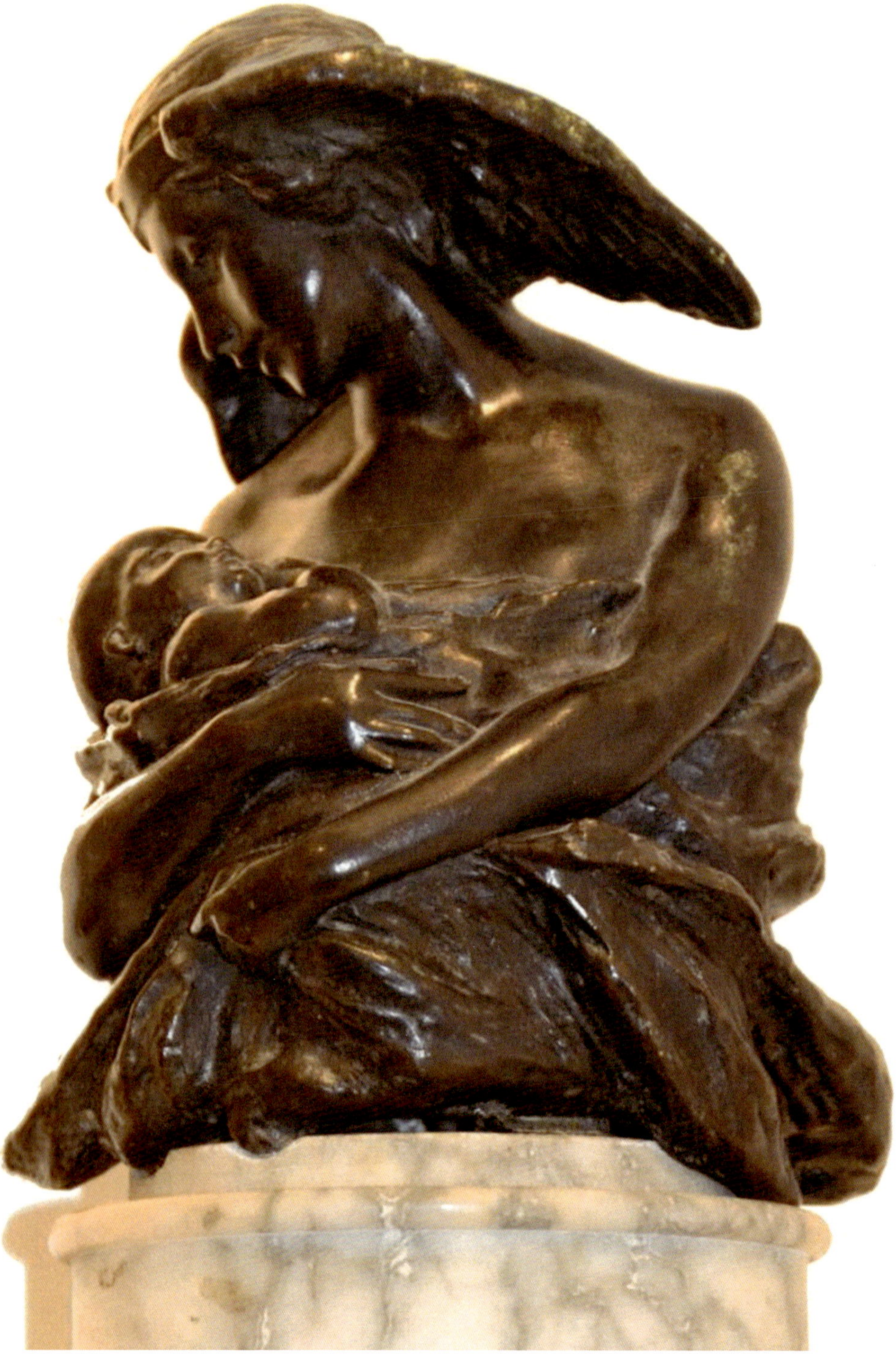

10. Lucy Gwendolen Williams, *Queen of Dreams*, 1905–06

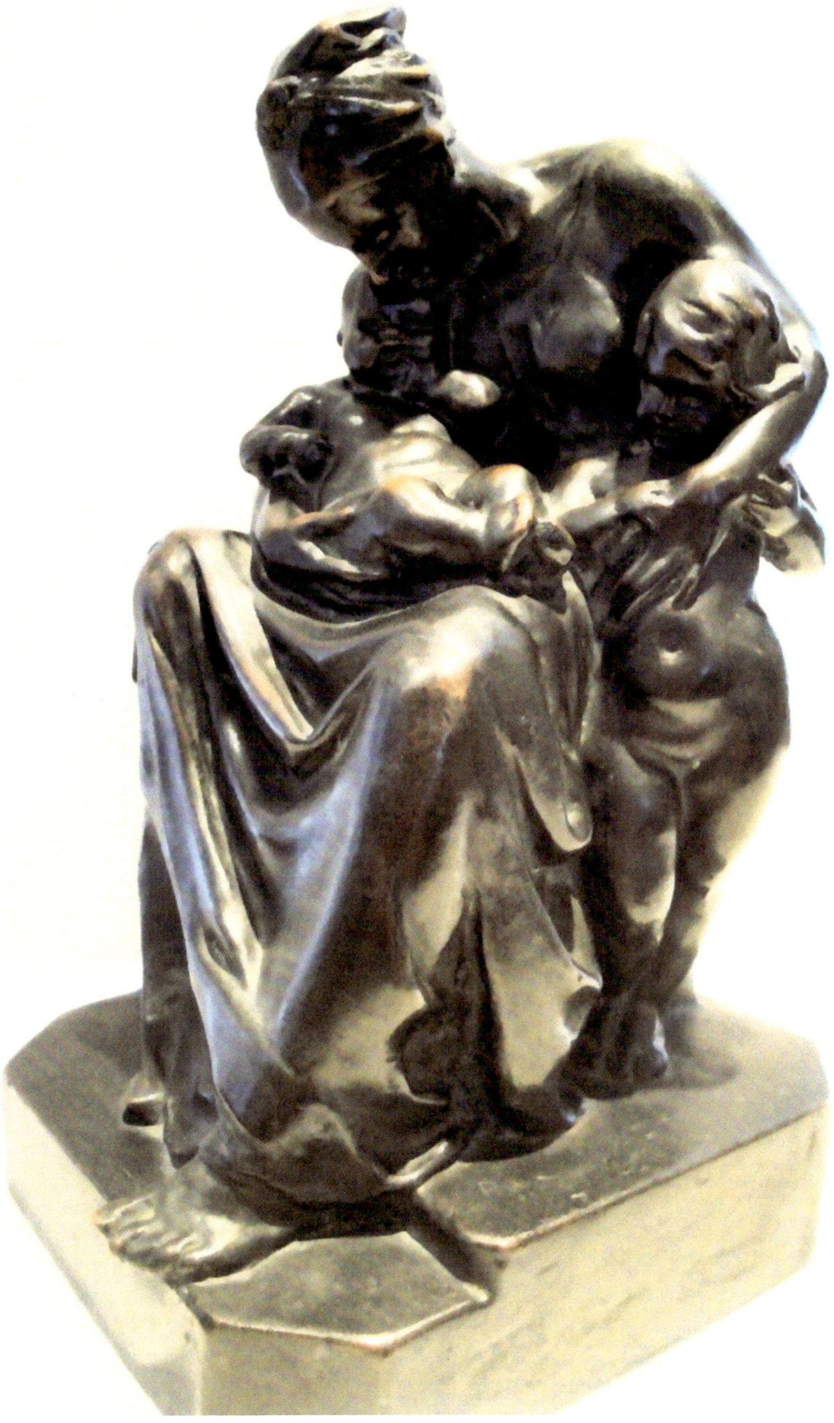

11. Phoebe Stabler, *Untitled (Mother and Child)*, c.1907

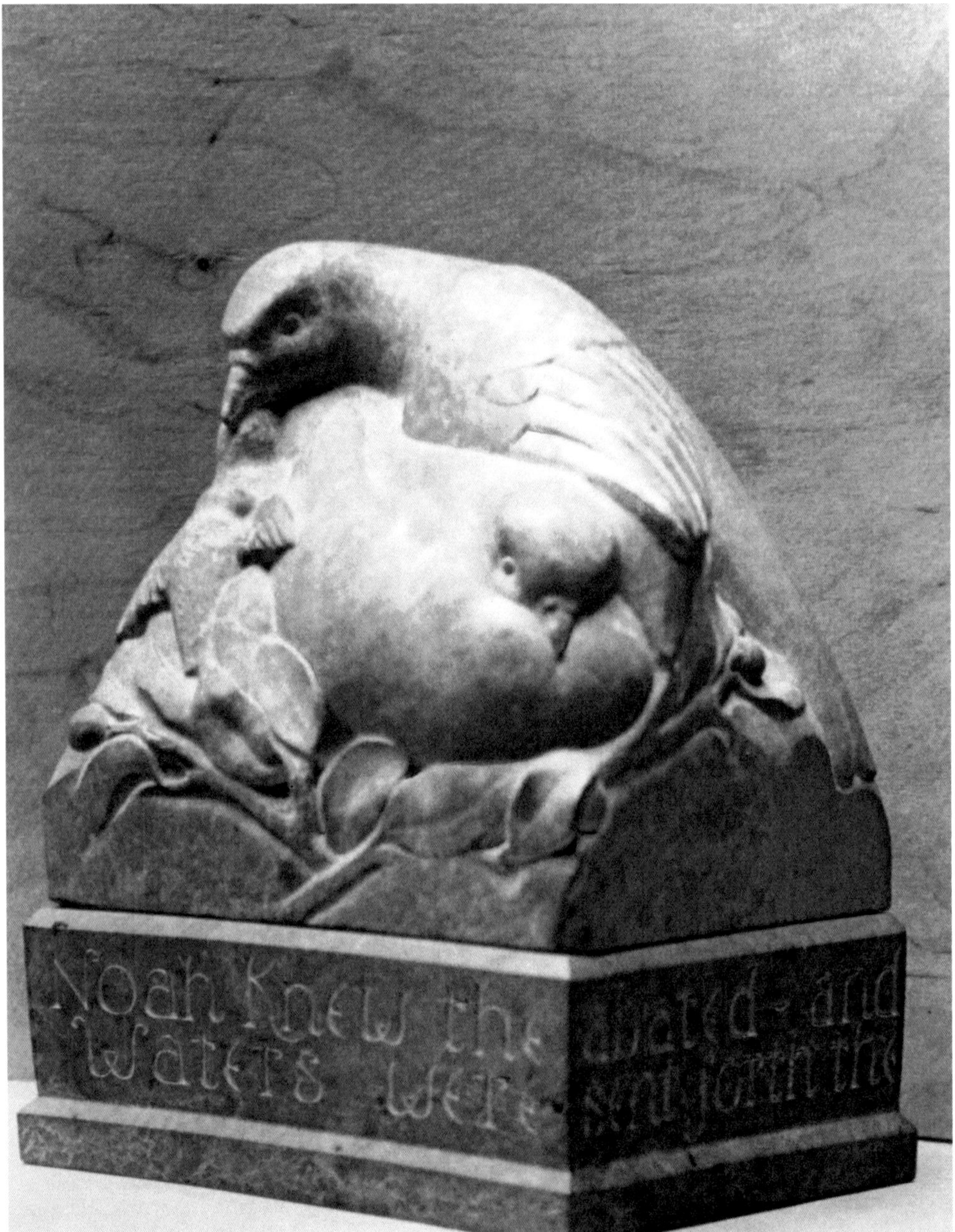

12. Josefina de Vasconcellos, *Dove from the Ark Nesting after the Flood*, undated

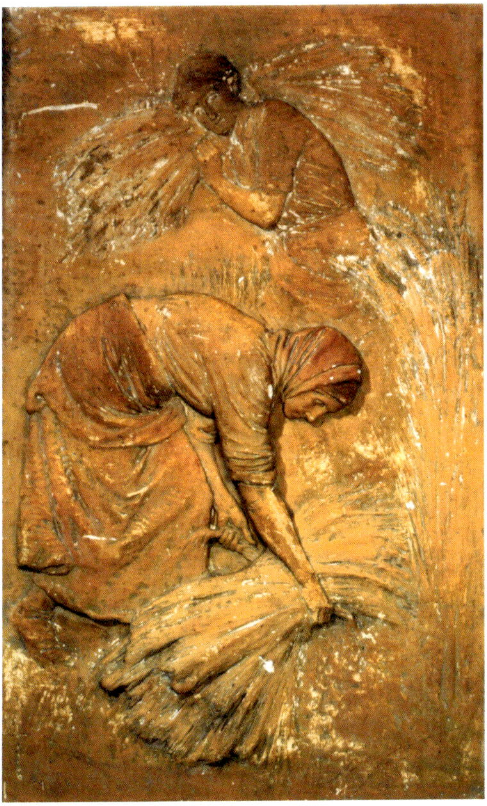

13. Rosamund Praeger, *Harvest*, c.1905

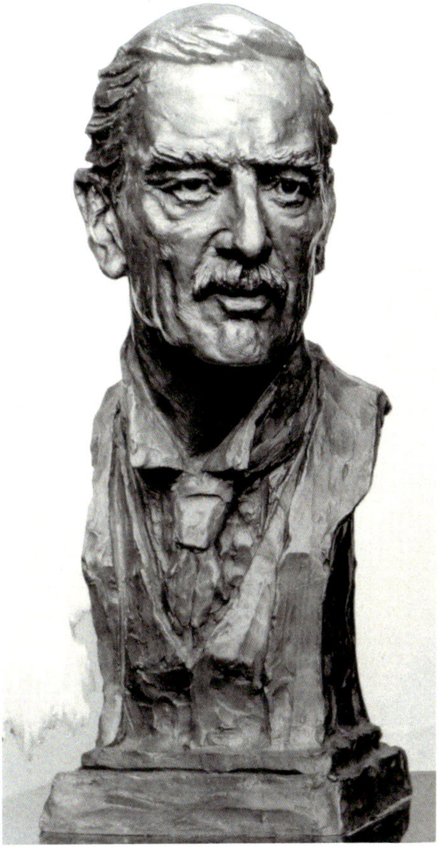

14. Kathleen Scott, *Neville Chamberlain*, 1936

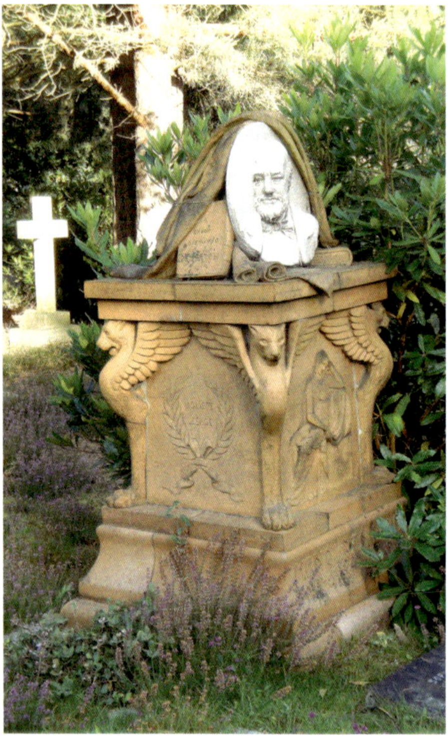

15. Emmeline Halse, *Monument to Henri Van Laun*, c.1897

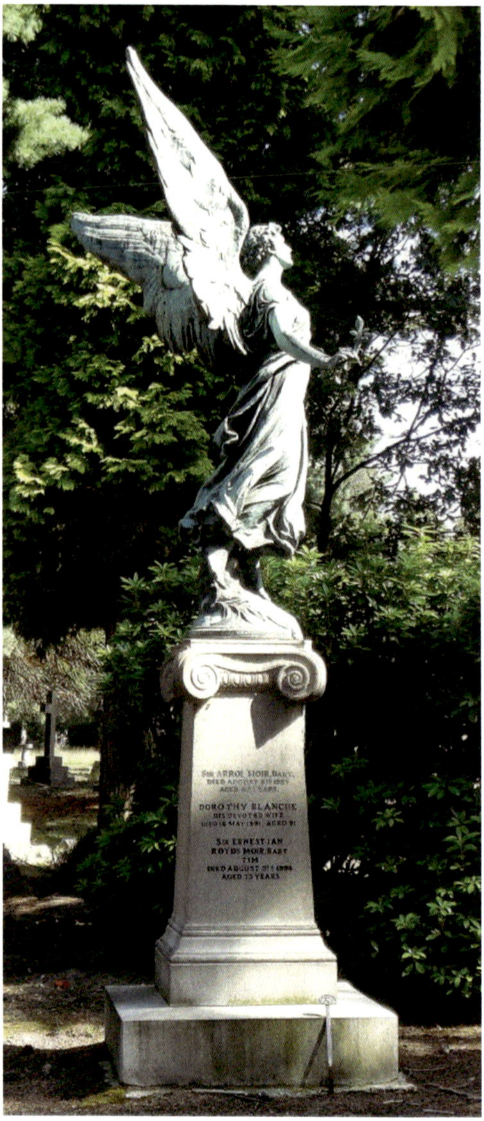

16. Lilian Maud Wade, *Monument to 2nd Lieutenant Rex Moir (1898–1916) and his father Sir Ernest William Moir (1862–1933)*, Brookwood cemetery, before 1923

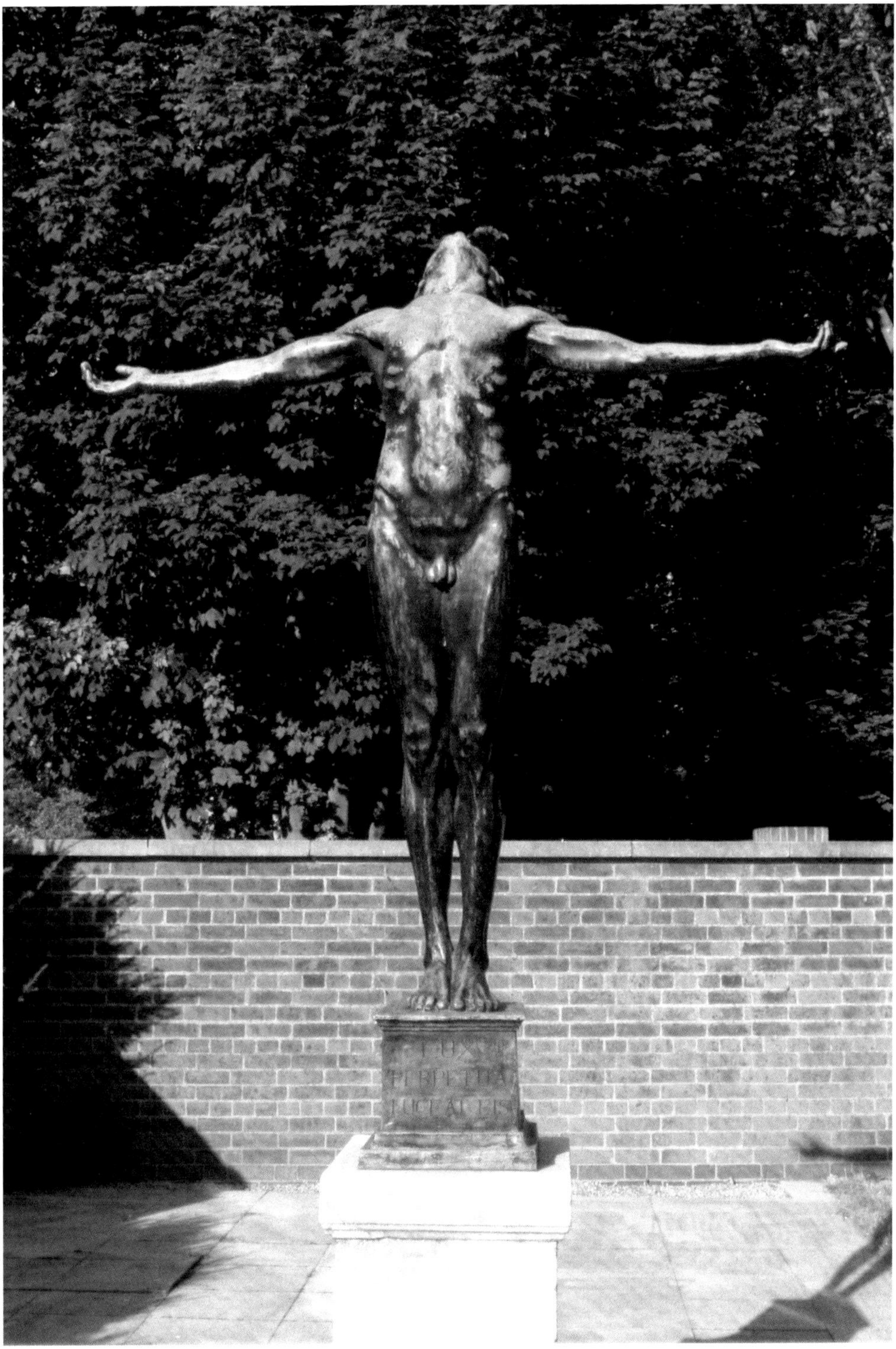

17. Kathleen Scott, *These Had Most to Give*, 1922–23

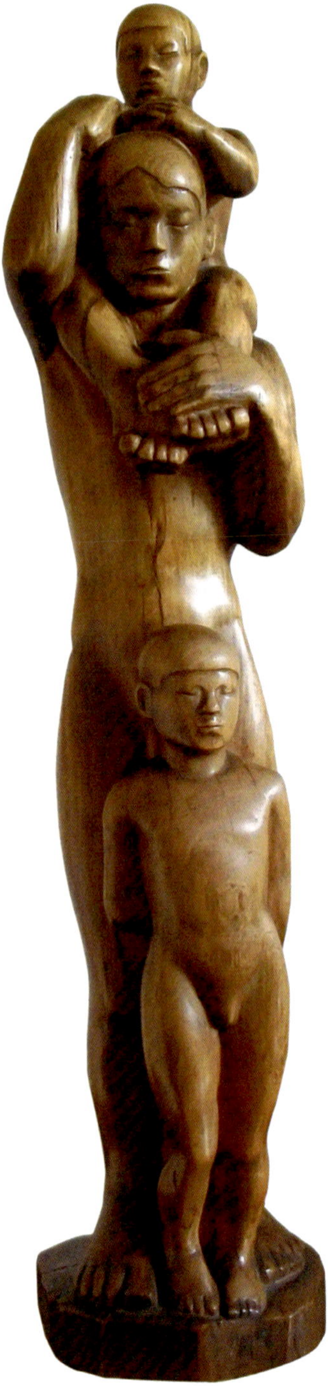

18. Anne Strauss, *Family Group*, c.1930

19. Frances Burlison, *Beaumont College War Memorial*, Windsor, 1921

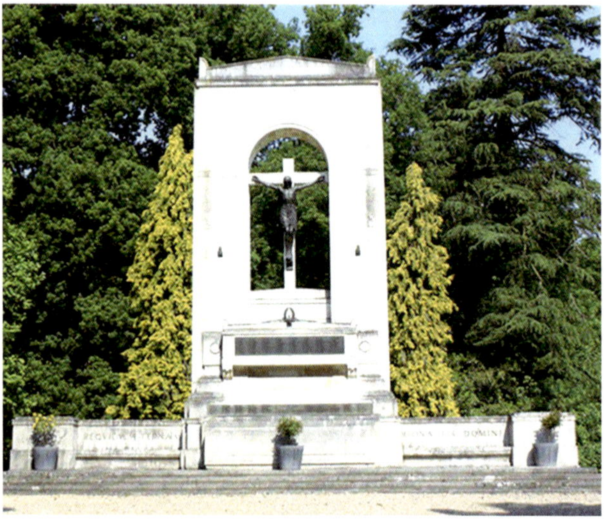

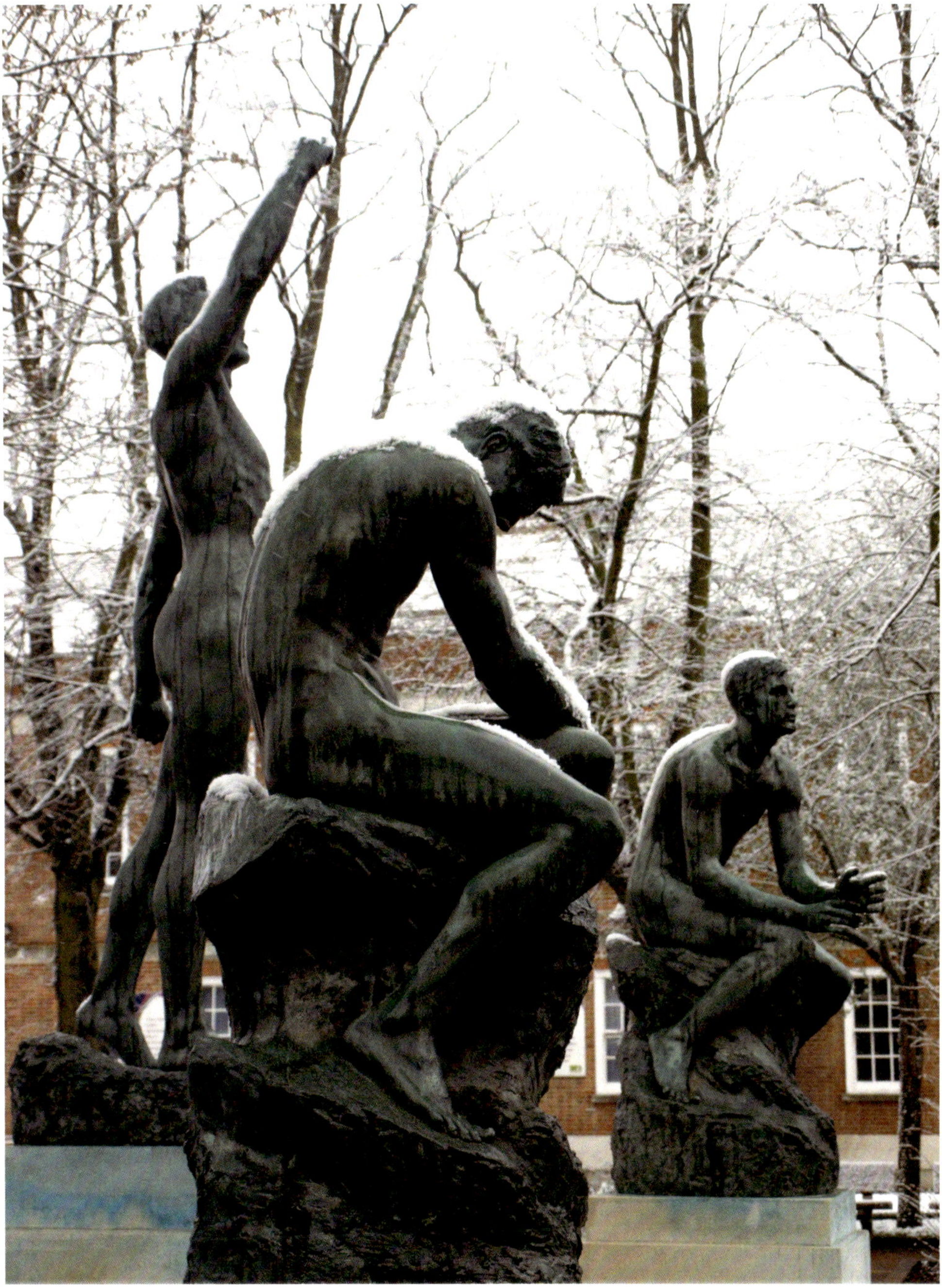

20. Mary Pownall Bromet, *Watford War Memorial*, 1928

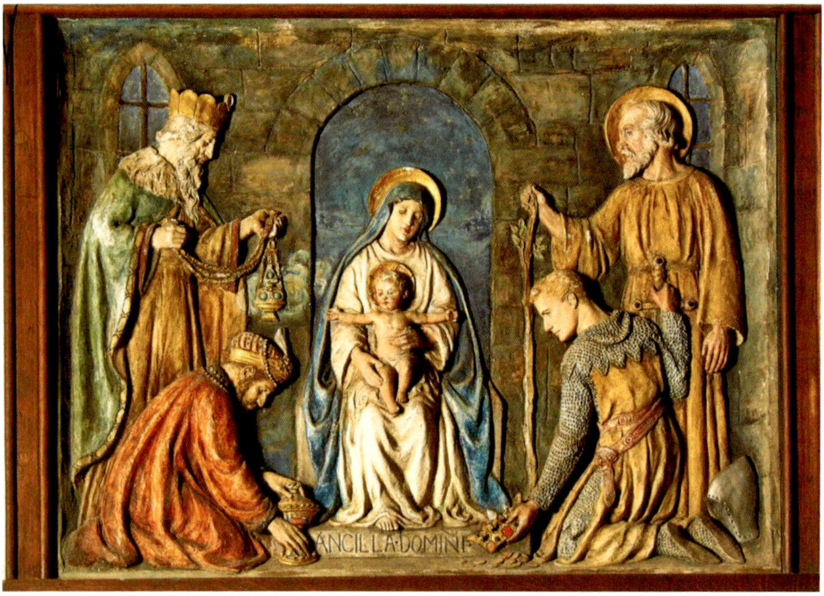

21. Frances Darlington, *Ancilla Domini, the visit of the Magi*, St Wilfrid's Church, Harrogate, c.1914–18

22. Ellen Mary Rope, *The Guardian Angel*, St Margaret's Church, Leiston, 1897

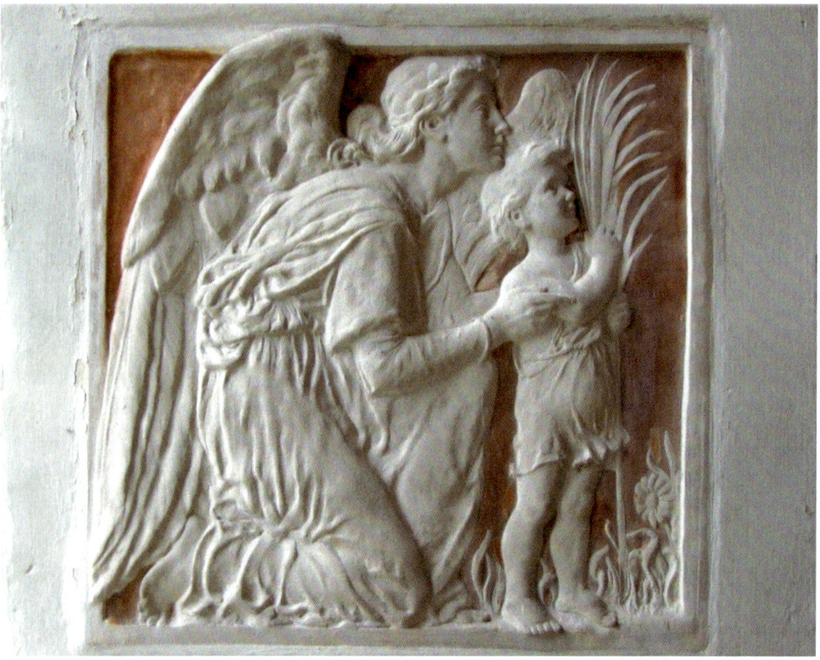

5

The Sculpted Body

5.1 Portrait busts

Sculpted busts were in demand for at least a century after the invention of photography, which speaks to the prestige of such objects and their makers. The more compelling experience of seeing a likeness in the round clearly resonated with prospective patrons who were able to afford this more expensive option. However, the genre has remained somewhat on the periphery of the discipline of art history, rarely being the subject of publications or exhibitions, despite the fact that during at least the first half of the period covered by this book it was popular and attracted highly regarded sculptors. Whereas the painted portrait has been placed at the heart of the discipline, sculpted portraits have tended only to be acknowledged in monographs on key historical artists. Because of the sheer number of such sculptures produced in the nineteenth century, some were inevitably formulaic, but the same could be said of many painted portraits. Unarguably, the unique feature of the sculpted portrait bust is that, as a fragment of the body, it is both highly artificial yet very 'real' in its three-dimensionality.

Queen Victoria was the subject of numerous public sculptures, starting as early as 1842 when she had been on the throne for only five years, and continuing after her death. Many were locally funded, both in Britain and across the Empire. These works carried great significance and the commissioning of such sculptures was, of course, in large part to do with the reach of Empire. However, the power of celebrity also played its part, since the queen's public image became increasingly accessible through the expansion of mass communication in the nineteenth century. The way in which she was represented remained largely consistent throughout and after her reign, but could be understood in different ways according to an individual sculpture's location.[1] Princess Louise became interested in sculpting through sitting for two other women sculptors. Susan Durant was commissioned by Queen Victoria to make medallion portraits of the royal children for the Albert Memorial Chapel at St George's, Windsor. The queen allowed Louise to study with Durant in the mid-1860s. When Durant became ill, the princess's second tutor was Mary Thornycroft, who was appointed to teach her in 1867. Princess Louise's artistic ventures have been described thus:

> Victorian England ... loved to think of a lady painting. Drawing was an integral part in the curriculum of a gentlewoman's education, almost as important as playing the piano. They all played 'nicely' and drew 'nicely'. But Princess Louise went far beyond these narrow limits. She drew and painted remarkably well ... had she been born in other circumstances she would have been quite capable of taking up an artistic career.

There was initial resistance on the part of the queen to allowing the princess to study, but eventually she was won over and doubtless was proud when Louise's work went on display at the Royal Academy before she was 20.[2] Osborne House became the location for her main studio; at Windsor she used rooms next to Mary Thornycroft, and she had a bespoke studio constructed in the gardens of Kensington Palace. There is some evidence of Thornycroft and Louise working collaboratively, with Louise doing some modelling in clay which Thornycroft would then carve.

Thornycroft was determined that the princess be allowed to follow more formal training.[3] She began to introduce her to other artists, and in spring 1866 they visited the studios of Baron Marochetti and William Theed.[4] In 1868 the queen agreed that Princess Louise could study at the National Art Training School which had been one of Prince Albert's innovations, established with money raised by the Great Exhibition, and thus she became the first princess to be publicly educated. At the school she only attended modelling classes, and irregularly because of her mother's commitments. The Hungarian-Viennese sculptor Edgar Boehm became her tutor, having arrived in London in 1862. To give her work additional realism he taught her to model in bronze, producing the type of statuette which he had made popular. Sir Alfred Gilbert was also a pupil of Boehm (and later an assistant), and he and Louise were friends until Gilbert's death in 1934.

Writing in 1868 Marion Spielmann commented on Princess Louise's first exhibition in a public gallery. He praised her sculpting abilities, but pointed to a tendency for prominent people to not be given due credit for their artistic work, the inference being that they received an excessive amount of help. Spielmann refuted this in the case of the princess:

> Her sculpture is … the stronger for the impress of a vigorous individuality. Much of it is excellent – surprisingly so when the relatively limited time which has been at her disposal for art study and practice is taken into consideration. Her busts show sensitiveness, great refinement, and appreciation of delicacy of form.[5]

Louise's marriage to the Marquess of Lorne in 1871 greatly expanded her social and artistic circle. In the same year she exhibited at the Old Bond Street Gallery of the British Institution. She met Gertrude Jekyll, who introduced her to a younger generation of architects and also to garden design, and as a result Louise met Edwin Lutyens and his former assistant E. Bayes Badcock, who worked for her at Cowes. Louise also became friends with Sir Edward Poynter and James McNeill Whistler. She was fortunate in marrying someone who appreciated art and at a time when the British art world was becoming influenced by developments in France, especially from the Impressionists and Rodin, although Louise resisted the latter's influence. In 1876 she made a marble bust of Queen Victoria and donated it to the Royal Academy the following year (**Figure 54**). There are some skilful elements to this work, notably in the drapery, although the portrayal is somewhat flattering when compared with contemporary photographic records. However, it still conveys a realistic presence, down to the rather fleshy chin and neck. We are left in no doubt that this represents a woman with an assertive personality.[6]

The most vivid account by far of Princess Louise's life is that by Lucinda Hawksley, who has described how the princess's files in the Royal Archives were closed to her. She was also unable to gain access to the Marquess of Lorne's family collection in Inveraray, being told that access to the archives for researchers was 'almost impossible'. She discovered that information about many individuals who had played a role in Louise's life, including royal servants and her art tutors, was hidden away:

> A great many items about these people that one would expect to be in other collections have been absorbed into the Royal Collection. Archivists at the National Gallery, Royal Academy and the Victoria & Albert Museum … were bemused to discover that primary sources I requested had been 'removed' to Windsor. Over the decades, there has been some very careful sanitising of Princes Louise's reputation and a whitewashing of her life, her achievements and her personality.

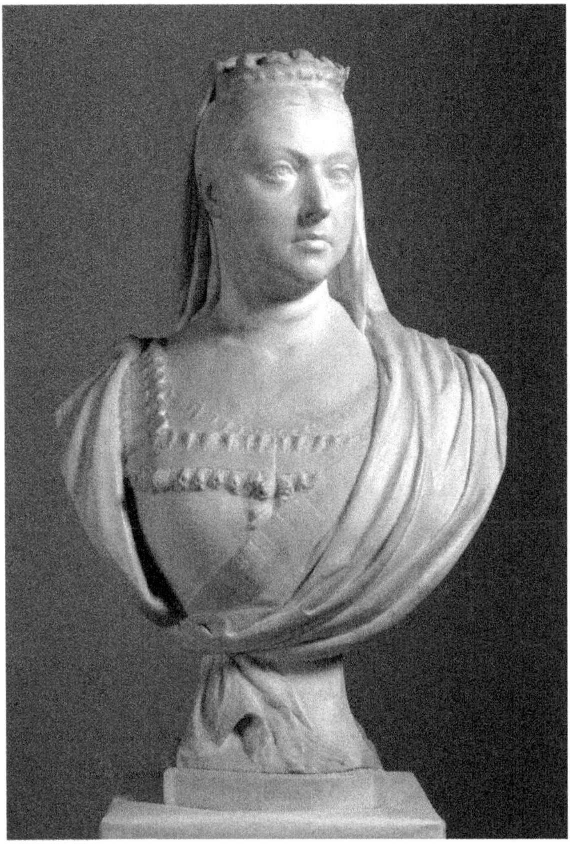

54. Princess Louise, Duchess of Argyll, *Queen Victoria*, 1876

Hawksley's original intention for her book was that it should be a full artist's biography, but it became clear that this would prove impossible. However, she realized that the process of trying to 'discover' the princess could be her focus.[7] This chimes with my experience when searching for information about many of the women sculptors included in this book – so often all that is available are tantalizing fragments. I was also unsuccessful in my attempts to access material on Princess Louise through the Royal Archives and the Lorne family papers, and completely understand how Hawksley

> became fascinated by how history has tried to tame and trivialise this astonishing woman; how often she has been dismissed with comments that she was 'unhinged' or 'paranoid': there has been a concerted effort to try and make people believe that nothing Princess Louise said or did could possibly have any credence. The opposite is true. Louise was

> a powerful voice for women of her generation. She was a princess who sought not to be 'royal', a Victorian woman who strove to break into a masculine world, and a fiery, intriguing, often confusing personality. She challenges many preconceptions that we, in the twenty-first century, have of women who lived under the long reign of Princess Louise's formidable and – it has to be admitted – often extremely unpleasant mother.[8]

Just before Christmas 1890 Boehm died at the age of 56. There had been many rumours about Boehm and Louise, often in the context of her supposedly less than happy marriage. These came to a head when there was some confusion over who had discovered Boehm's body – Princess Louise or Alfred Gilbert, whose studio was next door. Because from the outset there were so many versions of Boehm's death, this strengthens the suspicion that something was being covered up.[9]

In contrast, Jessie Lipscomb (1861–1952) benefited from parents who wished her to be well educated and who supported her artistic ambitions, being happy to let her travel alone to Paris, where by January 1884 she was living with Camille Claudel's family. Lipscomb had already been on her own as an art student in London and evidently enjoyed her independence, and so it was natural that she should go to Paris. Her parents recognized her early ability and supported her wish to have an art training, choosing the South Kensington School where she attended life classes and was taught by both Legros and Lantéri. She won the two prizes offered by the school – the Queen's Prize in 1882 and the National Silver Medal in 1883 – and at this point knew that she wanted to become a sculptor. Legros and Lantéri encouraged her to study in Paris: other women students from South Kensington also went to France, including Amy Singer and Emily Fawcett, Camille Claudel's studio partners. A paying guest in the Claudel home, Lipscomb worked with Claudel in her studio, which Rodin regularly visited and where he gave guidance. Lipscomb became proficient at drapery whereas Claudel excelled at modelling, and in 1885 Rodin needed reliable assistants to work on his latest commission for *The Burghers of Calais*. Claudel and Lipscomb took on these roles and joined the previously all-male atelier at rue de l'Université. As with other assistants they would have prepared Rodin's materials for him, enlarged or reduced maquettes, and assisted with various studies for both *The Burghers of Calais* and *The Gates of Hell*. They would also be involved in adding the drapery to the figures that Rodin preferred to first create as nudes.[10]

In 1885 Lipscomb exhibited her first sculpture at the Royal Academy, a terracotta *Portrait Study*, also shown that autumn in Nottingham alongside two other terracotta busts, one of her father and one of her fiancé William Elborne. In 1886 she exhibited a remarkable terracotta bust, *Day Dreams* (1886), which received Rodin's praise when he viewed it at the Royal Academy in the same year (**Figure 55**). Elborne's sister Polly was the model, and the emotional sensitivity of the work suggests an intimacy between sitter and sculptor. The downcast eyes and tilt of the head reflect a young woman who appears to have her mind elsewhere. William Elborne was in tune with Lipscomb's ambitions, and with her artistic friends, socializing with Rodin in Parisian bars and cafés, as he enjoyed spending time with artists and photographing them at work. Lipscomb does not appear, however, to have exhibited in France. Her work was essentially rooted in the English portrait tradition and she was not drawn to either large works or to subjects involving allegorical content, which would have appealed to a French audience.[11]

When she married in December 1887 she made the choice to forego her professional ambitions and moved to Manchester, although she continued to work intermittently. After having four children, Lipscomb did produce some sculpture in a top-lit studio which she had built at the end of the garden. She modelled family portraits, including a small, expressive bust of her eldest son Sydney aged 7 in 1897, a bust of her husband a year later, and another of Sydney aged 9 (1899). She also sculpted portraits of local people, but the only surviving one is a bust of Alderman Redhead, mayor of Peterborough. Lipscomb's last sculpture was made in 1925, a plaster head of Cavil, the new wife of her eldest son. A particularly strong portrait was Lipscomb's 1907 study of her husband, so reminiscent of Rodin's portraiture (**Figure 56**). In 1914 the latter's *Burghers of Calais* was installed in London: Rodin came to supervise the building of the plinth, and Jessie and Sydney joined him at the dedication ceremony. This was the last time Jessie saw him before he died in 1917. Exacerbating the invisibility of this highly talented sculptor, many of Lipscomb's clay and plaster works were left outside in a garden and did not survive the weather and neglect.

In 1900 Frances Darlington exhibited two works at the annual exhibition of the Society of Women Artists: a medallion portrait of Miss Palmer, the Lady Superintendent of Queen Alexandra's House, and a bust of its founder, Sir Francis Cook. Like Princess Louise, Darlington was commissioned to make a bust of Queen Victoria, in this instance by Morley Town Council for its town hall: this work is less austere than the

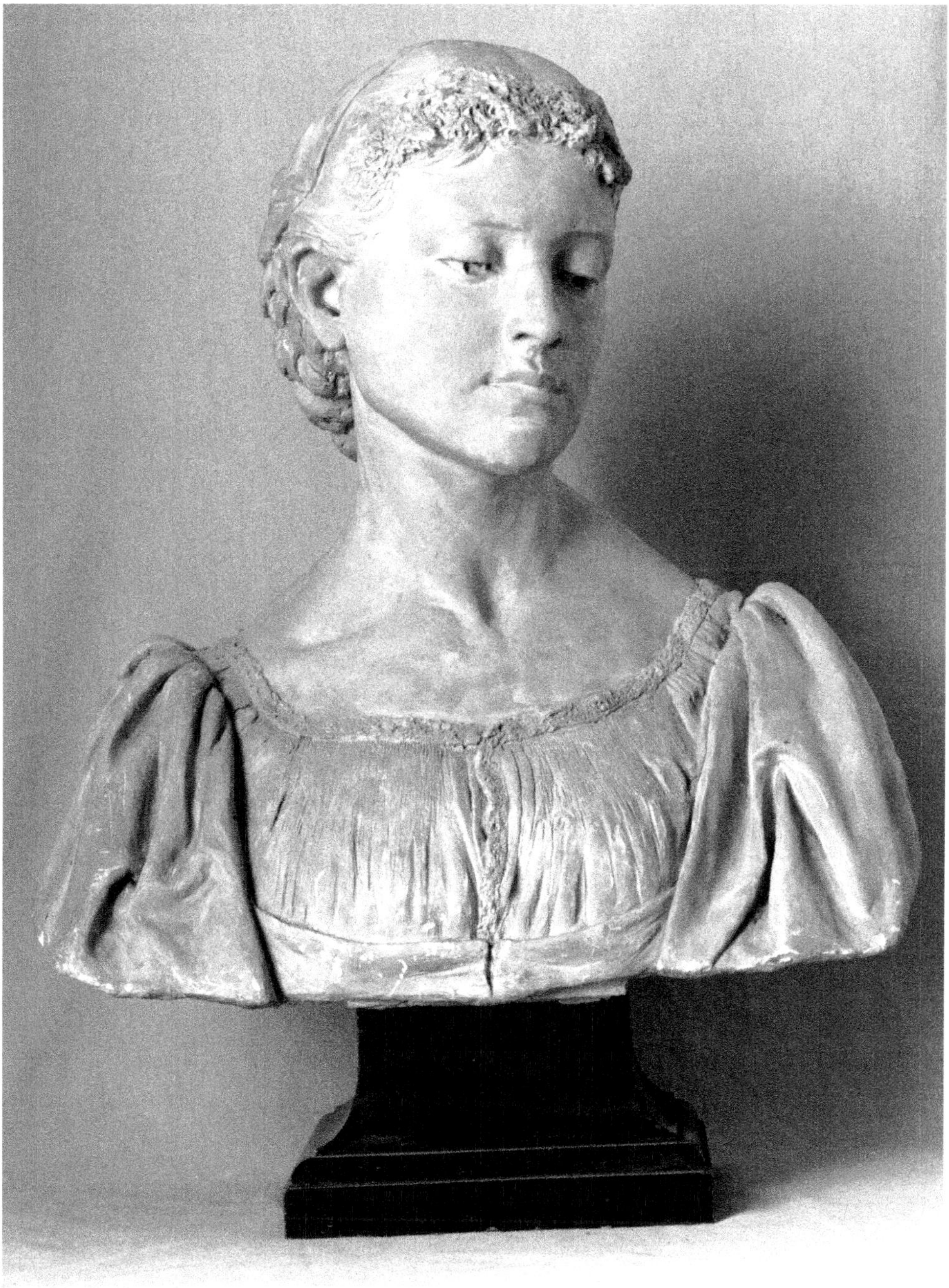

55. Jessie Lipscomb, *Day Dreams*, 1886

version by Princess Louise (**Figure 57**). At a meeting of the town council on 28 August 1901 members voted in favour of accepting Darlington's offer to produce a marble bust of the queen for their stairwell, to cost no more than £40. A subscription fund to recognize the queen's 1897 Diamond Jubilee had been launched in 1896 by the wives of Morley councillors and local dignitaries. The project grew out of a less ambitious one through which it had been intended that a painting be produced to mark the event, and it is possible that the strong reaction to the death of Queen Victoria in 1901 may have persuaded the council to follow a more impressive decorative scheme for the town hall staircase. Darlington's marble sculpture is on an alabaster stand, set into a niche.[12] Clearly, unlike the Princess Louise sculpture, Darlington's was produced without personal contact with the sitter, and given her known interest in

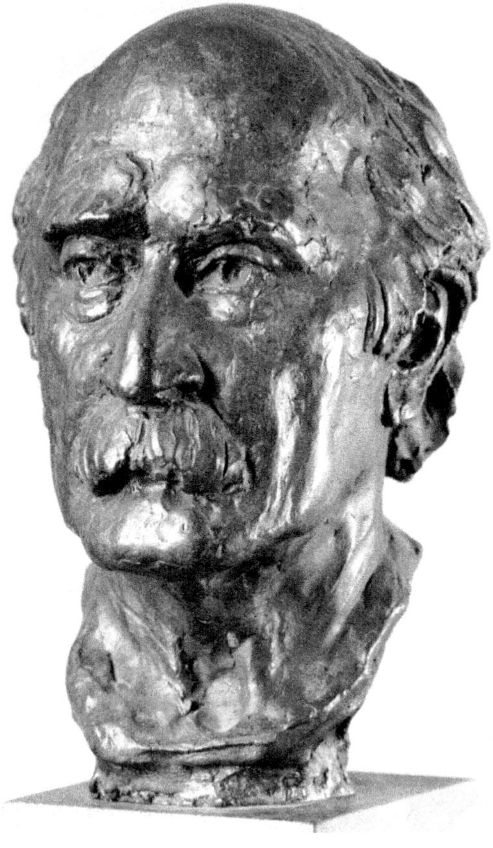

56. Jessie Lipscomb, *William Elborne*, 1907

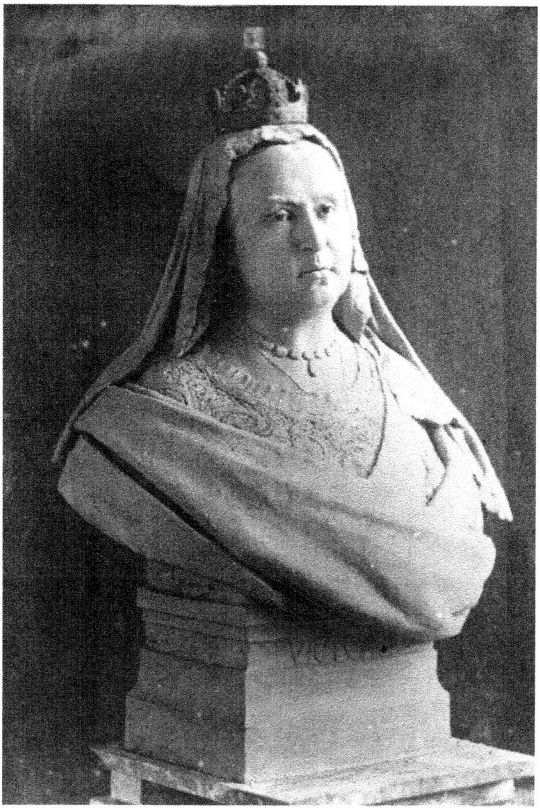

57. Frances Darlington, *Bust of Queen Victoria*, c.1902

photography it is likely that her source material comprised photographs of the queen.

Dora Gordine's *Chinese Head/The Chinese Philosopher/Chia-Chu Chang* (1925–26) caused a sensation when it was exhibited in Paris and drew the attention of several major collectors (**Figure 58**). This was one of Gordine's most celebrated portrait heads and was widely praised by art critics when it was first exhibited in 1926. The sitter Chia-Chu Chang was a Chinese student who was studying philosophy at the Sorbonne when Gordine spotted him while travelling in Paris; she spent time there during the interwar years and worked from non-Western models, reflecting the current popularity of 'the exotic'. Her sculpture could be seen as reaching back to Rodin via Epstein, although Gordine's sculptures were more stylized, drawing not just on live models but also on antique pieces, for example from Egypt. She travelled widely and thus saw her models in real life. In the autumn of 1924 she moved to Paris

58. Dora Gordine, *Chinese Head/ The Chinese Philosopher/Chia-Chu Chang*, 1925–26

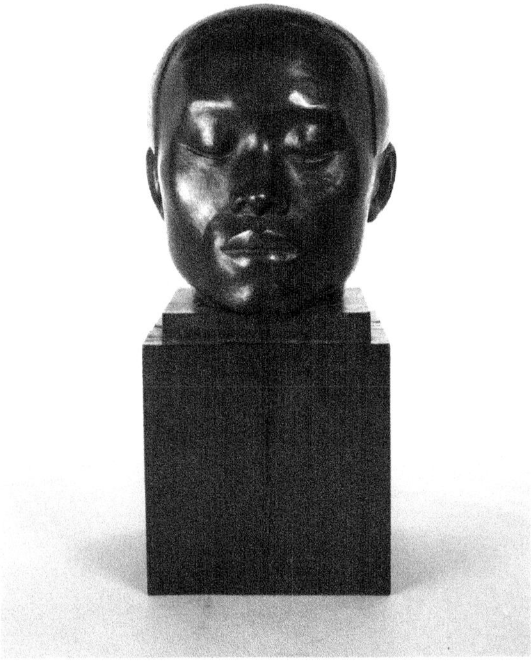

where the majority of young sculptors were concerned with the 'New Classicism' or 'Rappel a l'Ordre'. In spring 1925 she worked as a painter of murals for the interior of the main British pavilion at the Exposition Internationale des Arts Decoratifs et Industriels Modernes, and became friends with William Reid Dick after seeing some of his sculptures on display at the Exposition.

Robert Rattray Tatlock, a close friend of Roger Fry, editor of the *Burlington Magazine* and an art critic for the *Daily Telegraph*, gave a highly favourable review of Gordine's October 1928 exhibition at the Leicester Galleries.[13] This was regarded as the prime exhibiting venue for an 'ambitious cosmopolitan sculptor'.[14] Gordine's work sold well and from the beginning she made in excess of £1,000 from her exhibitions.[15] A review of her 1928 show appeared in the *Daily Express* entitled 'Amazing Studies by Girl Sculptor'. The heads were particularly selected for attention: 'No girl of her age has made bronzes of such expressive character and sculptural quality in our day.'[16] Reginald Wilenski wrote about Gordine in the *Evening Standard*: 'Girl sculptor Genius ... Her bronze heads are most sensitively seen and they are also more like a real sculpture than anything I have seen at the Royal Academy.'[17] He bought four such heads. From the 1930s to the mid-1950s Gordine received consistent praise for her portraiture and figure sculptures.

In 1936 Gordine married her second husband, the Hon. Richard Hare, and so moved into influential circles. Before they married Hare had purchased some of her work and in 1933 he donated one sculpture to the then National Gallery of British Art (now Tate Britain). In 1928 the director of the gallery brought Gordine's work to the attention of Sir Michael Sadler and also introduced her to Samuel Courtauld. A cast of the *Chinese Philosopher* was bought from Gordine by Ernest Franklin, a senior partner in the banking firm Samuel Montagu and Co. and an important collector. Between 1929 and 1960 Gordine exhibited with the Women's International Art Club and the Royal Academy, and Charles Wheeler, William Reid Dick and Gilbert Ledward were among the sculptors who tried unsuccessfully to get her made an associate member of the Academy in January 1942. Reid Dick got her elected as a member of the RBS in 1938 and she rose to full academician status in 1949. Her Russian heritage made her an exotic presence in the British art world. The combination of her husband's independent means and her own critical and commercial success enabled her to design and have built modernist studio/houses in Paris, Singapore and finally Kingston Vale.

In November 1927 Anne Acheson was offered a commission for an internationally important work which would confirm her reputation as one of the period's best modellers. This was to make a portrait bust of the explorer and Middle East expert Gertrude Bell, who was regarded as a celebrity, having helped to create Iraq from Mesopotamia following the collapse of the Ottoman Empire, and who had practically single-handedly established what would become the Baghdad Archaeological Museum. The serious tone of this work appeared in marked contrast to Acheson's garden statues of children (**Figure 59**). Bell had died in 1926; as she and Acheson never met, the portrait was modelled from photographs. In the summer of 1929 the sculpture was cast in bronze and put on display at the Forum Club where Acheson was a member. Many newspapers and periodicals announced the completion of the bust: in *The Times* it was described as being excellently modelled in the round, and it was stated that it would be placed on a wall in an

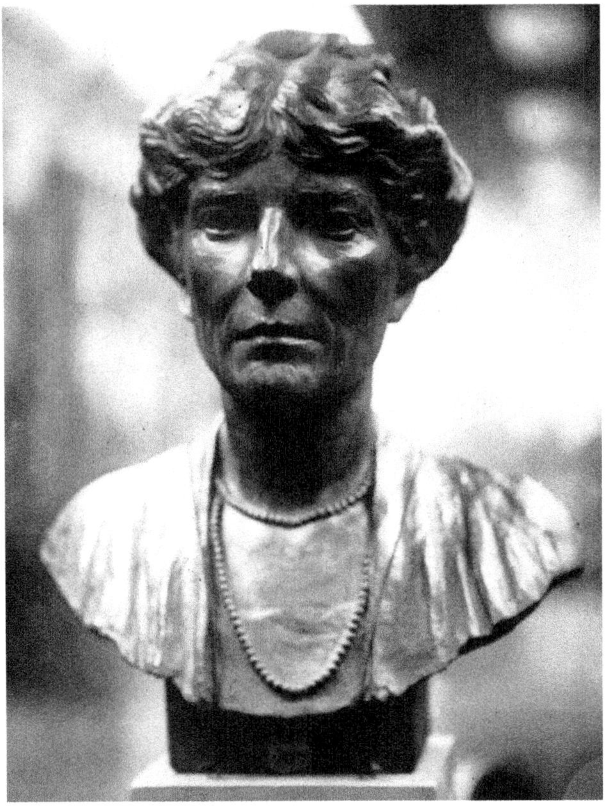

59. Anne Acheson, *Gertrude Bell*, 1928–29

arched recess at the Iraq Archaeological Museum, Baghdad. Acheson took the opportunity to promote her other work, as some of her garden figures were also on display at the Forum Club. The periodical *The Woman's Leader – And The Common Cause* described the bronze as 'a live thing, dominating the room'. The bust and bronze tablet were to have a background of yellow Yorkshire stone, sent to Iraq directly from the United Kingdom. It was unveiled on 18 January 1930 by King Faisal I and it was believed that Acheson had achieved 'a vital likeness of a very vital woman'.[18] The whereabouts of the original sculpture is unknown, although a replica is held by the Royal Geographical Society in Kensington.

During the 1930s the work of Kathleen Scott broadly comprised two categories. Her idealized statues of male youths, sometimes also used as war memorials, will be looked at later. The second group of work is her portraiture – these are usually busts, but she also made statues and statuettes of her well-known male sitters, and there are nearly 130 documented portrait busts and statuettes.[19] Scott emphasized the importance of knowing her sitters and preferred male subjects since she felt that men's features suggested either power or intellect, and given her social milieu she was in a perfect position to find such sitters. In an article published in 1927 under the title 'Are we vain and uninteresting', the writer challenged Scott over her claim that women made unsatisfactory subjects. Perceptively they commented that 'it takes a woman sure of her own powers and of the steady flow of a masculine clientele to say such a thing'. The writer concluded that:

> if you can pick your subjects, and they include such men as Lord Oxford, Mr Lloyd George, Mr. Baldwin, Lord Reading, the late Captain Scott, Mr. Bernard Shaw, and Mr John Galsworthy, you are bound to find women who are just great beauties or great social figures a little dull. There are women who have carved lines of intellect and character into their faces ... but, as a rule, the modern woman is more concerned in ridding her face of lines of any description. Is it by chance possible that the critic of her own sex may be right?[20]

Scott was not above advising others on the importance of gender differentiation. At a prize-giving event for Sevenoaks schoolgirls at Walthamstow Hall she warned them that copying

> the self-indulgencies of men – smoking, drinking, cocktails and wearing shorts – was not helping to add men's qualities to their own but merely resulted in a superficial imitation. There were three great women who had never 'imitated' – Jane Austen, Gertrude Bell and Florence Nightingale ... The nicest thing women could do was to make things easier for the 'great ones', and this was the shortest cut to becoming a great one themselves. They should train to be alert for emergencies, and get ready to help in the way that was most fitting ... Many of them had great advantages; they came from a grand stock. This was a great responsibility, too, for they must never let the stock down.[21]

This is a strange statement, not the least given the sheer determination of Scott's named examples, especially Nightingale, who certainly could never be accused of making things 'easier for the "great ones"'. Perhaps it also says something about social class in the pre-war period and the continuing expectations of those from Scott's privileged background. However, despite her divided life as wife, mother and socialite, she was remarkably productive, particularly since she delegated very little work apart from casting.

Scott's work was consistently searching and rigorous. The portraits particularly demonstrate this, and the responses to some of her exhibitions give a sense of how her work was perceived by her contemporaries. In 1913 she took part in a group show at the Fine Art Society's galleries. The *Illustrated London News* of 15 February contained a ten-page appraisal, and by the 1920s she was attracting significant press interest. Scott commented that

> with the recognition came responsibilities: unfortunately one of the first was a dinner about women sculptors – I don't believe in them, I don't consider them helpable or worth helping, but I didn't think it would sound nice to say so I held my peace. What help did I have or need – less than none.[22]

Scott's sculpture of the *Rt. Hon. David Lloyd George* (1922) was widely reviewed in the press but was rejected by the Royal Academy in 1924. This was one of several refusals over the following 15 years, the reasons for which are unclear. In November 1929 the sculptor had her second solo show at the Greatorex Galleries, Grafton Street. She is quoted thus:

> Hundreds and hundreds of people came. I hated it. Silly asses. I had some lovely things there and they say such silly things. I had a lovely pair of arms stretched up (out of a pool of water), with (a fountain of) water coming between them, and a lovely boy blindfolded. Did I mean this? Did I mean that? I could bear the frank jesters better, who said I should call the arms SOS etc. The press said I had a tremendous success because all fashionable London was there – I wanted to take all their stupid heads and bang them together. But I didn't, I just cackled like the rest of them. One is supposed to create and then put one's babies naked for anyone to palaver over, and to be quite insensitive impervious and polite. Well I was, as far as anyone in the world saw.[23]

Scott's bust of King George V was unveiled in June 1935 and was shown at the Royal Academy in that year. Reportedly the king offered her £100 to destroy an Epstein bust that he particularly disliked.[24] The king's portrait was considerably over life-size and showed him in naval uniform. The work was exhibited at the Royal Academy in 1935, a review in *Country Life* describing it as a good likeness as well as a 'dignified and vital monument ... [which] should have been given the place of honour [at the RA] occupied by Sir. W. Reid Dick's rather lifeless marble bust in the Central Hall'.[25] Another article comparing the two sculptures described the Reid Dick work as conventional, whereas Scott's employed a

> rougher and more powerful technique [which] manages to convey a much finer picture of the Sovereign and becomes a better piece of work. This bronze bust has excellent character and fine sculpturesque qualities. It has a vigorous achievement which secures complete unity, only to be found in a work of real inspiration; and it shows that the Royal bust can be made a work of art if the sculptor has the necessary power and intuition.[26]

Scott's 1936 bust of Neville Chamberlain was also rejected by the Royal Academy, despite its appeal as showing this controversial figure in a convincingly humane light (**Plate 14**). The photograph from the Kennet family papers has suffered from water damage at some point but still vividly illustrates the sculptor's ability to convey an individual personality. Correspondence between Scott and Chamberlain was markedly informal, with the latter writing to her in advance of a sitting in 1936:

> I postponed answering your letter for several days, in the hope that I might think of some good reason why I should not comply with your request; but Annie says that I had better get it over. I will, therefore, meekly obey and come on Friday, the 28th, at 11 o'clock, if this will suit you. I would have taken an earlier date, but I must get my hair cut, and I imagine that you like a shaggy subject, so I must give it a few days to grow again.[27]

Later in the year he wrote to her in the context of what appears to have been some confusion over this portrait:

> My dear Kathleen. It is evidently just an honest misunderstanding. You meant to convey that the bust was for yourself and not a commission from me. I understand that you were going to keep it in a cellar till I was dead and then produce it as a happy surprise. I didn't mind that because (1) I should be dead (2) I know you would make it better looking than the original and there could be no odious comparisons with the subject … PS I am in bed with gout *again* and in a disgusting temper.[28]

Chamberlain gave three or four sittings and the sculpture was warmly praised as maintaining dignity, yet going beyond the popular image of the 'Iron Chancellor'. One reviewer believed that 'his features are lit with humanity with a hint of cheerfulness and a suggestion of the lover of nature which led him to publish a charming story of a bird that amused him as he recovered from a summer indisposition at his official residence in Downing Street'.[29]

In the late winter of 1936 Scott had a show at Ackermann's Gallery in Bond Street. The most expensive work was *H.R.H. The Duke of York,*

K.G. at 320 guineas, and there was also a 'small' version of this available for 120 guineas. The cheapest sculpture was *Aspiration (sketch)* at 25 guineas, and 19 works in total were shown. A large version of *H.M. King George V* appears in the catalogue as unpriced, and therefore presumably not for sale, but a small version was available for 150 guineas. *These Had Most to Give* (**Plate 17**) was on sale for 40 guineas – presumably therefore being the statuette version.[30] One review noted that this exhibition had attracted much attention in artistic circles. It was felt that the portraits were unusually forceful for a female sculptor and that this aspect was Scott's strength; they were 'rugged' whereas the statues of young men were 'graceful, fanciful'.[31]

In 1937 Scott appeared on television, probably through Sir John Reith, as part of 'The World of Women' series. She spoke for 17 minutes, showed 15 works, and 'made dreamy generalizations about sculpture', describing her approach as 'emotional and pragmatic rather than intellectual'. This was the BBC's first television programme on sculpture, focusing on her portraits and working methods.[32] In 1938 Scott produced a photographic book of her sculptures (published by Geoffrey Bles) which in some sources is referred to under the title *Homage*. It was reviewed in the *Times Literary Supplement*, where Scott was applauded for being particularly able in rendering 'the hard clear dynamic features of statesmen and men of action'.[33] The book contained 40 photogravures of sculptures and was described as a beautiful work in terms of print and illustration quality. It was stressed that although no photograph could do more than suggest what an original artwork might look like, especially in the case of sculpture, the photographs in this book were of especial quality.[34]

Scott was included in Eric Newton's 1947 book *British Sculpture 1944–46* and died in London in July of the same year.[35] In 1948 a memorial exhibition was organized at Heal and Son's Mansard Gallery.[36] Unsurprisingly, the catalogue emphasized the prominence of Scott's sitters and thus the fame of her sculptures through their subject. She was quoted as believing that sculpture should serve the practical needs of both architecture and furniture. Fifty-seven works were shown: prices were available on application, and it was also indicated that works in plaster could be cast in bronze by arrangement. Many very prominent works were therefore apparently available in editions, as at the 1936 Ackermann Gallery exhibition, although the extent of these is unknown. They included *King George V* (1935, bronze), *King George VI* (1936, Hoptonwood stone) and *Adam Lindsay Gordon* (1934, bronze).

Overall the exhibition comprised large and life-size busts, life-size figures, statuettes, portrait statuettes and other works. Reviewing this exhibition, *The Times* correspondent was of the opinion that Scott's successes were in the realm of portrait busts and statues, rather than sculpture that lent itself to symbolism or decoration. He described her likenesses as 'exact and penetrating'.[37] He also mentioned Scott's focus on making statuettes in the last year of her life, and the domestic, decorative possibilities of sculpture were noted by G. M. Trevelyan, who opened the memorial exhibition and said:

> I am glad this exhibition and sale is being held on Heal's premises, because one of the merits of her portrait busts and ideal figures is that they fit into people's rooms and gardens. Sculpture is apt to be formidable, and the place that it can be induced to take in the home is a difficult problem, which interested her, and which she did something to solve.

He was emphatic that Scott's success in portrait sculpture was due to her close relationship with 'some of the most able and keen-witted men of her time, many of whom became her friends, whom therefore she understood better than some artists can understand the victims they are called on to delineate at a few hours' notice'.[38]

5.2 Statues and individual memorials

The public function of the sculpted portrait is even more explicit when realized in the form of a statue where, positioned in a public space and on a pedestal, its isolation and singularity attract the viewer's attention. In 1922 Kineton Parkes pinpointed some of the problems encountered in the placement of statues. Particularly critical of the positioning in 1914 of Rodin's *Burghers of Calais* at the base of the Victoria Tower at the Houses of Parliament, he described how the sheer height of the tower behind the sculpture reduced its 'noble simplicity'. He pointed out that there was a highly suitable area of grass nearby which would have provided a far superior location. In contrast, he complained that an exhibition of Rodin's work at South Kensington, although 'lavish', was not very good. 'There is too much Rodin for the proportionate value of sculpture to be properly observed. There is only one Rodin, but there are other sculptors: there are several phases of Rodin, and not all are of equal value.'[39] Hence he was acutely aware both of the impact of placement and the possible unevenness of an artist's output.

Princess Louise's marble statue of *Queen Victoria as a Young Monarch* (1887–93), sited in Kensington Gardens, is an example of a sculptural memorial situated in an entirely appropriate context. It was instigated by a committee of the Women's Golden Jubilee Fund, the principal donors also being women as well as the residents of Kensington (**Figure 60**). Chosen by a vote, the princess proposed that the sculpture should depict her mother being crowned. Although intended to mark the 1887 Golden Jubilee of Victoria's coronation, the sculpture was not completed and unveiled until the summer of 1893, an event attended by about 2,000 people to great acclaim. Its location makes it exceptionally visible and many observers drew attention to the importance of this highly public and popular site. They characterized the princess as a pioneer: both *Building News* and the *Art Journal* praised the sculpture from the perspective of its being the first memorial in London made by a woman. The latter publication moreover felt that the princess's sculpture certainly held its own when compared with many similar statues.[40] Spielmann described this as Princess Louise's most notable sculpture, indeed a work that would have been a credit to some sculptors who were fully professional and well regarded.[41] However, many observers assumed that Louise had received expert help – chiefly from Boehm, even though he had died in 1890. Nonetheless the newspapers were full of praise: 'There is no gainsaying that a true artist had been born in the Royal Family.' The monument was 'a labour of love' and the princess's name was linked with that of Rosa Bonheur, both to become examples to other women and art students.[42]

Louise worked on the statue in her garden studio at Kensington Palace, and then made a statuette of the queen to be placed over the western porch of Manchester Cathedral, showing Victoria as she was when she visited the city in 1857. Louise often had to imagine what the queen looked like when young, such as when she was aged 19 at the time of her coronation. Victoria had been at Kensington Palace when she heard of her uncle's death and her imminent accession to the throne. Shown wearing her coronation robes and seated on a throne, the statue in Kensington Gardens is positioned on a large stone plinth, the base made of buff-coloured stone and the pedestal of fashionable white Portland stone to match the marble of the statue. Louise had referred to paintings and illustrations of her mother's coronation when designing the statue, which was positioned within sight of the window of the room in which the young Victoria had slept.[43] Armed with this knowledge the viewer can relate the form of the statue to that of the

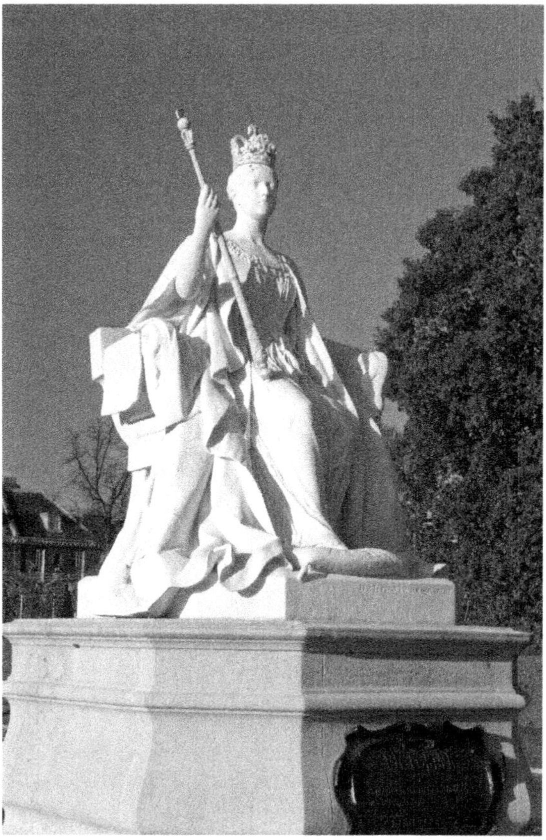

60. Princess Louise, Duchess of Argyll, *Queen Victoria as a Young Monarch*, Kensington Gardens, 1887–93

young woman who would so many years before have gazed out of the window in Kensington Palace. However, this depiction of a youthful queen was in marked contrast to the elderly, widowed monarch who unveiled it.

Ellen Mary Rope was born in Blaxhall, near Woodbridge, Suffolk, a member of a creative family of artists, farmers and engineers. She attended the Nottingham Place School, Marylebone, where she was taught drawing by its founder, the philanthropist and social housing reformer Octavia Hill, a pupil of John Ruskin and a woman who would be a continuing source of useful contacts. From here Rope returned to Suffolk to study at the Ipswich School of Art, and then went to the Slade School of Art between 1877 and 1885. In an 1895 interview for *Woman at Home* she made it clear that she did not think that there was much opportunity for women to have a career in sculpture:

> On the whole, men are not much inclined to encourage women in this department of art ... The woman-sculptor has often to earn a good part of her income by teaching. The class to which she appeals is small and select, and even after she has gained her name, there may be long intervals between commissions ... sculpture is not a very hopeful 'women's employment'.[44]

At the Slade she joined Legros's sculpture course and his work, in addition to early Florentine Renaissance decorative sculpture, was her greatest influence, much of her output taking the form of low plaster bas-reliefs. She began exhibiting in 1885 at the Royal Academy, and between 1889 and 1906 she exhibited mainly small-scale decorative works in plaster and bronze with the Arts and Crafts Society: 'a cinerary urn (1889), an electric light bracket (1893), a bronze mirror frame and three panels in coloured plaster (1896), panels for "ceiling or wall decoration" (1903) and a "sketch for a capital, St. Peter's Church, Cricklewood" (1906)'.[45] Few examples of her work are in public collections, one exception being a bronze panel, *Boy with Palms* (1907), in Ipswich Museum.

Many of her patrons requested personal memorials, and after the outbreak of the First World War this became a more important area of her work. It would appear from her collection of photographs that clients were able to choose from a range of standard designs which could be personalized in detail, medium and cost. One impressive example was a composition that depicted an angel sounding the last trump, which Rope reworked on at least three occasions. The initial marble commission in 1890 was for a *Memorial to Mrs. Mary Anne Moberly*, wife of George Moberly, Bishop of Salisbury (**Figure 61**).[46] A newspaper review referred to its recent unveiling:

> a figure of an angel standing waiting, intently watching for the dawn of the day of the Lord, after the night of watching and sorrow. The face depicts intense longing for the signal to sound the trumpet of the Resurrection, and of triumphant expectation. In front is the Sea, trembling and restless, emblematic of this troubled life, and the horizon shews [*sic*] clouds fleeing before the coming sun, the rays of which creep up the sky and light the tops of the waves. There is a fine suggestion of the breath of the coming day in the movement of the hair and drapery. In the right corner the springing growth of lilies and irises round a stone bearing the inscription 'Until the day break and the shadows flee away,' – which words also give the clue to the angel's attitude of expectation – is typical of the Resurrection.[47]

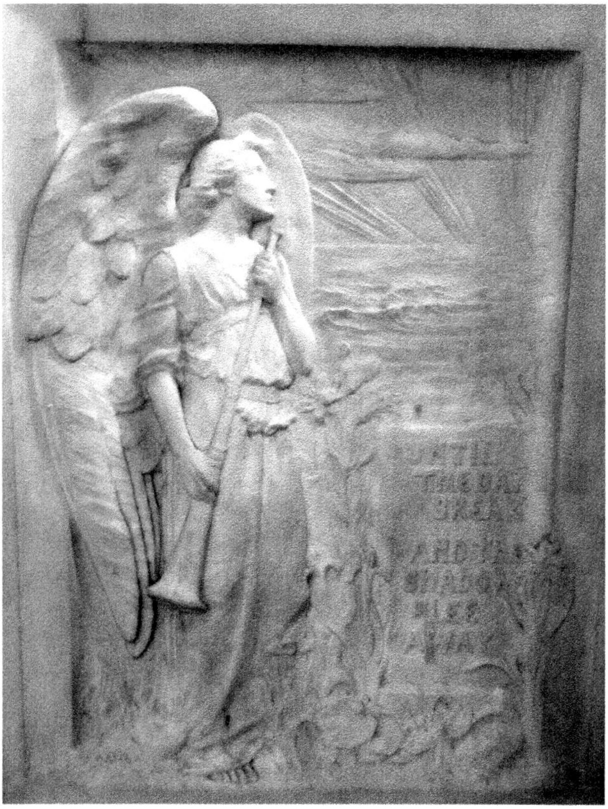

61. Ellen Mary Rope, *The Angel of the Resurrection*, Salisbury Cathedral, c.1902

Given its shallow relief, the sculpture shows a high level of skill in its illusion of depth. Depressingly, as is the fate of much sculpture made by women, in order for me to photograph this relief in the cathedral a cupboard placed in front of it first had to be moved to one side.

Emmeline Halse (1853–1930) was a sculptor and medallist who studied at the Royal Academy Schools between 1876 and the early 1880s, and then trained in Paris. Halse's memorial to Belgian critic and writer Henri Van Laun is an interesting work made from terracotta and marble (**Plate 15**). Van Laun died in 1896 and his memorial in Brookwood Cemetery, Woking, was made in about 1897. The oval portrait relief is glazed white, partially draped and set against books and scrolls. Underneath is a square plinth with griffon monopeds at the corners, and each of the depicted books have inscribed titles which include histories of English and French literature by Van Laun. The four faces of the plinth bear different designs: a relief of a classical mourning figure to the front; an inscription 'Erected to the memory of my father' at the back; and pairings of the names 'Taine' and 'Labruyere', and of 'Moliere' and 'Lesage'. This very unusual monument has some of the characteristics of the Coade stone factory Georgian memorials, and so it is possible that its conception might have been influenced by the nearby centre of terracotta production at Compton.

Halse lived in Clarendon Road, on the northern edge of Holland Park. In the late nineteenth century the area to the south of the park was home to several artists, including Frederic Leighton and Thornycroft, both of whom would certainly have been known to the Halse family because they both taught at the Royal Academy schools.[48] At the latter, Halse's understanding of anatomy would have been based on studying classical plaster casts. She won two silver medals and a £30 prize, and a relief entitled *The Swing* was shown at the Royal Academy in 1878 and also illustrated in a contemporary journal. In Paris she studied at the studio of French neoclassical sculptor F. L. D. Bogino, who sculpted pediments for the south wing of the Louvre, and Halse showed five works at the Paris Salon in the 1880s and 1890s. She exhibited 31 works at the Royal Academy between 1878 and 1918, 22 at the Glasgow Institute of Fine Arts, 12 at Liverpool's Walker Art Gallery, four at the Paris Salon, two at Manchester, seven at the New Gallery and one at the Royal Miniature Society. Her professional career began in the early 1880s with her reconstruction of the incomplete *Hermes of Praxiteles*: the statue was cast in bronze and presented to the British Museum. There were also probably many private commissions and it is known that she made portrait heads mainly of young children and babies as well as some religious and mythological subjects. Two of Halse's sculptures were acquired by public institutions. One of these was an allegorical relief, *The Pleiades*, which was bought by Glasgow Corporation and apparently caused a sensation when first exhibited at the Royal Academy in 1887. However, it was made of plaster and got broken. *Earthward Bound* was bought by St Bartholomew's Hospital, having been shown at the Royal Academy in 1917. Depicting a band of angels with clasped hands, this relief has also disappeared, possibly lost when the east wing was rebuilt in 1930 or when the hospital was bombed during the Second World War.

Rosamund Praeger also produced memorials: from 1910 onwards she sculpted a series of monumental commissions for some of the leading figures and families in Edwardian Belfast, such as Thomas Andrews and Walter Henry Wilson, who were two of the founders of the Harland and Wolff shipyard. In 1914 she was awarded the commission to decorate the Thomas Andrews Memorial Hall in Comber, Co. Down, built after Andrews had died on board the *Titanic* in April 1912.[49] She used cherubs for decoration and inside the building she made a bronze monumental portrait plaque of Andrews. She completed a second portrait memorial to him, showing the Harland and Wolff shipyard in the background, for the stairwell of the Ulster Reform Club in Belfast. Other important works included commissions from mercantile patrons such as the Inglis family who ran a successful bakery in Belfast (**Figure 62**). Praeger also designed the figures of *Hope* and *Memory* for her family grave in Holywood.

Aside from the Halse sculpture, another impressive funerary monument in Woking's Brookwood Cemetery was made by Lilian Maud Wade. It is to 2nd Lieutenant Rex Moir (1898–1915) and his father Sir Ernest William Moir (1862–1933), and was made some time before 1923 (**Plate 16**). The monument comprises a bronze depiction of *Peace* holding an olive branch, standing on a pink granite base above a stylized ionic column containing a relief profile portrait set within a laurel wreath. Moir Senior was an engineer who designed the Blackwall and Hudson

62. Rosamund Praeger, *Memorial for the Inglis family*, Belfast city cemetery, c.1905

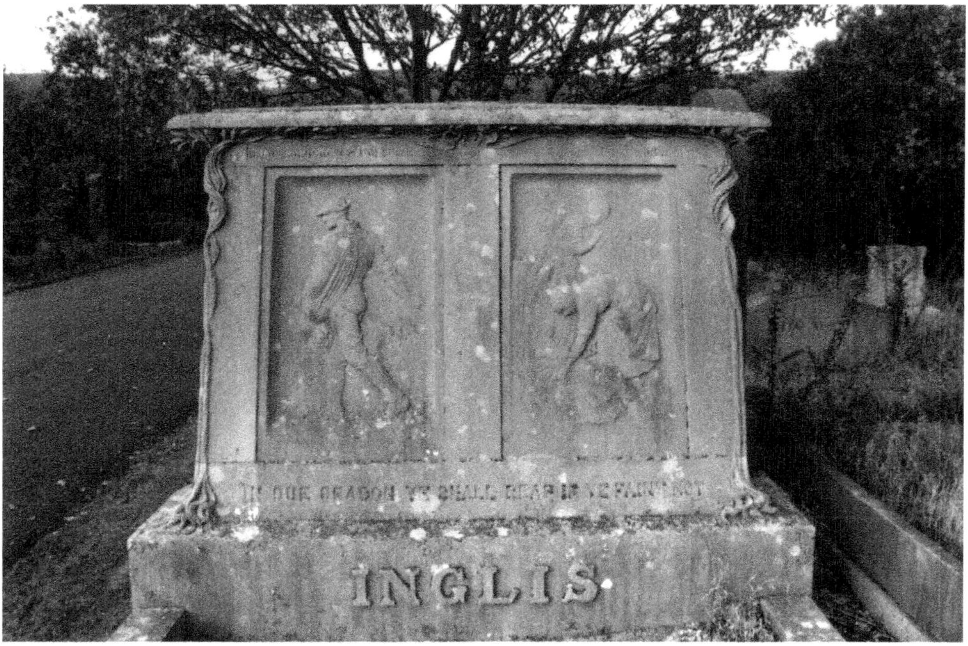

river tunnels. It appears from correspondence with Sir Ernest's great-grandson that Lilian Wade lived quite near his great-grandparents, so that might have led to the commission.[50] Given that Wade died in 1923 we might conclude that Moir Senior commissioned the memorial to his son, and that his name was added after his own death in 1933. Stylistically it bears some similarities to Wade's statuette *Victory* (c.1907) (**Figure 31**).

From around the 1890s we can trace a development in ambitious public decorative projects in London. Most such works by women sculptors were made during this period and were chiefly the result of private initiatives. Waterloo Place, for instance, was lined with statues on high pedestals, including a 1915 bronze statue of polar explorer Robert Falcon Scott made by his widow Kathleen (**Figure 63**). The monument was initiated by Royal Navy officers and financed by public subscription. Scott's free-standing statue is highly visible because of its size, material, genre and its placement on a tall granite pedestal in a central London square, in a garden to the rear of the United Services Club and fronting Waterloo Place. Scott is shown in full polar exploration attire, his right hand outstretched and holding a skiing stick. A letter dated 19 January 1914 from the Admiralty to HM Office of Works recorded the Navy's wish to erect the memorial, suggested an appropriate site and advised that Kathleen Scott should be engaged as the sculptor. The First Commissioner made some comments on a suitable site but was not keen on Scott: 'Personally I think it would be the greatest mistake to entrust such a work to Lady Scott's hands. From all I hear, she may be an admirable woman, but is absolutely devoid of all real artistic sense.' He also referred to a Scott memorial committee having decided to install a tablet in St Paul's Cathedral to commemorate the explorer, and which was also planning a statue; he queried whether this would make the Navy reconsider its plans for a memorial figure. However, by 4 May 1914 the site facing Waterloo Place was under consideration and the Admiralty asked whether the Office of Works would take charge of the statue and look after it; the negative view of Kathleen Scott appears not to have been shared by the Admiralty. In 1923 the names of the other four men who died with the explorer were included on a replacement plaque made by the sculptor.[51] The over life-size monument cost £1,500 and was unveiled by Arthur Balfour, who apparently said 'Now at last we have got a good statue in London.'[52] It is Scott's best-known work, following the tradition of late Victorian realism expected of such a memorial, albeit handled in a forceful manner.

Scott's first public commission had been a life-size monument to Charles Rolls, who founded Rolls-Royce in 1904. Unveiled in April

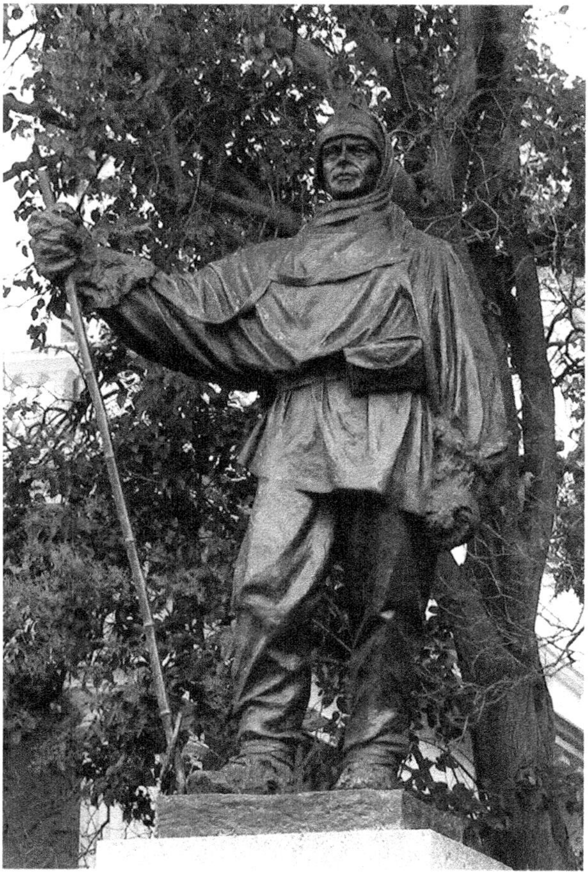

63. Kathleen Scott, *Robert Falcon Scott*, Waterloo Place, London, 1915

1912, it is positioned in a garden on the sea front at Dover. Rolls was the first Englishman to fly the Channel, but in July 1910 he was killed in a flying accident over Bournemouth. Scott asked John Tweed for advice on making a large sculpture as she was inexperienced and was working on a maquette at this time; apparently he gave her a book and told her that she must 'work it out' for herself.[53] A press photographer visited her to record the completed statuette, of which casts were sold, earning her £40. The monument was generally praised as being both life-like and expressing the character of its apparently modest subject. Another posthumous sculpture was Scott's statue to Captain Edward Smith of the *Titanic* in Beacon Park, Lichfield Public Gardens. Unveiled on 29 July 1914, it is 7 feet 8 inches high and positioned on a pedestal of Cornish granite. Smith came from Hanley, Staffordshire, and a statue had been intended for that town but was rejected. He had no connection with Lichfield, but the official explanation for the choice was that it was more convenient for visitors travelling from London or Liverpool than Hanley, and that in any case a memorial plaque had already been placed in Hanley Town Hall. Apparently some Lichfield citizens were unhappy with this turn of events.[54] The sculpture depicts a stoic Smith with folded arms and bears an inscription referring to him as 'bequeathing to his countrymen the memory and example of a great heart, a brave life, and a heroic death'. As he went down with his ship he was at the time regarded as a hero, although subsequently questions were asked about the decisions he made and in particular his failure to take notice of ice warnings.[55] However, at the unveiling there were many tributes voiced, including a message from Queen Alexandra and from others who had sailed as passengers with Smith, several of whom were American subscribers to the memorial. Equally, parallels were drawn between Smith and the bravery of Captain Scott, since they shared the same sculptor.

In 1928 Scott was working on a figure of the Right Honourable Edwin Samuel Montagu. It was unveiled in 1931 at Assembly House, Calcutta, and is now located on the Old Flagstaff House grounds, Barrackpore, the country residence of the Governor of West Bengal. Scott

> engaged a man to help but he was idle slow and clumsy, so I dispensed with him and I am getting on like anything alone. I have already put up a ton and a half of clay. If only I could leave it nude. If this thrill lasts I should have it finished in a fortnight ... I work like a fury till dark. God how I love big work. I push the great eight-foot thing out into the garden and back like a great juggernaut into its cage at night. The weather is glorious and I am so happy.

Later she made a statuette version:

> It is nasty niggly work but I stick to it because it seems I can sell half a dozen or so at £45 ... I don't want the money ... but even so I would like to make my garden pretty and mount my statues well. I shall have had a turnover of £2,700 this year. Pays for the studio all right![56]

5.3 The body

Some of the stylistic characteristics of the statuette can also be seen in sculptures of the nude body from the same period. It was normal for both the statuette and its larger equivalent not to be made to commission, thereby offering their makers a degree of freedom. A direct comparison can be made between Margaret Giles's 1902 statuette *Hero* (**Plate 7**) and Feodora Gleichen's almost contemporaneous *Diana*, installed in 1906 on top of a fountain in Hyde Park (**Figure 64**). This sculpture was donated by Lady Walter Palmer and is constructed from bronze and coloured marbles. *Diana* is presented in an assertive, active pose, quite different from more traditional portrayals of the huntress. The activity of the figure also reduces its erotic capability and might well have been perceived as referencing the fashionable rise in sport for women. The Giles statuette is more forceful in character, but of course was not a public work. Gleichen's *Diana* was also known as the *Artemis Fountain* and was originally located in woodland at Frognal before its relocation to the Rose Garden in the south-east corner of Hyde Park, with the fountain at its centre. Maquette versions were also sold.[57]

Katharine Maltwood's maquette for her monument *Primeval Canada Awakening to Her Destiny* (c.1912) attracted considerable attention, but sadly only the head survives. It was originally shown at the Arts and Crafts Society exhibition at the Grosvenor Gallery in 1912 and at the London Salon in 1913. Photographic evidence shows that the head was intended to be attached to a figure clothed in forest leaves, and a 1914 review confirmed the composition:

> The conception is that of a colossal woman, clothed in pine forests, with her head upturned to the skies and her hands at her sides protecting symbolic figures of moose and buffalo which rest upon the rectangular blocks forming the base of the monument. Between the feet of the woman stands a bearded figure, small in proportion, of a pioneer backwoodsman with an axe, his arm being outstretched as if in worship of Canada rising before and above him ... the suggestion might be that of a mountain coming to life before the impassioned gaze of the pioneer [**Figure 65**].[58]

The raised face was much admired; for instance, the *Observer* art critic wrote that 'the striving after the broad simplification of Egyptian or Assyrian archaic art must be welcomed', and he believed that the sculpture could be one of the most noteworthy pieces to be made by an English sculptor.[59] Stylistically there are some similarities to the work of Eric Gill, and both sculptors were rooted in the Arts and Crafts movement. Kineton Parkes had praised *Magna Mater* (**Plate 2**) but believed that *Primeval Canada* was an even better work. Writing particularly about the raised head, he described how 'the features, of Indian type, are slightly simplified, and their type-expression increased by the treatment, which is further emphasized by the straight folds of

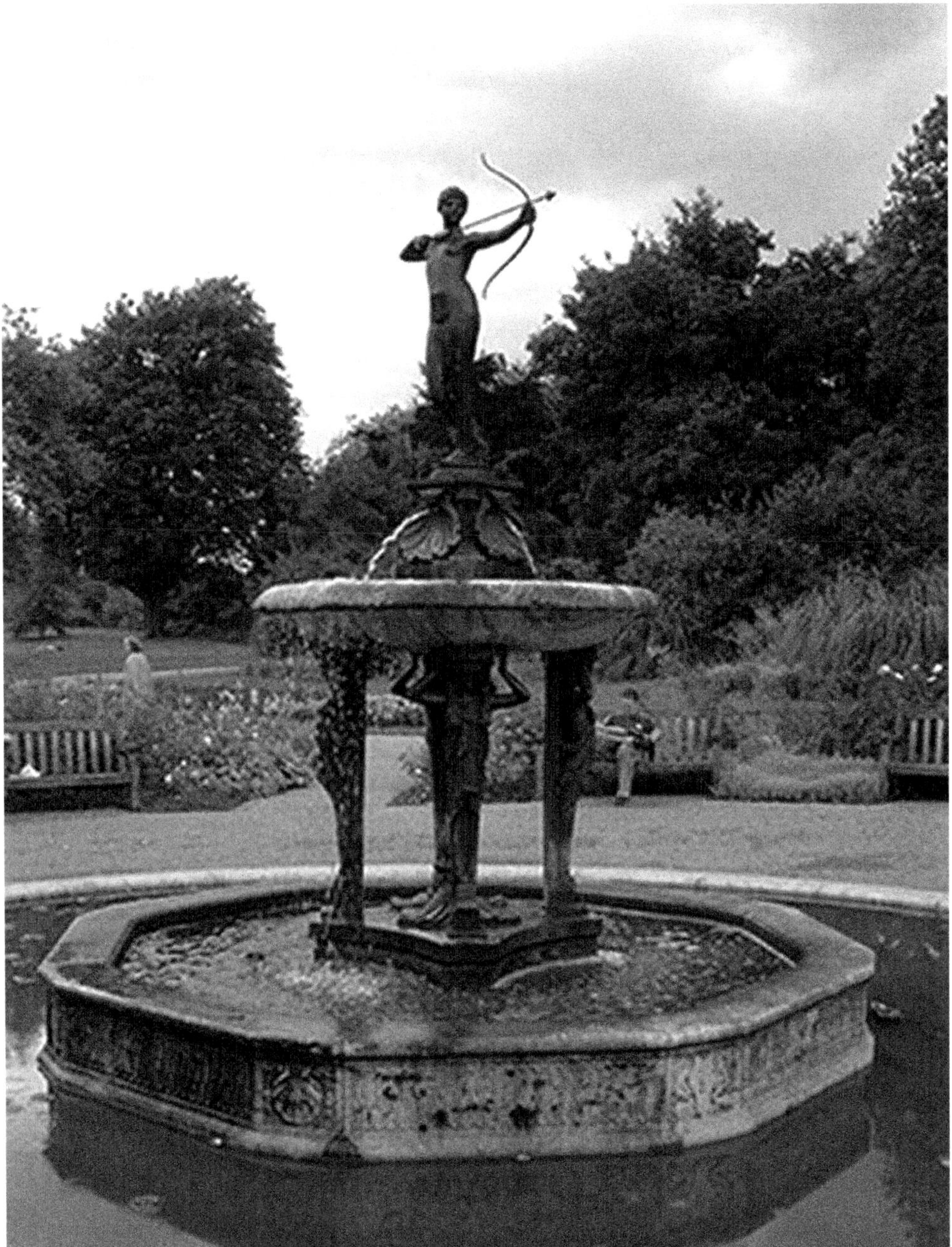

64. Feodora Gleichen, *Diana/Artemis Fountain/The Huntress*, Hyde Park, 1899

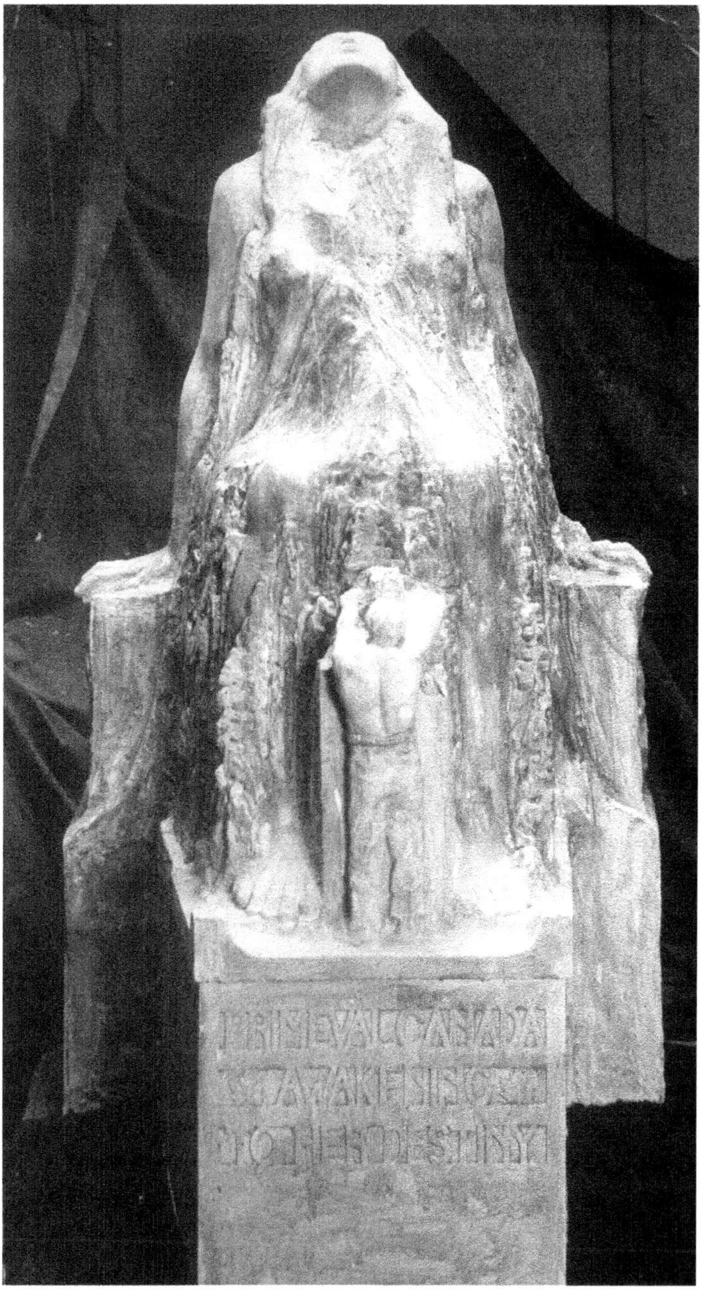

65. Photograph of Katharine Maltwood's *Primeval Canada Awakening to Her Destiny*, c.1912

drapery and the geometrical treatment of the muscles of the neck. This is colossal in size, hence its simplification.'[60] Maltwood's work reflected the artistic taste of the early twentieth century in her admiration for primitive and archaic art. Her simplified approach, which echoed the contemporary stylistic decorative treatment of architecture, meant that she was often referred to as 'the Epstein among women'.

Another example of her work that bears the alternative titles of *Adam* or *Primitive Man* (c.1912) has been likened to Rodin's work in both theme and handling (**Figure 66**). As with *Magna Mater*, the sculptor has used the device of small entwined bodies struggling up from the figure's arms, seemingly to represent humankind. Maltwood's *Mills of God* (1910) also attracted considerable praise: 'The writhing, but rhythmically linked, mass of agonized humanity, inexorably crushed between two solid stone wheels, is like a Michelangelo "Last Judgement" compressed into a few figures – it would lend itself to treatment on a larger scale, and it might even serve as a War Memorial' (**Figure 67**).[61] The sculpture comprised a giant wheel with multiple bodies helping one another to reach its top. The wheel was employed as a symbol of reincarnation, and Kineton Parkes applauded its 'simple but impressive conception'.[62] This sculpture was first exhibited in October 1919 at the Ridley Art Club and the Grafton Galleries, and a bronze version at Olympia in 1922. A 1924 appraisal in the *Studio* proposed that whereas much contemporary British sculpture lacked inspiration and originality, Maltwood's work had continually evolved, showing a freshness and breadth that was striking. Her work reflected aspects of both Christianity and Buddhism, yet also dealt with 'the mysterious force of growth which permeates all life'. Her sense of form was praised and it was noted how her bas-reliefs demonstrated her understanding of light and shade.[63]

Apart from her highly successful portrait sculptures, Kathleen Scott was also well known for her idealized, male nude figure bronzes which were produced between 1920 and 1938. In total she made 12 such sculptures in a variety of sizes: over life-size, life-size or large statuette. Reviewers at the time noted her two very different genres and styles of working, her forceful portrait busts and her graceful male nudes. Mark Stocker has pointed to a parallel that can be made here with Epstein, whose more creative work was essentially paid for by his lucrative portraiture, and it is the former for which he is admired. In the case of Scott, the reverse is true, it being her bronze heads of famous men that are best known.[64] However, Scott was thoroughly committed to her ideal nude sculpture, saying that 'really the only thing I've cared about

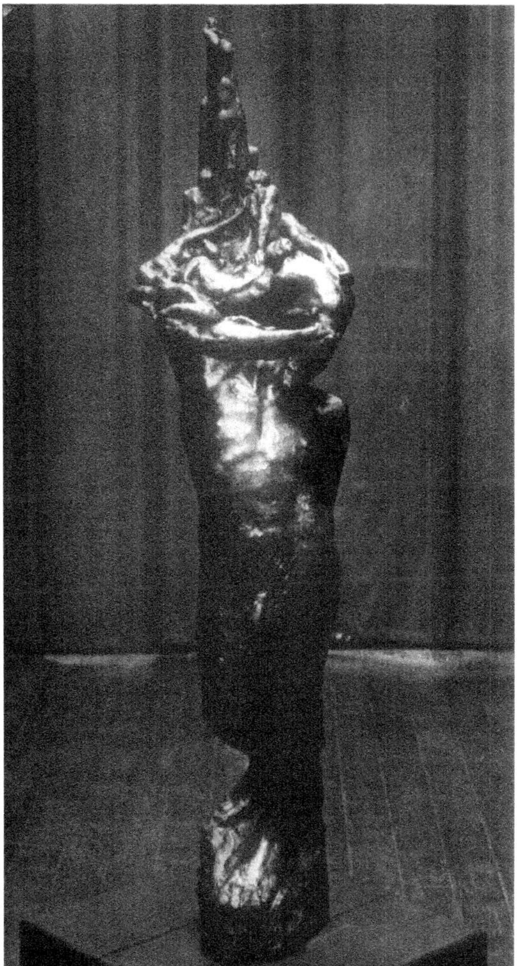

66. Photograph of Katharine Maltwood's *Adam* or *Primitive Man*, c.1912

are young male objects'.[65] Stocker has suggested that Scott's subjection of the young male body to her gaze was 'uncomplicated, loving and idealised' and that in neither intent nor outcome was this examination at all threatening to male identity. He makes a parallel with Renoir's sensuous treatment of female nudes, arguing that these paintings had 'their sculptural counterpart in the flawlessly chased surfaces of Kathleen's boys'.[66] However, from this analogy the logical conclusion is that Scott's gaze is indeed sensual and at the very least reflects her known preference for male companionship and sculptural subjects. Certainly it is interesting to imagine how we might interpret them were the sculptor

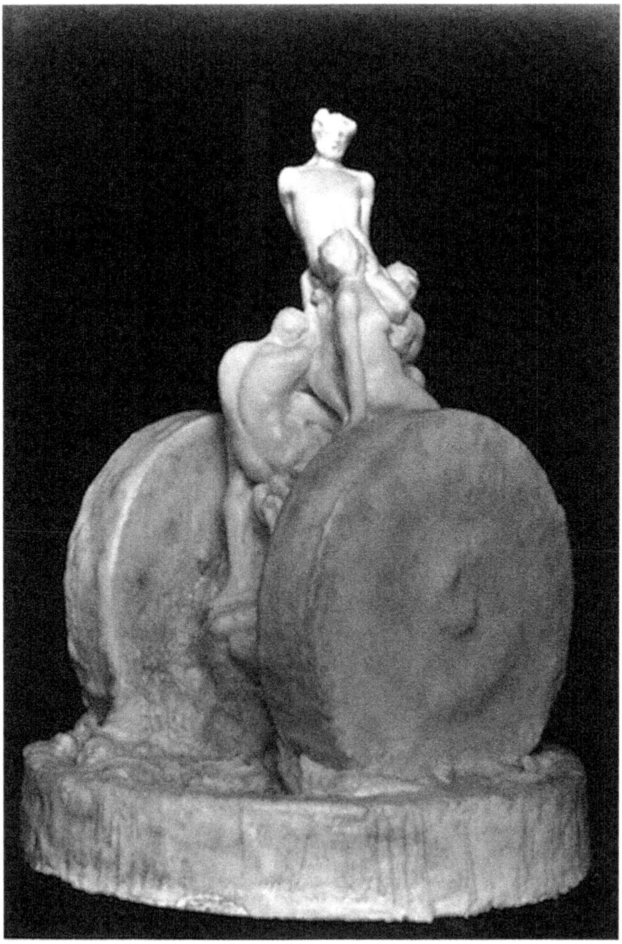

67. Katharine Maltwood, *Mills of God*, 1910

male: there is undoubtedly a fetishizing of the young masculine anatomy in these works. As in the rest of Scott's output, the influence of Rodin can be seen, but her male nudes are more direct than his. The smoother surfaces more closely equate to the realities of skin and of the body. Maybe, to paraphrase John Berger and Sir Kenneth Clark, they are more 'naked' than they are 'nude'.[67]

Scott's *These Had Most to Give* (1922–23) was also intended to be a war memorial: it is arguably her most important ideal sculpture and it was her favourite work (**Plate 17**). The model was 18-year-old Arnold Lawrence, brother of T. E. Lawrence. The life-size bronze was shown at the Grosvenor Gallery and the Royal Academy in 1923. It was also one of three works by Scott on display at the British Empire Exhibition in 1924. Subsequently it was exhibited at the 1925 Salon de la Societé des Artistes Français in Paris, where it was awarded a bronze medal and was praised in *Le Temps* for the honesty of its form and perfect modelling. The writer commented that English sculpture in its precision often became lifeless, but that in this particular example such exactitude had strengthened the work.[68] No sale resulted, however, and it stayed in Scott's garden until 1933, when she presented it to the Scott Polar Research Institute, for which she also sculpted a head of her husband to go in a niche above the entrance.

Stocker has drawn another parallel between Scott and Rodin with regard to the latter's retrospective titling of works, their possible meaning only resulting from their finished form. Scott changed the title of this sculpture from *Offering* to *1914–1918: These Had Most to Give*, to *Aspiration*, and finally to the more generic *Youth*. However, the second title, without dates, is the one most commonly used. Through its placement outside the Scott Polar Research Institute it would eventually stand as a memorial to the polar expedition, despite the incongruity of its nudity. The statue was nearly bought for the Tate Gallery. Sir Joseph Duveen visited Scott in July 1926 and she recalled that he

> professed simply to adore my work, used most extravagant adjectives, and finally said that he wanted to buy 'These Had Most to Give' … for the Tate Gallery … oh dear I mustn't count my chickens, especially such a sudden chicken, but it would be very nice to be represented in the Tate, and me a woman and alive and all.[69]

However, this did not materialize; instead in 1929 Duveen gave the gallery Scott's bust of Herbert Asquith (1913).

Geoffrey Dearmer, who was sculpted by Scott, particularly praised *These Had Most to Give*:

> The figure is … the embodied personality of self-sacrifice. If good modelling were enough, such a figure in repose would be enough; but beautiful execution is lifeless without beautiful conception. The life-size figure is erect; the head thrown back, the arms outstretched. It is intense but not restless, for it has about it the poise of perfect balance … Here the upturned and averted face admirably restrains the passionate quality of the figure. That may be the technical explanation; but the significance is deeper since, to our dull eyes, the human body is impersonal but the face personal. We cannot see the averted face, and the figure is unknown. It is this impersonal quality that makes the work a full, perfect and sufficient emblem of sacrifice.[70]

Scott, who rarely commented on the specifics of her sculptures, did echo Dearmer's analysis when she said that the 'outstretched hands and the upturned head are expressive of sacrifice, of absolute surrender to ideas, and I intended it to typify the holocaust of youth during the war'.[71] She also later said that 'I should like to see it placed on the top of some hill so that it could stand outlined against the sky.'[72]

Scott's intention that some of these ideal nudes should serve as war memorials was not realized, even at a time when memorials were greatly needed, and she complained that memorials showing figures in full uniform were preferred.[73] However, some critics seemed to find the ideal sculptures either empty of meaning or overly theatrical.[74] Indeed there was some opposition to *These Had Most to Give* at the Institute, as it was thought to refer too much to death and martyrdom. The site is also rather unsatisfactory, as the sculpture is placed on a narrow strip of ground between the building and a busy road, only separated from the latter by a low wall. It looks at its best when viewed from the front against a background of trees which form the boundary with the adjacent property. The Master of Downing College, Albert Seward, told Frank Debenham, an expedition veteran and then director of the Institute, that he could not

> really applaud the kind of spirit in which the sculptor gave it (it having been executed for an entirely different motive) and ... its position in the front of the building is likely to arouse comment just of the kind I should like to avoid, some of it surprise at the sacrifice idea, and some of it mere ribaldry.[75]

It was, however, not really feasible to refuse this gift from Scott's widow.

Scott's life-size bronze *Ad Astra* (1937–38) was shown at Ackermann's in 1936 and at the Royal Academy in 1938. This sculpture, along with *The Kingdom is Within* (**Figure 2**), did not attract as much comment as had *These Had Most to Give* and, as was the case with the latter, the title *Ad Astra* (literally *To the Stars*) was changed several times. It was originally called *The Strength Within*, which temporarily became the somewhat bizarre *Strength through Joy*, and then later *Ready to Pounce*. This in turn seemed problematic in the uncertain political climate, and so for a time its title became simply *England*. In March 1940 Scott recorded that she had sold her 'big nude boy for a site at Welwyn Garden City. To an unknown solicitor for a very reduced price. **£267.** Still I'm absolutely delighted. I so love to get good homes for my boys & I'm to design the pedestal.'[76] The following year she approved its location: 'set up in the parky wood in the middle of the town ... I think it looks very lovely in its original surroundings – tall lovely trees – tall lovely men – lovely.'[77]

Frances Darlington's seated figure *The Little Sea Maiden* (1905) was shown at Leeds City Art Gallery's 1906 Spring Exhibition (**Figure 68**). It could be seen as related to *The Magic Crystal* (**Figure 48**), since the girl appears similar in her age and hairstyle. Writing about *The Little Sea Maiden*, several contemporary critics focused on the girl's gaze as

> infused with so many different emotions ... at once ... gazing to the furthest possible distance, yet inwardly contemplating something equally deep within ... In contrast to *The Magic Crystal*, the spectator's focus, as well as the subject's has shifted away from the object to the gaze (and imagined thoughts) of the subject.

The Little Sea Maiden was bought by Leeds City Art Gallery, giving Darlington some independence of income. It appears that the unrealized

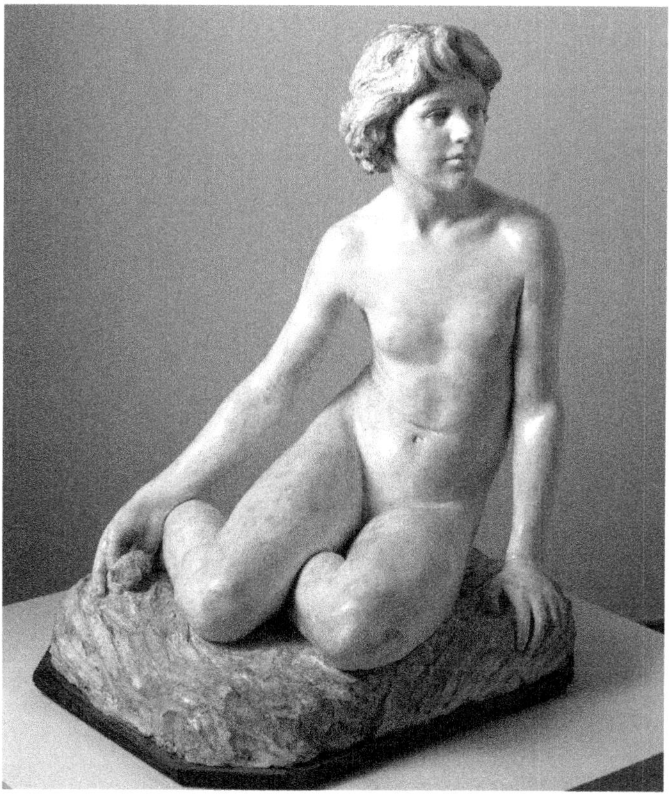

68. Frances Darlington, *The Little Sea Maiden*, 1905

intention was that the figure should function as a design for a bronze statue to be situated on Liverpool's waterfront.[78]

A strikingly different yet almost contemporaneous sculpture was Edith Downing's *Avarice* of 1908 (**Figure 69**). The *New York Times* noted that this sculpture, whose alternative title was *The Spirits of the Trusts*, was much admired by visitors to the 1908 Paris Salon, being 'regarded with both admiration and wonder – admiration because of its artistic excellence, wonder because of the strange conception it embodies'.[79] The accession note for this sculpture in the National Museum of Wales describes it as depicting 'an old haggard woman, kneeling on a rectangular block. Right arm outstretched as if to grasp something. Her left hand is at her side and is clutching a money-bag.' Goscombe John wrote to the National Museum of Wales in December 1928 stating that Downing had sent him several photographs of her past work, which he recommended that the museum acquire. He had asked Downing to forward some of these images to the museum for inspection, and John particularly noted *Avarice*.[80] Subsequently the museum's keeper wrote to Downing in 1930, sending photographs of her now acquired sculptures, and saying that he would like, for comparative purposes, to see her own photograph of *The Spirit of the Trusts* (*Avarice*).[81] Why he wanted this is unclear – possibly it was to confirm the best placement of the piece – but it remains an intriguing request. Downing duly replied with two photographs of the sculpture, and also made the comment that she felt that photographs of her sculptures would 'look softer and less metallic if they were printed on tinted paper'.[82] In 1901 Spielmann had described her work as characterized by 'its sweetness and grace and charming feminine quality', so it is interesting to speculate on what he might have thought of *Avarice*.[83]

Audiences admired Dora Gordine's bronze portrait heads, whose simplified modern style was seen as the antithesis of their academic equivalents. However, many were less happy with her treatment of the female body, for example the life-size *Javanese Dancer* (1927–28), which some saw as using distortion for the sake of it (**Figure 70**).[84] The exaggerated swing of the hips deviated markedly from Aristide Maillol's classically inspired forms, although the frequent comparisons between the two sculptors' work undoubtedly helped Gordine's reputation, since he was regularly referred to as the greatest living sculptor. In explicitly referring to Maillol's work, Gordine positioned herself within the currently admired French figurative tradition, which comprised a modernist reworking of the classic female nude. Maillol's

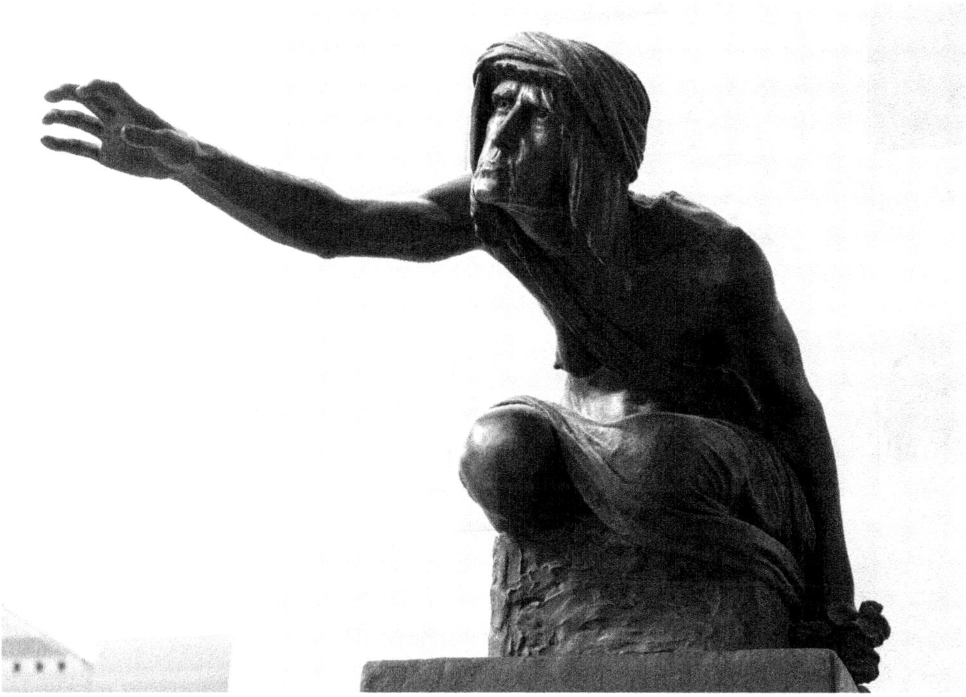

69. Edith Downing, *Avarice*, 1907–08

work was seen by many as indicating the way in which sculpture might develop following the First World War, 'after the "painterly" excesses of Rodin'.[85] Gordine certainly took Maillol's advice on working from life and relying on her own aesthetic sense as her guide. This tactic was vital in enabling her career in Paris and London, and between the wars she was also routinely compared with Epstein, Hepworth and Dobson. However, her approach to representing the female and male nude was different from these other sculptors. Gordine's *Javanese Dancer* drew on the popular image of the erotic dancer, with the body opened up to the viewer. With a less smooth surface than that seen in Maillol's work, we are even more aware of the figure's physicality, the result being 'an uneasy tension between the material object occupying the viewer's space and the represented female body'.[86] Against an increasing emphasis in the interwar years on materials and processes, and the masculinity of the act of direct carving, Gordine's life-size figures proved uncomfortable viewing. They are physically strong

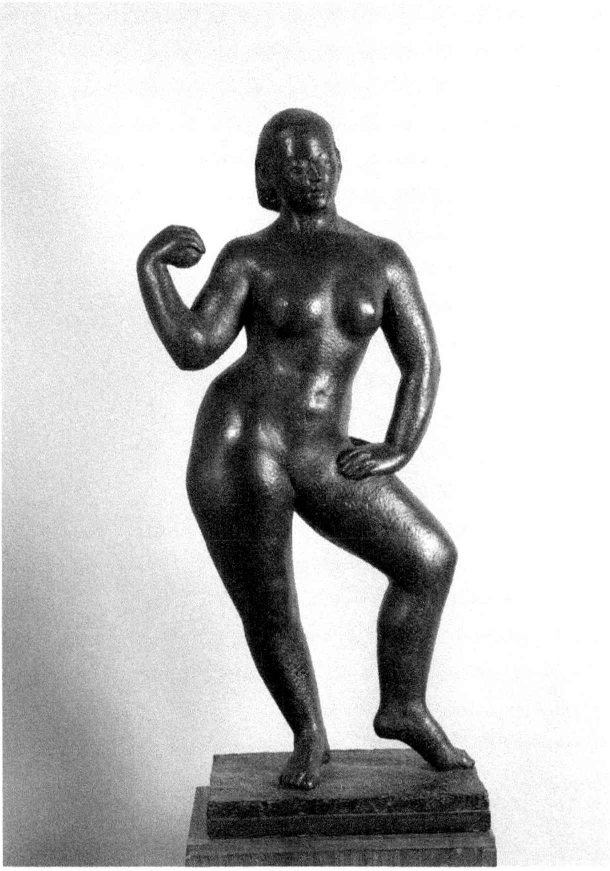

70. Dora Gordine, *Javanese Dancer*, 1927–28

sculptures but were also, for some, 'not sufficiently removed from the "real" bodies which they evoke'.[87]

It is possible to approach Gordine's female sculptures as an alternative to Moore's monumental figures such as the Leeds *Reclining Figure* of 1929 or to Hepworth's early 1930s sculptures based on stones, which related more obviously to the English landscape. Gordine's sculpture is more in line with Epstein and his interest in the various bodies 'that tell of empire and the cultural diversity of cosmopolitan London in the 1930s'.[88] However, Gordine did not like contemporary sculptural developments, stating in her second television appearance in 1938 that sculpture was 'going through a very bad time'.[89] Nonetheless, the truncation evident in her two male nudes places her firmly within a modernist framework. *Walking Male Torso* (1927–28) and *Dyak/Headhunter* (1931–32) (**Figure 71**) were both greatly admired, and in 1938 the latter was shown at the Royal Academy and in 1951 at the Festival of Britain. Arthur Symons described *Dyak* as

> magnificently masculine and there is an intense simplicity and that intensity of life which seems to exist in every limb. She has given him neither head nor feet. What she gives is the body of a primitive animal, ready to seize his prey like a wild beast, virile and capable of any violent action. And you feel the solidity of that immense weight, what force and reality, what sudden arrested life in those long arms and furiously clenched hands.[90]

These sculptures of male bodies are in stark contrast to those made by Kathleen Scott, which are vulnerable in their open poses, more youthful and sensuous.

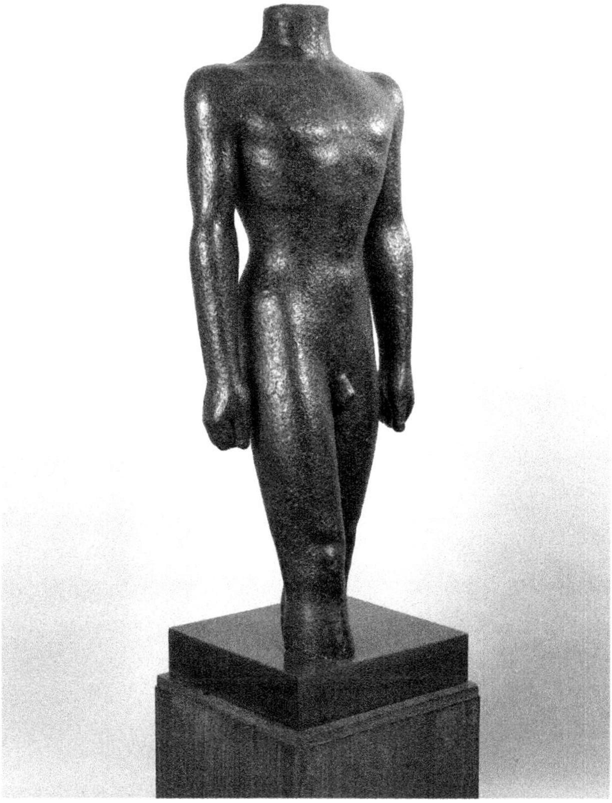

71. Dora Gordine, *Dyak/ Headhunter/Man*, 1931–32

In the late 1940s, partly due to a scarcity of materials, Gordine decided to concentrate on making small statues, but the production of multiple casts adversely affected her critical reputation, and at the 1949 Leicester Galleries exhibition her portrait heads were preferred. Unlike many other modellers, Gordine exercised direct control over her work by not using assistants and not translating her work into stone versions. She worked in clay with the live model in front of her; plaster casts were made in her studio-homes and she spent days at the foundry overseeing the casting of her work.[91] After the unexpected death of her husband in 1966 she practically ceased exhibiting and producing work; however, in later life her reputation had a resurgence. In particular she was shown in the important exhibition *Sculpture in Britain between the Wars*, curated by Peyton Skipwith at the Fine Art Society, London in 1986. An obituary described her as 'one of the more talented among the honourable band of sculptors who managed to develop a distinctive modern style in the 1920s and yet remained within the figurative tradition'.[92] Sir Anthony Caro described his time as a student in the 1940s:

> The English artists that we looked to were Jacob Epstein and Dora Gordine. In the 1940s Henry Moore's work was not known at all to us students ... Gordine never had the wildness or taste for experimentation of Epstein, but she was an ambitious artist and her work has strength. It is clear that she looked at Indian art and her sculpture has ... serenity ... steadiness ... It may not seem so very extraordinary to us nowadays, but when we place her work against that of the much more successful academic sculptors of the time it is a million miles better.[93]

The emphasis on direct carving negatively affected Gordine's reputation, following a lineage through from Epstein to Gill to Moore in the 1920s, and the latter's dominance of British sculpture in the 1950s.[94]

Barbara Hepworth's truncated bodies are less dynamic than both Scott's and Gordine's sculptures, having a quality of stillness. Undoubtedly the modernist bias of her sculpture worked in Hepworth's favour from the 1930s onwards, when artists not adopting this approach were marginalized within art history, and her move into abstraction allowed her to engage with public commissions. As we have seen, the linking of Hepworth's work to that of Henry Moore could be problematic; however, it undoubtedly had the benefit of keeping her name in the public consciousness. As with Moore, too much reliance has been placed on her own words as a means whereby to understand her practice; neither sculptor's work was consistent, and some of their later work raised issues of quality as their fame increased and commissions

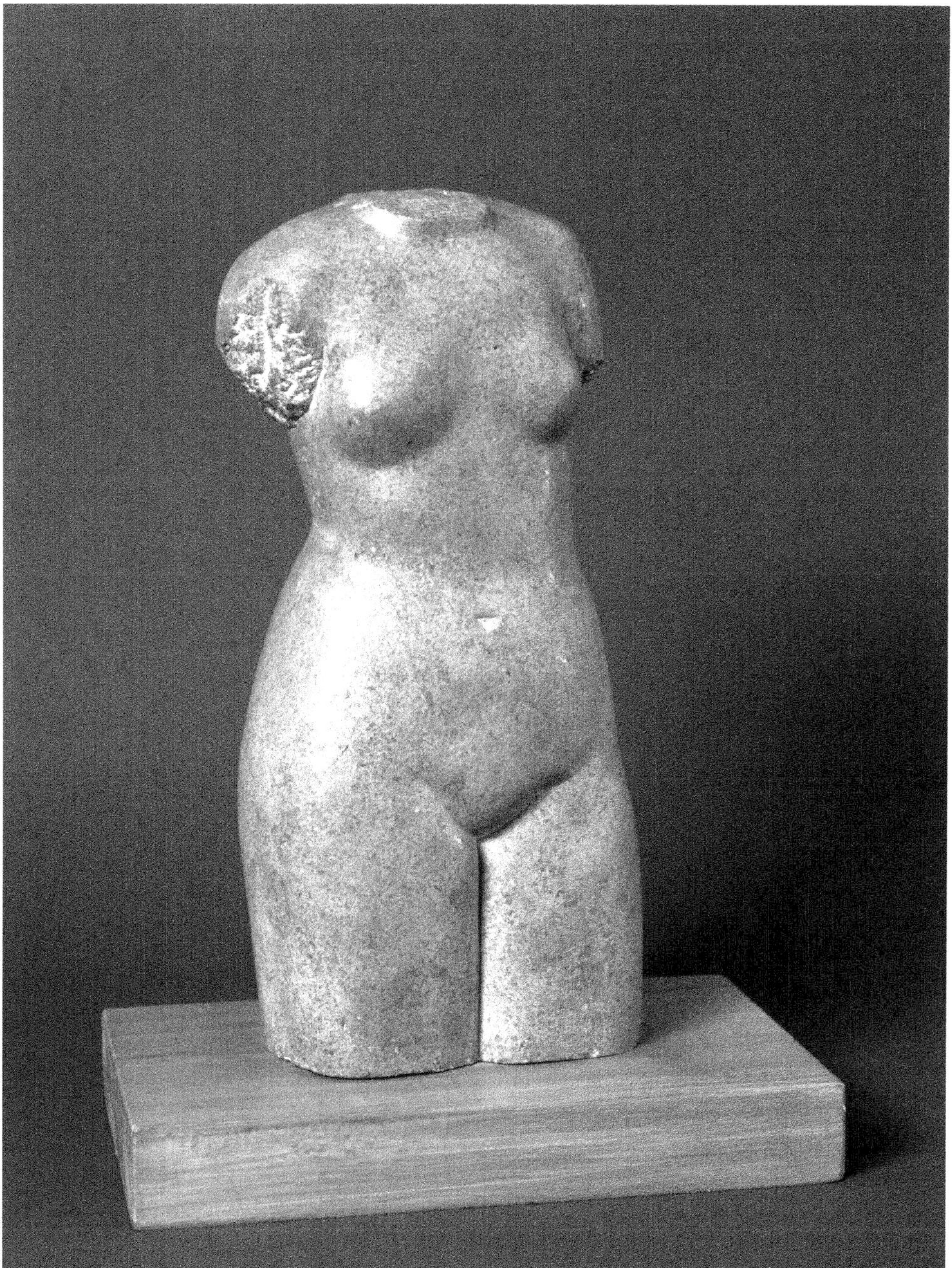

72. Barbara Hepworth, *Torso*, 1928

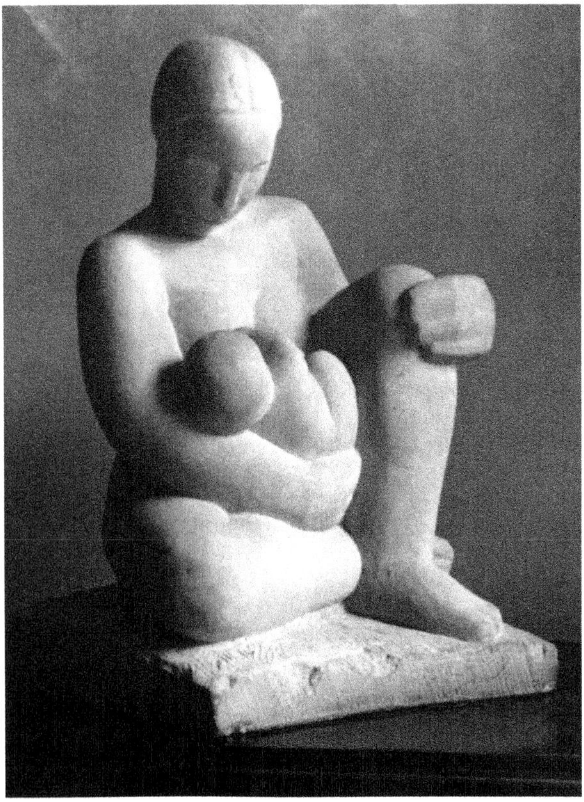

73. Betty Rea, *Mother and Child*, c.1932

were gained. In 1928 Hepworth and her then husband John Skeaping produced their first show at the Beaux Arts Gallery. In 1931 Kineton Parkes mentioned Hepworth briefly in *The Art of Carved Sculpture*, but placed no more emphasis on her than any other woman sculptor discussed, which is in stark contrast to subsequent accounts, in which Hepworth came to the fore and other women artists disappeared from view. Parkes stated that she had made three important torsos, presumably *Torso* of 1928 being one of these (**Figure 72**). He referred to another joint exhibition with Skeaping at Arthur Tooth's Gallery in October 1930, complaining that the gallery was cluttered with 50 sculptures that did not show much progress from earlier exhibited work. He understood that the aim of the exhibition was to show a variety of materials, but he found the execution of individual works to be 'monotonous'.[95] George Eumorfopoulos admired Hepworth's work and bought her *Doves* (1927) (**Figure 41**) from Hepworth and Skeaping's studio show in late 1927.

If we return to the 1928 carving *Torso* we see a sculpture that embodies both the contemporary ethos of direct carving and the widespread sculptural representation of the truncated female torso. Possibly Hepworth's version is more contained and less overtly sexualized than many of the versions produced by male sculptors. Hepworth's 1932 *Kneeling Figure* in rosewood was acquired by the Wakefield City Art Gallery (and is now at the Hepworth Wakefield) as a result of Hepworth reducing its price, a Victoria and Albert Museum purchase grant, and a donation from Hepworth's former school. This acquisition took place around the time that Hepworth had an exhibition in Wakefield, being keen to exhibit in her home city. In 1944 she wrote to Ernest Musgrave, the director at the Wakefield City Art Gallery, thanking him for the show and enquiring about the local response to it: 'I don't mind the hard facts because I know you must have a very uphill task! I saw the Express notice of Saturday and I think it is, without any doubt, the worst press notice I've had in 16 years, to say nothing of the grudging appreciation for *your* work.'[96] Later that year she wrote to say how pleased she was that there was hope of raising sufficient money to acquire her *Kneeling Figure*, which she characterized as 'a good early work and early works are important because the thread runs right through, and abstraction comes from something and not as a bolt out of the blue. In my case I feel increasingly in touch with the human figure and landscape every year.'[97]

It is clear that the acquisition of Hepworth's sculptures by public galleries around this period was not a straightforward matter. For example, in October 1937 the director of the Lefevre Galleries wrote to Musgrave in the context of a forthcoming exhibition in Wakefield, saying that Hepworth would be happy to lend one or two of her sculptures if Wakefield would agree to acquire one work for its permanent collection. The reply was not promising. Musgrave responded that this was an unusual request; he was at pains to point out that on a personal level he was keen to acquire Hepworth's work, but that it was difficult to raise funds to purchase contemporary work. However, he was clearly nervous of public response since he felt that he would first

> like the public to become a little more familiar with her. Any work she sends will be in good company. Henry Moor [*sic*] and other advanced sculptors are exhibiting. I sincerely hope that Miss Hepworth will favour us by sending us works despite the fact that we cannot commit ourselves to purchase.

From the third letter in this exchange from the Lefevre Galleries it is clear that Hepworth had given way on the acquisition issue and would be lending two sculptures. However, the pressure on Musgrave was reasserted on the basis of Hepworth being a native of the county and also because she had been generous in the loan of her sculptures. It was probably not wise to add that 'The artists in London who are keen about modern sculpture have been greatly interested in her present Exhibition, which has been quite an artistic and financial success.'[98]

Betty Rea (1904–65) studied at the Regent Street Polytechnic between 1922 and 1924 and at the Royal College of Art from 1924. Her earliest sculpture reflects the emphasis on direct carving espoused in the 1920s, and she was taught at the Royal College by Moore. She was a founder member of the Artists' International Association (AIA) and its secretary between 1934 and 1936; she was also chair of the Arts Peace Campaign and worked on a mural in the Unofficial Peace Pavilion at the 1937 Paris World Fair. In the introduction to the 1935 publication *Five on Revolutionary Art*, Rea argued that the artist had a responsibility to address contemporary issues.[99] This commitment required the defeat of fascism and the construction of a society rooted in communist ideas. It also aligned to contemporary Marxist ideas such as those advocated by John Berger, who throughout the 1950s championed social realism, Rea being among the artists whom he supported. At the AIA there was much discussion on the issue of artistic style, the particular merits of abstract or realist art, and the relevance of Social Realism. It is important to consider how we might understand the term 'realism' in relation to Rea, and how the figurative nature of her work (as with the majority of sculptors discussed in this book) should not consign it to a regressive, essentially academic lineage. Sculpture that is as much about content as it is about form needs to be reinstated in its rightful place within the history of the medium. Rea's work in particular was largely driven by social or political ideas and as such had to be visually coherent.[100] **Figure** 73 shows her addressing the established subject of *Mother and Child* (c.1932) in a work shown that year at the London Group exhibition. The distractions of other concerns and responsibilities that dogged so many women sculptors is exemplified in this description of Rea by Bryan Robertson in the catalogue introduction for a 1965 retrospective of the artist's work. He wrote:

> Responsible and impulsive; always involved in household activities and her children; a superb cook, creating happy, festive occasions that were totally unpretentious and easy but quickened by an aristocratic (a

> word she would have detested) sense of style; engaged by good causes, including educational enlightenment – I felt that her earlier sculpture was unforced, absolutely true to its subject, and often alive with a personal, quiet beauty but still a by-product, almost, of other aspects of her life. Making a good dinner, putting a child to bed, working for refugees – or modelling a figure – seemed too near each other: different facets of a happily domesticated nature that also embraced issues and people outside her home.[101]

In his *A Short History of English Sculpture* Eric Underwood proposed that Anne Strauss preferred carving to modelling, and he illustrated and wrote about her work *Family Group* in tulip wood (c.1930) as one that proved her concern with mass, handled with dignity and restraint (**Plate 18**).[102] Apart from Barbara Hepworth, Strauss is the only woman sculptor to have her work illustrated in Underwood's publication. Another of Strauss's works is her 1926 *Torso* in Verde di Prato marble, a confident work completely in line with avant-garde practices of the decade. She exhibited throughout the 1930s and continued to carve after the war, but withdrew from exhibiting.[103] In 1936 her alabaster carving *Man on a Dragon* from 1928 was shown at the Venice Biennale's British Pavilion alongside works by Hepworth and Ethel Walker. She exhibited at the Royal Academy annual exhibition, at the Goupil Gallery between 1937 and 1939, and at the Women's International Art Club between 1934 and 1938, but is little known today.

Mary Spencer Watson also produced work which centred on the human as well as animal body. In 1923 her parents bought Dunshay Manor, located three miles outside Swanage, where in 1926 stonemason Titus Lander of the Purbeck stone quarry provided Spencer Watson with tools and showed her how to work the stone. Aged 15 she went to Bournemouth Municipal College in 1928, chiefly to prepare a portfolio with which to apply for entry to the Royal Academy Schools. The latter rejected her application as they felt she needed more experience, and so she went to the Slade instead where she modelled portrait heads and drew from the antique. A year later she was accepted by the Royal Academy Schools and studied there between 1930 and 1934. But she was only taught life modelling, not carving. She moved to the Central School of Arts and Crafts for a year, studying with Alfred Turner and John Skeaping, under whom she was taught to carve stone. **Figure 74** shows Spencer Watson's striking early work *Thought*, dated 1928, made when she was just 15. There had been a possibility that Spencer Watson might study with Eric Gill when she was looking to work in the studio of an established sculptor. However, in 1937 she visited the International Exhibition in Paris. There she saw the work of Ossip Zadkine and as a result wrote to him. Whereas Skeaping had taught Spencer Watson to produce smooth surfaces, Zadkine encouraged her to leave a surface where the chisel marks were evident. She also toured the French cathedrals, examined the medieval carvings at the Musée Cluny and visited Autun to study the work of Gislebertus. In the mid-1930s Spencer Watson met Elizabeth Muntz and they became friends and relatively close neighbours in Dorset. After the war Spencer Watson taught art in five schools. These included Clayesmore where she had a studio and taught until 1948.

Concerning her affinity with blocks of stone, Spencer Watson believed that Victorian sculptors had lost touch with the material they were working, and that even someone of the stature of Rodin made stone models and then passed these to his assistants who would use pointing machines to produce a finished marble sculpture, and so he hardly touched these works. Spencer Watson read Eric Gill's 1934 book *Art and a Changing Civilisation* and no doubt was in agreement with his belief that an artist needed to be a craftsman. Spencer Watson's work is neither naturalistic nor non-figurative. This could be seen as reflecting her wide interests, such as in Greek and medieval carving, as well as the work of Zadkine, Gill and Epstein. Much of her larger work was intended for a garden setting and the sculptures seem best to fit an outdoor rather than indoor environment, particularly when made from her favourite material of Purbeck stone.[104]

She was still only 24 at the time of her 1937 solo exhibition at the Mansard Gallery, showing sculptures in green marble, alabaster and wood, as well as terracotta figures and plaques, the latter arising from a study made at the Academy Schools of the collection of Tanagra figures at the British Museum.[105] Eric Newton accepted her invitation to visit the show and it appears that this was his first encounter with her work.[106] Apart from this correspondence there is little archival evidence of significant response to her diligent mass-typed invitations to journals and newspapers:

> Dear Sir, I enclose a notice of my first exhibition in London, also a few photos. John Skeaping with whom I have worked says 'I like all the works for the strength and guts which they have ... The little (Terracotta) Figures are most attractive.' I hope you will come. Yours truly ... P.S. I shall be much obliged if you will kindly return the photos in the enclosed stamped addressed envelope.[107]

74. Mary Spencer Watson, *Thought*, 1928

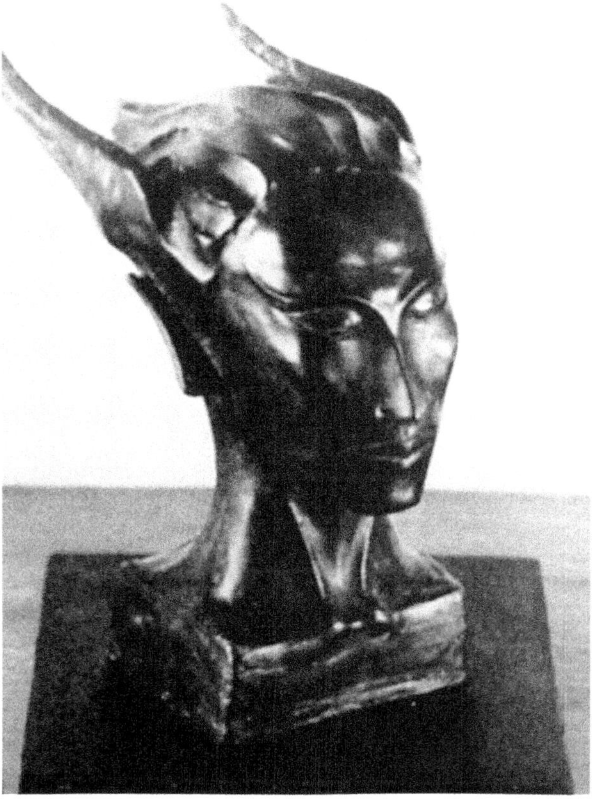

Her *Mother and Child* from the mid-1930s was also exhibited at the Mansard Gallery show, as was her *Young Beast* from the same period. She exhibited at Shire Hall, Dorchester in 1945, at Foyles Art Gallery in 1946, and participated in group shows at the Royal Academy. She also exhibited with the National Society of Painters, Sculptors, Engravers and Potters in the 1940s, the Women's International Art Club, RBA Galleries between 1947 and 1951, and with the 1950 Arts and Crafts Exhibition Society at the Victoria and Albert Museum. Her *Auccassin and Nicolette* (c.1946) particularly showed Zadkine's influence (**Figure 75**). The title is taken from a thirteenth-century French love song about a romance between a young knight and a captive Saracen slave. The stone, Purbeck Burr, is relatively rare and thus it is unusual to source large blocks. Spencer Watson emphasized the integrity of the block by leaving parts of it uncut: the effect is like a two-sided relief, but the carving is pierced so that the shapes continually shift as you move around the sculpture.

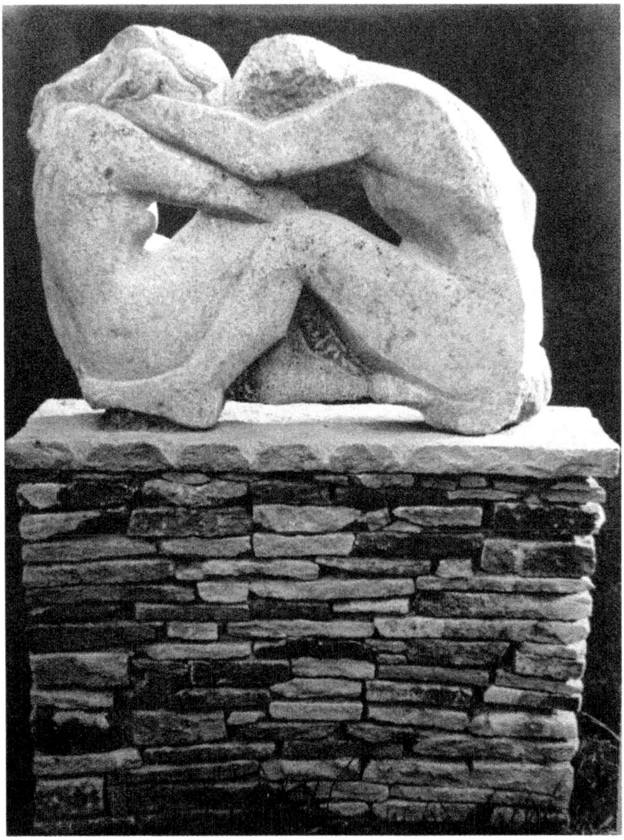

75. Mary Spencer Watson, *Auccassin and Nicolette*, c.1947

After the war Spencer Watson received important commissions from some of the best architects involved in post-war reconstruction, including Sir Frederick Gibberd at Harlow New Town and Sir Edward Maufe at Guildford Cathedral. In 2004 her first retrospective of more than 50 sculptures was held in Salisbury; reviews noted that she had been working for more than 70 years in rural Dorset, remaining relatively unknown. A reviewer for *Country Life* wrote 'When I met her at Dunshay Manor, the mellow 15th-century house where she has lived since 1923, I was struck by her animated blue eyes, thick mop of silvery hair and strong, sculptural hands. This is a woman in her nineties who reveals no hint of frailty.'[108] The exhibition comprised both wood and stone carvings, as well as some early terracotta works. The strong sense of plane in Spencer Watson's carved work resulted in sculptures that retained a vivid sense of the weightiness of the original block of stone.

At the time of her death at the age of 92 Spencer Watson remained undervalued.

This chapter has covered a wide range of work both in terms of timespan and stylistic characteristics. In the work of the more academically minded sculptors, such as Kathleen Scott, the conventional genres of the portrait bust and statue were handled in a particularly robust and expressive manner. Other sculptors, such as Katharine Maltwood, produced work that easily sits alongside contemporary avant-garde practices, and the work of Mary Spencer Watson has an individualized vigour that speaks to a range of European sculptural languages. The variety of work produced by these women sculptors makes clear their distinctive practices. It certainly weakens claims that their work was inevitably derivative and a pale imitation of the supposedly innovative sculptures produced by their male colleagues.

Notes

1 Eoin Martin, 'Framing Victoria: royal portraiture and architectural sculpture in Victorian Britain', *Sculpture Journal*, 23.2 (2014), p. 197.
2 David Duff, *The Life Story of H.R.H. Princess Louise, Duchess of Argyll* (Bath: Cedric Chivers, 1940), pp. 100–01.
3 Elizabeth Longford (ed.), *Darling Loosy: Letters to Princess Louise 1856–1939* (London: Weidenfeld and Nicolson, 1991), pp. 14–15.
4 Hawksley, *The Mystery of Princess Louise*, p. 76.
5 Spielmann, *British Sculpture and Sculptors of To-Day*, pp. 160–61.
6 Hawksley, *The Mystery of Princess Louise*, pp. 110–11.
7 Hawksley, *The Mystery of Princess Louise*, pp. 2–3.
8 Hawksley, *The Mystery of Princess Louise*, p. 5.
9 Hawksley, *The Mystery of Princess Louise*, p. 237.
10 Odile Ayral-Clause, *Camille Claudel, A Life* (New York: Harry N. Abrams, 2002), p. 51.
11 Ayral-Clause, *Camille Claudel, A Life*, p. 78.
12 Marchal, *Finding Frances*, p. 102.
13 Robert Rattray Tatlock, *The Daily Telegraph*, 6 October 1928, p. 15.
14 Fran Lloyd in Black and Martin, *Dora Gordine: Sculptor, Artist, Designer*, p. 76.
15 Evelyn Silber, 'The Leicester Galleries and the promotion of modernist sculpture in London, 1902–75', *Sculpture Journal*, 21.2 (2012), p. 139.
16 'Amazing studies by girl sculptor', *Daily Express*, 6 October 1923, p. 3.
17 Reginald Wilenski, 'Girl sculptor genius', *Evening Standard*, 5 October 1928, n.p.
18 Llewellyn, *The First Lady of Mulberry Walk*, pp. 93–95.
19 Stocker, '"My masculine models"', p. 51.
20 'Are we vain and uninteresting?', *The Bulletin and Scots Pictorial*, 1 April 1927. University of Cambridge Manuscripts Library, GB/NNAF/P 162494, NCUACS 87.8.99.167/1, Press Cuttings.
21 '"Do not imitate men"', *Kent Messenger*, 18 July 1931. University of Cambridge Manuscripts Library, GB/NNAF/P 162494, NCUACS 87.8.99.167/1, Press Cuttings.
22 Young, *A Great Task of Happiness*, p. 213.
23 Young, *A Great Task of Happiness*, p. 230.
24 Young, *A Great Task of Happiness*, p. 227.
25 *Country Life*, 11 May 1935, n.p. University of Cambridge Manuscripts Library, GB/NNAF/P 162494, NCUACS 87.8.99.167/1, Press Cuttings.
26 *The Builder*, 24 May 1935, n.p. University of Cambridge Manuscripts Library, GB/NNAF/P 162494, NCUACS 87.8.99.167/1, Press Cuttings.
27 Letter from Neville Chamberlain to Kathleen Scott, 18 February 1936. University of Cambridge Manuscripts Library, GB/NNAF/P 162494, NCUACS 87.8.99, Kennet Manuscripts, E-H, K. Letters. Kennet 120/1-3. Neville Chamberlain. Reproduced by kind permission of the Syndics of Cambridge University Library and the Kennet family.

28 Letter from Neville Chamberlain to Kathleen Scott, 14 November 1936. University of Cambridge Manuscripts Library, GB/NNAF/P 162494, NCUACS 87.8.99, Kennet Manuscripts, E-H, K. Letters. Kennet 120/1-3. Neville Chamberlain. Reproduced by kind permission of the Syndics of Cambridge University Library and the Kennet family.
29 'A human chancellor', *Birmingham Daily Mail*, 21 November 1936. University of Cambridge Manuscripts Library, GB/NNAF/P 162494, NCUACS 87.8.99.167/1. Press Cuttings.
30 *Sculpture by K. Scott*, Arthur Ackermann and Son, 19 November–19 December 1936. Catalogue in *Register of Sculpture by Kathleen Lady Kennet (Lady Scott) 1878–1947*, compiled by Lord Kennet (1948).
31 'Lady Kennet's one-man show', *Eastern Daily Press*, 23 November 1936. University of Cambridge Manuscripts Library, GB/NNAF/P 162494, NCUACS 87.8.99.167/1, Press Cuttings.
32 Young, *A Great Task of Happiness*, p. 244.
33 Young, *A Great Task of Happiness*, p. 244.
34 Wilfred Salter, 'The library', *The Parthenon* (1939). University of Cambridge Manuscripts Library, GB/NNAF/P 162494, NCUACS 87.8.99.167/1, Press Cuttings.
35 Eric Newton, *British Sculpture 1944–46* (London, 1947).
36 *Memorial Exhibition of the Work of Kathleen Scott (Lady Kennet of the Dene), A Fellow of the Royal Society of British Sculptors*, Heal and Son's Mansard Gallery, 5–29 May 1948. Catalogue in *Register of Sculpture by Kathleen Lady Kennet (Lady Scott) 1878–1947*, compiled by Lord Kennet (1948).
37 'Kathleen Scott: memorial exhibition', *The Times*, 18 May 1948, p. 8. University of Cambridge Manuscripts Library, GB/NNAF/P 162494, NCUACS 87.8.99.167/1, Press Cuttings.
38 Dr G. M. Trevelyan, OM, transcript for *Speech delivered on opening of the memorial exhibition of the work of Kathleen Scott (Lady Kennet of the Dene) at The Mansard Gallery, on 5th May, 1948*. University of Cambridge Manuscripts Library, GB/NNAF/P 162494, NCUACS 87.8.99, Kathleen Scott catalogues. Reproduced by kind permission of the Syndics of Cambridge University Library and the Kennet family.
39 Parkes, *Sculpture of To-Day*, pp. 17–18.
40 Duff, *The Life Story of H.R.H. Princess Louise*, p. 207.
41 Spielmann, *British Sculpture and Sculptors of To-Day*, pp. 160–61.
42 Jehanne Wake, *Princess Louise: Queen Victoria's Unconventional Daughter* (London: Collins, 1988), p. 305. Newspapers unidentified.
43 Hawksley, *The Mystery of Princess Louise*, pp. 225–26.
44 *Woman at Home* (1895, precise date not given), p. 477, quoted in Elizabeth Crawford, *Enterprising Women: The Garretts and Their Circle* (London: Francis Boutle, 2002), pp. 291–92.
45 Beattie, *The New Sculpture*, p. 196.
46 Read, (introduction) *Ellen Mary Rope: The Poet Sculptor*, pp. 14–15.
47 'Memorial to the Late Mrs. Moberly', newspaper and date unknown (c. August 1890). Copy sent to the author by Arthur Rope.

48 Farningham, *Emmeline Halse, Sculptor,* p. 5.
49 Joseph McBrinn, '"A populous solitude": the life and art of Sophia Rosamond Praeger, 1867–1954', *Women's History Review,* 18.4 (2009), p. 584.
50 Email from Nick Moir to the author, 13 September 2013. There seems to be some confusion between the names of Lilian Maud Wade (Morris) and Lilian N. Morris (active 1899). The latter appears on the *Victorian Web,* accompanied by an illustration of *Arts Fortune.* However, on the *Mapping Sculpture* database, only the name of Lilian Maud Wade (Morris) appears (c.1870–1923). From looking at the work, it appears that this is one and the same person, supported by the fact that the contemporary publication *Academy Architecture* attributed *Arts Fortune* to Lilian Maud Wade.
51 Work 20/127, http://yourarchives.nationalarchives.gov.uk/index.
52 'Lady Kennet', obituary, *The Times,* 26 July 1947, p. 6.
53 Young, *A Great Task of Happiness,* pp. 125–26.
54 Ann Savours, 'Kathleen Scott's statue of Captain Smith of the *Titanic*', *Mariner's Mirror, Journal of the Society for Nautical Research,* 95.4 (2009), p. 478.
55 Geoff Archer, *Public Sculpture in Britain* (Kirstead, Norfolk: Frontier Publishing, 2013), p. 155.
56 Young, *A Great Task of Happiness,* p. 219.
57 For example, Bonhams sold a small version, 54 cm high, in a sale on 9 June 2009, 'Carpets and Rugs', probably cast from the model made for presentation to the committee dealing with the commission.
58 Review in *The Standard,* 12 June 1914, quoted in Brown, *Katharine Emma Maltwood,* p. 23.
59 Brown, *Katharine Emma Maltwood,* p. 23. No further details are given for this 1914 *Observer* article.
60 Parkes, *The Art of Carved Sculpture,* pp. 122–23.
61 Brown, *Katharine Emma Maltwood,* pp. 23–29.
62 Parkes, *The Art of Carved Sculpture,* p. 123.
63 Vivian Usborne, 'The sculpture of Katharine Maltwood', *The Studio* (15 April 1924), pp. 197–99.
64 *Weekly Despatch,* 3 April 1927, n.p., quoted in Stocker, '"My masculine models"', pp. 47–54.
65 J. Lees-Milne, *Fourteen Friends* (London: John Murray, 1996), p. 10.
66 Stocker, '"My masculine models"', p. 50.
67 John Berger, *Ways of Seeing,* Episode 2, BBC 1972; Kenneth Clark, *The Nude* (Harmondsworth: Penguin, 1993 [1956]).
68 *Norfolk News,* 1 August 1925. Translation from *Le Temps,* 10 May 1925, p. 3.
69 Young, *A Great Task of Happiness,* p. 227.
70 Geoffrey Dearmer, 'A modern sculptor', *Empire Review,* 65.312 (1927), p. 166.
71 *Eastern Daily Press,* 28 March 1927, n.p.
72 Patmore, 'Other People's Homes – No. 10: the studio of a famous woman sculptor', p. 11.
73 *Dundee Courier,* 1 April 1927, n.p.

74 Sir Claude Phillips, the veteran critic of the *Daily Telegraph*, found it difficult to pinpoint what it lacked: 'There is … notwithstanding the audacious movement of the Figure, a certain uncertainty, a certain emptiness', *The Daily Telegraph*, 23 October 1923, p. 14. Similar misgivings were echoed by a review in *The Times* in which it was stated that it showed 'only illustrative and dramatic expression … though very well executed', *The Times*, 29 March 1927, p. 12.
75 Frank Debenham to Albert Seward, 20 April 1933. Scott Polar Research Institute Archives, History of SPRI Collection.
76 Note, 19 March 1940. Kennet Papers, Department of Manuscripts, Cambridge University Library, D/32. Reproduced by kind permission of the Syndics of Cambridge University Library and the Kennet family.
77 Note, 22 May 1941. Kennet Papers, Department of Manuscripts, Cambridge University Library, D/33. Reproduced by kind permission of the Syndics of Cambridge University Library and the Kennet family.
78 Marchal, *Finding Frances*, p. 131. Original source unknown.
79 *The New York Times*, 24 May 1908, n.p.
80 Letter from Goscombe John to National Museum of Wales, 19 December 1928. Edith Downing file, Archives, National Museum of Wales, Cardiff.
81 Letter from the Keeper, National Museum of Wales, to Edith Downing, 18 June 1930. Edith Downing file, Archives, National Museum of Wales, Cardiff.
82 Letter from Edith Downing to Mr Williams, Keeper, National Museum of Art, 26 June 1930. Edith Downing file, Archives, National Museum of Wales, Cardiff.
83 Spielmann, *British Sculpture and Sculptors of To-Day*, p. 163.
84 P. G. Konody, *The Observer*, 7 October 1928, p. 14, quoted in Black and Martin, *Dora Gordine: Sculptor, Artist, Designer*, p. 76.
85 Black and Martin, *Dora Gordine: Sculptor, Artist, Designer*, p. 75.
86 Fran Lloyd in Black and Martin, *Dora Gordine: Sculptor, Artist, Designer*, pp. 75–78.
87 Fran Lloyd in Black and Martin, *Dora Gordine: Sculptor, Artist, Designer*, pp. 80–82.
88 Fran Lloyd in Black and Martin, *Dora Gordine: Sculptor, Artist, Designer*, p. 84.
89 *Picture Page*, BBC TV, 24 November 1938, BBC Written Archives, Reading, quoted in Black and Martin, *Dora Gordine: Sculptor, Artist, Designer*, p. 51.
90 Arthur Symons, 'Sculpture: Dora Gordine', *The Spectator*, 14 July 1933, pp. 45–46.
91 Fran Lloyd in Black and Martin, *Dora Gordine: Sculptor, Artist, Designer*, p. 82.
92 Peyton Skipwith, 'Dora Gordine obituary', *The Independent*, 4 January 1992, p. 10.
93 Anthony Caro, 'Introduction', in S. MacDougall and R. Dickson (eds), *Embracing the Exotic: Jacob Epstein and Dora Gordine* (London: Ben Uri Gallery/Papadakis, 2006), p. 17.
94 Fran Lloyd in Black and Martin, *Dora Gordine: Sculptor, Artist, Designer*, p. 73.
95 Parkes, *The Art of Carved Sculpture*, pp. 129–30.
96 Barbara Hepworth, letter to Ernest Musgrave, Director, Wakefield City Art Gallery, 22 February 1944. Hepworth Archive, Hepworth Wakefield. By permission of Hepworth Estate.
97 Barbara Hepworth, letter to Ernest Musgrave, Director, Wakefield City Art Gallery, 16 March 1944. Hepworth Archive, Hepworth Wakefield. By permission of Hepworth Estate.

98 D. M. Macdonald, Director, The Lefevre Galleries, London, letter to Ernest Musgrave, Director, Wakefield City Art Gallery, 7 October 1937; letter from Musgrave to Macdonald, 8 October 1937; letter from Macdonald to Musgrave, 18 October 1937. Hepworth Archive, Hepworth Wakefield.

99 Betty Rea, Foreword, *Five on Revolutionary Art* (London: Wishart Books, 1935), p. 7.

100 Gillian Whiteley, *A Context of Commitment: The Sculpture of Betty Rea*, The Henry Moore Institute Essays on Sculpture, no. 40 (n.d.), p. 2.

101 Bryan Robertson, *A Retrospective Exhibition of Sculpture 1925–1965*, June–July 1965 (London: Zwemmer Gallery, 1965), p. 2.

102 Underwood, *A Short History of English Sculpture*, pp. 164–65.

103 Email to the author from Martin Strauss, 9 February 2015.

104 Peter Davies, 'Mary Spencer Watson', exhibition, Pelter/Sands Art Gallery, Bristol, 8–29 October 1988. Dorset History Centre, Mary Spencer Watson Archive MSW, Solo Exhibitions, A–Z.

105 Peyton Skipwith, 'Mary Spencer Watson. Redoubtable sculptor best known for her work in Purbeck stone', *The Independent*, 10 March 2006, n.p.

106 Letter from Eric Newton to Mary Spencer Watson, 17 October 1937. Dorset History Centre, MSW: 9209, Sculpture, Exhibition Catalogues, Ephemera.

107 Standard letter from Mary Spencer Watson addressed 'Dear Sir' (undated, but autumn 1937). Dorset History Centre, MSW: 9209, Sculpture, Exhibition Catalogues, Ephemera.

108 Mary Miers, 'Poetry in stone', *Country Life*, 2 September 2004, pp. 96–97.

6

A Public Practice

6.1 Architectural sculpture

The architect Somers Clarke stressed the value of sculptural architectural work when he wrote about stone and wood carving in 1893. A Gothic revivalist by training and a member of the Art Workers' Guild, he believed that decorative work needed to be taken seriously by sculptors. He argued that beauty was a crucial component of public life, and so architectural sculpture was important since it was made with its location in mind, unlike art, which often bore no relation to its surroundings, being transferable between the drawing room, the conservatory or the public square. Clarke referred to periods when stone and wood carving were of the highest standard: Greek craftsmen and Florentine sculptors could produce a door, choir stall, pulpit or a tomb, such sculpture forming part of the buildings it adorned. He believed that this flexibility was not evident in contemporary working relationships between sculptors and architects, the result being that sculptures in this context were '"stood about" like ornaments on the mantelpiece. The architect seems as unable to prepare for them as the sculptor to make them. We seldom see congruity even between the figure and the pedestal on which it stands.' He believed that improvements to this situation would not materialize until stone and wood craftsmen became more like architects and vice versa.[1]

Another example of an attempt to align fine and decorative arts, and to harness both to architecture, was evident in a lecture given a year later by Lawrence Alma-Tadema at the Guild and School of Handicraft, London. He described sculpture as being neglected in England despite the presence of so much great work in the country's cathedrals. It is interesting in light of my earlier comments that he also remarked on the essential difference between painting and sculpture, in that the former encouraged the viewer to forget that they were looking at an object, whereas a sculpture remained a material fact. He referred to the presence of numerous empty pedestals all over London, and bemoaned this missed opportunity to bring colour into contemporary life via sculpture. He believed that the blame could be attributed to Britain's system of running competitions for sculptural commissions, particularly for public buildings. 'Competition and Officialism! There is one nice kind of tape which I hate, and that is red tape.'[2]

However, Marion Spielmann would probably have disagreed. Writing in 1901 he advocated the notion of some kind of official body of individuals knowledgeable about sculpture who might oversee an annual grant to commission works for public parks and squares. In this way London and other British cities might become as beautiful as Paris, and Spielmann was convinced that there were sculptors of great merit who could fulfil such commissions. He described bad sculpture as 'a public nuisance', but he did think that architects were increasingly recognizing how well sculpture could perform in such contexts and that now

> our streets are accordingly assuming an air of interest till lately absent from them. Ordinary business houses and tradesmen's premises are now being embellished with excellent work. Restaurants in some number … and other owners of business places, have made their premises beautiful with decorative sculpture of a high class properly applied; while private houses and great offices … have been carrying forward the same movement.

However, he also commented on the well-rehearsed conflict between sculptor and architect whereby the architect was the dominant figure.[3]

Despite these concerns, it was common practice in the nineteenth century for sculptors to make autonomous statues and busts and for decorative work on buildings to be designed by architects and produced by craftsmen stone carvers, trained in the increasing number of government-sponsored schools of art and design. Continued industrialization and increased prosperity did create a higher demand for the adornment of the outside and inside of important city centre building projects, and at the turn of the century increasing numbers of established sculptors were co-opted by architects to apply sculptural decoration to their buildings. The outcomes were improved when such partnerships resulted in sculpture being better integrated into the design of a building rather than looking like (and indeed being) applied afterwards. However, professional tensions remained. Kineton Parkes argued that

> unfortunately our publicly-exposed sculpture has not always been the best fitted for the purpose, and the consequence has been that it has earned derision and defacement. Public sculpture should be of such a character that an appeal should be made in the twinkling of an eye to the best receptive faculties of the beholder, if its appeal is of any lower order it is a failure. The great work of art can subdue the rabble as well as the connoisseur.[4]

In the early 1930s Eric Underwood reflected the change in taste when he acknowledged that for much contemporary architecture, sculptural decoration was inappropriate. However, he believed that there were still buildings, private as well as public, that would benefit from the beauty of such decorative work. He referred to the steady source of architectural sculptors working in Greece and Gothic Europe whom he likened to public servants for the state, the Church or a city: they had an adequate wage and recognized social position. This was in marked contrast to the contemporary sculptor, and Underwood quipped:

> The mere fact that an artist today chooses to be a sculptor is evidence certainly of great courage, possibly of incipient lunacy, but undoubtedly of immense sincerity. At the best he cannot hope to make more than a fraction of the income which would be his if he were a successful painter.

As a symptom of the problem, Underwood criticized what he regarded as mass-produced war memorials that took no regard for siting, choice of materials or style.[5] Like others, he also complained about many contemporary sculptures being placed in an architectural context as an 'afterthought'. Again he attributed this to a lack of communication between architect and sculptor, and also to the sculptor regarding his work as autonomous.[6] He was deeply critical of local authorities that interfered with sculptors' designs: 'No paid civil servant nor bribed alderman would think of calling in a surgeon to remove his appendix and then dare to give him instructions as to how to perform the operation.' He argued that there were plenty of competent craftsmen and sculptors but many patrons took insufficient care when deciding on details of scale, placement and even pedestal design.[7]

Architecture has been described as the greatest consumer of sculpture between 1925 and 1950, but for the most part architectural sculpture has been overlooked by historians, apart from the work of prominent British modernists. Certainly the major building programme in London in the interwar period did present opportunities for sculptors working in a variety of styles, but because of the fierce competition for such work it was vital that a sculptor received architectural patronage.[8] However, when we look at contemporary writings it is clear that the friction between architects and sculptors continued well into the twentieth century. In an article published in the *Studio* in 1930 this disconnection between architecture and sculpture was criticized, but it was suggested that the proliferation of war memorials had 'at last forced attention to the deplorable position, and hastened reaction'.[9] Critical positions may have also been distorted by the increased demand for war memorial sculptures in the 1920s, which was obviously finite, as well as by the 1929 stock market crash which adversely affected sculptors' livings. Although the development of modernist architecture reduced the demand for decorative sculpture on stylistic grounds, such work remained highly regarded by sculptors.

Several women practitioners sought these commissions, including Elizabeth Muntz and Barbara Hepworth, and the fact that architectural decoration attracted lively discussion both in the press and in lectures underscores the fact of its continuing importance. In 1947 Hepworth wrote to Sigfried Giedion in response to a questionnaire dealing with collaboration between artists and architects. Giedion had recently visited Hepworth and the latter wrote critically of contemporary architects, in that she had been left with

> a very sad feeling that the gulf between architects and sculptors is a very large one and that it can only be bridged by a change of heart in the architects. I felt that the questions to be asked should not be 'should the architect and sculptor collaborate from the beginning?' but 'why do the architects and sculptors not collaborate from the beginning!' ... I feel as a sculptor that we have said what we have to say and played our part and that architecture, as the co-ordinating part of our culture, has failed so far, to unite (and even to understand!) the work that has been done in our time by painters and sculptors. Without this unity we cannot achieve a robust culture. During my last exhibition I found there was a keen sense, among all kinds of people, of the part that sculpture plays in life, *except* among the architects. They all stood with their backs to the sculpture and bewailed their lot, or chattered about new materials. I was shocked by this attitude because we are working, all of us, for something much greater than planning.[10]

On completing her training, Ellen Mary Rope worked as an illustrator and painter but continued to model in clay, until in 1885 the Royal Academy accepted three low-relief terracottas including *David playing before Saul* (**Figure 3**). She had submitted this work as an unframed panel but the Academy was apparently so impressed that it paid for it to be mounted. It attracted very positive reviews and was instrumental in consolidating her reputation as an important sculptor. The poetic nature of Pre-Raphaelitism offered Rope, as it did other sculptors, a particular type of realistic sculptural language which could be adapted to fit individual commissions. This influence comes through strongly in Rope's work where she harnessed this language to the concerns of the New Sculpture and Arts and Crafts movements. As was the case with Frances Darlington, Rope was very interested in the addition of colour to sculpture, again paralleling the work of her contemporaries George Frampton and Robert Anning Bell. Her use of colour on some of her bas-reliefs can be linked to Frampton's 1894 explanation that he preferred to colour his plaster works as the 'only treatment which can make the repeats interesting'.[11] An article in the *Builder* noted how Rope's panels could be made at a modest cost and if required could be replicated, which would widen her potential clientele.[12] Rope clearly wished to work with architects and said so in an interview for *Woman at Home* in 1895.[13] Sadly, despite its importance at the time, very little of this work has survived.

Rope's alliance to the Arts and Crafts movement particularly came through in the ceramics that she produced for the Della Robbia Pottery in Birkenhead after joining the firm in 1896 and with which she was associated until its closure in 1906. Rope produced both plain and coloured relief works for Della Robbia, her designs showing figures, especially children, and often images relating to the sea. She experimented with new techniques and sometimes collaborated with other artists; for example her 1889 cinerary urn was made by W. Allen, and in 1896 a bronze mirror frame designed and modelled by Rope was electro-deposited by F. Schaub.[14] Rope exhibited from 1889 with the Arts and Crafts Exhibition Society, showing designs for functional objects such as panels for ceilings and walls, mantelpieces and nursery decorations, as well as for practical everyday items such as an electrical bell push, doorplates, a tea caddy and a letterbox. As her status increased, so did the prestigious commissions from leading architects of the day wishing to incorporate her work into their decorative schemes. Rope seems to have been commercially adept and able to manoeuvre her career in directions responsive to the marketplace, and thus she was able to practice as a professional fine art sculptor as well as a decorative artist. She exhibited widely and internationally, received considerable respect in the art press of the day, and also wished to make her work affordable to people of relatively modest means.[15]

Rope visited Italy, and although she had previously been able to look at reproductions of Italian Renaissance sculpture, a small sketchbook from her visit records excursions to Venice, Padua and Milan. Such first-hand experience underscores the impact of Florentine Renaissance sculpture on her work. Among her most notable architectural commissions was the design of four polychromed classical plaster-relief spandrels, comprising 6-feet-tall images of *Faith, Hope, Charity* and *Heavenly Wisdom* for the vestibule of the Women's Building at the 1893 Columbian World's Fair in Chicago. The building's architect was Sophia Hayden and women from many countries provided additional decoration, the project being conceived as providing a focal point for the emerging women's movement. It is possible that Rope gained this prestigious commission through Octavia Hill, who was a member of the British organizers' committee. Apparently G. F. Watts admired Rope's spandrels and wished to place them in the South London Art Gallery, Camberwell. In the event, and possibly prompted by Hill, Rope arranged for the reliefs to be installed at the Chenies Street Ladies Dwelling.[16] In 1894 Hill was instrumental in commissioning from Rope a series of bas-reliefs for the Women's University Settlement in Nelson Square, Southwark, which Hill had established as a place where women could be trained and accommodated in order to work with the poor in this disadvantaged part of London.[17] Rope also received a commission for Morley Town Hall in Yorkshire, which opened in 1895, and where Frances Darlington's sculpture of Queen Victoria would also be installed at a slightly later date. Rope produced three large, plaster, female allegorical figures, *Faith, Hope* and *Charity,* in a similar classical style to her Chicago spandrels, and probably commissioned by local suffragist Alice Cliff Scatcherd. The bas-reliefs were positioned high on an end wall of the Alexandra Hall and appear to have been over seven feet tall, but some time after 1921 they were removed and their current whereabouts is unknown.

Rope produced much architectural sculpture, such as her impressive Rotherhithe frieze. The plaster maquette model for the 20-feet-long relief commissioned for the council chamber of Rotherhithe Town Hall in 1897 is held by the Museum of London. The careful and detailed study of nature advocated by William Rossetti can be seen in the realism of the figures. An image of the plaster panel appeared in the *Builder* on 3 December 1898 and the actual title of the piece was *Relief: The Shipping and Timber Trade of the Thames of 1700–1894*. Rotherhithe held a limited competition for its new town hall design in which six architects were invited to compete, and the winners were Murray and Foster of Adelphi Chambers. The design was characterized as Italian Renaissance in style and was notable for its incorporation of good architectural sculpture, both on the interior and exterior, of which Rope's relief for the council chamber was perhaps the most remarkable example. Writing in the *Artist* B. Kendall stated:

> Miss Rope's masterly treatment of a difficult subject has been duly recognised; the breadth and power displayed is leavened by that poetic charm which is never absent from her work. She is a worker who takes infinite pains to be accurate down to the minutest details, so day after day saw her in the timber yards or on the wharves that line the river, making studies from life. The result is the striking realism of the figures. The models for the ships Miss Rope obtained from the South Kensington Museum.[18]

The building was formally opened on 28 April 1897. In May 1900 a writer in the *Magazine of Art* noted that this was Rope's largest work to date and described it as highly skilful and important as a work produced by a female sculptor.[19] Sadly the building was gutted during an air raid in the Second World War, and was demolished in early July 1974. Rope's relief must have been in fairly good condition judging from the photograph that was taken before the building's destruction (**Figure 76**). Framed with oak panelling above and below, the relief was described by Kendall as having at its centre the vestry arms, designed by the vestry clerk James Stokes. The *Southwark Annual* of 1902 noted the relief's topographical accuracy:

> It has a ship in the centre, whilst two shipwrights uphold the shield, and thus remind one of the industry of ship-building, which made Rotherhithe famous in the past. On the right is another ship in dry-dock, and the representation of a granary which calls to mind the immense business of the Surrey Commercial Dock Company, whose efforts have drawn to Rotherhithe so much trade, not only in grain but also in wood which is also illustrated in the panel by the porter engaged at his daily task. The shipping interest is also illustrated on the left of the panel, whilst the rising sun naturally symbolises the prosperity which trade has brought to the old riparian parish.[20]

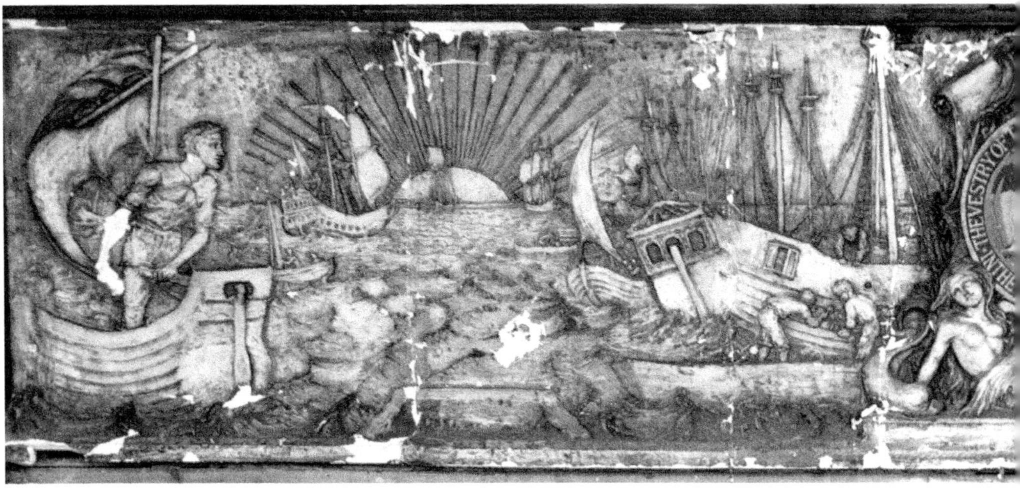

76. Ellen Mary Rope, Rotherhithe Library Frieze, *Relief: The Shipping and Timber Trade of the Thames of 1700–1894*, 1897–98, photograph 1941

To counteract the flattening effect of the light in the council chamber Rope applied raw umber and wax to the relief.

An article in the *Studio* praised Rope's ability to portray children in ornamental form and described her bas-relief *Christ Blessing the Little Children* (1898) as well balanced, with the modelling being enhanced by a thin brown wash that flowed into the hollows of the plaster composition (**Figure 77**).[21] Two years later in his *British Sculpture and Sculptors of To-Day*, Spielmann referred to Rope's reliefs exhibited at the Royal Academy, in particular the panels commissioned for the Women's Building at the 1893 Chicago Exposition, but he also noted *Christ Blessing the Little Children* as a particularly sensitive work. However, he had some reservations about the Rotherhithe Town Hall frieze, remarking that 'clever and decorative as it is, [it] seems to lack something of her usual qualities of composition and balance'; nonetheless he described her as having 'considerable talent'.[22] Two contemporary assessments reveal how Rope was regarded at the opening of the twentieth century. The first is from the Kendall article already quoted: he believed that she was the ideal sculptor of small children, able to empathize with their imagination and extremes of emotion.[23] The second is a 1900 article in the *Magazine of Art* which described how, in the main, Rope's work comprised small decorative reliefs which showed a creative sense of conception and a high technical skill. It was acknowledged that her panels depicting

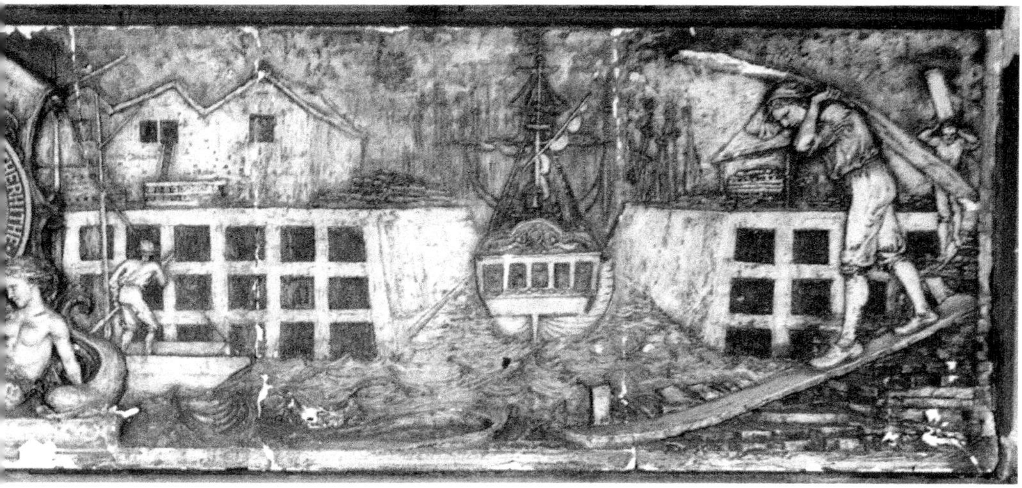

children were probably more familiar to the public than her more serious works, but that they alone were of sufficient standard to place her among the best of decorative sculptors. A direct analogy was made to the early Renaissance sculpture by the Della Robbia family through 'the beauty

77. Ellen Mary Rope, *Christ Blessing the Little Children*, 1898

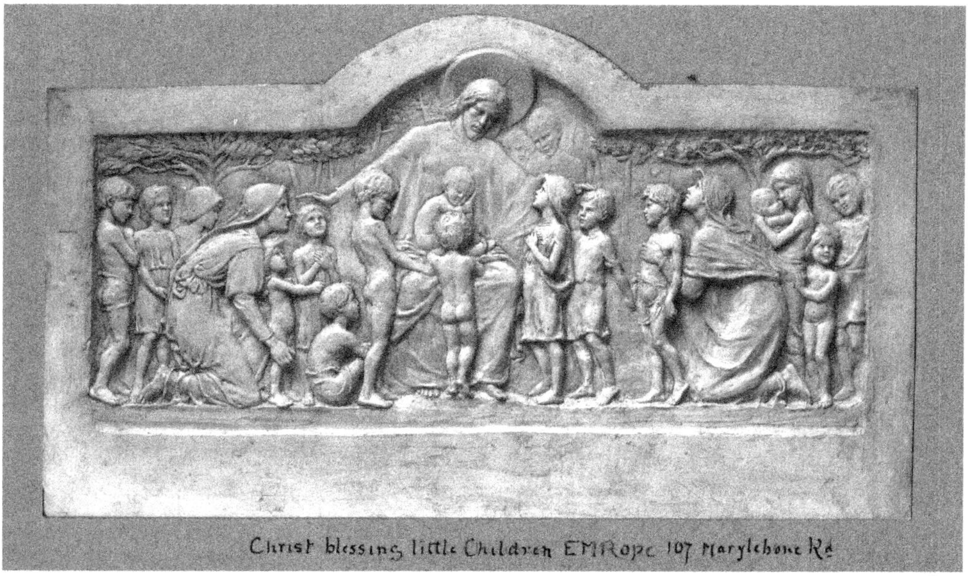

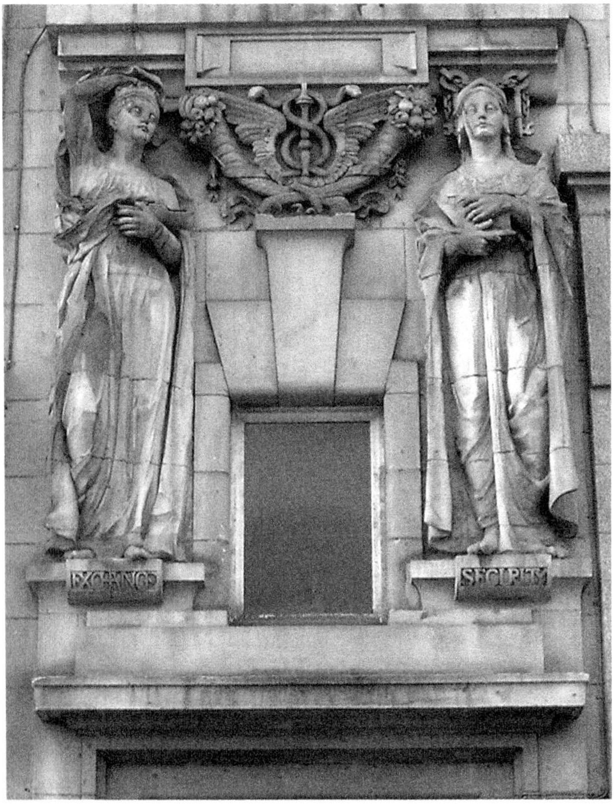

78. Phyllis Archibald Clay, *Exchange and Security*, 1906–07

and simplicity of the child-forms'.[24] Rope exhibited internationally and through many commissions she was able to work full-time as a professional sculptor. Ben Read described her as an artist 'who successfully combined a delicate sensitivity and considerable technical skill, with a lively imagination and intellect. Her work is a lasting testament to this achievement.'[25]

Phyllis Clay studied at Glasgow School of Art, gaining her diploma in 1908.[26] Around 1906 she married Charles Clay, moving first to London and then to Grasmere, Westmoreland. She exhibited frequently at the Royal Society of Arts. A major architectural work comprised her figures representing *Exchange, Security, Prudence* and *Adventure* on the Royal Bank of Scotland, 30 St Enoch's Square, Glasgow (1906–07), executed by Clay and sculptor Richard Ferris, the architect being Alexander Nisbet Paterson. Functioning as caryatids, the two pairs of full-length standing figures are approximately two metres high, placed in compartments above the side entrance and ground-floor window of the outer bays, and representing the four principal emblems of banking. From the left we have *Exchange* holding a model ship, *Security* bearing a casket with keys and chains above, *Prudence* carrying a scroll, and *Adventure* whose attribute is unclear. **Figure 78** shows *Exchange* and *Security*. The space between each pair of figures is occupied by an identical decorative scheme comprising pairs of outstretched wings, crossed cornucopias and entwined snakes. Their placement on either side of the pink granite facing on the ground floor marks out that section of the building as belonging to the bank, since the upper storeys comprised warehouses and offices, and as they were fairly low they were unusually visible from street level. The design and execution of the sculptures was overseen by the architect, and sources are unclear as to how the modelling and carving were divided between the two sculptors, although the *Building News* reported that Clay modelled the figures while Ferris made the ornamental decoration.[27]

George Frampton's commitment to painted relief sculpture would be crucial for the development of Frances Darlington's practice. Frampton worked in this genre with Anning Bell, with whom he shared a studio between 1889 and 1895, and he published an article on the subject in the *Studio* in 1894.[28] Bell left London in 1895 so it is feasible that Frampton would have been looking out for a suitable sculptor with whom he could continue his collaboration. No relief works from Darlington's time at the Slade survive, only those produced later, but the painted relief became a major component of her practice. The inspiration of the Della Robbia family of sculptors is again relevant here, as with some of the other sculptors I have discussed such as Ellen Rope: these women sculptors were of the right generation to see the Della Robbia collection at the South Kensington Museum, later the Victoria and Albert Museum. During the nineteenth century Luca Della Robbia emerged from the then forgotten period of early Italian sculpture to become a key artist. In part this was aided by Walter Pater's important 1873 text *The Renaissance: Studies in Art and Poetry*, which included a chapter dedicated to the artist. Pater believed that the use of low relief essentially resulted in a painterly effect. He proposed that Luca Della Robbia used terracotta in order to more widely disseminate his work, allowing access to a broader audience. He also suggested that Della Robbia, 'inspired by easily distributable pottery, was led to the application of colour which, in the darkened churches, cool streets and monotony of daily life, would provide a sensual, vibrant experience for the everyday viewer'. The Italian

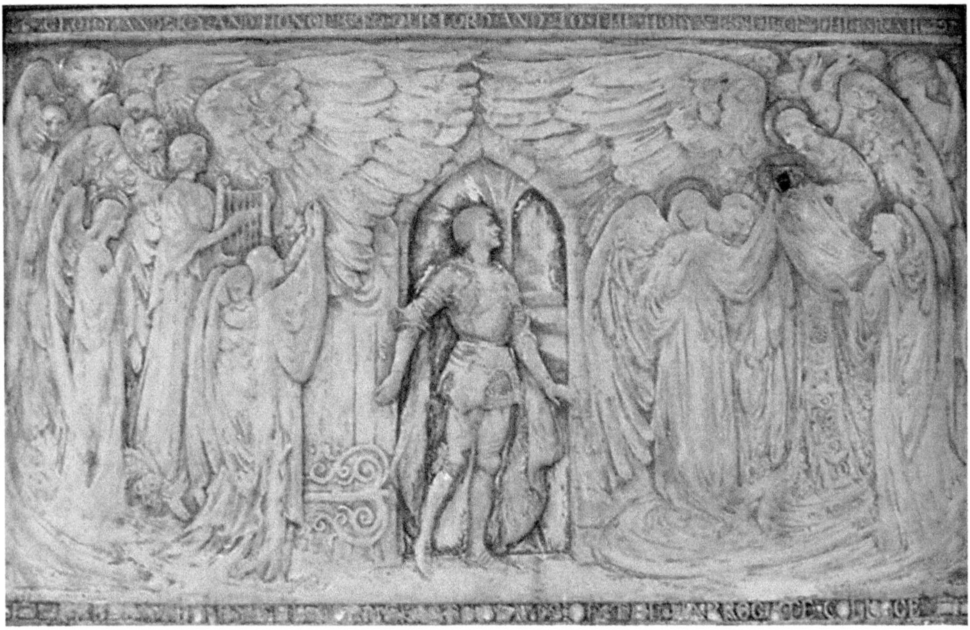

79. Frances Darlington. *Sir Perceval and the Vision of the Holy Grail*, c.1907–08

sculpture collection of the South Kensington Museum was developed in the mid-nineteenth century through the acquisition of numerous medieval and Renaissance sculptures, ceramics and decorative items. By 1862 the Della Robbia family's sculpture dominated the collection; however, to revive Luca della Robbia's reputation it was necessary to present his work as combining Early Renaissance and Victorian ideals, achieved mainly through linking Della Robbia with the values propounded by John Ruskin. In the mid-nineteenth century Ruskin had found the colour in Della Robbia's sculptures problematic. However, a few decades later he bought Andrea Della Robbia's *Adoration of the Virgin* (c.1477), believing it to be by Luca; its colour was apparently no longer problematic and the work was given pride of place in Ruskin's home. It seems that Ruskin's espousal of 'truth to nature' in art allowed for his warming towards the vivid colour in Luca Della Robbia's glazed terracottas, the colour arguably being an aid to naturalism.[29]

Darlington produced relief panels of *Sir Perceval and the Vision of the Holy Grail* in 1907–08. There appear to be two versions: the first was reproduced in *Academy Architecture* in 1907 and was shown at the

Royal Academy and therefore probably sold. The second version is in the Hewlett Reading Room of Harrogate Ladies' College (**Figure 79**). Darlington had been a pupil at the college, which might explain the commissioning of the panel to be positioned over the fireplace in the library, but no records confirm this.[30] This work is directly inspired by Tennyson's poem *The Holy Grail*. The version exhibited at the Royal Academy in 1907 was the only one of Darlington's sculptures to be illustrated in any of that institution's catalogues. It appears that this panel was particularly important to the sculptor, since three photographs taken by her survived, more than any of her other works. In 1908 a similar panel was shown at the Leeds spring exhibition, listed as 'a fireplace panel in plaster', and this is probably the panel over the library fireplace in Harrogate Ladies' College. The two panels seem to have been conceived as a sequence from the same story; the first has been described as comprising

> eight angels holding the Sword Excalibur, echoing the form of the Cross as a central symbol which is held over the grail. Sir Percival kneels before the Heavenly Host and other human figures bear witness to the Glory. The whole background texture and rhythm is beaten with angel wings and drawn on with flowing drapery. There are more human participants than in the second panel; it is a moment of honour and acknowledgement of human virtue which is centred on God and surrounded by angels.[31]

Rosamund Praeger achieved considerable success with monumental architectural works in Belfast's key buildings such as the cathedral, as well as in schools, libraries, hospitals and the shipyards. These are very different from her sculptures of children. Praeger became a leading exponent of a fusion between the New Sculpture and the ideals of the Arts and Crafts movement, aligned to Celtic Revivalism. However, she met with some initial resistance in seeking patronage in Belfast; as early as the late 1890s she even offered to donate her work, but this was declined.[32] Praeger was overlooked when the commission for the decoration of the new city hall arose, the work going instead to established London-based sculptors such as Hamo Thornycroft, Frederick Pomeroy and Thomas Brock.[33] She completed several sculptures at the newly constituted Queen's University in Belfast, including the *Reverend Thomas Hamilton Memorial*. In 1908 she carved the allegorical figures of *Art, Literature* and *Science* on the façade of the Carnegie Library in the Falls Rd, Belfast, thought by some to be among her best works. The central figure of

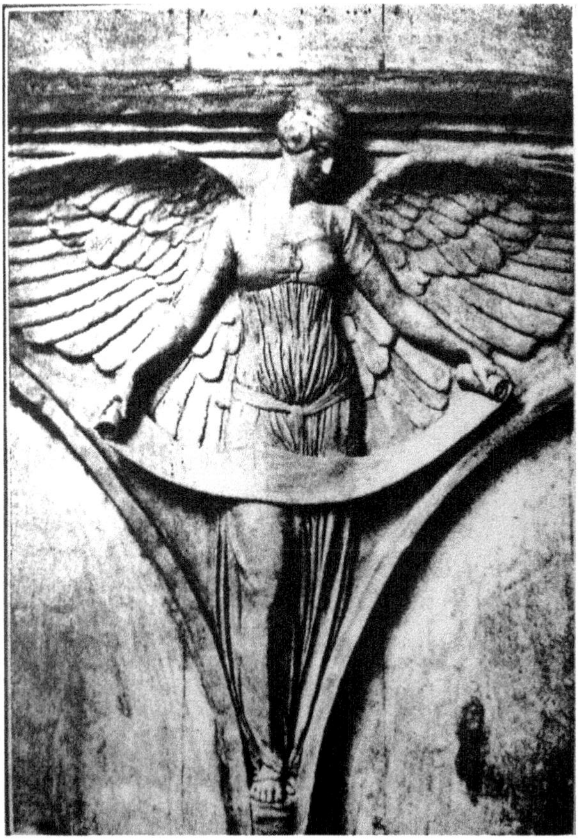

80. Rosamund Praeger, *Literature*, Carnegie Library, Falls Rd, Belfast, 1908

Literature shows a typically New Sculpture treatment, reminiscent of Pre-Raphaelitism (**Figure 80**). It seems possible that one influence on this work could have been the carvings made by Praeger's friend Ellen Rope, namely the *Faith, Hope, Charity* and *Heavenly Wisdom* spandrels for the 1893 World's Fair.[34] Praeger's façade decorations clearly demonstrate her ability as a designer of monumental architectural decoration, and in her 1912 solo exhibition at Pollack's Gallery, Belfast, particular notice was taken of her skills in this area. After the First World War she received many commissions broadly in the areas of memorials and portraits. She increasingly worked with direct carving, and her choice of local Irish limestone and marbles links her work to Irish medieval sculpture.[35]

Another woman sculptor who worked with architects was Julian Phelps Allan (1892–1996), who studied sculpture at the Westminster School of Art and then at the Royal Academy Schools roughly between

1923 and 1926, winning during this period the Landseer Scholarship for Sculpture and a gold medal. She was awarded the Edward Scott Travelling Studentship through which she studied in Florence under Libero Andreotti in 1926. She then travelled to Yugoslavia in 1933 and met the sculptor Ivan Meštrović in Zagreb in 1936, and also studied Romanesque sculpture in France. She exhibited at the Royal Scottish Academy, the Royal Academy summer exhibitions and the Royal Society for the Arts, becoming an RBS associate member in 1938 and a Fellow during the period 1948 to 1969. In 1947 she was nominated by Phyllis Bone for membership of the RSA. She changed her name from Eva Dorothy Allan to Julian Phelps Allan in 1929, following a contemporary trend of using a masculine name to declare a lesbian identity. She produced bas-reliefs at Lambeth and Maudsley hospitals and elsewhere, and after 1947 carried out many ecclesiastical commissions. In 1938 she wrote:

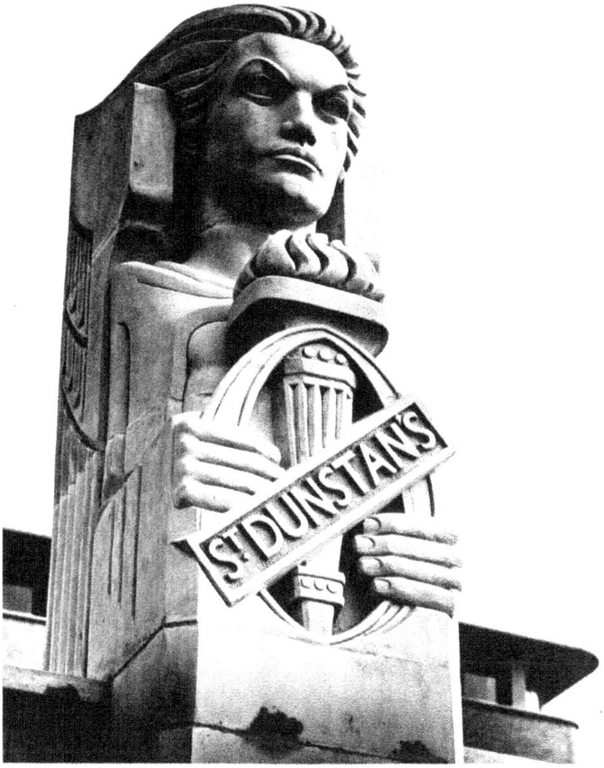

81. Julian Phelps Allan, *Winged Victory*, St Dunstan's, Brighton, 1938

> I am now working on what will be a 20ft figure for the new St. Dunstan's Convalescent Home which is being built outside Brighton. This is a 'Winged Victory' holding the insignia of St. Dunstan's. It is rather an adventure, especially as no one knows whether the floor of my studio will hold it![36]

Figure 81 shows the sculpture on the exterior wall of the chapel at St Dunstan's where it was installed in the same year. She is one of the many female sculptors about whom very little has been written.

6.2 Collective monuments and memorials

After the death of Queen Victoria the demand for monuments lessened until the cessation of the First World War. However, from the 1920s debates began over the precise role and form of public monuments and sculpture, both in themselves and as part of an architectural scheme, debates that continued into the second half of the century. This type of work was crucial for sculptors' careers as such commissions provided significant income and the nature of the works gave them much-needed public visibility. After the First World War the surge in the production of war memorials was mainly carried out by the male sculptors of the New Sculpture generation, as well as by local stonemasons and tradesmen. For modernist sculptors, engaging with the monumental tradition had clear problems. Negotiation and consensus were required for the realization of public work, and the inherent isolationist stance adopted by studio-based sculptors separated them from potential civic and other urban patrons.[37]

In 1922 Kineton Parkes wrote disapprovingly about what he saw as a pernicious trend in recent sculpture. This was the production of work on a very large scale, made in the belief that

> a great mass is equivalent to a great impression … Big arid masses of granite, largely without ornament and certainly without meaning, were accepted as impressive and commanding. The acceptation was so complete that there are monuments in existence now that it were better they had never been achieved. The principle even spread to London, but so slowly do the English absorb ideas from without in art, it was not until after the war that it appeared there. It was not welcome, and I hope it will not make any headway. London suffered late, but in its war memorials seriously, and the undoubted tendency is greatly to be deplored.[38]

Despite these issues, an enormous number of war memorials were erected after the First World War, representing the largest public art project ever seen in Britain. Where sculpture formed part of the design it was overwhelmingly figurative in nature. Lively debates about precisely how one should memorialize occurred in the years following the cessation of hostilities. Often marginalized on aesthetic grounds, these memorials are a real reflection of contemporary life, as historically rooted artefacts and symbols expressive of the national mood and values.

Constructing a predictable meaning for memorials was tricky. A traditional form was more likely to succeed in providing a focal point for mass grief and memory, since modernist designs could eloquently express the feelings of an individual but were less amenable to a more generalized, collective remembrance and acknowledgement of sacrifice. An essential aspect of the war memorial, and the act of remembering, was the idealization of the fallen. To fulfil this purpose visual references to the realities of war were discouraged.[39] War memorial iconography could have a powerful effect on the viewer and for the sake of national unity these designs had to be carefully handled. If the designs that were approved often appear pedestrian, they nevertheless speak to us of the taste of the day and thus are a mirror held up to history. Rather than searching for a way to mitigate grief, discussions about the form a memorial should take were largely directed towards the expression of a moral and/or political perspective. It was this ambition that was most discussed in committee meetings and at unveiling ceremonies. Since memorials were such a sensitive and pervasive form of 'public' art, it is clear that there was much concern that they should present a 'correct' idea, and this concern was reflected in the sheer number of articles on the subject in art and architecture periodicals, as well as in newspapers. Contemporary debates about memorials often showed that too much was expected by way of change in public taste, and many campaigns to 'improve' such taste foundered. However, despite the understandable desire to gloss over the realities of warfare, many First World War memorials made visible its real effects and so differed from memorials to earlier conflicts.[40]

The Civic Arts Association was formed in late 1915 to encourage good design in all aspects of the physical reconstruction of the country post-war, but especially in relation to the erection of war memorials. The intention was that a committee of experts should act in an advisory capacity with public bodies or private individuals involved in such projects. In 1915 Lawrence Weaver's book *Memorials and Monuments* focused attention on good design, and articles on this topic appeared in professional journals. In 1918 the Royal Academy of Art proposed the formation of an advisory committee on war memorials, issuing a pamphlet entitled *Suggestions for the Treatment of War Memorials* which was distributed to public bodies that might instigate a commission. The committee's recommendations were that designs should only be accepted from recognized artists; that siting should be given careful attention; that materials should be appropriate both in terms of appearance and available funds; that the architectural context should be taken into account when designing interior memorials; that lettering should be legible; and that an emphasis should be placed on simplicity and clarity. On 26 June 1918 the Academy hosted a conference on war memorials and in 1919 organized an exhibition of war memorial designs which it hoped would help authorities when selecting designs and artists. In addition the RBS circulated advice to local authorities as did civic societies: for example, in 1920 the Leeds Civic Society held an exhibition of war memorial designs.[41] Thus the subject was clearly deemed a sensitive and important matter. It was political in the broadest sense since it needed to be supported by the public from whom funds might have to be raised, and it needed not to attract concerted opposition.

Civic pride was linked to urban improvement, and both were linked to social cohesion. Civic societies were important in promoting these ideas and they were formed widely in larger towns in the years preceding and following the First World War; the individuals involved were often businessmen, other professionals and academics. There were alternatives to the large expensive memorial, such as smaller tablets and monuments which could be sourced from the catalogues of church furniture firms and monumental masons. Naturally artists were active in responding to such competition and so presented their work as offering a higher-quality product supported by a professional service. However, architects often employed masons to work to their designs, which subsequently caused some difficulty in being certain about just who had produced a given work, particularly in the case of memorials as well as ecclesiastical work. There is evidence of friction between bodies such as the RBS and architects, particularly when the latter were seen to be employing mason-sculptors rather than professional sculptors.[42] Nonetheless some architects did approach sculptors to work with them on monuments and several female examples are discussed below. Professional bodies such as the Royal Institute of British Architects, the RBS and the Royal Academy were on hand to offer expert advice in response to approaches from memorial committees and naturally they argued for the employment of properly trained sculptors.

Those designing First World War memorials had a broad range of styles on which to draw. The legacy of Pre-Raphaelitism had merged with the style of work generally seen at the Royal Academy and thus appealed to a broad audience, and the characteristics of the New Sculpture movement were also still in evidence. In the early twentieth century, the nature of sculpture generally, including memorials, was more complex than a binary choice between conservative or modern approaches. The result was that some previously ignored or disregarded sculptors might now gain an enhanced profile.[43] Apart from local stonemasons and architectural practices, companies such as R. L. Boulton, H. H. Martyn and the Bromsgrove Guild provided commemorative work which might extend from stained glass to bronze sculptures, and from modest wall plaques to monumental works.[44] In March 1922 a conference took place at the Royal Academy at which architect Aston Webb mooted the idea of forming a Commission of Fine Arts. This was realized in 1924, its members including George Frampton and Edwin Lutyens. Items within its remit included

> the location of statues, fountains and monuments in public squares, streets and parks, both in London and in the provinces, and ... the selection of designs for statues, fountains and monuments or any artistic matters in the open air, such as alterations to buildings, town planning and landscape gardening and public parks.[45]

The commissioners were often consulted about the positioning of sculptures and were aware of the 'growing difficulty of harmonizing the new with the old, and preserving the old while doing justice to the new'.[46]

Appropriate representations of masculinity were a concern when conceiving memorials. Clearly there was a reluctance to depict a wounded or injured soldier, despite the dire reality of the First World War, since this would disrupt the overall aim of memorializing in what might be termed a positive manner. Moreover, social conventions made it problematic to reconcile 'manly' behaviour with an acknowledgement of what combatants had endured. Therefore few war memorials showed an obviously shell-shocked soldier, although there are some that clearly do not aim to glorify war. For example, Kathleen Scott's Huntingdon memorial (1923) shows a soldier deep in thought (**Figure 82**). This ambitious over life-size seated figure was unveiled on Armistice

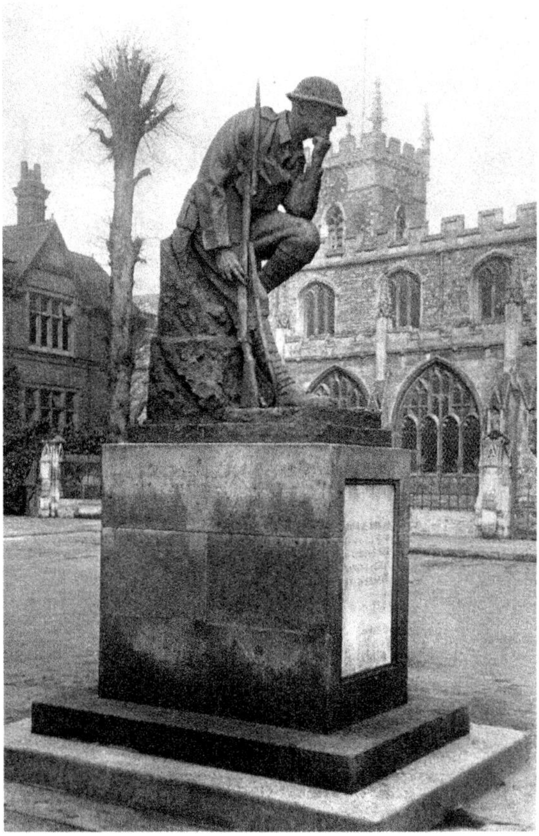

82. Kathleen Scott, *Huntingdon War Memorial*, 1923

Day, 11 November 1923. Although the work is made from bronze, the impression is of the figure emerging from an unfinished block, thus being slightly reminiscent of Rodin's *The Kiss* or the pensive stance of his *Thinker*. Whether Scott's gender had any effect on the non-combative presentation of this soldier is a matter of speculation.[47] At least one newspaper review noted its ambiguity:

> It represents a steel-hatted soldier, characteristically seated upon the trench side, deep in thought, his chin thrust into his hand. So calm and steady is his gaze that it will hold the attention of the most casual passer-by. He is in this case portrayed not so much as the fighter, but as the thinker and watcher, with a unique quality of quick concentration and a tender earnestness as he seems to weigh and probe the problems of War and Peace. In his person he would appear to draw together and unite the symbols of the spiritual and civic life of the town he has come

> to dwell in: the church on the one hand, the Town Hall on the other; whilst at his feet and round him surge the hum and business of the market week by week.[48]

An organization called Sculptured Memorials and Headstones was formed in 1934 to enable artists and craftsmen to more readily access potential clients. Recent work by its members was illustrated in a 1937 book, *Sculptured Memorials and Headstones Designed and Carved in Sculptors' Studios in British Stones,* a copy of which was owned by Elizabeth Muntz. The foreword referred to the 'deplorable increase during the last hundred years of mass-produced imported white marble and granite memorials', which 'had practically killed public appreciation of good work'. Also regretted was the loss of the

> lovely traditional tombstone art of the country ... as a result, the countryside, both in churchyard and cemetery, has been desecrated and made ugly. It is our aim ... to help to change that in a practical way, by making it possible for the public who appreciate good design, material, and workmanship, to obtain the work of sculptors at prices which even compare favourably with the much inferior ready-made product.[49]

In addition to memorial work the organization began to recommend contemporary British sculpture and carving, including garden sculpture, bronzes and portraiture, and as a result changed its name to Sculpture and Memorials. They deplored the use of white marble referred to above, describing it as being 'glaring', 'alien' and 'distressing'.

Reference was made to a publication produced by the British Institute of Industrial Art, *The Art of Graveyard Monuments,* in which familiar complaints were repeated, the importation and use of Italian marble being particularly criticized. The fact that monuments were being imported from Italy caused further controversy, and it was felt that public taste was producing this undesirable result. A strong element of nationalism was evident in the criticisms made of 'foreign' materials and labour, whereas it was felt that the public should be employing British labour and using British stone in order 'to maintain British traditions of quietness and dignity in their monuments'.[50] The Society was, however, pessimistic about change, although positive about the good work carried out by the Imperial War Graves Commission in its use of native Portland stone. It was hoped that this organization would raise the standard of graveyard memorials and so enable the emergence of a reinvigorated school of sculptors and masons who had the ability to create skilful designs and lettering to equal both good examples of past

British headstones and sculpture, as well as great historical sculpture in general.[51] Apart from memorials the publication also encouraged sculpture for the garden and for interior decoration, particularly noting how it could be harnessed to modern lighting, examples of which have been seen in Chapter 4.2.[52]

Even towards the end of the period covered by this book the issue of memorial sculpture was still a matter for concern. In 1949 Elizabeth Muntz was a founder of the Guild of Memorial Craftsmen, instigated to uphold and develop the standard of memorial sculpture. Eric Kennington and Gilbert Bayes also exhibited with this organization, which in its second (undated) brochure reported that it was not difficult to produce good memorials, but the most difficult task was to challenge poor taste and vested interests.[53]

Despite potential disapproval there were a significant number of monuments that did make reference to injury and sacrifice. In such instances they were often modest works, some located inside a building – especially in churches – and some commissioned by private patrons. In this way sculptors seem to have avoided the constraints placed on those designing a memorial for a village or town centre. Some of the works took the form of reliefs, which allowed for a more pictorial type of representation. Ellen Mary Rope produced a small war memorial for her local church of St Peter's in Blaxhall (1914–18) which contains a number of her works (**Figure 83**). It depicts a fallen soldier on the battlefield, with Christ looking over him, set against a backlit landscape of trenches and cannon.

In 1905 Princess Louise's bronze Boer War memorial was installed in St Paul's Cathedral. The Boer War had ended in 1902 and plans for a memorial were initiated jointly by the Colonial Troops Club and Princess Louise. A memorial committee was formed of which the Dean of St Paul's and Lawrence Alma-Tadema were members. A letter establishing the required 'tone' of the work set out the priorities of good workmanship and sensitivity to its context. Some irritation was expressed concerning sculptors with whom the writer had worked: too often they completely misjudged the scale required to place a work in the cathedral. To address this issue a full-size model would first be installed to check the sculpture's suitability. Fortunately, Princess Louise was seemingly happy with such an arrangement, being both approachable and open to discussion.[54] Although the letter bears no signatory, it may have been from Somers Clarke, Surveyor of the Fabric at St Paul's Cathedral 1896–1906, and it is known that he was concerned

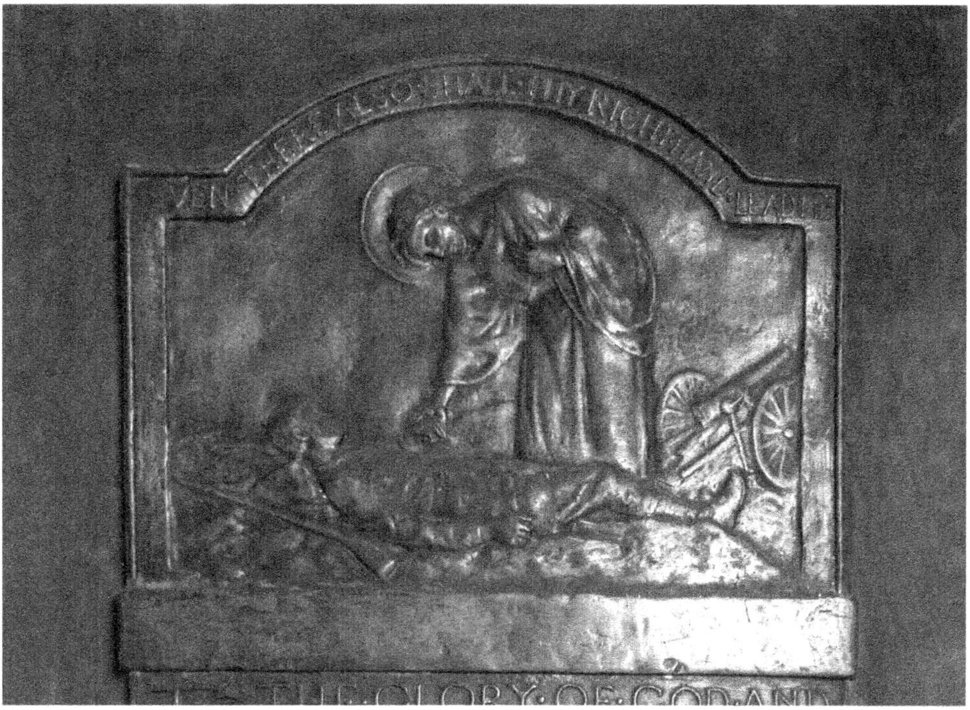

83. Ellen Mary Rope, *Blaxhall War Memorial*, St Peter's Church, 1914–18

to encourage collaboration between architecture and other art forms within the cathedral. The princess seems to have been meticulous in having a clear overview of the whole installation. Writing on her behalf from Kensington Palace, W. G. Probert emphasized to Somers Clarke that Louise would check that the inscription was 'in character with the whole design. I am to say that it certainly will not have the appearance of an advertisement with a long collection of names.'[55]

In October 1903 the committee met in the cathedral to assess the princess's chosen site, and a cartoon painted by her was positioned in the south transept. A life-size Angel of Mercy leaned protectively over an effigy of Christ on the cross, supporting his hands. On each side of the cross the angel's robes billowed downwards and around Christ's feet. The large outstretched wings rose high, meeting nearly exactly above the lowered head of the angel, and swept down so as to form a frame around Christ's trailing robes. The committee observed how light from a window on the west wall would illuminate the statue and there was unanimous approval of both its design and placement.[56] Louise modelled the tablet and wreath, executed by Farmer and Brindley, with the princess having the final word on the colour of bronze to be used.[57] There was some dispute over the nature of the inscription, whether it should comprise a Shakespearean quotation or not; this dithering clearly irked Somers Clarke, who drafted a letter describing the changes being made

> not at the eleventh but I may even say at the nineteenth hour … an inscription of this sort is not an advertisement or an effort of the Bill Poster … As I once heard an eminent artist remark. A fine inscription is not set out so that he who *runs* may read. It is intended to be gazed upon and taken in as a part of the artistic effect which should be manifested throughout the whole monument … now, so late in the day I cannot make alterations, nor indeed have I any right to do so.[58]

In another draft letter dated ten days later Somers Clarke agreed to changes to the order in which the colonial dead were listed, and to the number of lives lost, but ended his letter with: 'You must however permit me to say that you have used me very ill over this business. No end of unnecessary trouble which might have been avoided … had I received proper instructions at first.'[59] As is so often the case with such records, the precise details of disputes are only hinted at. The friction clearly extended to the stage of fixing the sculpture to the cathedral walls, when in April 1905 Probert informed Somers Clarke that the cathedral authorities were not allowing the bracket fastenings to go further into the wall than one foot, whereas the foundry insisted that a depth of two feet minimum was needed in order to take the weight of the sculpture. However, once the work was completed Princess Louise was praised for possessing 'no little ability', and her sculpture as being 'surely her masterpiece, as well as an example of virtuoso bronze casting, which used its slender site cleverly'.[60] Stylistically the work owes some debt to late Pre-Raphaelite painting: a professional model, Mrs Lloyd, posed for the figure of the angel, having been recommended to Louise by Sir William Blake Richmond who was a friend of several Pre-Raphaelite and Aesthetic artists. The model for the dying Christ was the Italian Antonio Corsi, who had previously modelled for the princess.[61]

Frances Bessie Burlison (1875–c.1974) studied at the Slade School of Art. She exhibited with the Society of Lady Artists in 1898 and an exhibition review in *The Times* particularly noted her promising decorative sculpture.[62] She worked for Adrian Gilbert Scott and made sculptural figures for various cathedrals, including Liverpool, and showed at the Royal Academy between 1889–94 and 1911–27. Her father, John Burlison, was half of the Burlison and Grylls stained glass company; it is possible that a couple of the Grylls daughters also studied at the Slade, which may explain the continuing professional connection between the two families. Grylls involved several of his daughters in drawing and modelling for him, so it is quite possible that he similarly employed Burlison.[63] Burlison's impressive First World War memorial at Beaumont College was unveiled on 13 November 1921 (**Plate 19**). Beaumont was a Jesuit public school, which had opened in 1861 and eventually closed in 1967. The memorial comprises a Portland stone arch framing a life-size sculpture of Christ crucified, beneath which are the names of the dead, the whole mounted above an altar, symbolic of sacrifice.[64] The unveiling was described in 1922:

> the memorial ... occupies a prominent site in the midst of the college lawns, with a background of trees originally forming part of Windsor forest. The memorial, which is 33 feet in height, and constructed of white Portland stone, has been designed by Mr. G. Gilbert Scott ... and Mr. A. Gilbert Scott ... both of them old Beaumont boys. It takes the form of a large Greek cenotaph, embodying a calvary, with a life-size bronze figure modelled by Miss Frances Burlison, well known by her work at the Royal Academy. The figure is set in an arch, through which the background of trees is seen, and at the foot of the memorial is a massive stone altar for use in memorial services, and lateral wing walls extending some 50 feet in length.[65]

Frances Darlington also made a war memorial, for St George's House, Northern Police Orphanage, Otley Road, Harrogate, between 1914 and 1918 (**Figure 84**). This First World War memorial was in memory of old boys and girls; unveiled in December 1918 it was the gift of Dr and Mrs Crawford Watson, who were friends of Darlington, and it is now in the Ripon Police Museum. This work harnessed Darlington's religious beliefs with her ongoing interest in medieval knighthood. Comprising a very large relief, the sculpture depicts the Vision of St George offering succour to Richard the Lionheart on the First Crusade. The focus of the panel is a portrayal of the saint on a white horse, with St Joan of Arc kneeling before him, holding a banner with the red and white cross of St George. Here the enemy is generic, a threat to Christianity and to human morality. It glorifies courage rather than war and there is no reference to the actual enemy faced during the war. The quasi-medieval imagery was popular at this time, and in comparison with other 1918

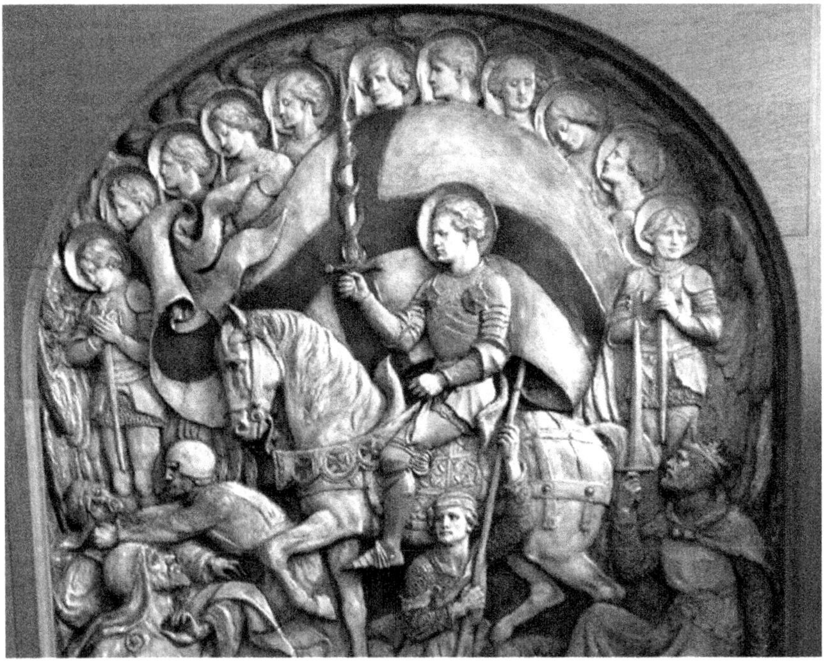

84. Frances Darlington, *St George's Police Orphanage Memorial*, Ripon, c.1918

war memorials it is 'complex and delicate and ... comparatively very feminine'.[66]

Rosamund Praeger completed in excess of ten First World War memorials in town squares, schools, hospitals and Presbyterian and Anglican churches. Her most important was her commission for Belfast's Workman and Clark's shipyard. As well as being a public war memorial, it was also intended to commemorate the family's only son, Edward Workman, who died in January 1916 from injuries sustained in battle. The design comprised his portrait flanked by the names of over 120 men from the shipyard. This was supported by a pictorial frieze divided into three parts, showing first the men at work in the shipyard, then leaving home after enlisting, and finally wounded men being cared for on the battlefield. The memorial was unveiled on 8 August 1919, and after the shipyard closed part of the memorial was transferred to the Thompson Pump House in the Harland and Wolff shipyard. One of Praeger's most striking memorials comprised a bronze panel showing an angel with outstretched wings hovering over two dying young soldiers. This was for Richard Caulfield Orpen's First World War memorial in Omagh,

Co. Tyrone, which was unveiled in September 1927 (**Figure 85**). The memorial takes the form of a large obelisk of hammered granite and Praeger's panel is set in the lower half.

Ursula Edgcumbe also made a war memorial, installed in 1922 in the grounds of Zennor Parish Church in rural Cornwall. It is an unusual work, now badly weathered and covered in lichen, comprising a squat pillar of local granite surmounted by small high-relief figures standing in a mourning position. The First World War dedication is carved on to one side of the pillar, with a bronze plaque below carrying the Second World War dedication. Kineton Parkes described Edgcumbe as 'a woman carver who has done some excellent architectural work', and stated that the Zennor memorial was 'one of the most significant of the British war memorials'. He defined the subject as Shadrach, Meshach and Abednego in flames, and the figures surmount a column designed by architect George L. Kennedy. Parkes believed that the memorial's significance lay in its being almost the sole example in England of 'simplified direct carving in granite, at the quarries, unpolished and unsophisticated'.

85. Rosamund Praeger, *War Memorial*, Omagh, 1927

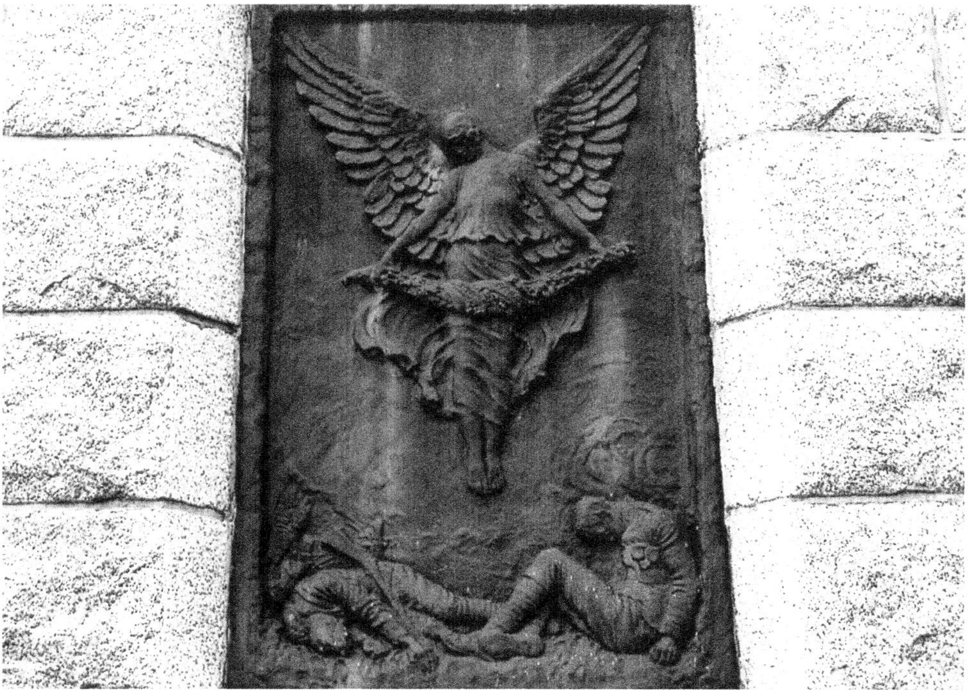

He noted Edgcumbe's five years of study under sculptor Havard Thomas at the Slade School, and that she followed him into architectural carving of which, in Parkes's opinion, there was too little that was good in Britain.[67]

Gertrude Alice Meredith Williams's *Spirit of the Crusaders* monument (1924) was an ambitious work, as can be seen from the bronze maquette held by the National Museum of Wales, which was the competition model for Paisley's war memorial (**Figure 86**). Placed alongside a staircase, this model is a rarity among the works discussed in this book as it is on permanent display, albeit in a rather out-of-the-way position where it might easily go unnoticed. On 27 July 1924 the imposing Paisley memorial was unveiled. It comprised a 25-feet-high square pillar by the architect Sir Robert Lorimer, topped with a larger than life-size medieval knight on horseback, wearing mail and carrying

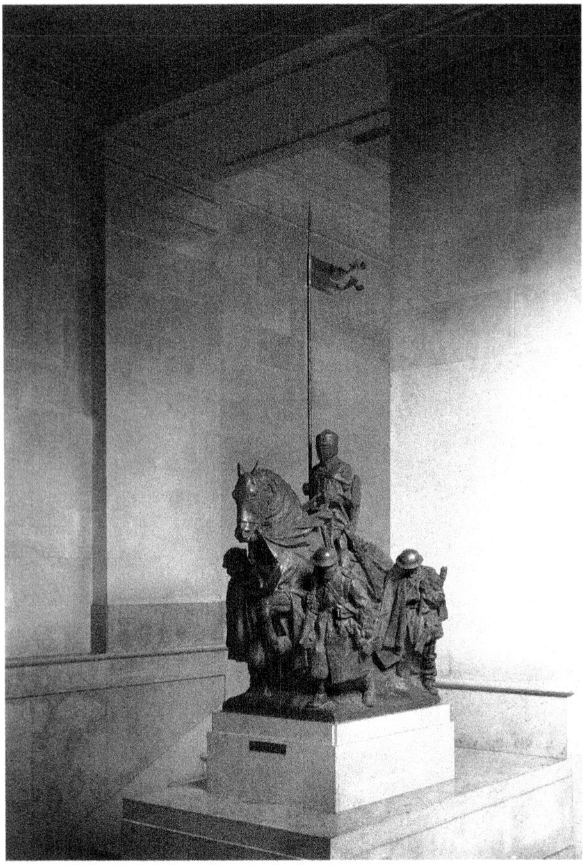

86. Gertrude Alice Meredith Williams, *Spirit of the Crusaders*, 1924

an upright lance. He is closely surrounded by four British soldiers in full marching dress appropriate to the 1914–18 conflict. Although allegorical figures were popular for war memorials, the most common motif was that of the ordinary soldier. Williams, wrongly identified as a man in the press, was commissioned after winning a competition which attracted 195 entries, her second entry being placed third. There appears to have been some friction between the city council and Lorimer and Williams. The town clerk wrote to Lorimer on 17 April 1923 complaining about the projected completion of the memorial in July 1924, since he had anticipated the summer of 1923 as marking its dedication. He rather sharply expressed the opinion that 'the Memorial Committee ... cannot help feeling that Mrs. Williams is not giving the Memorial the attention to which it is entitled'.[68] Lorimer's response was decisive:

> You must remember that this group of sculpture [*sic*] is one of the largest things that has ever been done in Scotland. When your Committee come to see the full size model I think they will be impressed. If we get the memorial completed by Midsummer 1924 I think that everyone concerned will have done uncommonly well. In this connection I may point out that the Gladstone Memorial erected in George Street here took 14 years to complete, and that the famous Rodin spent most of his life over the group known as the 'Burghers of Calais' – a copy of which was erected on the Thames Embankment not long ago. This 'Burghers of Calais' group is a small affair compared to what you are going to get at Paisley.[69]

The attitude of the stoical soldiers in their thick clothes is suggestive of determined resistance rather than victory. The sculpture was originally shown as a small terracotta at the 1921 Royal Scottish Academy Exhibition, and since the collaboration with Lorimer has been stated as arising from his recognition of the sculpture's potential qualities, this suggests that the original small piece might have been a stand-alone work, only later adopted for the Paisley war memorial. A review in *Country Life* from 16 May 1925 admired this sculptural group as commanding 'reverence and respect because of the spirit of romance and sober purpose animating it; because ... of the unforced sculpturesque power pervading it, and the unaffected sobriety of achievement by which it is distinguished; it is a masterpiece of modern sculpture'.[70] The large plaster cast of this final model was shown at the 1922 Wembley British Empire Exhibition, and Williams let the National Museum of Wales have a bronze cast of the work at cost price as she felt it an honour to be represented in the museum's collection.[71]

During his war service, her husband, the painter Morris Meredith Williams, made drawings which would be shared with his sculptor wife. The couple had met in Paris in 1904 when Alice was travelling on a scholarship granted by Liverpool Council in 1901. She had studied at Liverpool University's School of Architecture, and a glowing 1917 reference from Vice-Principal Charles J. Allen showed how highly she was regarded.[72] After their meeting in Paris, Morris returned to get a job in Edinburgh and Alice went back to Liverpool in 1905, working at the Della Robbia Pottery for three months just before it closed. The couple married and settled in Edinburgh in 1906, and retired to Devon in 1929. Gertrude was four-and-a-half years older than her husband; she declared her age incorrectly when she married and so some documentation records it inaccurately. She was the ninth of ten surviving children and her siblings all had good careers; this was clearly a family that believed in education for girls as well as boys. By all accounts it was she who negotiated prices after her marriage, her husband being 'hopeless' with such finances.[73]

Robert Lorimer was the architect for the Scottish National War Memorial in Edinburgh (1924–27) and Williams worked with him again when she made the principal sculptures. Once more she worked with her husband, producing an impressive bronze frieze encircling the shrine. The design by Morris drew attention to the individuality of those involved in war, constructed in the format of the classical processions of ancient Greece and Rome (**Figure 87**). Many different roles are depicted and the frieze includes men and women, mules, weaponry and aeroplanes. It is both a comprehensive record as well as a highly coherent and effective design. Alice also designed the casket located within the shrine which holds the Rolls of Honour inscribed with the names of the dead; this she decorated with angels and statues of St Andrew and St Margaret of Scotland. It is constructed from steel, which although hard to work is appropriate as the metal of war. The entire composition of angels and casket stands upon a pillar of dark green Italian marble, which in turn stands on the actual rock of Edinburgh Castle at its highest point. Suspended from the roof in the centre of the shrine is Williams's oak carving *St Michael*, again well over life-size at 11 feet in height, and on the northern face of the outside of the shrine is her stone group *The Calling of St Andrew*. Williams hoped that an unrealized work, known as *The Lost Legion* (1918), would be placed over the door of the Hall of Honour, but this position was to be occupied by Pilkington Jackson's *Reveille*.

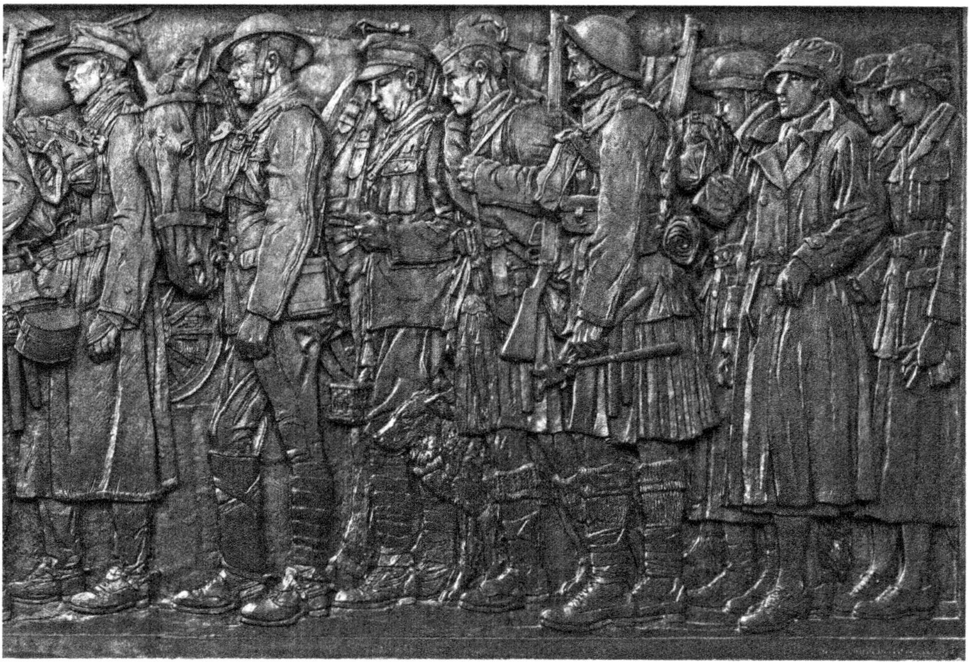

87. Gertrude Alice and Morris Meredith Williams, *Frieze*, first right-hand panel, Shrine east side, Scottish National War Memorial, Edinburgh, detail, 1927

Figure 88 shows the clay version of what would have been a particularly poignant and expressive figure of a combatant. The Scottish National War Memorial was widely commented on, and a publication produced some time after 1945 (since it referred to the dead of the Second World War) characterized it as

> a wholly Scottish achievement conceived in the Scottish spirit, designed, built and made a proud fact by Scottish brains and hands [and] it has won the admiration and touched the hearts of people from all over the world ... Our sorrow and our pride were personal, and our builders and our artists expressed them personally. But for that very reason they were not private. If a feeling is deep enough and sincere enough ... it is universally recognized.[74]

In an obituary in *The Times* Williams was described as chiefly an architectural sculptor with a highly developed sense of the interdependence between the two art forms.[75]

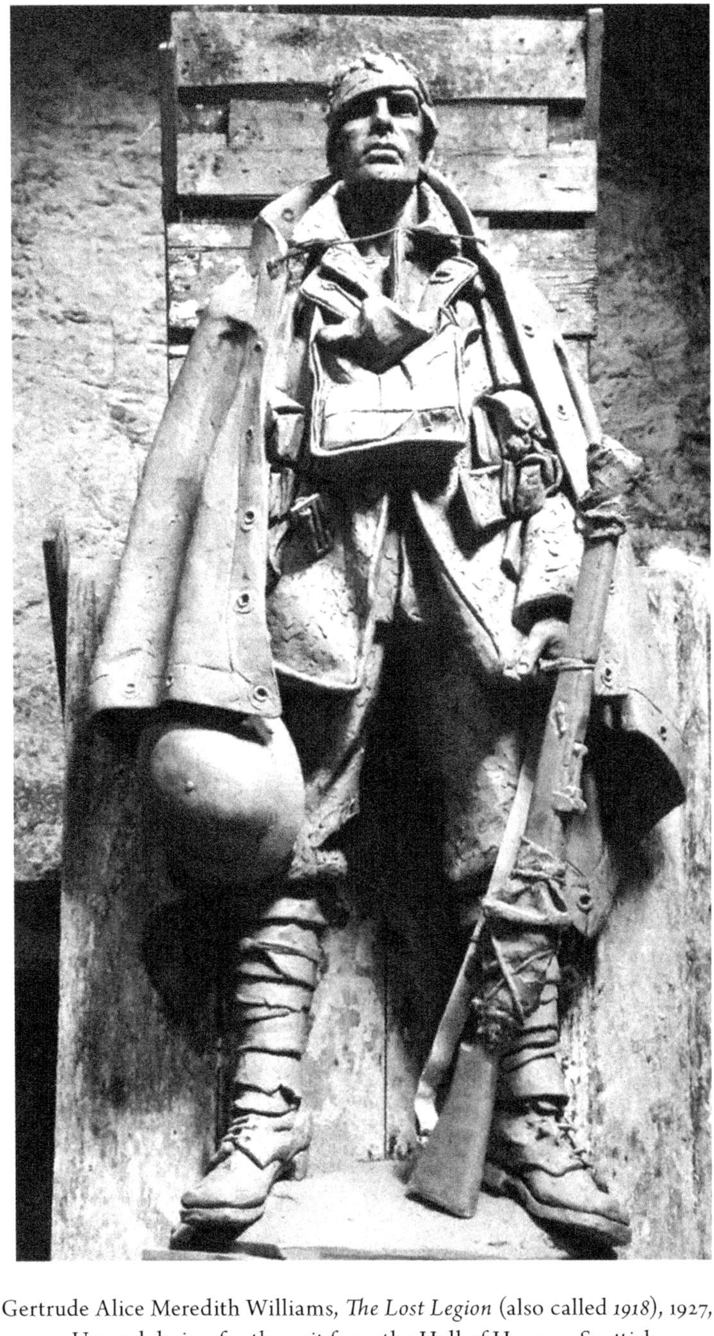

88. Gertrude Alice Meredith Williams, *The Lost Legion* (also called *1918*), 1927, clay. Unused design for the exit from the Hall of Honour, Scottish National War Memorial

At the young age of 16 Phyllis Mary Bone (Hornby) (1894–1972) entered the Edinburgh College of Art, and by 1918 had gained a diploma in sculpture. She then studied in Paris with Edouard Navellier as well as in Italy. In 1939 she was elected an associate member of the Royal Scottish Academy and in 1944 was the first woman to be elected an Academician. She was one of several artists who worked on the Scottish National War Memorial. Robert Lorimer was noted for encouraging women sculptors, and he seems to have treated Bone as an equal collaborator on the project, despite the fact that she had only recently graduated. She produced all of the animals bar one on the memorial, including capitals for the niches and the heraldic beasts of England and Scotland, the *Heraldic Lion* and the *Unicorn*, for the entrance to the memorial (**Figure 89**); she also made a relief, *Remember also the Humble Beasts*, and in the south-west bay *The Tunnellers' Friends*. Her work here established her reputation and led to further commissions, while at the same time she continued to produce

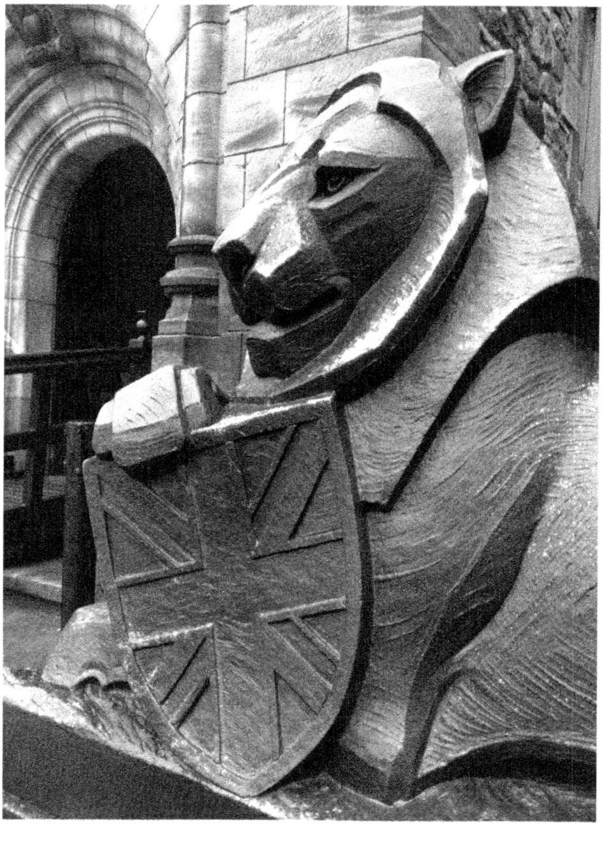

89. Phyllis Bone, *Heraldic Lion*, Scottish National War Memorial, Edinburgh, 1924–27

small bronze works. In 1949 Bone moved to the Galloway countryside so that she could focus on more personal sculpture; she watched animals in the wild, even on occasion taking her modelling materials out with her.[76]

Phoebe Gertrude Stabler's Durban Cenotaph is a truly unusual work (**Figure 90**). This Art Deco First World War monument erected in Farewell Square, Durban, was unveiled on 7 March 1926. The design was by A. L. Gordon Pilkington, who was born in Cape Town and went to Europe for further experience on completion of his articles. Unusually it is made from granite and blue and gold glazed ceramic tiles, and was constructed in England by Phoebe and her husband, and shipped to Durban for assembly. Phoebe was responsible for modelling the figures. The glazed structure is some 21 feet high and on it are two large winged angels in white and lapis lazuli who are raising up the soul of a dead

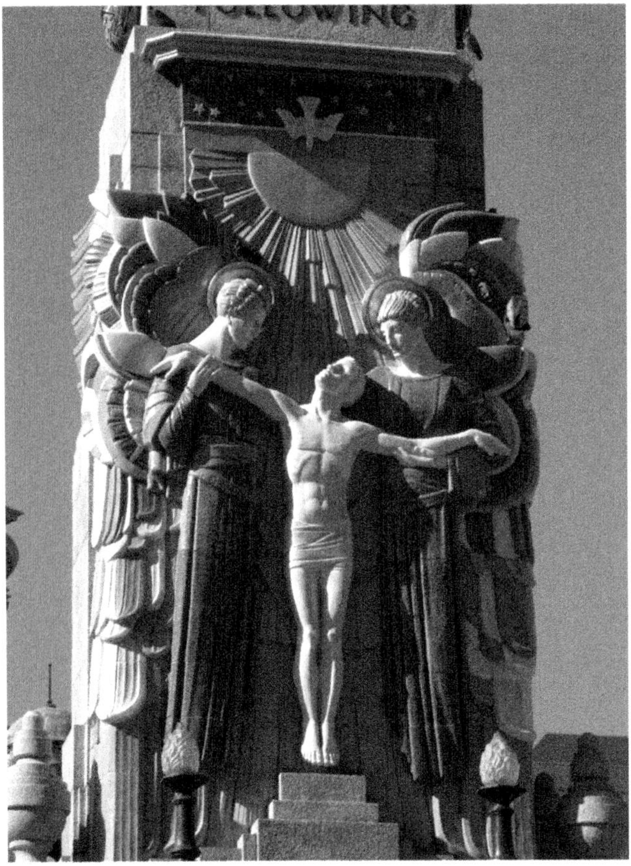

90. Phoebe Stabler, *The Durban Cenotaph*, Great War Memorial, Gardiner Street, Durban, 1926

soldier. Heaven is presented symbolically by a blue starlit sky and a yellow sun, accompanied by the white dove of the Holy Spirit. The vivid colour of the figurative decoration made the cenotaph very distinctive. The stone elements of the monument are in a neoclassical style and as with other Commonwealth cenotaphs a wreath crowns the top, in this case made of green ceramic. The legend 'Tell it to the generation following' appears just below, and a metal statue of a dead soldier lies stretched out on a plinth in front of the monument. Initially locals were unhappy with its bright colours, supposedly influenced by the tomb of Tutankhamen, but it appears that the public eventually warmed to the distinctive nature of their striking monument and the colours have softened somewhat over time.[77]

Mary Pownall Bromet (c.1862–1937) studied in Frankfurt for a year and spent four years in Rome. Around the period 1897–98 she was a pupil of Rodin in Paris. In 1902 she married Alfred Bromet, a friend of Stanley Baldwin. Pownall Bromet exhibited at the Royal Academy and throughout Europe, as well as in British municipal galleries, and she also served as president of the Society of Women Artists. Her technical virtuosity led to several commissions which required emotive figures, such as her 1928 Watford war memorial (**Plate 20**). Under each of the men, from left to right in this photograph, are the words *Victory, To The Fallen* and *To The Wounded*. The three male nudes show the clear influence of Rodin and are designed to represent the three main aspects of war. Two of the figures are dated, one inscribed 1914 and the other 1916, so they were produced prior to the eventual memorial design, possibly explaining the nudity, which would be more conventional in a gallery setting. When seen in a memorial, as with Kathleen Scott's statues of young men, they convey both

> vulnerability and moral integrity ... As mind and body were believed to be directly related it was assumed that strengthening the body consequently strengthened the will and so helped the development of character ... the finely honed body served as a metaphor for the effectual society and it is in this sense that memorialists who revealed the exposed male body as muscular and athletic, literally laid bare their images of manhood, suggesting not only physical, but moral strength.[78]

In this way the heroic bodies make reference to Renaissance and thus Classical ideals. The war memorial was moved in 1987 from in front of the Peace Memorial Hospital when the road was widened, and is now beside the town hall. The three bronze sculptures are placed on a stone base which was originally white but is now badly stained due to the weathering of the bronze.

The March family of sculptors was responsible for the Canadian National War Memorial (also known as *The Response*), a tall granite cenotaph with bronze sculptures sited in Confederation Square, Ottawa, which serves as the country's federal war memorial. Built to commemorate the First World War, it was rededicated in 1982 to include the Second World War and the Korean War. In 2000 the Canadian Tomb of the Unknown Soldier was added to the memorial site, symbolizing the sacrifice made by every Canadian who has died or may yet die for their country. In 1925 a competition was held to invite designs, with entrants to be residents of the British Empire or citizens of allied nations. There were 127 entries; seven were requested to submit scale models and Vernon March was named the winner in January 1926. His approach to the commission was to show the response of Canada to war in the form of service personnel marching through a triumphal arch. Two 17-feet 6-inch allegorical figures of peace and freedom are placed at the apex of the arch, and below are 22 Canadian servicemen, from all branches of the forces that served in the First World War, dressed in historically correct uniforms. March was assisted by his brothers and his sister Elsie, all of whom completed the work after his death in 1930. However, the idea persists that women could not work on such large projects. It was suggested to the author that it was unlikely that Elsie would have been involved:

> I would say not, at least the physical working of the memorial, a bit heavy work for a young lady!! (and little sister!!) although they did have a team of men and a foreman doing the heavy work. I would think she helped in kitchen table chat about the overall effect … Although the finished work involved at least three of the brothers, I would think she would have been given credit if actually involved. Being 'just a woman' and keeping house, which she did, would not [have] been upgraded to helping … although they could not have managed one suspects without her doing so!![79]

The bronzes were cast in the Marchs' foundry; the work was finished in July 1932 and put on display in Hyde Park before being shipped to Ottawa in 1937. The entire cenotaph was completed on 19 October 1938 and on 21 May 1939 was officially unveiled by George VI. It was filmed twice for British Pathé in 1932. The title of the first film was *Farnborough, Kent. Canada's National Memorial – to her 68,000 dead. Colossal group of bronze Figures – after 6 years unremitting labour, by the famous 6 March*

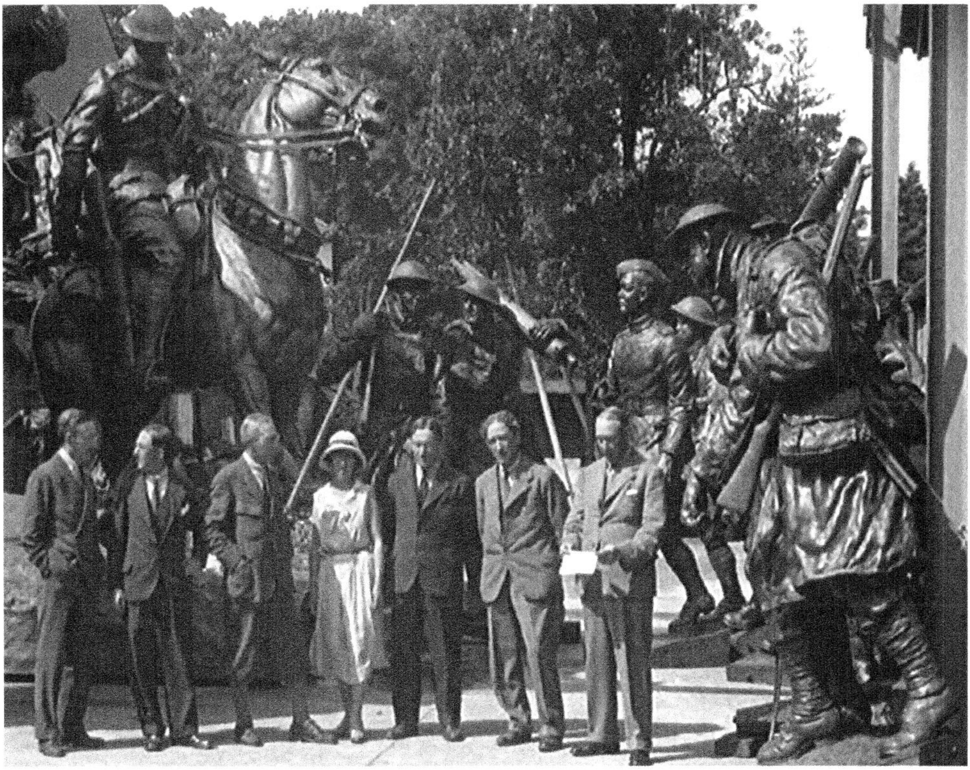

91. March Family, *Figures for the Canadian War Memorial, Ottawa*, Ontario, Canada, 1938

brothers & their sister – completed! (**Figure 91**). In this still image we see the March family standing in front of some of the bronze components of the memorial. In the film there are various shots of this impressive monument's figures, close-up details and images of the maquette.

6.3 Ecclesiastical sculpture

Kineton Parkes included ecclesiastical work in *The Art of Carved Sculpture* (1931), for example noting sculptor Alan Durst's processional crucifix for St Matthew's Church, Brixton, carved from ivory and ebony, as well as illustrating an altar crucifix. Stylistically the latter work is somewhat similar to Devon wood carver Violet Pinwill's reredos at Ermington, which will be examined in this chapter. Like Pinwill, Durst was described as a wood carver, rather than solely a sculptor, and it is interesting that Parkes made the specific point that wood sculpture received too little official recognition.[80] It is clear that contemporary writers saw less of a distinction between what we might now define as ecclesiastical sculpture – tombs and memorials – and items that we would regard as 'furnishings', such as screens, pulpits, bench ends and so on. This overlap is important in drawing together a broad range of practices, and in rehabilitating 'the decorative' into the narrative of public and, in this case, ecclesiastical sculpture. A 2008 exhibition mounted jointly by the Henry Moore Institute and the John Paul Getty Museum in Los Angeles examined the frequently close relationship between sculpture and the decorative arts[81] and such a comparison can equally be mapped on to ecclesiastical sculpture in all of its forms. There are many similarities and crossovers between sculpture and decoration, which have often been regarded as polar opposites. Qualities normally associated with sculpture, such as creative freedom and autonomy, could very often be traded with qualities that have ordinarily been ascribed to decorative work, such as craftsmanship and functionality. So we can conceive of sculpture as existing within some 'decorative' work and also understand that it is possible for sculpture to work in a 'decorative' manner. Of course, we need to be mindful of the contemporary understanding of how objects functioned for their original audiences and how such terminology was conceived.[82]

An understanding of ecclesiastical sculpture is not helped by the practical constraints of exhibitions. The latter play a key role in bestowing the label 'art' on work that can be displayed in a gallery, and thus make it more difficult for a sculptural and artistic object that cannot be moved from its fixed location to lay claim to such qualities. Of course, there are exceptions to this, most notably in the famous statuary contained in the great European cathedrals which can hold their own through the fame of their maker. But where such fame does not exist, the absence of public display in a curatorial context discourages critical attention and reduces public familiarity. The materials used for so-called decorative art objects have also been an issue for some, yet

> the same materials and techniques appear across different practices, and their resonance shifts dramatically in different contexts. For example, while a pair of bronze baroque putti, originally made for an altar but immediately collected as works of art in their own right, may strike as sculpture *par excellence*, bronze turned into functional objects has a more ambiguous aura.[83]

Equally the attention to material differs according to how the viewer understands the object at which they are looking. We assume that the material used for sculpture is a means to an end – we take it for granted. Whereas with the decorative arts, the materials – how they are crafted and the level of skill on display – are frequently the focus. This despite the fact that sculptors needs a sophisticated understanding of working with a material's inherent properties that goes beyond technical facility.[84]

In the late nineteenth century there was a noticeable increase in firms or individuals that traded in the area of church furnishing.[85] There was also much general discussion about the decoration of churches, in the same way that there would later be debates about war memorials. Organizations were established to try and rectify what was seen as a lowering in the standards of ecclesiastical taste. In 1896 the Clergy and Artists' Association was formed with a view to bringing both groups together and to make improvements overall in the artistic standards of church furnishings and fittings.[86] They held exhibitions of members' work, sometimes jointly with the Church Congress, and generally acted as agents, responding to applications made by clergymen seeking advice and suggesting names of craftsmen and artists. An organization with a similar intent was the Church Crafts League, founded in 1899 by John Ruskin and G. F. Watts, which was an offshoot of the Arts and Crafts Society.[87] The League had been established to give fresh artistic inspiration to church commissions as well as to facilitate ecclesiastical commissions being awarded to credible artists and craftsmen.[88] Also in 1899 Percy Dearmer wrote the *Parson's Handbook*, which was revised and enlarged in 1903 and 1907. Here he argued that

> the Church of England had neglected the great artists and craftsmen of the last generation ... Never had there been so many first class makers of furniture, interior decorators, sculptors, stone and wood carvers and metal workers working in England. The Church missed a great opportunity in not employing them.[89]

Dearmer headed the advisory committee of the Warham Guild, which was founded in London in November 1912 to augment the directives of the *Parson's Handbook* by providing altars, acting for metal and wood carvers, and offering advice on any work connected with the fabric of churches. From the outset several women were members of its committee. The Guild published between 1912 and 1963, and through its activities and its Handbook had a great influence on the appearance of English churches well into the mid-twentieth century.

Some time in the 1920s H. H. Martyn and Co. published *Memorials*, which combined a trade catalogue with text, setting out the firm's aims and beliefs. The text focused mostly on the responsibilities of the architect rather than those of the sculptor. However, it is significant that in this essentially trade catalogue it was argued that ecclesiastical furnishings and fitments could function as ideal memorials, giving the opportunity to display the highest standard of craftsmanship. The skills needed for good ecclesiastical woodwork were high, since 'the traditions are exacting and perfection is the aim'.[90] Based on this and many other sources it is clear that from the late nineteenth century until at least the 1920s there was considerable flexibility around the concepts of memorials, sculpture, decorative carving and so on. However, this fluidity is rarely reflected in recently published texts on public sculpture.[91] 'Public' in the latter sense seems necessarily to mean 'outside', which leaves important ecclesiastical works unconsidered and, crucially, separated from such surveys. In this way they remain largely beyond critical attention, and so ecclesiastical and decorative sculpture are further marginalized.[92]

Apart from drawing on texts concerned with the decorative arts, equivalent publications on the history of interior design can also be helpful in thinking about how we might bring sculpture, applied art and architecture closer together. In *Craft, Space and Interior Design, 1855–2005* (2008) it was proposed that one only has to look at the key historical writers on craft and design history to realize that architects were keenly aware of the importance of the relationship between architecture and the decorative arts.[93] Writing on 'Space and the Victorian Ecclesiastical Interior', Jim Cheshire notes that although the Victorian church furnishing business became increasingly commercialized, there was still an appreciation of skill and of making on an individual scale. Addressing the Oxford Movement's interest in medievalism, he made the link to a renewed appreciation for ecclesiastical decorative arts, in that

> there was a perceived need for new churches, ecclesiologists were waging an influential campaign for the revival of highly ornate interiors and Victorian England was the richest country the world had ever known. It is perhaps not surprising in this context that a whole range of artists, artisans and manufacturers arose to meet the demand.

There was some debate over how much craftsmanship was used in the production of church woodcarving, although even large companies such as Cox and Son used hand-carving methods, and it appears that substantial businesses coexisted with small craft practices.[94] Indeed, by the 1880s

92. Frances Darlington, *Madonna Della Rosa*, c.1906–07

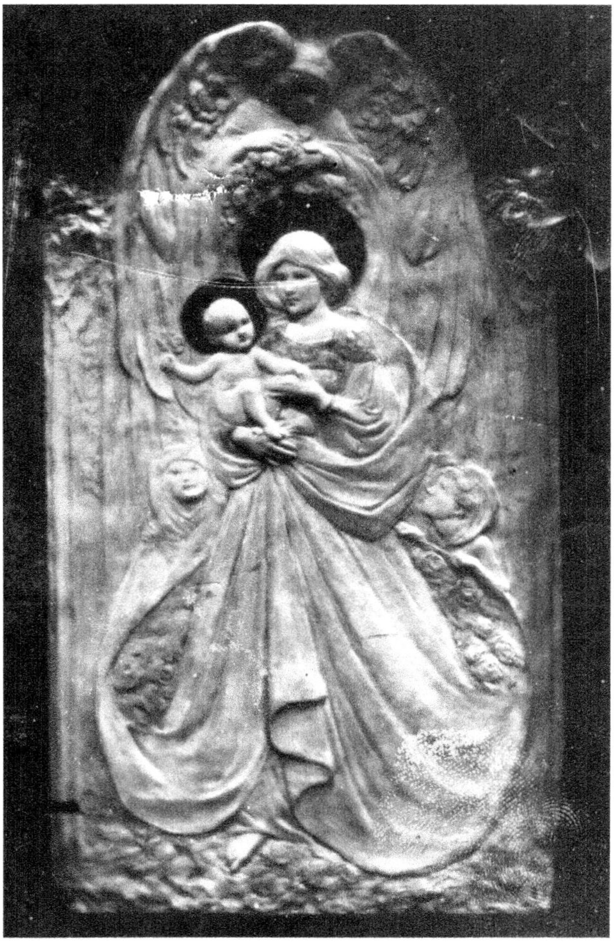

church furnishers' designs were seen as dated, having 'no place in the more eclectic and self-consciously individualistic interiors produced by Arts and Crafts architects'.[95] This shift in taste could well have facilitated the engagement of individual decorative craftsmen and sculptors.

At least one of the sculptors included in this book, Frances Darlington, was certainly influenced by the Oxford Movement, in relation not only to its beliefs but also to the art with which it became associated.[96] This was possibly also the case with Violet Pinwill, not the least since her father was a clergyman. Darlington's relief panel *Madonna Della Rosa* (c.1906–07) lay undiscovered until 2003, when it was found in the crypt of St Wilfrid's Church, Harrogate (**Figure 92**). It is not clear whether this was a commission, but the sculpture is known to have first been exhibited at the spring exhibition in Leeds in 1907. The subject was popular in High Renaissance art, although most treatments showed the Virgin and Child holding a single rose. In contrast Darlington depicted the Madonna surrounded by angels bringing her roses, while others assist in carrying them in her skirts and veil. Between 1913 and c.1920 Darlington made coloured plaster relief panels depicting scenes from the Nativity and Stations of the Cross for St Wilfrid's Church, which was designed by Temple Lushington Moore. Darlington and her mother were now living in a house situated such that St Wilfrid's was between her home and studio, which might well have smoothed the way for her discussions with the architect and clergymen. Moore was a High Anglican architect and St Wilfrid's was his most famous building, the commission originating in a bequest to build a medieval style church on the site. He was prolific and popular, working on both new and existing churches throughout the United Kingdom. The title of Darlington's *Stations of the Cross* is somewhat misleading, since to truly fit that category the work would need to comprise 14 stations whereas Darlington made only nine panels. The Christmas story is depicted on panels on the opposite wall, **Plate 21** showing a detail from *Ancilla Domini, the visit of the Magi* (c.1914–18). The panels were sculpted and painted by Darlington using the polychrome techniques of her former teacher Frampton, and in terms of subject, dimensions and colour they relate directly to the Scrovegni Chapel decorated by Giotto.[97]

Wood carving was at the heart of the ecclesiastical practice of Violet Pinwill, and her work can be seen in more than 200 churches in Devon and Cornwall. She used mainly oak or chestnut, and her career demonstrated one of the ways in which women artists of the period could engage in important three-dimensional and relief work. Some of her practice involved the restoration of medieval churches, but in the first half of the twentieth century she also decorated newly built churches. The particular beauty of West Country churches, especially those in Pinwill's native Devon, lies in their lavishly carved woodwork, including magnificent roodscreens. Cornish churches also are noted for outstanding woodwork, and most of Pinwill's work was carried out across the two counties. Many of Devon's medieval roodscreens remain substantially complete, with minimal restoration, and they dominate parish churches, being massive and often displaying similar decorative elements of trailing vines, animals and birds, while being varied in their ornamental edgings. From the 1880s onwards churches were influenced by the Arts and Crafts movement, and this coincided with a revival in the craft of Devon wood carving. The carvers generally copied medieval designs and the subjects were usually drawn from nature rather than referencing religious themes.

The late Victorian architect John Dando Sedding was important in setting some precedents for the Pinwill practice and he is likely to have played a part in her training. His restoration of the church at Holbeton in Devon has been highly praised, 'completed at astronomic expense between 1884 and 1889 (c.£25,000)'.[98] Sedding was involved with the Art Workers' Guild and was inspired by Ruskin and Morris. Indeed, much of the most innovative early work of the Arts and Crafts movement can be seen in the furnishing schemes for churches, rather than solely in the domestic sphere which is the usual focus for scholars of the movement. Sedding's aim was to preserve where possible, and he became interested in post-medieval designs such as Jacobean. Importantly for a discussion of Violet Pinwill, a central theme in his plans was the use of 'sculpture in architecture as a means to attain expression',[99] and for Sedding this alliance could become more varied, in both form and materials. 'Sculpture could be employed throughout a building, in wood as well as stone; indeed, this "decorative carpentry" increased the opportunity for expression, creating more complex interiors, texts rich with a symbolic vocabulary.'[100] Edmund Harold Sedding was John Dando's nephew and carried on the latter's work, setting up his own practice in Plymouth shortly after his uncle's death in 1891. He would go on to work with Pinwill on some of her church restoration and new-build projects.

As with many of the women discussed in this book, archival material for Pinwill is very slight; the main holding is a large collection of photographs of her work in the Plymouth and West Devon Record Office, but reproduction of these is not permitted. Pinwill's premises suffered a fire in 1905 and were bombed in the Second World War, and so any chance of useful written material surviving was at that point decided. Apart from working with Edmund Sedding she also collaborated with R. F. Wheatly of Truro, and in many instances the architects sent her full working drawings.

The fifth of seven daughters, she had moved with her family to Ermington vicarage in 1880. Her father, Reverend Edmund Pinwill, was determined to see the restoration of his church. John Dando Sedding was invited to oversee the work, calling upon the skills of a team of craftsmen and his nephew Edmund, who became a firm friend of the family. In the late 1880s the Mildmay family of Fleet in Devon had wanted to undertake restoration work in churches at Ermington and Holbeton, the latter being carried out first. When the Holbeton restoration was complete, a team of church craftsmen was assembled for Ermington, and the head of carving agreed to teach three of the Pinwill girls, including Violet. The sisters reportedly produced much of the church woodwork, starting with the pulpit and followed by the reredos and font cover. The fact that they learned to carve was not so strange, since wood carving was not regarded as an unusual practice for young ladies, but rather as an 'accomplishment'. The sisters Mary, Ethel and Violet became highly proficient, making the unusual move of forming their own company to carry out commissions. It was named Rashleigh, Pinwill and Co. in order to disguise their gender through the use of Mary's middle name. Some time around 1911 Violet became the sole proprietor of the business in Plymouth, gradually changing the name to V. Pinwill Carver, and she ran the firm for the next 50 years until her death in 1957. During this time she employed up to 29 wood carvers and joiners.[101]

The bulk of the work for an individual church would be hewn and carved in the company's workshop, while the final assembly was carried out on site.[102] It has been suggested that the speed with which her business expanded was in part due to the fact that Edmund Sedding designed much of her early work, thereby establishing high standards. One of Pinwill's carvers was Hubert Charles Minchinton, and a letter from his granddaughter to the West Devon Record Office describes how Pinwill gave Minchinton an album of about 50 photographs of carvings on his retirement, inscribed 'To my chief carver, in remembrance of many years excellent work.' These photographs may well be part of the deposit held by the Record Office.[103]

In 1934 an article was published on Pinwill for a series about *Westcountry Women's Careers*:

> Miss Pinwill carries on the tradition of those craftsmen of centuries ago who took infinite pains over their labours more for the pleasure and pride they felt in their work than for personal gain, yet this Westcountry woodcarver is not only an artist, but a business woman also. She has founded a carving and joinery business that is known throughout the country, and employs a staff of men, many of whom have been trained in her workshop ... When I walked up the stairs to her workshop I found a slight woman with simply-dressed grey hair and the light of enthusiasm in her eyes. Her vivid blue smocked overall made a brilliant note of colour among the drab clothes of the men who work under her and the planks of wood piled on the floor.

The article noted that Pinwill had won several prizes in the South Kensington examinations for her subject; this is the only source that makes any reference to Pinwill's involvement with a formal educational system, which thus remains a mystery. Her methods were then described, in that she worked to an architect's design but drew out the details of the carving herself. The article continued:

> As I walked down the steps that lead from her workshop to St. Lawrence Yard I realized that she had made an unqualified success of a job which most of her sex could not undertake, for there must be few women, or men either for that matter, who can combine such artistic talent with a business head and the gift of organizing a staff of skilled carvers and joiners.[104]

Pinwill's obituary in *The Times* applauded her deep knowledge of hagiology as well as her exceptional achievements in running a business at a time when this was extremely unusual for a young woman.[105]

Examples of her domestic carving remain with her heirs. Her great-nephew Robert Ward remembered her well, being 18 when she died. He recalled as a child watching Pinwill carving in her workshop:

> It was fascinating. She hardly ever followed a pattern, a lot of it coming straight out of her head like a painter painting from memory … a little old lady, by then well into her seventies and not five feet tall, carving great pieces of wood, always oak, with the facility of a man.[106]

This again raises questions about Pinwill's practice: to what extent was she carving from her own or from architects' designs, and how much work did she produce by her own hand? It is true that this lack of clarity sometimes raises attribution problems in relation to historical sculpture and painting workshops run by male artists. That said, observers seem to have been too quick to suggest that female sculptors had necessarily needed significant male assistance. However, Ward's memories of Pinwill's creativity are substantiated by a 1976 film made about her and the church at Ermington, in which her nephew Henry Caunter participated. According to his account, the first thing attempted by the Pinwill girls in the church at Ermington was indeed the pulpit, most of it carved by Violet when she was only 16 years old. Caunter speaks on the film to presenter Clive Gummell, describing the loyalty of Pinwill's workmen, given their unusual position working for a woman. Significantly, Gummell admired the Tudor rose on the Ermington reredos (c.1889) and argued that it and its surrounding foliage 'sums up for me all that is best in the work of Violet Pinwill. It's the looseness,

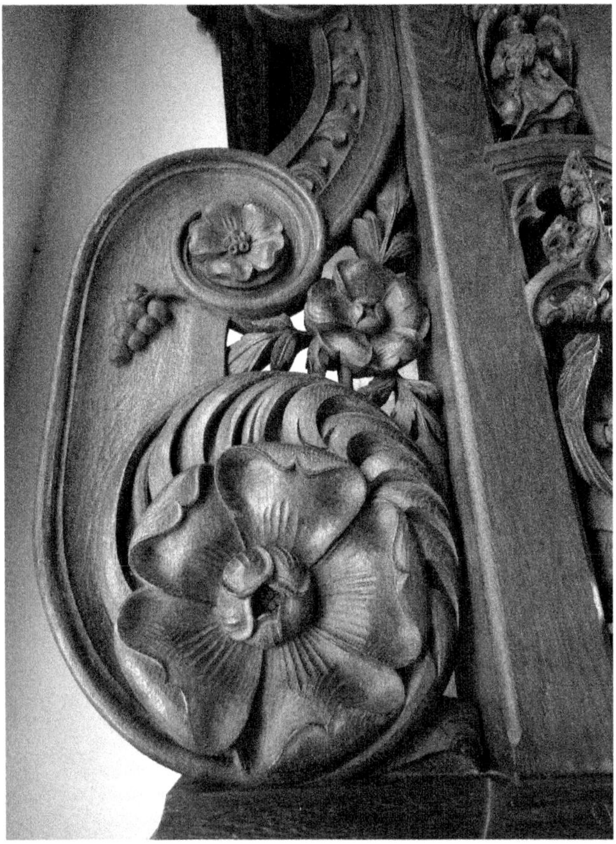

93. Violet Pinwill, left side of reredos, c.1889, detail. Church of St Peter and St Paul, Ermington

the freedom of movement, which she had.' On the film he points to the foliage and directs the viewer's attention to

> all one long chisel stroke all the way round like a good draftsman who never needs to take his pencil off the page. You can see gauge marks and then another. No uncertainty, no messing about. It has a freedom, a technical flow about it which I find very beautiful and the overall thing is full of life. She had a unique technical ability.[107]

Figure 93 shows the left-hand side of the reredos to which he motions on the film.

In 1899 Edmund Sedding wrote about Ermington church, although he did not describe the restoration, the new woodwork, or indeed the Pinwill sisters.[108] However, attached to a copy of this essay held at the Devon Record Office there are some plans, on the back of which is written 'Ermington Church by E. H. Sedding. To be preserved [?], V. Pinwill. Kindly return this to V. Pinwill, No. 9 Queen Anne Terrace, Plymouth.' This is definitively in Violet Pinwill's handwriting.[109] Given its unusually personal iconography, the pulpit (c.1889) is surely the Pinwill sisters' work. It is full of detail, indeed perhaps overcrowded, and stylistically is more heavily worked than the reredos surround. However, it is a highly individual work, containing at the base of the panels portraits of the three sisters. Thus it is a work which explicitly refers to its authorship and the portraits lay claim to their makers' skills, as was often the case in artworks of the past. It is unusual in being 'one of the few contemporary instances of women being directly involved in the practical, manual work within architecture, rather than the decoration of a church through embroidery or painting'.[110]

94. Violet Pinwill, alabaster and wood reredos, 1911. Church of St Peter and St Paul, Ermington

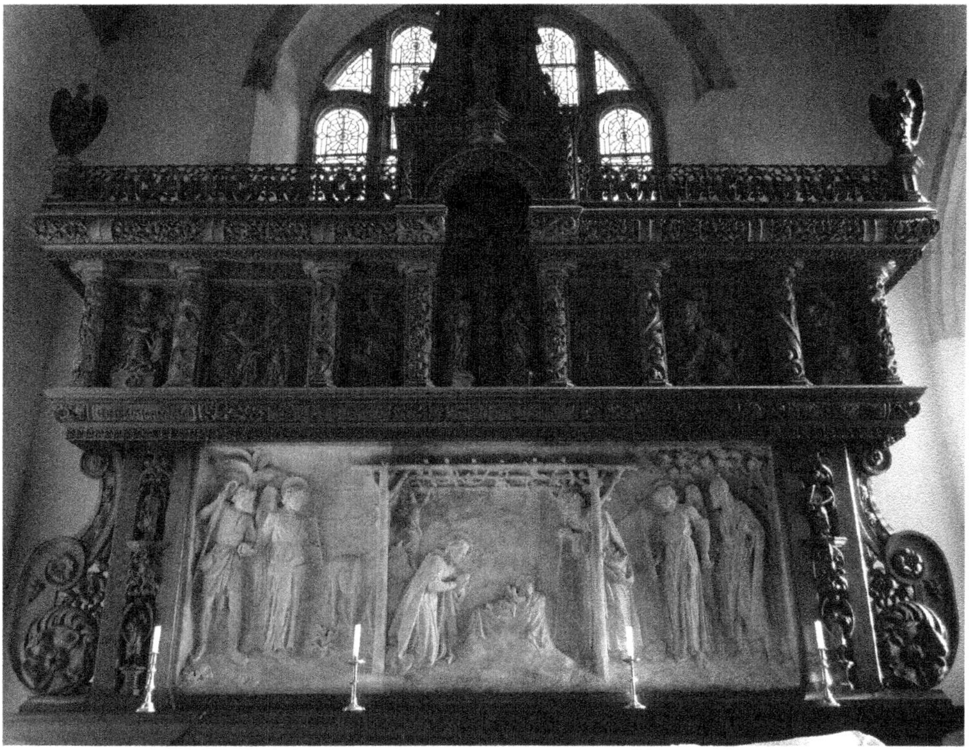

The remarkable and huge reredos does appear to have been designed by Edmund Sedding, with wooden figured panels above a large alabaster scene of the Nativity. It is described in the church literature as being after Burne-Jones, who was clearly a favourite of Pinwill's as his work was used for inspiration in her other churches. It was dedicated in May 1911 (**Figure 94**). Despite the alabaster carving being an exception in Pinwill's work, there is no evidence to suggest that the Ermington reredos was not hers. Nothing has come to light that might indicate the involvement of a sculptor known for working in stone, either at this or any other time during her career. Indeed, a contemporary newspaper reviewed the unveiling of the reredos and reinforced its attribution to Pinwill:

> The reredos is a costly work of oak and alabaster ... [and] consists of notable scenes in Gospel history. The large panel at the base, about 10ft. by 4ft. long, by 4ft. high, represents the adoration of the Shepherds and the Magi, carved in high relief; the sides are trimmed in traceried oak work, with large carved scrolls. The upper portion of the reredos is of dark oak, very beautifully carved, and is divided into compartments. The centre one represents the Crucifixion; the two larger ones the Annunciation and the Burial; the smaller one the Four Evangelists. The cornice above these subjects is surmounted by an elaborate cresting, and in the centre of all is a very richly carved niche with the figure of the Risen Saviour. Two angels, one at either end of the cresting, complete this splendid work. Miss Rashleigh Pinwill, of Plymouth, carried out the designs which were made by Mr. Edmund Sedding (Sedding and Wheatley), of Plymouth and London, and the people at Ermington are to be congratulated upon so beautiful an addition to their church.[111]

Figure 95 shows the highly accomplished Nativity section. Pinwill's relatives collaborated on a book of reminiscences, *Ermington Days*, giving us an important primary source. Here it is stated that 'after becoming thoroughly established as a wood-carver, Miss Pinwill became known as a worker in stone also, though this was not the medium most generally used by her', hence reinforcing the attribution of the alabaster work to Pinwill.[112]

The tiny Dartmoor church at Postbridge contains other beautiful but simple examples of the work carried out by Pinwill's firm, which was responsible for the whole interior, comprising the pulpit, reading desk and screens. The woodcarvings of wildlife and biblical scenes were commissioned by a Mrs Pethybridge of Hartyland, who was a great benefactor, donating £1,250 in 1936 for the restoration. The rear of the

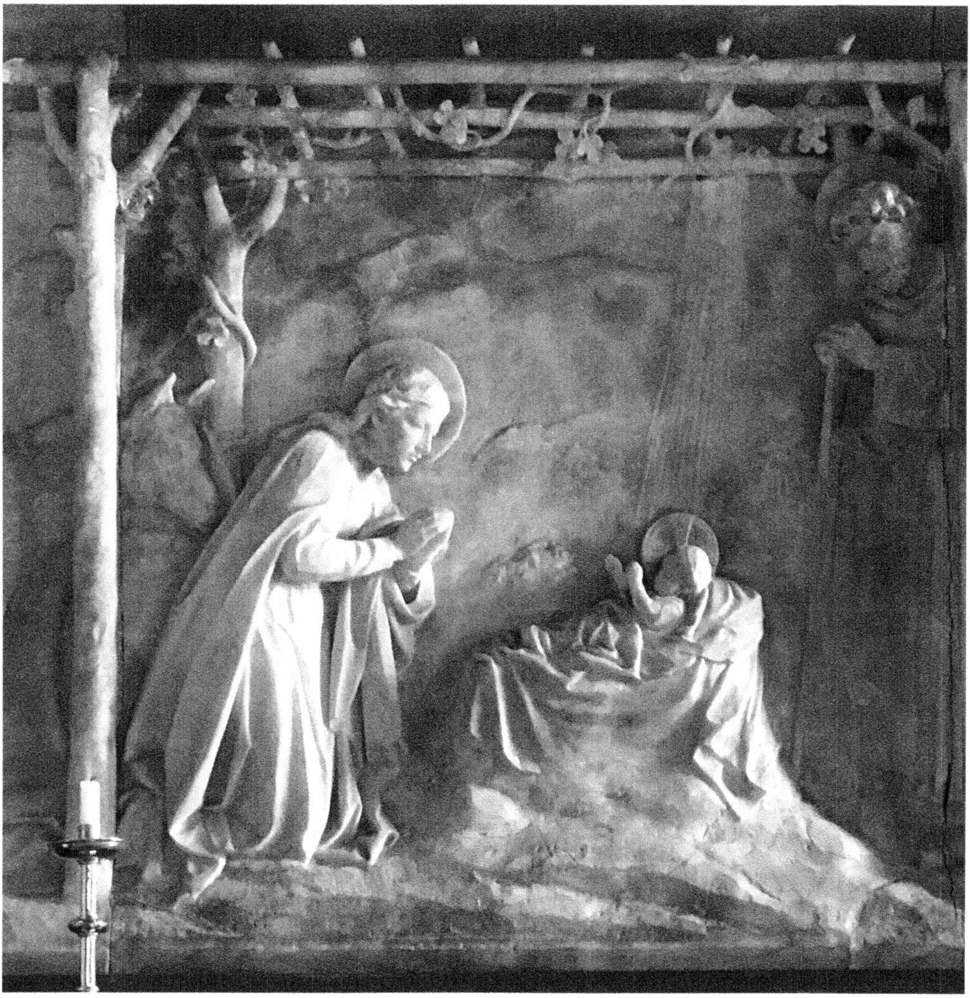

95. Violet Pinwill, *The Nativity*, 1911, alabaster, reredos. Church of St Peter and St Paul, Ermington

pew just inside the church entrance contains a shallow relief depiction of the Garden of Eden, somewhat reminiscent of Ellen Mary Rope's relief work. The pulpit, as at Stoke Fleming (**Plate 1**), is vigorously carved, and depicts a substantial number of wild animals (**Figure 96**).

Pinwill's designs, carving and business comprise a vivid account of a woman's engagement with and success in the generally masculine world of architectural collaborations. Unlike Rosamund Praeger,

96. Violet Pinwill, pulpit, St Gabriel's Church, Postbridge, detail, after 1936

perhaps because she was working mainly in rural locations, Pinwill's role appears not to have been challenged by male sculptors employed in the same field.

Emmeline Halse's most prominent ecclesiastical work is her 1890 reredos for St John's Church, Ladbroke Grove, Notting Hill. **Figure 97** shows it during restoration in 2015. The central sculpted group portrays the Crucifixion, with the Virgin, Mary Magdalene and St John at the base of the cross. The left-hand recess contains a sculpture of a young St John as a fisherman mending his nets, and the recess to the right holds a sculpture of the elderly St John on the Island of Patmos. There are two small free-standing angels in the central niches, an unusual aspect being their wings, which protrude to the sides. Flanking the altar are angels in high relief. The reredos was designed by Aston Webb and both he and Halse were parishioners of the church. The commission gave Halse the opportunity for a major work comprised of three-dimensional figures and reliefs within an architectural framework, and she worked on the sculptural groups for at least two years. Her statue of the saint as a young fisherman, *The Call of St John*, was also shown at the Royal Academy in 1889. The reredos figures are half life-size and are, unusually, made of terracotta and placed within an architectural frame made of the same material. The whole design is contained within a traceried architectural framework designed by Webb. This was one of his early works and there were no subsequent collaborations with Halse. On 23 August 1890 the *Builder* described the reredos then on display at Messrs. Doulton and Co.'s works at Lambeth Potteries, Albert Embankment, where the work had been fired. It was especially noted that it had been made from a new 'cellular' terracotta, which allowed for ornamental detail to be produced without moulds; in this way each piece of ornamentation was modelled separately and therefore there are no exact replicas in the overall structure. In December of the same year the *Builder* carried an illustration of the sculpture without its architectural framework. This was after the dedication, so this seems to be an illustration of what had been on show earlier at the Lambeth Potteries.

An unidentified newspaper review described the dedication of the reredos at the Harvest Festival in 1890:

> One great proof of the high artistic merit of Miss Halse's work is that it bears looking at again and again, and grows upon one. We cannot imagine anyone tiring of it, as one might do of a merely 'pretty' design. The work has already received the approval of highly competent judges, and we hope it will secure for the artist the reputation she deserves. She herself, we believe, thinks most of the privilege of doing something for God's church, by contributing to its beauty what may teach as well as charm; but there are substantial earthly rewards for a conscientious and gifted artist, of which we trust she may be allowed to obtain her just share.

Further comment in the *Builder* stated that the subject was 'treated with great feeling and expression'.[113] However, in his *Buildings of England* Pevsner merely stated that the reredos was by Aston Webb, an example of a woman being written out of history.

In announcing Halse's death, an article in the parish magazine from 1930 recalled this commission, and she was described as having had 'a distinguished career at the Royal Academy School, winning three medals and a £10 prize ... All her works show great anatomical knowledge, poetical treatment, and refinement of touch.'[114] During restoration it was discovered through paint analysis that the reredos was probably

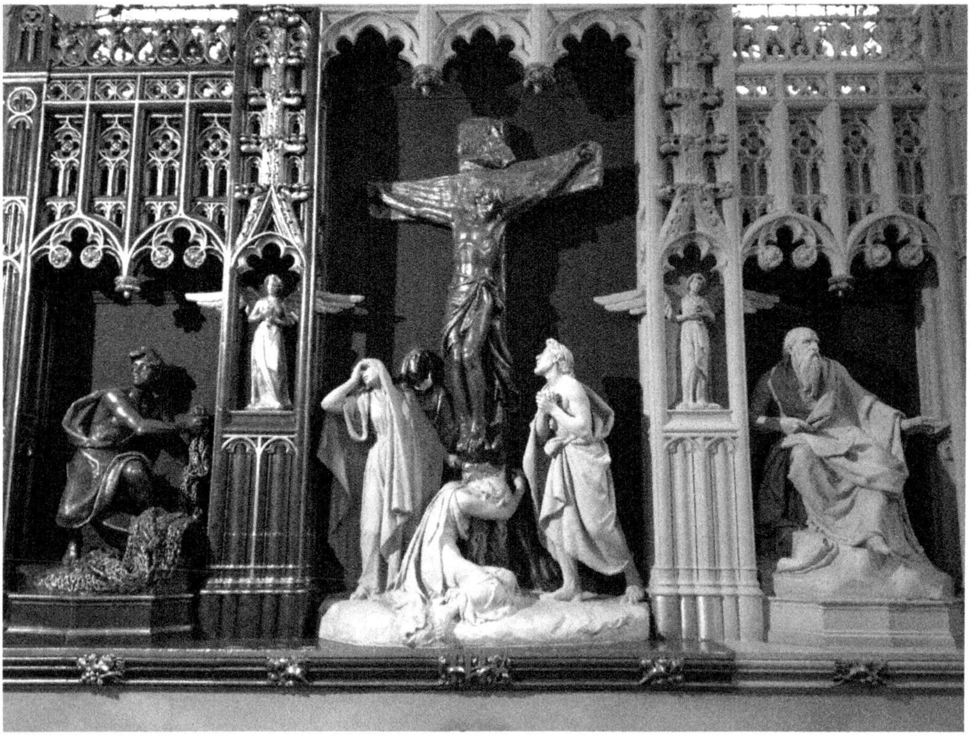

97. Emmeline Halse, reredos, 1890, terracotta. St John's Church, Ladbroke Grove, Notting Hill, London, during 2015 restoration

decorated in places so as to imitate bronze and gilding. The sculptures showed thin paint layers, a darker glaze having been applied to the pink terracotta ground to imitate flesh tones. Behind the central group there was some painting which had possibly suggested a landscape.[115] Halse made sculpted portraits throughout her career, in particular allegorical subjects and studies of children. Many of the child studies, in the form of plaster statuettes, remained in the family, but because of the fragility of the material few have survived. The sculptor may well have benefited from the fashion for statuettes for the home at the end of the nineteenth century: a letter of her father's from 1895 to an unknown recipient refers to a statuette, *Joybells*, which was made from tinted plaster:

> I send a photo of her *Joybells*, a competition work for the *Art Union of London*. Alas! the man who cast it, and the man who silvered it spoilt her delicate work between them and it is unsuccessful. It was a charming and original work and deserved a better fate.[116]

Like Praeger and Rope, Halse's work was influenced by Italian Renaissance sculpture. This is especially noticeable in the young St John on the reredos, who is essentially classically inspired.

By the time the Della Robbia Pottery closed Ellen Mary Rope had created a successful business especially in the area of memorial church decoration. For St Peter's Church, Blaxhall, as well as the war memorial, she also produced the *Bates Monument* and some stained glass for the porch. It is feasible that Rope's success in ecclesiastical work arose from the links she had with a number of religious groups that promoted church

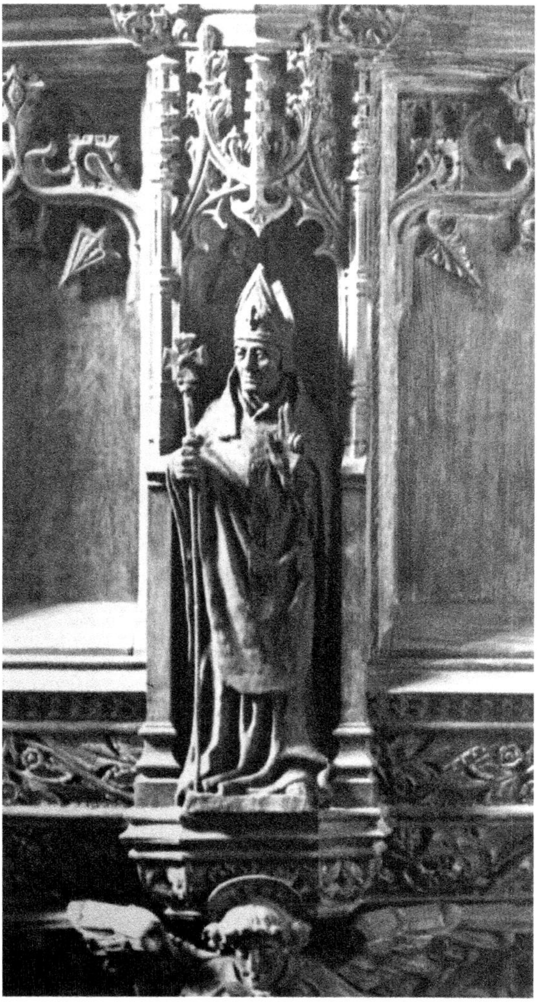

98. Kathleen Scott, *Bishop Warham*, 1913, bronze. Winchester College Chapel

art, for example the Church Congress and the Church Crafts League.[117] She exhibited initially at the fourth Clergy and Artists' Association exhibition in 1900, which was reviewed by the Reverend Haweis for the *Magazine of Art*. He stated that Rope's work added 'lustre to the Church Congress', and continued: 'Let us hope ... that such seemly and inexpensive decorations may supersede the hideous beady ornaments and china flowers under glass which now turn our church yards into the semblance of a Whiteley's variety counter about Christmas time.'[118] The chairman of the Crafts League was the sculptor Thomas Stirling Lee, and Rope would have come into contact with him in Liverpool. Her work was included in a 1916 book *Church Crafts League, List of Artists and Craftsmen*, published in memory of Lee. Rope's *The Guardian Angel* from 1897 was a panel that originated from the larger relief *Children Bringing Lilies to the Holy Child* (1897) in St Peter's Church, Blaxhall. In its reduced version shown in **Plate 22** it was installed in St Margaret's Church, Leiston, Suffolk.

A highly unusual departure from Kathleen Scott's secular work can be found in Winchester College chapel, where she made four bishops on a third life-size scale. The sculptures were donated for the screen by Lord Muir-Mackenzie, Warden of the college from 1904–15. The gallery in the chapel was erected in 1908 and in 1913 the bronze statues were added, chosen to represent four distinguished Wykehamists – Thomas Beckington, John Russell, William Warham and Robert Sherborne. Warham (**Figure 98**) was Archbishop of Canterbury, Russell Bishop of Lincoln, Sherborne Bishop of Chichester, and Beckingon Bishop of Bath and Wells. In a note dated 18 June 1912 signed by Muir-Mackenzie, he offered the sculptures to the college and referred to the Arts and Crafts architect William Douglas Caröe:

> I beg leave to present to the College four bronze figures for the niches on the face of the gallery in Chapel. Although the eye has become used to empty niches in the most exquisite relics of Gothic art, and although few restorations have been so calamitous as those which have evolved [*sic*] modern figures – new wine in old bottles – no one would deliberately design bare niches as a decoration, and the gallery cannot be considered satisfactory until completed with appropriate figures. I have consulted Mr. Caroe on the point, and he cordially agrees.

Muir-Mackenzie proposed that clay models, painted to look like bronze, should be placed in the location to be approved by the Warden and Fellows. Although the decorative quality of the works was most

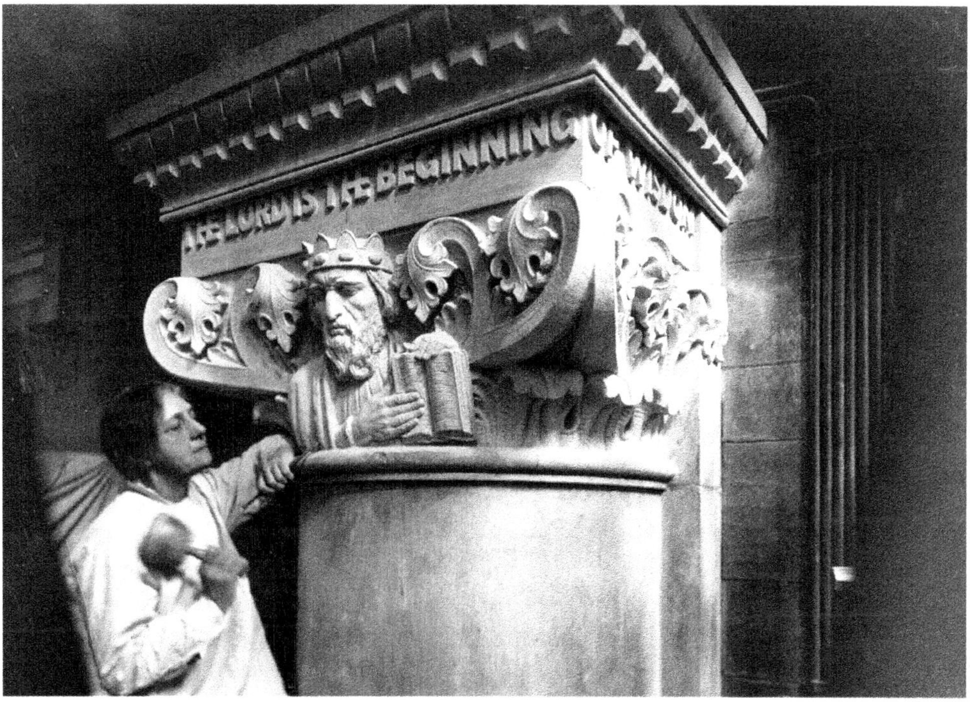

99. *Miss Praeger working on the figure of 'Solomon' on the Pillar of Wisdom,* Belfast Cathedral, 1928

important, he felt that careful thought should be given as to whom the statues depicted, and it was his preference that these should be the four fifteenth-century Wykehamist scholar bishops. He proposed commissioning Scott because

> she is the artist of the fine statue of [Charles] Rolls ... lately set up at Dover. There was an exhibition of her works at the Grafton Gallery [*sic*] last winter; and I believe that every one who saw them recognised their high merit: amongst them were several small bronze figures, which suggested to me her qualification for the work which I had in mind.[119]

The secretary to the governing body, Herbert Chitty, was informed by Muir-Mackenzie that Scott had requested an engraving of Warham to refer to.[120] Scott wrote to Chitty some time in 1912 thanking him for information about the bishops she was to portray. She recorded that she had been to see (presumably an effigy of) Archbishop Warham at Lambeth, and thanked Chitty for the loan of the print to aid her likeness.

She stated that she also intended to visit Wells to search out information on Beckington, and told Chitty that any details he could give her about any of the men – 'such as Russell's "mild disposition"' – would be most useful.[121] There is not much information in the college governing body minutes about the whole process of commissioning Scott or of the installation, although the Fellows are recorded as having made a visit in November 1912 to view the plaster casts of the proposed sculptures, and it is noted that they agreed to the designs.[122]

In 1924 Rosamund Praeger began her carvings in the nave of Belfast Cathedral. Although she made several major memorials for the cathedral she was the architect's second choice for the decorative elements of capital and façade carvings. The architect was Sir Charles Nicholson, a pupil of John Dando Sedding, and he chose Harry Bates's nephew Morris Harding, brought over from London to work on the inside and portal decorations. Praeger was the only local sculptor working on a monumental scale, and when Harding arrived from London she generously offered him space in her studio and rented his family some lodgings. Their friendship outlasted the commission, and when it was completed Harding and his family remained in Northern Ireland.[123] Harding was awarded most of the commissioned work, but it was Praeger's sculpture that received positive comments. Given the baptistery

> to display her talent ... true to form she was asked to reduce it to carving children's heads as bosses on supporting buttresses. Indeed Nicholson was even credited with key involvement in some of her designs such as the William Reeves Memorial ... which has her unmistakable profile portrait head, Celtic scrollwork and letter-cutting.

Thus Praeger's work was symbolically given Nicholson's 'signature'. Praeger undoubtedly noted this 'demarcation between professional male architect and amateur female craftworker'.[124] She received further commissions to work on the capitals of *Wisdom* and *Justice* and was photographed in June 1928 on scaffolding, carving the figure of *Solomon* in situ 50 feet off the ground (**Figure 99**). Completed between 1925 and 1937, Belfast Cathedral contains a monumental scheme of interior decoration in the Arts and Crafts style.

It is clear that many female sculptors were able to engage with public commissions, but equally that some were hampered by not being part of professional networks, which often originated through art school professors and later through engagement with institutional frameworks such as committees. In part this reflects social norms and a tendency for women sculptors to work alone. It also reminds us of how they were often regarded by their tutors: if the expectation was that they would not follow a professional career, but instead marry and have a family, the establishment of potentially useful contacts would have been difficult. Despite this situation, we come across some striking instances of women sculptors' generosity of spirit: Rosamund Praeger's kindness towards Morris Harding, effectively a competitor, is impressive, and one wonders whether a male sculptor would have been so accommodating in such circumstances.

Notes

1 Somers Clarke, 'Stone and wood carving', in Arts and Crafts Exhibition Society, *Arts and Crafts Essays by Members of the Arts and Crafts Exhibition Society* (Rivington: Percival and Co., 1893), pp. 81–88.
2 Lawrence Alma-Tadema, 'Sculpture: a lecture by Alma Tadema, before the Guild and School of Handicraft, London', Toynbee Hall, reproduced in *The Decorator and Furnisher,* 24.6 (September 1894), pp. 227–28.
3 Spielmann, *British Sculpture and Sculptors of To-Day,* pp. 8–11.
4 Parkes, *Sculpture of To-Day,* p. 14.
5 Underwood, *A Short History of English Sculpture,* pp. 9–10.
6 Underwood, *A Short History of English Sculpture,* pp. 48–49.
7 Underwood, *A Short History of English Sculpture,* p. 136.
8 Sarah Crellin, 'Infrastructures: formations and networks: 1925–50', in Henry Moore Institute, *Sculpture in 20th Century Britain: Identity, Infrastructures, Aesthetics, Display, Reception* (Leeds: Henry Moore Institute, 2003), vol. 1, pp. 88–89.
9 Jellicoe, 'Modern British sculpture', pp. 26–31.
10 Barbara Hepworth, letter to Sigfried Giedion, from Chy-an-Kerris, Carbis Bay, 10 September 1947, in response to Giedion and Jean Arp's questionnaire concerning collaboration between artists and architects for the 1947 CIAM VI conference at Bridgwater, Somerset, in Sigfried Giedion (ed.), *A Decade of New Architecture* (Zurich, 1951). Quoted in Bowness (ed.), *Barbara Hepworth: Writings and Conversations,* p. 40.
11 George Frampton, 'On colouring sculpture', *The Studio,* 3 (1894), p. 78, quoted in Read, *Ellen Mary Rope: The Poet Sculptor,* p. 12.
12 *The Builder,* 3 December 1898, p. 508.
13 *Woman at Home* (1895, exact date unknown), p. 477.
14 Read (preface), *Ellen Mary Rope: The Poet Sculptor,* p. 7.
15 Arthur Rope, 'The poet sculptor Ellen Mary Rope', in *Blaxhall's Creative Past: Snapshots of Village Life* (Blaxhall, Suffolk: The Blaxhall Archive Group, 2009), p. 76.
16 *Magazine of Art* (December 1900), p. 234, quoted in Read, *Ellen Mary Rope: The Poet Sculptor,* pp. 8–9.
17 Read (preface), *Ellen Mary Rope: The Poet Sculptor,* p. 14.
18 B. Kendall, 'Miss Ellen Rope, sculptor', *The Artist* (December 1899), p. 209.
19 *Magazine of Art* (May 1900), p. 326.
20 Read (preface), *Ellen Mary Rope: The Poet Sculptor,* n.p.
21 'Arts and Crafts', *The Studio,* 18 (1899), p. 271.
22 Spielmann, *British Sculpture and Sculptors of To-Day,* p. 162.
23 Kendall, 'Miss Ellen Rope, sculptor', p. 209.
24 'A.F.', 'The Art Movement: the work of Miss Ellen M. Rope', *The Magazine of Art* (1900), p. 323.
25 Read (preface), *Ellen Mary Rope: The Poet Sculptor,* p. 17.
26 Also known as Miss Phyllis Clay, Mrs Archibald Clay, or Mrs Phyllis Muriel Cowan Archibald.

27 Ray McKenzie, *Public Sculpture of Glasgow* (Liverpool: Liverpool University Press and Public Monuments and Sculpture Association, 2002), p. 360.
28 Frampton, 'On colouring sculpture'.
29 Charlotte Drew, 'Luca della Robbia: South Kensington and the Victorian revival of a Florentine sculptor', *Sculpture Journal*, 23.2 (2014), pp. 171–83.
30 Marchal, *Finding Frances*, p. 61. The school had opened its doors to girls in 1893.
31 Marchal, *Finding Frances*, pp. 131–32.
32 McBrinn, *Sophia Rosamond Praeger*, p. 18.
33 McBrinn, 'A populous solitude', p. 584.
34 McBrinn, 'A populous solitude', pp. 587–88.
35 McBrinn, *Sophia Rosamond Praeger*, p. 22.
36 www.publicsculpturesofsussex.co.uk > object > id=155 (accessed 13 February 2020).
37 Sue Malvern, 'The identity of the sculptor 1925–50', in Henry Moore Institute, *Sculpture in 20th Century Britain: Identity, Infrastructures, Aesthetics, Display, Reception* (Leeds: Henry Moore Institute, 2003), vol. 1, p. 80.
38 Parkes, *Sculpture of To-Day*, pp. 23–24.
39 Geoff Archer, *The Glorious Dead. Figurative Sculpture of British First World War Memorials* (Kirkstead, Norfolk: Frontier Publishing, 2009), pp. 8–9.
40 Archer, *The Glorious Dead*, pp. 9–10. The construction of monuments is generally well documented since the memorial committees that oversaw their creation would hand over future responsibility to the relevant local authorities. Thus committee minutes survive quite consistently in various record offices.
41 Alex King, *Memorials of the Great War in Britain: The Symbolism and Politics of Remembrance* (Oxford: Berg, 1998), p. 71.
42 King, *Memorials of the Great War in Britain*, pp. 101–08.
43 Archer, *The Glorious Dead*, p. 321.
44 Archer, *The Glorious Dead*, p. 249.
45 Cowdell, 'The Role of the Royal Academy in English Art 1918–1930', p. 22. Expanded in footnote. See Royal Academy Annual Report (1923), p. 9.
46 Cowdell, 'The Role of the Royal Academy in English Art 1918–1930', p. 24. See Royal Fine Art Commission Second Report (1926), 3, paragraph 1.
47 Stocker, '"My masculine models"', p. 50.
48 'An inspiring statue: Huntingdon soldiers' memorial', *Peterborough Standard*, 16 November 1923, n.p. University of Cambridge Manuscripts Library, GB/NNAF/P 162494, NCUACS 87.8.99.167/1, Press Cuttings.
49 'Sculptured memorials and headstones designed and carved in sculptors' studios in British stones', *Sculpture and Memorials*, London (January 1937), p. 5. Elizabeth Muntz Archive, Dorset History Centre.
50 'Sculptured memorials and headstones', p. 5.
51 'Sculptured memorials and headstones', p. 5.
52 'Sculptured memorials and headstones', p. 13.
53 Sir Charles Tennyson, Foreword, *Memorial Craftsmanship*, Guild of Memorial Craftsmen, undated. Elizabeth Muntz Archive, Dorset History Centre.
54 Unknown author, letter to Sir Arthur Birch, 4 July 1903. St Paul's Cathedral Archives, Princess Louise, Colonial Forces Monument, SPCAA/SP/3/18, 1903–1905.

55 Letter from W. G. Probert to Somers Clarke, 31 August 1903. St Paul's Cathedral Archives, Princess Louise, Colonial Forces Monument, SPCAA/SP/3/18, 1903–1905.
56 Wake, *Princess Louise*, p. 368.
57 Letter from W. G. Probert to Somers Clarke, 20 May 1904. St Paul's Cathedral Archives, Princess Louise, Colonial Forces Monument, SPCAA/SP/3/18, 1903–1905.
58 Draft letter from Somers Clarke to Sir Arthur Birch, 15 January 1905. St Paul's Cathedral Archives, Princess Louise, Colonial Forces Monument, SPCAA/SP/3/18, 1903–1905.
59 Draft letter from Somers Clarke to Sir Arthur Birth, 25 January 1905. St Paul's Cathedral Archives, Princess Louise, Colonial Forces Monument, SPCAA/SP/3/18, 1903–1905.
60 Derek Keene, Arthur Burns and Andrew Saint (eds), *St Paul's: The Cathedral Church of London 604–2004* (New Haven, CT: Yale University Press, 2004), p. 291.
61 Hawksley, *The Mystery of Princess Louise*, p. 294.
62 *The Times*, 2 February 1898, p. 11.
63 Emails from Peter Moore to the author, July 2013.
64 'War memorials. Beaumont College', *The Tablet*, 23 December 1922, p. 27.
65 'War memorials. Beaumont College', *The Tablet*, 23 December 1922, p. 27.
66 Marchal, *Finding Frances*, pp. 176–81.
67 Parkes, *The Art of Carved Sculpture*, pp. 101–03.
68 Letter from J. F. Johnstone, Town Clerk, Paisley to Robert Lorimer, 17 April 1923. Gertrude Alice Meredith Williams Archive, Somerset.
69 Letter from Robert Lorimer to Town Clerk, Paisley, 19 April 1923. Gertrude Alice Meredith Williams Archive, Somerset.
70 James A. Morris, 'A monument to chivalry', *Country Life*, 16 May 1925.
71 Letter from Mr Meredith Williams to Isaac Williams, National Museum of Wales, 15 October, year unclear. Sculpture bought by the museum on 27 July 1925. Archives, National Museum of Wales, Cardiff.
72 Reference for 'Mrs. G. Williams', Charles J. Allen, 24 October 1917. Gertrude Alice Meredith Williams Archive, Somerset.
73 Conversation between the author and Phyllida Shaw, Somerset, 26 April 2016.
74 The Right Hon. Sir Andrew H. A. Murray, Lord Provost of the City of Edinburgh, *The Scottish National War Memorial* (no date or pages). Gertrude Alice Meredith Williams Archive, Somerset.
75 'Mrs. Meredith Williams: An Architectural Sculptor', *The Times*, 7 March 1934, p. 16.
76 Adam Bruce Thomson, undated manuscript concerning Phyllis Bone. Manuscript Collections. National Library of Scotland, Deposit 199/15, Phyllis Bone, Letters and miscellaneous papers 1937–1961.
77 Padaruth Raksha, *The use of ceramics as an aesthetic element in Durban architecture (1914–2012)*, 2013. http://hdl.handle.net/10321/945, p. 55 (accessed 12 February 2020).
78 Archer, *The Glorious Dead*, p. 310.
79 Email from Paul Rason to the author, 19 February 2014.

80 Parkes, *The Art of Carved Sculpture*, p. 98.
81 Martina Droth, *Taking Shape: Finding Sculpture in the Decorative Arts* (Leeds/Los Angeles: Henry Moore Institute/J. Paul Getty Museum, 2008).
82 Droth, *Taking Shape*, pp. 4–6.
83 Droth, *Taking Shape*, p. 14
84 Droth, *Taking Shape*, pp. 14–16.
85 James Bettley, '"An earnest desire to promote a right taste in ecclesiastical design": Cox & Sons and the rise and fall of the church furnishing companies', *Decorative Arts Society Journal*, 26 (2002), p. 9.
86 *The Builder*, 70 (1896), p. 417.
87 Bettley, '"An earnest desire to promote a right taste in ecclesiastical design"', p. 19.
88 Revd Percy Dearmer, *The Parson's Handbook* (London, 1903), pp. 76–77, quoted in Read, *Ellen Mary Rope: The Poet Sculptor*, p. 14.
89 Peter F. Anson, *Fashions in Church Furnishings 1840–1940* (London: Studio Vista, 1965), pp. 306–07.
90 H. H. Martyn and Co., *Memorials* (Cheltenham: H. H. Martyn and Co., 1920s), p. 22, archive.org > details > H.h.MartynCoLtd.SpecialistCraftsmenInMemorial Architecture.
91 For example, Geoff Archer in his *Public Sculpture in Britain* (2013) stated that he would not cover sculptural work in churches, nor do the county volumes published under the auspices of the Public Monuments and Sculpture Association's National Recording Project, which was instigated to catalogue all public sculpture and monuments in the United Kingdom.
92 Archer, *Public Sculpture in Britain*, pp. 8–9.
93 Sandra Alfoldy and Janice Helland (eds), (introduction), *Craft, Space and Interior Design, 1855–2005* (Farnham: Ashgate, 2008), p. 2.
94 Jim Cheshire, 'Space and the Victorian ecclesiastical interior', in Sandra Alfoldy and Janice Helland (eds), *Craft, Space and Interior Design, 1855–2005* (Farnham: Ashgate, 2008), pp. 27–30.
95 Cheshire, 'Space and the Victorian ecclesiastical interior', p. 41.
96 Marchal, *Finding Frances*, p. 109.
97 Marchal, *Finding Frances*, pp. 151–52.
98 Paul Snell, '"The Priest of Form". John Dando Sedding (1838–91) and the Languages of Late Victorian Architecture', PhD dissertation, University of Manchester, 2006, p. 77.
99 Paul Snell, 'John Dando Sedding and sculpture in architecture: the fulfilment of a Ruskinian ideal?', in Rebecca Daniels and Geoff Brandwood (eds), *Ruskin and Architecture* (Reading: Spire Books, 2003), p. 331.
100 Snell, 'John Dando Sedding and sculpture in architecture', pp. 345–46.
101 Anthony Lewis, reports of meetings and events, *Helen Wilson, 'Violet Pinwill: Woodcarver of Ermington and Plymouth'*, 6 September 2013, Friends of the Tamar Valley, newsletter (spring 2014).
102 Tony Dustan, script (undated), Plymouth Museum and Art Gallery Archives. His father, Ron Dustan, worked for Violet Pinwill as one of her carvers.
103 Kathleen B. Green, letter to Mr P. Brough, West Devon Record Office, Plymouth, 20 August 1996. Plymouth Record Office, ACC 2139.

104 Betty Crisp, 'Westcountry Women's Careers: No. 4 – a Plymouth woodcarver', *Western Weekly News*, 22 September 1934, n.p.

105 'Miss Violet Pinwill', *The Times*, 20 January 1957. According to Maggie Ward, this was written by her late husband Robert's mother, Charlotte Alice Greatorex Ward. Pinwill was Robert Ward's great aunt.

106 Letter from Robert Ward to Sue Andrews, 16 January 2005. Private collection.

107 Clive Gummell, presenter, South West Film & Television Archive, Plymouth. Tape number 180876, recorded and transmitted 18 August 1976. No title for programme available.

108 Edmund Sedding, 'Ermington Church', *Transactions of the Exeter Diocesan Architectural and Archaeological Society*, 6, 1st series (1899), pp. 56–59. Westcountry Studies Library, Exeter Central Library.

109 Devon Record Office. Ermington 548M/2/1.

110 Snell, 'John Dando Sedding and sculpture in architecture', p. 345.

111 Sent to the author by Clare Pawley, 7 April 2012. Source unknown.

112 Elaine Chaytor, *Ermington Days* (Melinga Publishing, 2000).

113 Farningham, *Emmeline Halse, Sculptor*, pp. 18–20.

114 Anon., 'In Memoriam', *St. John's Church, Notting Hill. Parish Magazine* (1930), quoted in Farningham, *Emmeline Halse, Sculptor*, Appendix.

115 Helen Hughes – Historic Interiors Research & Conservation (HIRC), St John's Church, Ladbroke Grove, London W11. Research to determine the decoration of the Mini-North Transept (1845–1873) and the Terracotta Reredos (1890) (October 2012). Copy supplied by the church to the author.

116 Farningham, *Emmeline Halse, Sculptor*, p. 26.

117 F. J. Maclean, 'The art of E. M. Rope', *The Expert* (1907), p. 252, quoted in Read (preface), *Ellen Mary Rope: The Poet Sculptor*, p. 12.

118 Revd H. R. Haweis, 'The Art Movement, church art and the Church Congress', *Magazine of Art* (1900), p. 134, quoted in Read (preface), *Ellen Mary Rope: The Poet Sculptor*, pp. 13–14.

119 Signed 'K. M. M.', note headed 'Winchester College Chapel', 18 June 1912. Winchester College Archives.

120 Letter from Muir Mackenzie to Herbert Chitty, 16 October 1912. Winchester College Archives.

121 Letter from 'KS' to Herbert Chitty, undated, marked as 'answered 18 October 1912'. Winchester College Archives.

122 Email from Suzanne Foster, Archivist, Winchester College to the author, 2 May 2014.

123 McBrinn, 'A populous solitude', p. 586.

124 Joseph McBrinn, 'Craft as union, craft as demarcation: the decoration at Belfast Cathedral', in Sandra Alfoldy and Janice Helland (eds), *Craft, Space and Interior Design, 1855–2005* (Farnham: Ashgate, 2008), p. 80.

7

Conclusion

Although British female sculptors tended not to benefit from being part of the institutional networks that were more easily accessible to their male peers, some did participate in national and international events, enabling them to be part of the presentation of Britain on the world stage. For example, a bust by Princess Louise of Queen Victoria was displayed at the 1893 Chicago World's Fair; Margaret Giles was one of the female sculptors proposed by the RBS for inclusion in the 1908 Franco-British Exhibition of Science, Art and Industries which took place in London, as were Esther Mary Moore and Princess Louise. In 1924 and 1925 the British Empire Exhibitions were staged at Wembley, and in the 1924 RBS *Annual Report* it was noted how its members had formed part of the sculpture committee and were involved with the details of the displays. The work of about 1,130 living artists was on display, and it was claimed as 'the most important showcase for the arts in London in the immediate post war period'.[1] Anne Acheson, Katharine Maltwood and Rosamund Praeger were among the exhibitors in the 1925 exhibition.

There were many British female sculptors from the mid-nineteenth century onwards, despite the common perception that it was a masculine practice. Early in this period many of them attended the classes for women artists being established at some art schools. However, it appears that in the second half of the century art societies were generally not in favour of recognizing women artists, either abolishing the previously established category of 'honorary' membership for women or marginalizing female artists into women-only categories.[2] So while some gains were made, these were often counterbalanced by reversals. After women gained access to formal training the debate moved to questions of quality, and successful women artists were frequently characterized as the exceptions among their sex. Towards the close of the nineteenth century female artists were taking part more frequently in exhibitions;

between 1870 and 1880 the percentage of women exhibiting at the Royal Academy nearly doubled: 'at the start of the decade they made up 7.6 percent of the participants, by the end they numbered slightly over 15 percent'.[3] Women-only exhibitions did allow for focused attention on their work, making a space for discussion and analysis, without facilitating repetitive arguments concerning their supposed inferiority to male practitioners. However, participation in single-sex exhibitions must have felt a mixed blessing: such women quite naturally would wish to be valued for their achievements as sculptors, rather than as female sculptors.

Ellen C. Clayton's 1876 book *English Female Artists* made quite clear how they were perceived towards the end of the nineteenth century: 'Artists, especially English artists, and above all, English Female Artists, as a rule lead quiet, uneventful lives ... In the majority of instances, their daily existence flows tranquilly on within the limited precincts of the studio ... Eminently respectable, they affect little display.'[4] Thirty years later, Mary Fanton Roberts pinpointed the cultural and social constrictions still being experienced by female artists. A regular contributor to the *Craftsman*, in 1908 she argued that

> The question is ... not one of sex discrimination, but of fundamental sex variations in expression ... true art must forever reflect existing conditions of life ... The monk and the non-conformist alike are bound back from productive art by the limitations of renunciation; the scientist by the limitations of mathematics; the royal man by the limitations of formalities. And so, great art does not flourish in the monastery, in the laboratory or in the palace. For it has always demanded freedom, the liberty to think straight and to see clear, a perfect freedom of observation and experience ... woman, the world over ... has not this freedom.[5]

This statement is a remarkable forerunner of the arguments made by Linda Nochlin in her 1971 essay 'Why have there been no great women artists?', in which she pointed to the absence of professional artists from the aristocracy, whose time was committed to running large estates, or from women, whose role it was to raise and care for families.[6]

Given the obstacles that women sculptors faced, their achievements were significant, all the more so since they tended to work alone, often with the other responsibilities of being a wife and a mother. Until the 1950s, generally speaking they could not indulge themselves in the egocentric conduct enjoyed by some of their male counterparts. Double standards where behaviour was concerned were in evidence well into the second half of the twentieth century. Unsurprisingly, there is also evidence of gender inequality with regard to payments made to women sculptors. A document lodged in the Imperial War Museum mentions a letter dated 25 November 1918 from sculptor Countess Feodora Gleichen to Lady Norman, the latter presumably Florence Norman who after the First World War supported the establishment of the Museum. The letter asked of Lady Norman that women sculptors be better paid, and was signed by 15 additional women, including Esther Mary Moore, Ellen Mary Rope, Phoebe Stabler and Florence Steele.[7] There is no evidence of the outcome, if any, of this request.

Undoubtedly women sculptors faced difficulties from all quarters, whether social, cultural or financial. Looking at those included in my book, the ones who married seem in the main to have had supportive husbands who in many cases were able to facilitate useful contacts. The women who chose to remain single had more time for their work, but surely suffered from restrictions not experienced by male sculptors. The first half of the twentieth century was a very different world indeed, but even well into the second half of the century it appeared normal to trivialize and make generalized statements about women artists.

Despite the fact that the British art school system in the first half of the twentieth century militated against women being taken seriously as aspiring sculptors, many did achieve their goals. Some supported themselves through teaching within the growing secondary school system for girls or through offering private classes. Many enjoyed successful and extensive exhibiting careers; however, they did face difficulty in becoming part of the art world's infrastructure, such as sitting on selection juries, organizing exhibitions, or working as art critics or museum curators.[8] There are numerous references to women sculptors in catalogues and exhibition reviews, but trying to locate their work is a huge challenge. By the end of the period covered by my book, arguably only the work of Hepworth among the many sculptors I have included was being given serious critical attention. The rest were considered 'traditional' in style and subject matter, and did not attract the attention of influential art critics.

The tombstone of Gertrude Alice Meredith Williams bears a simple inscription arranged by her husband Morris, which speaks to important issues. First, the sole affiliation given is to her profession, as an associate member of the Royal Society of British Sculptors. Her husband has not included his name as her spouse: he has effectively stepped aside from the conventions of tomb inscription in order to emphasize his wife's professional status. Secondly, it reminds us that women sculptors who had sympathetic and supportive husbands or parents undoubtedly had a greater chance to practise their profession and, perhaps even more importantly, had a family member who could guard their legacy through the organization and preservation of archival material. Lord Kennet assembled comprehensive photographic albums of his wife Kathleen Scott's work, noting sales, and including the full range of her output. The only sculptor included in this book who showed a conscious wish to preserve similar records and thus construct her own legacy was Barbara Hepworth. My impression has been that women sculptors, whether single or married, had enough to do, whether solely pursuing a career or trying to juggle professional and family commitments.

Despite all of these difficulties, gaining at least a glimpse of this other narrative reveals much work of quality and presents a more accurate picture of what was being produced by British female sculptors during this long half-century. To believe that a woman sculptor cannot be of importance because she has not been the subject of a major exhibition or book is to set up a circular argument: the existence of such women first needs to be known before such attention can be given to them.

Notes

1 Compton, 'Infrastructures: formation and networks 1900–25', p. 23.
2 Waller, *Women Artists in the Modern Era*, pp. 98–99. Specifically the Royal Academy and the Society of British Artists abolished such honorary membership categories in the 1850s and 1860s, and watercolour societies established a 'ladies' category rather than, as previously, allowing women artists to be full members.
3 Waller, *Women Artists in the Modern Era*, p. 186.
4 Ellen C. Clayton, *English Female Artists* (London: Tinsley Brothers, 1876), vol. 1, p. 1.
5 Mary Fanton Roberts, 'The quality of women's art achievement', *The Craftsman*, 15 (December 1908), pp. 292–98.
6 Linda Nochlin, 'Why have there been no great women artists?', in Thomas B. Hess and Elizabeth C. Baker (eds), *Art and Sexual Politics: Why Have There Been No Great Women Artists?* (New York: Macmillan, 1971), pp. 1–39.
7 List of documents headed 'Imperial War Museum. Manuscript Material', 19 October 1987, including document E/15 'Countess Feodora Gleichen', letter of 25 November 1918 to Lady Norman. Gertrude Alice Meredith Williams file, Archives, National Museum of Wales, Cardiff.
8 Deepwell, 'Women Artists in Britain between the Two World Wars', p. 385.

Bibliography

A major resource is the live online database *Mapping the Practice and Profession of Sculpture in Britain and Ireland 1851–1951*, https://sculpture.gla.ac.uk/. It comprises 'the first authoritative study of sculptors, related businesses and trades investigated in the context of creative collaborations, art infrastructures, professional networks and cultural geographies. This database is the main outcome of the research and contains over 50,000 records about sculptural practice. The information has been entered so that the numerous connections between different areas of practice can be explored.'

'A.F.', 'The Art Movement: the work of Miss Ellen M. Rope', *The Magazine of Art* (1900)

Alfoldy, Sandra, and Helland, Janice (eds), *Craft, Space and Interior Design, 1855–2005* (Farnham: Ashgate, 2008)

Alma-Tadema, Lawrence, 'Sculpture: a lecture by Alma Tadema, before the Guild and School of Handicraft, London', *The Decorator and Furnisher*, 24.6 (September 1894), pp. 227–28

Anson, Peter F., *Fashions in Church Furnishings 1840–1940* (London: Studio Vista, 1965)

Archer, Geoff, *The Glorious Dead. Figurative Sculpture of British First World War Memorials* (Kirkstead, Norfolk: Frontier Publishing, 2009)

– *Public Sculpture in Britain* (Kirkstead, Norfolk: Frontier Publishing, 2013)

The Arts Council of Great Britain, *Sculpture in the Home – 1st Arts Council Exhibition* (London: The Arts Council of Great Britain, 1946)

– *Sculpture in the Home, 2nd exhibition* (London: The Arts Council of Great Britain, 1950–51)

'Arts and Crafts', *The Studio*, 18 (1899), p. 260

Arts and Crafts Exhibition Society, *Arts and Crafts Essays by Members of the Arts and Crafts Exhibition Society* (Rivington: Percival & Co., 1893)

Ayral-Clause, Odile, *Camille Claudel, A Life* (New York: Harry N. Abrams, 2002)

Barron, M., 'Dorich House Kingston Vale', *Country Life*, 5 November 1938, pp. 456–57
Beach, Jeremy (ed.), *Public Sculpture of Birmingham, including Sutton Coldfield* (Liverpool: Liverpool University Press and Public Monuments and Sculpture Association, 1998)
Beattie, Susan, *The New Sculpture* (New Haven, CT: Yale University Press, 1983)
Bergstein, Mary, 'Lonely Aphrodites: on the documentary photography of sculpture', *The Art Bulletin*, 74.3 (1992), pp. 475–98
Bettley, James, '"An earnest desire to promote a right taste in ecclesiastical design": Cox & Sons and the rise and fall of the church furnishing companies', *Decorative Arts Society Journal*, 26 (2002), pp. 8–26
Black, Jonathan, and Martin, Brenda, *Dora Gordine: Sculptor, Artist, Designer* (London: Dorich House Museum, Kingston University, in association with Philip Wilson Publishers, 2007)
Blizard, Francis S., 'L'Art Nouveau: What it is and what is thought of it: a symposium', *Magazine of Art* (1904), Part I, pp. 209–13; Part II, pp. 259–64; Part III, pp. 324–27
Bowness, Sophie (ed.), *Barbara Hepworth: The Plasters. The Gift to Wakefield* (London: Lund Humphries and The Hepworth Wakefield, 2011)
– (ed.), *Barbara Hepworth: Writings and Conversations* (London: Tate Publishing, 2016)
Broadbent, Arthur J., *Sculpture Today in Great Britain, 1940–1943* (London: John Tiranti, 1944)
Brown, Rosemary Alicia, *Katharine Emma Maltwood, Artist, 1878–1961* (Saanich, BC: Maltwood Art Museum and Gallery, 1981)
Burstow, Robert, *The Sculpture in the Home Exhibitions: Reconstructing the Home and Family in Post-War Britain* (Leeds: Henry Moore Institute, 2008)
– '"Sculpture in the Home": selling modernism to post-war British homemakers', *Sculpture Journal*, 17.2 (2008), pp. 37–50
Campbell, Louise, 'Women, architecture and the Aesthetic Movement', in Brenda Martin and Penny Sparke (eds), *Women's Places: Architecture and Design 1860–1960* (London: Routledge, 2003), pp. 3–9
Casson, Stanley, *Twentieth Century Sculptors* (Oxford: Oxford University Press, 1930)
Cavanagh, Terry, *Public Sculpture of South London* (Liverpool: Liverpool University Press and Public Monuments and Sculpture Association, 2007)
Chaytor, Elaine, *Ermington Days* (Sutton: Melinga Publishing, 2000)
Cheshire, Jim, 'Space and the Victorian ecclesiastical interior', in Sandra Alfoldy and Janice Helland (eds), *Craft, Space and Interior Design, 1855–2005* (Farnham: Ashgate, 2008), pp. 27–30

Clark, Kenneth, *The Nude* (Harmondsworth: Penguin, 1993 [1956])
Clarke, Somers, 'Stone and wood carving', in *Arts and Crafts Essays by Members of the Arts and Crafts Exhibition Society* (Rivington: Percival & Co., 1893), pp. 81–88
Clayton, Ellen C., *English Female Artists*, 2 vols (London: Tinsley Brothers, 1876)
Clement, Clara Erskine, *Women in the Fine Arts from the Seventh Century B.C. to the Twentieth Century A.D.* (Boston: Houghton, Mifflin, 1904), https://archive.org/details/womeninfineartsooclemgoog (accessed 25 November 2019)
Clifford, Linda, *Sculptor: Josefina de Vasconcellos* (Linda Clifford, 2000)
Codell, Julie F., 'The art press and the art market: the artist as "economic man"', in Pamela Fletcher and Anne Helmreich (eds), *The Rise of the Modern Art Market in London, 1850–1939* (Manchester: Manchester University Press, 2011), pp. 128–50
– 'From English School to British School: modernism, revisionism, and national culture in the writings of M. H. Spielmann', *Nineteenth-Century Art Worldwide: a Journal of Nineteenth-Century Visual Culture*, 14.2 (2015), http://www.19thc-artworldwide.org/summer15/codell-on-modernism-revisionism-and-national-culture-in-the-writings-of-spielmann (accessed 25 November 2019)
Compton, Ann, 'Infrastructures: formation and networks 1900–25', in Henry Moore Institute, *Sculpture in 20th Century Britain: Identity, Infrastructures, Aesthetics, Display, Reception* (Leeds: Henry Moore Institute, 2003), vol. 1, pp. 21–32
– 'Affirmative action: *British Sculptors and Sculpture* and the monographic form in twentieth-century sculpture studies', *Sculpture Journal*, 22.2 (2013), pp. 77–88
– *Facing the Future: Sculpture from the Harrogate Collection* (Harrogate: The Mercer Art Gallery, 2014)
– 'Crafting modernism: Hepworth's practice in the 1920s', in Penelope Curtis and Chris Stephens (eds), *Barbara Hepworth: Sculpture for a Modern World* (London: Tate Publishing, 2015), pp. 12–19
Cowdell, Theophilus Paul, 'The Role of the Royal Academy in English Art 1918–1930', PhD dissertation, University of London, 1980, available at British Library e-theses online service, https://ethos.bl.uk/
Cran, Marian, 'Lead garden figures', *The Queen*, 9 August 1923, p. 65
Crane, Walter, *Ideals in Art* (London: George Bell, 1905)
Crawford, Elizabeth, *Enterprising Women: The Garretts and Their Circle* (London: Francis Boutle, 2002)
Crellin, Sarah, 'Infrastructures: formations and networks: 1925–50', in Henry Moore Institute, *Sculpture in 20th Century Britain: Identity, Infrastructures, Aesthetics, Display, Reception* (Leeds: Henry Moore Institute, 2003), vol. 1, pp. 88–100

Cunliffe-Charlesworth, Hilary, 'The Royal College of Art: Its Influence on Education, Art and Design, 1900–1950', PhD dissertation, Sheffield City Polytechnic, 1991, available at British Library e-theses online service, https://ethos.bl.uk/

Curtis, Penelope, 'The landscape of Barbara Hepworth', *Sculpture Journal*, 2 (1998), pp. 106–12

Curtis, Penelope, and Stephens, Chris (eds), *Barbara Hepworth: Sculpture for a Modern World* (London: Tate Publishing, 2015)

Curtis, Penelope, and Wilkinson, Alan G., *Barbara Hepworth: A Retrospective* (Liverpool: Tate Gallery, 1994)

Curtis, Penelope, and Wilson, Keith (eds), *Modern British Sculpture* (London: Royal Academy of Arts, 2011)

Davies, Veronica, '"Steering a progressive course"? Exhibitions in wartime and postwar Britain', paper given at the *Sculpture in the Home* study day, Henry Moore Institute, Leeds, 5 December 2008, HMI archives

Deepwell, Katy, 'Women Artists in Britain Between the Two World Wars', PhD dissertation, Birkbeck College, University of London, 1991, available at British Library e-theses online service, https://ethos.bl.uk/

– 'Hepworth and her critics', in Katy Deepwell (ed.), *Women Artists and Modernism* (Manchester: Manchester University Press, 1998), pp. 97–109

– (ed.), *Women Artists and Modernism* (Manchester: Manchester University Press, 1998)

– *Women Artists between the Wars: 'A fair field and no favour'* (Manchester: Manchester University Press, 2010)

Dorich House, *Kathleen Scott Portraits* (Kingston: Kingston University Press, 1999)

Dorset County Museum, *Mary Spencer Watson: Catalogue of Sculptures* (Dorchester, 1998)

Drew, Charlotte, 'Luca della Robbia: South Kensington and the Victorian revival of a Florentine sculptor', *Sculpture Journal*, 23.2 (2014), pp. 171–83

Droth, Martina, 'The Statuette and the Role of the Ornamental in Late Nineteenth Century Sculpture', PhD dissertation, University of Reading, 2000, available at British Library e-theses online service, https://ethos.bl.uk/

– 'Conditions of display 1900–25', in Henry Moore Institute, *Sculpture in 20th Century Britain: Identity, Infrastructures, Aesthetics, Display, Reception* (Leeds: Henry Moore Institute, 2003), vol. 1, pp. 43–54

– 'Small sculpture c.1900: the "new statuette" in English sculptural aesthetics', in David J. Getsy (ed.), *Sculpture and the Pursuit of a Modern Ideal in Britain c.1880–1930* (Aldershot: Ashgate, 2004), pp. 141–66

– (ed.), *Taking Shape: Finding Sculpture in the Decorative Arts* (Leeds/Los Angeles: Henry Moore Institute/J. Paul Getty Museum, 2008)

Droth, Martina, Edwards, Jason, and Hatt, Michael, *Sculpture Victorious: Art in the Age of Invention, 1837–1901* (New Haven, CT: Yale University Press, 2014)

Droth, Martina, and Trippi, Peter, 'Change/continuity: writing about art in Britain before and after 1900', *Nineteenth-Century Art Worldwide: A Journal of Nineteenth-Century Visual Culture*, 14.2 (2015), http://www.19thc-artworldwide.org/summer15/droth-trippi-introduction-writing-about-art-in-britain-before-and-after-1900 (accessed 25 November 2019)

Duff, David, *The Life Story of H.R.H. Princess Louise, Duchess of Argyll* (Bath: Cedric Chivers, 1940)

Dunstan, Angela, 'Nineteenth-century sculpture and the imprint of authenticity', *Interdisciplinary Studies in the Long Nineteenth Century*, 19 (2014), https://www.19.bbk.ac.uk/articles/10.16995/ntn.704/ (accessed 25 November 2019)

Farningham, Elizabeth, *Emmeline Halse, Sculptor, 1853–1930* (Doncaster: L. E. Farningham, 2002)

Figures in a Landscape, directed by Dudley Shaw Ashton (British Film Institute Experimental Film Fund, 1953) https://www.bfi.org.uk/films-tv-people/4ce2b6aa1d0ac (accessed 20 February 2020)

The Fine Art Society, *Carving in Britain from 1910 to Now* (London: The Fine Art Society, 2012)

Foster, William, 'A clear look at the Royal Academy after 200 years', *Homes and Gardens*, 49.11 (May 1968), pp. 58–59

Fraser, Inga, 'Media and movement: Barbara Hepworth beyond the lens', in Penelope Curtis and Chris Stephens (eds), *Barbara Hepworth: Sculpture for a Modern World* (London: Tate Publishing, 2015), pp. 72–83

– '"The English independents": some twentieth century women carvers', *Sculpture Journal*, 23.3 (2015), pp. 369–78

Gale, Matthew, and Stephens, Chris, *Barbara Hepworth: Works in the Tate Collection and the Barbara Hepworth Museum St. Ives* (London: Tate Publishing, 2001)

Gardiner, Margaret, *Barbara Hepworth: A Memoir* (London: Lund Humphries, 1994)

Garrihy, A., 'Scott, Kathleen', in D. Gaze (ed.), *Dictionary of Women Artists*, vol. II (Chicago: Fitzroy Dearborn, 1997), p. 1253

Gaynor, Catherine, 'An Ulster sculptor: Sophia Rosamond Praeger (1867–1954)', *Irish Arts Review* (2000), vol. 16, pp. 34–43

Getsy, David, J., 'Sculpture in the home: the cult of the statuette in late Victorian Britain', in Martina Droth, Jason Edwards, David J. Getsy and Matthew Withey, *The Cult of the Statuette in Late Victorian Britain* (Leeds: Henry Moore Institute, 2000), pp. 2–4

– 'The identity of the sculptor 1900–25', in Henry Moore Institute, *Sculpture in 20th Century Britain: Identity, Infrastructures, Aesthetics, Display, Reception* (Leeds: Henry Moore Institute, 2003), vol. 1, pp. 9–20

Gibson, William, 'Art – two English sculptors', *Britain Today*, 129 (January 1947), pp. 30–31

Gosse, Edmund, 'The New Sculpture 1879–1884', *Art Journal*, 1894, pp. 138–42, 199–203, 277–82, 306–11

– 'The place of sculpture in daily life', *Magazine of Art*, January 1895, pp. 368–72

Gray, C. B., 'The lead tradition in gardens', *Landscape and Garden*, January 1939, p. 171

Gray, Sara, *The Dictionary of British Women Artists* (Cambridge: Lutterworth Press, 2009)

H. H. Martyn and Co., *Memorials* (Cheltenham, c. 1920s)

Hawksley, Lucinda, *The Mystery of Princess Louise: Queen Victoria's Rebellious Daughter* (London: Chatto and Windus, 2013)

Heal and Son's Mansard Gallery, *Memorial Exhibition of the Work of Kathleen Scott* (London: Heal and Son, 1948)

Hedgecoe, John, *Henry Spencer Moore* (London/New York: Nelson/Simon and Schuster, 1968)

– *A Monumental Vision: The Sculpture of Henry Moore* (London: Collins and Brown, 1998)

Henry Moore Institute, *Sculpture in 20th Century Britain: Identity, Infrastructures, Aesthetics, Display, Reception* (Leeds: Henry Moore Institute, 2003)

Hepworth, Barbara, *A Pictorial Autobiography* (London: Tate Publishing, 1998 [1970])

Hill, Jane, *The Sculpture of Gertrude Hermes* (London: Lund Humphries in association with the Henry Moore Foundation, 2011)

Hirons, Margot, 'The art of Anne Acheson – adorning the family garden with lead and bronze statuary', *The Lady*, 11 August 1927, p. 165

Holman, Valerie, 'A fruitful symbiosis: sculptors and publishers in Britain between the wars', *The Space Between: Literature and Culture, 1914–1945*, 7.1 (2011), pp. 109–23

Hosmer, Harriet, 'The Process of Sculpture', *Atlantic Monthly*, December 1864, pp. 734–38

Hurtado, Shannon, *Genteel Mavericks: Professional Women Sculptors in Victorian Britain* (Berlin: Peter Lang, 2012)

James, Duncan S., *A Century of Statues: The History of the Morris Singer Foundry* (London: Morris Singer Foundry, 1984)

Jellicoe, G. A., 'Modern British sculpture', *The Studio*, January 1930, pp. 26–31

Johnson, Geraldine A., 'Renaissance sculpture and the visual historiography of art history', *Art History*, 36.1 (2013), pp. 12–51

Keene, Derek, Burns, Arthur, and Saint, Andrew (eds), *St Paul's: The Cathedral Church of London 604–2004* (New Haven, CT: Yale University Press, 2004)

Kennet, Kathleen, *Self-Portrait of an Artist* (London: John Murray, 1949)

King, Alex, *Memorials of the Great War in Britain: The Symbolism and Politics of Remembrance* (Oxford: Berg, 1998)

Landow, George P., *Giles's Hero in the Context of Contemporary Women Sculptors*, www.victorianweb.org/sculpture/giles/hero3.html (accessed 25 November 2019)

– *Margaret M. Giles's Hero and the Sublime Female Nude: Introduction*, http://www.victorianweb.org/sculpture/giles/hero.html (accessed 25 November 2019)

Lane, John, *Devon's Churches: A Celebration* (Totnes: Green Books, 2007)

Lara-Betancourt, Patricia, 'Conflicting Modernities? Arts and Crafts and Commercial Influences in the Decoration of the Middle-Class Home 1890–1914', PhD dissertation, Kingston University, 2008, available at British Library e-theses online service, https://ethos.bl.uk/

Lees-Milne, J., *Fourteen Friends* (London: John Murray, 1996)

Lewis, Margaret, *Josefina de Vasconcellos: Her Life and Art* (Hexham: Flambard Press, 2004)

Lichtenstein, Jacqueline, *The Blind Spot: An Essay on the Relations between Painting and Sculpture in the Modern Age* (Los Angeles: Getty Research Institute, 2008)

Lieberman, Ralph, 'Thoughts of an art historian/photographer on the relationship of his two disciplines', in Helene E. Roberts (ed.), *Art History: Through the Camera Lens* (London: Gordon and Breach, 1995), pp. 217–46

Llewellyn, David, *The First Lady of Mulberry Walk: The Life and Times of Irish Sculptress Anne Acheson* (Leicester: Matador, 2010)

Longford, Elizabeth (ed.), *Darling Loosy: Letters to Princess Louise 1856–1939* (London: Weidenfeld and Nicolson, 1991)

MacDougall, S., and Dickson, R. (eds), *Embracing the Exotic: Jacob Epstein and Dora Gordine* (London: Ben Uri Gallery/Papadakis, 2006)

Malvern, Sue, 'The identity of the sculptor 1925–50', in Henry Moore Institute, *Sculpture in 20th Century Britain: Identity, Infrastructures, Aesthetics, Display, Reception* (Leeds: Henry Moore Institute, 2003), vol. 1, pp. 77–87

Marchal, Louise, *Finding Frances: The Biography of Frances Darlington (Sculptor)* (Thirsk: The Marble Press, 2013)

Marcoci, Roxanna, *The Original Copy: Photography of Sculpture, 1839 to Today* (New York: Museum of Modern Art, 2010)

Marshall, Christopher R. (ed.), *Sculpture and the Museum* (Aldershot: Ashgate, 2011)

Martin, Brenda, 'A house of her own: Dora Gordine and Dorich House (1936)', in Brenda Martin and Penny Sparke (eds), *Women's Places: Architecture and Design 1860–1960* (London: Routledge, 2003), pp. 125–47
Martin, Brenda, and Sparke, Penny (eds), *Women's Places: Architecture and Design 1860–1960* (London: Routledge, 2003)
Martin, Eoin, 'Framing Victoria: royal portraiture and architectural sculpture in Victorian Britain', *Sculpture Journal*, 23.2 (2014), pp. 197–207
McBrinn, Joseph, *Sophia Rosamond Praeger, 1867–1954, Art, Literature, Science* (Belfast: The Naughton Gallery, 2007)
– 'Craft as union, craft as demarcation: the decoration at Belfast Cathedral', in Sandra Alfoldy and Janice Helland (eds), *Craft, Space and Interior Design, 1855–2005* (Farnham: Ashgate, 2008), pp. 75–90
– '"A populous solitude": the life and art of Sophia Rosamond Praeger, 1867–1954', *Women's History Review*, 18.4 (2009), pp. 577–96
McKenzie, Ray, *Public Sculpture of Glasgow* (Liverpool: Liverpool University Press and Public Monuments and Sculpture Association, 2002)
Miers, Mary, 'Poetry in stone', *Country Life*, 2 September 2004, pp. 96–97
Milligan, Clare, 'Sculpture in the Home: A Case Study for Post-War British Life, Culture and Aesthetics', MA thesis, University of Leeds, 2003, Henry Moore Institute Archives
Moffat, Nan Muirhead, *Round the Studios 1939: Portraits of Twelve Lady Artists at Work* (1939) (originally published as 12 articles in the *Glasgow Herald* from April to June 1939. Milngavie: Heatherbank, 1982)
Moore, Meredith, 'The struggles of New Sculpture', 08 EL 156/HA 152, *Romans in Togas: Classicism and Empire in Victorian Literature and Art*, Brown University, http://www.victorianweb.org/sculpture/levick/moore.html (accessed 25 November 2019)
Morris, James A., 'A monument to chivalry', *Country Life*, 16 May 1925, n.p.
Nairne, Sandy, and Serota, Nicholas, *British Sculpture in the Twentieth Century* (London: Whitechapel Art Gallery, 1981)
Naylor, Gillian, 'Formative years of the Arts and Crafts Exhibition Society: 1888–1916', *Craft History*, 1 (October 1988), pp. 1–7
Newton, Eric, *British Sculpture 1944–46* (London: John Tiranti, 1947)
Nochlin, Linda, 'Why have there been no great women artists?', in Thomas B. Hess and Elizabeth C. Baker (eds), *Art and Sexual Politics: Why Have There Been No Great Women Artists?* (New York: Macmillan, 1971), pp. 1–39
Nunn, Pamela Geraldine, 'The Mid-Victorian Woman Artist: 1850–1879', PhD dissertation, University College London, 1982, available at British Library e-theses online service, https://ethos.bl.uk/
Padaruth Raksha, *The use of ceramics as an aesthetic element in Durban architecture (1914–2012)*, 2013. http://hdl.handle.net/10321/945, p. 55 (accessed 12 February 2020)

Palmer, Rodney, and Frangenberg, Thomas, *The Rise of the Image: Essays on the History of the Illustrated Art Book* (Aldershot: Ashgate, 2003)
Parkes, Kineton, *Sculpture of To-Day. Vol. 1, America, Great Britain, Japan* (New York: Charles Scribner's Sons, 1922)
– *The Art of Carved Sculpture, Vol. 1, Western Europe, America and Japan* (London: Chapman and Hall, 1931)
Patmore, Derek, 'Other People's Homes – No. 10: the studio of a famous woman sculptor: Lady Hilton Young's house in Bayswater', *Queen*, 3 February 1932, pp. 11–13
Peers, Roger, *The Sculpture of Elizabeth Muntz at the Dorset County Museum* (Dorchester, 1971)
Percifull, Elise, 'Arts and Crafts Influences in East Anglian Gardens: Gardens and Gardening in Norfolk and Suffolk 1885–1914', PhD dissertation, University of East Anglia, 1999, available at British Library e-theses online service, https://ethos.bl.uk/
Preziosi, Donald, *Rethinking Art History: Meditations on a Coy Science* (New Haven, CT: Yale University Press, 1989)
Purvis, June, *Women's History: Britain, 1850–1945* (London: Routledge, 1995)
R.B.S., *Modern British Sculpture* (London: Country Life, 1939)
Rea, Betty, Foreword, *Five on Revolutionary Art* (London: Wishart Books, 1935)
Read, Benedict, Preface, in *Ellen Mary Rope: The Poet Sculptor* (London: Joanna Barnes Fine Arts and H. Blairman and Sons, 1997)
– Introduction, in The Fine Art Society, *Carving in Britain from 1910 to Now* (London: The Fine Art Society, 2012)
Read, Herbert, *Barbara Hepworth: Carvings and Drawings* (London: Lund Humphries, 1952)
Reed, Christopher (ed.), *Not at Home. The Suppression of Domesticity in Modern Art and Architecture* (London: Thames and Hudson, 1996)
Register of Sculpture by Kathleen Lady Kennet (Lady Scott) 1878–1947, compiled by Lord Kennet (1948)
Reynolds, S., *Paris–Edinburgh: Cultural Connections in the Belle Époque* (Farnham: Ashgate, 2007)
Ritchie, Carson I. A., *Modern Ivory Carving* (New York/London: A. S. Barnes and Company/Thomas Yoseloff, 1972)
Roberts, Mary Fanton, 'The quality of women's art achievement', *The Craftsman*, 15 (December 1908), pp. 292–98
Robertson, Bryan, *A Retrospective Exhibition of Sculpture 1925–1965* (London: Zwemmer Gallery, 1965)
Rope, Arthur, 'The poet sculptor Ellen Mary Rope', in *Blaxhall's Creative Past: Snapshots of Village Life* (Blaxhall, Suffolk: The Blaxhall Archive Group, 2009), pp. 71–106

Rose, Pauline, *Henry Moore in America: Art, Business and the Special Relationship* (London: I. B. Tauris, 2014)
Ruskin, John, *The Seven Lamps of Architecture* (Orpington: Allen, 1880)
Savours, Ann, 'Kathleen Scott's statue of Captain Smith of the *Titanic*', *Mariner's Mirror, Journal of the Society for Nautical Research*, 95.4 (2009), pp. 478–83
'S.B.W', 'Handicrafts at the Women Artists' Exhibition', *The Studio*, 15 April 1924, pp. 200–02
Scott, L., 'Women at work: their function in art', *Magazine of Art*, 7 (1884), pp. 98–99
Sedding, John Dando, *Garden Craft Old and New* (London: Kegan Paul, 1895)
Shaw, Phyllida, *An Artist's War. The Art and Letters of Morris & Alice Meredith Williams* (Cheltenham: The History Press, 2017)
– *Undaunted Spirit, The Art and Craft of Gertrude Alice Meredith Williams* (London: Independent Publishing Network, 2018)
Silber, Evelyn. 'The Leicester Galleries and the promotion of modernist sculpture in London, 1902–75', *Sculpture Journal*, 21.2 (2012), pp. 131–44
Smith, J. C. D., *Church Woodcarvings: A West Country Study* (Newton Abbot: David and Charles, 1969)
Snell, Paul, 'John Dando Sedding and sculpture in architecture: the fulfilment of a Ruskinian ideal?', in Rebecca Daniels and Geoff Brandwood (eds), *Ruskin and Architecture* (Reading: Spire Books, 2003), pp. 321–53
– '"The Priest of Form": John Dando Sedding (1838–91) and the Languages of Late Victorian Architecture', PhD dissertation, University of Manchester, 2006, available at British Library e-theses online service, https://ethos.bl.uk/
Sparke, Penny, 'Domesticity in post 1945 England and the role of Sculpture in the Home', paper given at the *Sculpture in the Home* study day, Henry Moore Institute, Leeds, 5 December 2008, HMI archives
Spielmann, M. H., *British Sculpture and Sculptors of To-Day* (London: Cassell, 1901)
– 'The fine art section', in *Souvenir of the Fine Art Section, Franco-British Exhibition, 1908*, under the auspices of the British Art Committee (London: Bemrose and Sons, 1908)
Steggles, Mary Ann, and Barnes, Richard, *British Sculpture in India: New Views and Old Memories* (Kirstead, Norfolk: Frontier Publishing, 2011)
Stephenson, Andrew, 'Conditions of display 1925–50', in Henry Moore Institute, *Sculpture in 20th Century Britain: Identity, Infrastructures, Aesthetics, Display, Reception* (Leeds: Henry Moore Institute, 2003), vol. 1, pp. 111–24

Sterckx, Marjan, 'The invisible "sculpteuse": sculptures by women in the nineteenth-century urban public space – London, Paris, Brussels', *Nineteenth-Century Art Worldwide: A Journal of Nineteenth-Century Visual Culture*, 7.2, 2008, http://www.19thc-artworldwide.org/autumn08/38-autumn08/autumn08article/90-the-invisible-sculpteuse-sculptures-by-women-in-the-nineteenth-century-urban-public-spacelondon-paris-brussels (accessed 25 November 2019)

Stocker, Mark, 'Edmund Gosse on sculpture', *University of Leeds Review*, 28 (1985–86), pp. 283–310

– '"My masculine models": the sculpture of Kathleen Scott', *Apollo*, 150.451 (1999), pp. 47–54

– '"Young male objects": the ideal sculpture of Kathleen Scott', *Sculpture Journal*, 22.2 (2013), pp. 119–27

Stokes, Adrian, 'Art. Miss Hepworth's carving', *The Spectator*, 3 November 1933, n.p.

The Studio Yearbook of Decorative Art: A Guide to the Artistic Decoration and Furnishing of the House (London, Paris, New York: *The Studio*, 1906)

Thomas, Margaret, *How to Understand Sculpture* (London: G. Bell and Sons, 1911)

Tillyard, S. K., *The Impact of Modernism 1900–1920: Early Modernism and the Arts and Crafts Movement in Edwardian England* (London: Routledge, 1988)

Tinkler, Penny, 'Women and popular literature', in June Purvis (ed.), *Women's History: Britain, 1850–1945* (London: Routledge, 1995)

Towndrow, Kenneth Romney, 'Small sculpture in the home', *The Studio*, 134.654 (September 1947), pp. 57–63

Turner, Sarah Victoria, '"Reuniting what should never have been separated": The Arts and Crafts movement, modernism, and sculpture in Britain 1890-1914', *Nineteenth-Century Art Worldwide: A Journal of Nineteenth-Century Visual Culture*, 14.2, 2015, www.19thc-artworldwide.org/summer15/turner-on-the-arts-and-crafts-movement-modernism-and-sculpture-in-britain (accessed 25 November 2019)

Underwood, Eric G., *A Short History of English Sculpture* (London: Faber and Faber, 1933)

Usborne, Vivian, 'The sculpture of Katharine Maltwood', *The Studio*, 15 April 1924, pp. 197–99

Wake, Jehanne, *Princess Louise: Queen Victoria's Unconventional Daughter* (London: Collins, 1988)

Waller, Susan, *Women Artists in the Modern Era: A Documentary History* (Metuchen, NJ: The Scarecrow Press, 1991)

Whiteley, Gillian, *A Context of Commitment: The Sculpture of Betty Rea*, The Henry Moore Institute Essays on Sculpture, no. 40 (n.d.)

Witzling, Maria R. (ed.), *Voicing our Visions: Writings by Women Artists* (London: The Women's Press, 1992)

Wolfflin, Heinrich, 'How one should photograph sculpture', trans. Geraldine A. Johnson, *Art History*, 36.1 (2013), pp. 52–71

Wood, Jon, *Close Encounters: The Sculptor's Studio in the Age of the Camera* (Leeds: Henry Moore Institute, 2001)

Wood, T. Martin, 'A decorative sculptor: Miss Ruby Levick: (Mrs. Gervaise Bailey)', *The Studio*, 34 (1905), pp. 100–07

Young, Louisa, *A Great Task of Happiness: The Life of Kathleen Scott* (London: Macmillan, 1995)

Index